CHRISTIAN LIVES

The aim of this small collection of new biographies is to study outstanding Christians of the modern era, particularly some who have taken a lead in the ecumenical renewal of the Church in mission and unity.

Zinzendorf the Ecumenical Pioneer by A. J. Lewis, *A Man to be Reckoned With: The Story of Reinold von Thadden* by Werner Hühne and *African Saint: The Story of Apolo Kivebulaya* by Anne Luck have already been published.

———————

PAUL COUTURIER
AND UNITY IN CHRIST

The Abbé in 1947

GEOFFREY CURTIS
of the Community of the Resurrection

PAUL COUTURIER
AND UNITY IN CHRIST

72947

BX
6.8
.C67
C8

SCM PRESS LTD
BLOOMSBURY STREET LONDON

FIRST PUBLISHED 1964
© SCM PRESS LTD 1964
PRINTED IN GREAT BRITAIN BY
W. & J. MACKAY & CO LTD, CHATHAM

CONTENTS

Contents

ILLUSTRATIONS

*Copyright: Yves Guillemaut, Paris

ACKNOWLEDGEMENTS

The story told in this book, in so far as its details have not been supplied from my own personal memories and gathered by me from friends of the Abbé Couturier, is based upon the record given in the well-known book by Père Maurice Villain, S.M., *L'Abbé Paul Couturier, Apôtre de l'Unité chrétienne*, described below on pp. 11 and 16. Much use has also been made of the tributes to the Abbé from fourteen of his friends, collected by Père Villain in *Paul Couturier, Apôtre de l'Unité chrétienne. Témoignages*, Lyon: E. Vitte, 1954, and of the valuable brochure by Père Michalon, p.S.S., *L'Abbé Paul Couturier et l'unité chrétienne*, Lyon: Centre Unité chrétienne, 1963.

I have known all these friends of the Abbé, most of whom have given me their help. Indeed the kindness of Abbé Couturier's friends and relatives has been unforgettable, especially that of those who have been his hosts in France, England, Belgium and Switzerland. I owe much to the Abbé's young priest kinsmen, Père Robert Clément, S.J., and Abbé Marc Clément. I should have been helpless without the aid of Père Villain, S.M., and Père Michalon, p.S.S., each in his own way and sphere the worthy successor of the Abbé. The hospitality of the priests of St Sulpice at the Séminaire Universitaire of Lyons, now Père Michalon's home, has been from 1939 onwards most gracious and helpful. The Monks of Unity of the Abbaye de Chevetogne, Belgium, whom I first knew at the Priory of Amay-sur-Meuse, have not only been frequently—and twice for long periods—my kindly and patient hosts, but have also been as much a source of inspiration as of valuable information. My debt is almost as great to the Trappist monks of the Abbaye de Notre Dame des Dombes, to the Brethren of Taizé and to the Sisters of Grandchamp. I owe much to the Anglican Communities, both of men and of women, with whom Abbé Couturier had friendly relations—the Benedictine monks of Nashdom Abbey, the Society

8

of St John the Evangelist, Oxford, the Society of the Sacred Mission, Kelham; of women's communities especially the House of Prayer, Burnham, the Community of St Mary the Virgin, Wantage, the Sisters of the Love of God (Fairacres), Oxford, the Society of the Holy Cross, Haywards Heath, and St Mary's Abbey, West Malling.

I am indebted for the loan of letters or photographs to Archimandrite Abraham of Rozay-en-Brie, Professor Pierre Kovalevsky, Father Francis Tyndale-Biscoe, S.S.F., the Rev. Ivan Young, the Rev. A. Phyall, Miss Barbara Simonds, the Lady Abbess, West Malling, and to Brother George Every, S.S.M., who also procured for me the loan of the Abbe's letters to the late Father Reginald Tribe, S.S.M.

For personal information I am specially grateful to the Society of the Priests of St Irendaeus at Lyons, to Pastor Bruston, to the late M. Victor Carlhian, to M. Escoffier and to Dr Sergius Bolshakoff. Valuable help and criticism have been given by Père Guilter, S.J., the Rev. A. M. Allchin, the Rev. Anthony Andrews, Mr Desmond Parsons, who also read the proofs, Miss Maisie Spens, Miss M. V. Woodgate, Miss Cynthia Wood, Miss Irene Edmonds, who helped in the translation of various passages, the Community of the Holy Name, Malvern Link, who helped with regard to things Swedish, the Brethren of my own community, especially Father Martin Jarrett-Kerr, who corrected the whole in proof, and above all, by Sister Gabriel, S.S.C., of Ty Mawr, who besides correcting the proofs has fruitfully examined the structure of the whole book. I owe more than I can say to Miss Joan Petersen, who, when the prospect of carrying through my task seemed especially dark, offered her help simply as one who understood the mechanics of book production, but who provided wise and bracing counsel as well as generous technical and secretarial help. Others who have kindly done typing have been Miss Carole Copland, Mrs Roberts and Mlle Yvonne Derrien. The latter also read the proofs with special attention to the French background and nomenclature. Dr Martin Schor has given invaluable aid in the transliteration of Russian names.

I owe much, especially in chapter 5, to the *History of the Ecu-*

Acknowledgements

menical *Movement, 1517–1948,* London: S.P.C.K., 1954, by Ruth Rouse and Bishop Stephen Neill, and to the works of Père Yves Congar, O.P., and Père G. Tavard. I have made much use of the many ecumenical journals and reviews of which the library of the Abbaye de Chevetogne has an unrivalled collection. I should not have needed to make such laborious use of these if there had been earlier available to me Père Villain's collection of the Abbé's writings, *Oecuménisme spirituel: les écrits de l'Abbé Paul Couturier,* Tournai: Casterman, 1963. No bibliography that I could offer could excel that given by Père Villain in *Unity: a history,* London: Harvill Press, 1963.

The patience and encouraging kindness and understanding of the publishers of this book recall those of Abbé Couturier himself. It is greatly indebted in many ways to the labours of the Rev. Michael King. It was an earlier Managing Director and Editor of SCM Press, the Rev. David Paton, who first suggested that I should undertake this task. Conscious of other engrossing claims, I should have declined but that a like request, which was endorsed by my Superior, reached me at the same time from a senior official of the World Council of Churches and from intimate friends of the Abbé in his own country.

No one is more conscious than I of the shortcomings of what I have written. One would need a lifetime to speak adequately of Paul Couturier, but the length of life is uncertain and the times are pregnant. So I offer this work, imperfect as it is, as an act of obedience and love to Christ and his Church, in the hope that others worthier, more capable and with more time at their disposal, may make use of it when time is ripe, to do better than I have done.

G.C.

PREFACE

The life of Abbé Couturier of Lyons has been vividly described by his devoted and able disciple, Père Maurice Villain, S.M.[1] Although I had the privilege of being numbered amongst the Abbé's friends during the major part of his apostolic work for Christian unity, my own book is necessarily at many points wholly dependent upon that of Père Villain. As the Abbé's beloved disciple, intimate collaborator and trusted executor, his knowledge of the subject is incomparably greater than mine.

There remained, however, a real need for a book on the same subject by an English Christian, and in particular, by an Anglican. Our own debt to the Abbé is a special one. It is different in kind from that of which Père Villain is conscious. That debt too we share at least in part. It has been an indescribable source of blessing to us also to know Abbé Couturier. How could it not be? Aided as he was by new facilities of communication provided by scientific invention, I do not know that since the death of the apostles of Christ, any one of the saints has done more than Paul Couturier to draw the world into union with its Saviour. But there is something which Abbé Couturier has done for Christians of our land, necessarily different from what he has done for Père Villain. For the latter the Abbé has been spiritual father and master. It has been his to give the whole devotion of his mind and spirit to Christ Jesus in the great apostle of unity. For us Anglicans who have had the privilege of calling ourselves his friends, while the Abbé has been a revelation of the sympathy, courtesy and understanding, the patience, faithfulness and humility, of the strength in weakness and of the transparency of Christ, he has also rendered another invaluable service. He has fulfilled for Christ a unique ambassadorial service in his interpretation of the Roman Catholic Church, teaching us the lesson of the ancient anagram, *Roma amor*: that Rome at its essential best means *amor*—the love of Christ. He has done this through drawing us into the large circle of his friends, the communion of saints both living and departed, Protestant as well as Catholic, in fellowship with whom his life has been spent. This Catholic and Christian world of France and all its rich heritage belongs by right to Père Villain and his French readers. For an average Anglican, introduction to this is a new and wonderful experience to be shared,[2] so far as possible, with his fellow-Christians.

In performing this service Abbé Couturier effaced himself while his presence transfigured those around him. Professor Alexander Nairne used to point out as one of the loveliest traits of the Fourth Gospel, our Lord's way of drawing out into new and vivid life those whom he encountered. This was true of the Abbé. If in the first part of this book I seem to have devoted too much space to those around him in proportion to that given to himself, this is due to the Abbé himself. Someone who knew him very well remarked after reading this first part, 'The Abbé himself, in his love of hiddenness and his desire to draw out others, would be very pleased with it.' Lavelle has said, 'The saint is like a light which God has put into the world. The more it illuminates, the less we see its own blaze'. In later chapters using in part my own very limited experience, I have tried to bear witness to the light as it shone through this priest himself, from whom has flowed so much fresh and unifying light for others.

Most certainly God chooses the weak things of the world to confound the things that are mighty. None seemed less likely to prove an instrument used to alter the religious atmosphere of the world. The Abbé did not discover the full meaning of his life—his ecumenical vocation—until he had lived for more than half a century. He was then an obscure, fragile, ageing priest living in great poverty. Influence, distinguished family connexions, intellectual eminence (at least in the field of theology), grace of self-expression—all these things were lacking to him. When he saw the heavenly vision, instead of pleading, as would so many of us, lack of the necessary qualifications of health and position, his was the simple answer of the Blessed Virgin Mary, to whom he specially belonged—'Behold the servant of the Lord: be it unto me according to thy word.' And so the Spirit, the Word, the Sacrifice of God were given free course in and through his servant, and during the remainder of his life and since his death they have been more and more richly glorified.

The spread of his influence during the quarter of a century since he first proclaimed his message has been marvellous. The first official approval of the Call to Universal Prayer came in 1934 from Eastern Orthodoxy—from Metropolitan Eulogius, exarch (of the Ecumenical Patriarch) for Western Europe, followed soon after by that from the Ecumenical Patriarch of Constantinople himself and from many other prelates. In 1936 the Synod of the Reformed Churches of France recorded their resolution giving the cordial support of French Protestantism. Three years later the Archbishops of Canterbury and York and many other Anglican bishops were co-operating and the Superiors of the men's religious communities in the Church of England sent out a letter asking all Christians to join in observing the Week of Prayer for Unity. Anglican co-operation has been constant and increasing until in the 57th resolution of the last Lambeth Conference (1958) the bishops of our communion throughout the world 'commend to all Anglicans the observance of the Week of Prayer for Christian Unity in the spirit of the late Abbé Paul Couturier. . . .'[3]

The Abbé had already close ties with those who were engaged in planning the World Council of Churches before its actual emergence in the Assembly of Amsterdam (1948). From the first it has shown traces of his influence. This is most clearly seen in the Report of the second Assembly of the Council at Evanston (1954) in a section which might well have come from the Abbé's own pen.

> The measure of our concern for unity is the degree to which we pray for it. We cannot expect God to give us unity unless we prepare ourselves to receive his gift by costly and purifying prayer. To pray together is to be drawn together. We urge, wherever possible, the observance of the Week of Prayer for Christian Unity, 18–25 January (or some other period suited to local conditions) as a public testimony to prayer as the road to unity.[4]

In the preparatory Report published by the Central Committee before the Third Assembly of the Council at New Delhi (November 1961), only one Roman Catholic, besides Pope John XXIII, was mentioned by name—Paul Couturier.

The Roman Catholic Church, which in the person of the Archbishop of Lyons, Cardinal Gerlier, had always rewarded the Abbé's unfaltering obedience by wise discipline and faithful protection, has given signal commendation to his whole work which, since his death, it deliberately maintains and develops.

The great Dom Lambert Beauduin O.S.B., founder of the Monks of Unity, closed thus his reflections on the occasion of the jubilee in 1950 of his monastery:

> Here [i.e. in work for Christian unity] more than in any other domain, supernatural effort ought to occupy the first place. We are glad to pay our homage to the activity of the ecumenical group of Lyons, so remarkable from this point of view. Abbé Couturier is its indefatigable apostle. With an exemplary perseverance and tenacity, he succeeds in drawing workers for unity into a movement of real spiritual intensity—reciprocal love and union in the prayer and charity of Christ. He stands out as the zealous promoter of the novena [*neuvaine*] of prayer for unity from 18–25 January. We may say that it is thanks to him that this institution has had so great a development in all the Churches. His apostolate has been favoured by the attitude of the Holy See which approves the interconfessional recitation of the *Pater* and thus encourages the union of all Christians in the prayer of the Master.[5]

Seven years later there succeeded to the Holy See a Pope who showed himself in complete sympathy with the ideals of Dom Lambert Beauduin and Abbé Couturier, which were those also of Pius XI, *Papa unionis*.

> With Pope John XXIII [observes a Roman Catholic theologian in the famous German journal *Herder-Korrespondenz*], the accent is thrown back from the Roman Catholic form of unity (which is by no means abandoned) on to the Divine Persons. That means that in our prayer for the unity of the true Church we are to take a step farther away from the too conventional representations of it and to penetrate effectively in a deep manner to the source of unity, the

love of Christ in whom Roman Catholics are not alone in recognizing their Saviour. This 'shift of accent' Christians of *Una Sancta*[6] have waited for. What joy to find their aspiration confirmed by the highest authority!

Speaking of the Abbé's way of prayer for unity, Dom Sartory, O.S.B. (of Niederaltaich) writes:

> Catholics have found this manner of prayer recalled recently by Pope John XXIII who thus formulated the intention (of prayer) for January: 'That all those who seek the true Church, may recognize more profoundly the aspiration of the Heart of Jesus for the unity of his own and be in that manner drawn to unity.'[7]

His Holiness, the late John XXIII, in his youth came to Lyons as the emissary of Pius XI with a view to reorganizing an earlier world-transforming movement which originated in that city, the Propagation of the Faith. He recalled this mission when in September 1957, as Cardinal Roncalli, Archbishop of Venice, he addressed a gathering of theologians at Palermo:

> The thing most needed in work for unity at the present moment is this: it is still too little spread amongst the masses, though they would nevertheless be ready to appreciate it. My old friend, a Benedictine monk of Belgium, Dom Lambert Beauduin, said when I was beginning my work of co-operation in the Near East: 'A movement must be created in the West in favour of reunion with the separated Churches, a movement parallel to that of the Propagation of the Faith.' I had at the moment just completed reconstituting this in the world, under the direction of the new Pope, the glorious Pius XI. And I think we ought to return to the idea of Dom Lambert Beauduin.[8]

The movement His Holiness then demanded has been already created. Like the Propagation of the Faith, it arose in Lyons. It belongs not only to the West but has rooted itself in at least sixty nations all over the world. Its growth from year to year is overwhelming. All this derives from the obedience of a poor man unknown to the world who laboured to the very end, though during his last nine years, after imprisonment by the Gestapo, he was a man mortally stricken. Such is the power of faith working through love in union with the Prayer of Christ. So essentially is the whole movement centred in the heart of Christ crucified and glorified that the achievement is as surely qualitative as it is quantitative—it is a triumph of the Holy Ghost. Père Congar, O.P.[9] writes that the greatness of Abbé Couturier

> consists in his having given to the work of ecumenism its full dimension of *religion*, its heart of prayer. He has thus situated it on the mystical level in the sense that Péguy gives to the word: he has given it in a Catholic sense [*catholiquement*] its *mystique*. By this very fact—this is the discovery, the great poetic achievement of Abbé Couturier—he has freed the Week of January and the work of ecumenism itself from the mortgage of confessional quarrels of the controversial or proselytizing type without sacrificing in any way either the rights of truth or the duties of Catholic fidelity. This is what we owe him: nothing less. It is immense and it is decisive.

NOTES

[1] Maurice Villain, S.M., *L'Abbé Paul Couturier, apôtre de l'unité chrétienne: souvenirs et documents* (Collection Eglise Vivante) Tournai: Casterman, 1957.

I hope that many readers of my book will, if they have not already done so, read this book; and that some will proceed also to read the same author's *Introduction à l'oecuménisme* (Collection Eglise Vivante), Tournai: Casterman, 1958. An English translation of the third French edition of this book, revised and enlarged by the author in 1961, was published in 1963 by the Harvill Press under the title, *Unity: a history and some reflections*. This is a helpful book for any who seek to do service in the quest of Christian unity and one which is even fuller of the spirit and of the wisdom of Abbé Couturier than is the earlier book specially devoted to him.

[2] The testimony of Professor Zander, an Eastern Orthodox theologian, is similar. 'In him (Abbé Couturier) we encountered the fatherly attitude, the fraternal attitude which the Church of Rome reveals only rarely to those who do not belong to her' (Villain, *L'Abbé*, p. 108).

[3] See the *Report of the Lambeth Conference 1958*. I doubt whether in the history of Christendom any such tribute has ever been made before by the bishops of one world-wide Church to a lowly member of another Church not in communion with itself.

[4] *The Evanston Report*, London: SCM Press, 1954, p. 91.

16

⁵ Dom Lambert Beauduin, O.S.B., 'Jubilé du monastère de l'Union (1925–50)' (contd), *Irénikon* XXIV, Ier trimestre, 1951, p. 36.

⁶ The *Una Sancta* movement is a movement for the quest of Christian unity which is inspired by principles similar to those of Abbé Couturier. It was founded by his contemporary, the German apostle of unity, Padre Max Metzger. See pp. 124–6, below.

⁷ Dom Th. Sartory, O.S.B., 'L'esprit de l'oecuménisme en Allemagne', *Istina*, 1960, no. 1, pp. 27f. Both quotations are to be found in this article. (The former is a quotation by Dom Sartory from *Herder-Korrespondenz*. The theologians who contribute to that journal never sign their articles.)

⁸ Cf. the Italian text of this discourse in *Unitas*, March 1960, p. 42.

⁹ Yves M. J. Congar, O.P., review of M. Villain, *L'Abbé* in *Revue des Sciences philosophiques et théologiques*, XLI, No. 3, 1957, p. 590.

I

THE HIDDEN YEARS

PAUL Couturier was born at Lyons on 29 July 1881, the second and last child in a bourgeois family profoundly imbued with the faith of Christ and, in an age dominated by scientific progress, proud of their inheritance of the traditions of an older France. He had been preceded by a sister, Marie Antoinette, two years older than himself. His father owned a chemical factory close to the Prado on the left bank of the river Rhône.

The year 1880 has been claimed as being the highwater mark in a generation dominated by science, but as at the same time marked by the dawn of a spiritual renaissance. The Prado was itself a bright ray of this new light. It was situated in a surburban district which was grubby and unkempt and still insecure from river floods, but no longer disreputable. The world-famed apostle, Père Antoine Chevrier died there in 1879. By nineteen years of heroic labour he had transformed the Prado from being the most notorious dance-hall in Lyons into the *Providence du Prado*, the cradle of a great work for destitute children, and of much else that is good.[1]

Lyons, city of doctors, martyrs, and confessors without number, glories increasingly in the Prado—in the evangelical spirituality of its founder, in its challenging presentation of the Gospel, in its school for the re-education of delinquents, in its training ground for priest-evangelists, in the fervent holiness of its sons and daughters working in many lands. Of all the holy influences of that great city which were to play their part in marking Paul's life and work, none penetrated deeper than that of the 'father of the poor' of Lyons. It was with slag from the Couturier factory that Père Chevrier had built his chapel, the destitution of which recalls the cave of Bethlehem. He became confessor to the grandmother, mother, and aunts of the child whom he did not live long enough to baptize. Indeed Paul, who loved to introduce his friends to the Prado, will have known from childhood the great words that Père Chevrier inscribed on his wall for his first retreat for seminarists:

> A priest is a man stripped.
> A priest is a man crucified.
> A priest is a man devoured.

When the boy was 3 years old, financial misfortune led to the abandonment of the factory and to the family's withdrawal to Algeria. It was there that Paul received his earlier education, first at the school of the Brothers in El Biar, later from a priest of the parish of Agha. When he was 12 years old, his parents brought him back to Lyons. He made his first communion at the church of St Nizier where some of the earliest Christians of Lyons, so many of whom won martyrdom, had worshipped. Then he became a day-boy at the College of the 'Lazarists'[2] until his studies were completed by his securing in 1899 the *baccalauréat moderne* (in English education roughly equivalent to the General Certificate of Education with some subjects at 'A' level) and a further degree in mathematics in 1900.

Paul's upbringing was directed by his grandmother and his mother in strict obedience to a narrow interpretation, widely followed in those days, of the Catholic rule of life.[3] The rigid *conformisme* of the family circle left clear traces of itself in the life of one who was in youth no stranger to the agonies of scrupulosity: indeed they must have continued to trouble him until he was almost on the threshold of his ecumenical ministry. It was in 1935 that a concise and serene article of his appeared unsigned in *La Vie Spirituelle*[4] entitled 'Spiritual Therapeutics for the Scrupulous'. In this we find notes written by someone who has clearly suffered much and for a considerable time from this malady and whose counsel has therefore the value of springing from actual experience.

Convinced that the juridical point of view combined with a rigorist upbringing has led astray many souls and spread the disease of scrupulosity in the Latin West, the author pleads that the scrupulous should be given the benefits of a generous ἐπιείκεια, [A.V. 'moderation']. He must be freed from the bonds of legalism and restored to an atmosphere of liberty in which, without any other obligation save that of an act of perfect contrition, he will find nourishment in the Eucharist. Confession ought to be rare, i.e. monthly, preceded only by a short self-examination. No one was strictly obliged to more than this before the Council of Trent.

As a matter of fact, in these earlier centuries annual confession seems to have sufficed. However, the practice of monthly confession was for this writer a way of liberty and it brought him peace.

Paul's fellow-students recall a rather introspective soul, but one much admired for his transparent purity and for his keenness in work and games as well as in worship. There were two influences, besides those of college life, prevailing now to safeguard the boy's development. There was great-uncle Monsignor Louis Planus of the Society of the Priests of St Irenaeus (popularly known as *missionnaires Chartreux*), a renowned preacher, vicar-general of the diocese of Autun. It was he who, when Paul in his nineteenth year made clear his hope of dedicating his life to Christ in the priesthood, directed him to seek entry into his own brotherhood of the Chartreux. There was also Aunt Marie-Thérèse Lepage, a Sister of the Congregation of Nazareth, later stationed in Rome, always ready with wise counsel for her nephew who was later in life to repay the debt by himself directing his aunt's soul in the way of Christ.

After one year in the novitiate (1901) crammed full enough with the study of Latin, lectures on scholastic philosophy, and addresses on the spiritual life, followed by four years of theology in the Grand Séminaire on the hill of St Just where he numbered amongst his teachers Lepin, Tixeront and Pourrat, Paul was ordained priest on the feast of St Columba, 9 June 1906, and celebrated his first Mass next morning in the beautiful church of St Bruno des Chartreux, once the church of the Carthusian monastery, but now under the care of the Society of St Irenaeus. To the end of his life the daily Mass was for Abbé Couturier an *événement* as to the rich and crucial significance of which he was to leave behind copious notebooks full of exquisitely transcribed reflections. As to this his first priestly access to the holy mysteries we have only the recollection of a server that the movements of the new priest at the elevation, slow and full of adoration, 'would have moved an inveterate unbeliever'. The preacher was his uncle, Louis Planus, who bade the young man not to be over-anxious what use would be made of him in his ministry. Generosity in self-giving he counselled, detachment and abandonment—how faithful Paul was to prove to these priestly admonitions!

His superiors had decided that Paul Couturier was to teach. So he proceeded from the study of higher mathematics to spend the next three years qualifying at the Catholic University for a licentiate's degree in Physical Sciences.

Do not let us forget the fact of Paul's special training in the exact sciences. A distinguished philosopher and mathematician, his dear friend the late M. Victor Carlhian, has written with regard to this:

> Thanks to his scientific training he [Paul Couturier] had developed the precision of mind and the sense of approximations from which science can never escape. He had, along with a wise relativism, the horror of illegitimate extrapolations. He would have readily subscribed to such a formula as this: 'Never forget Reason, but never fall into the extravagance of allowing yourself to become its prisoner.'

In Paul these characteristics were compounded with a robust orthodoxy of faith, with a vivid and rich historical imagination and with a gift of prayer whose unusual strength went along with a profound sense of the power of prayer.

Thus equipped, the young Abbé became a master in the college known as the *Institution des Chartreux* in which his teaching was to continue for more than forty years. His tenure of this post was interrupted only by the Great War of 1914 during which he was mobilized as *infirmier* in the Health Service. As he was to devote so large a portion of his life to the laborious work of teaching boys, we must take a glance at the background of his labours.

The College of the Chartreux was, like the English Charterhouse, a school established in a dissolved Carthusian monastery; but unlike its English counterpart, founded in 1611 in the city of London but now flourishing at Godalming, this college continues on its monastic site. The monastery at Lyons, which came into being more than two centuries later than its sister in London (founded in 1371), was established in 1584 by the sickly King Henri III and called the Chartreuse du Lys-Saint-Esprit. After its dissolution in the Revolution it was refounded by Cardinal Fesch, the egregious uncle of Napoleon Bonaparte, to be the home of the Society of St Irenaeus, a company of mission-priests. This society had already done a century of valuable work, not least for education, throughout this region of France, when Abbé Couturier, as one of its members, became a schoolmaster in the college.

The buildings are on the slope of the Croix Rousse, the hill overlooking the Saône and flanking that part of the city which lies between the two great rivers, the other, and greater, being the Rhône. It is one of the oldest parts of the city. Indeed it has recently been discovered that the martyrs of Lyons and Vienne in the second century underwent their agony here in a Roman amphitheatre a short way below the school and not, as used to be thought, in the amphitheatre on the slopes of Fourvière, the hill on the other side of the Saône. The monks had chosen well, for their property commanded a wonderful view of the western parts of the city. Their church of St Bruno is a large baroque building of great interest and beauty, its rich interior decoration being in vivid contrast to the spirit of St Bruno, founder of this order of coenobitic solitaries, statues and pictures of whom are nevertheless conspicuous here. His sons have left to their successors in this place a more characteristic memorial in the atmosphere of august and serene adoration which clothes the church. Here this one at least of the latter so-called Chartreux was to learn, as St Bruno learnt, the priceless value of solitude. The school does not often worship here, for it has its own large chapel, a modern building with stained glass windows of real distinction. The Abbé prayed very often in both these buildings, and perhaps even more regularly in the little oratory in the Institute which belongs specially to the priests of the Society, a chapel where recollection is more easily attained. This chapel contains the memorial of the dedication of the Society in 1878 to the Most Sacred Heart of Jesus.

The priests of the Society live in a building close to the college and take their meals together. Those engaged in missions and parochial work are thus in continual relationship with those engaged in teaching in the college.

Within the Society the life of the Abbé was in one respect singular. His mother being no longer alive and his sister being regarded as too delicate to live alone, with the advice of his uncle, Mgr Planus, he judged it his duty, instead of residing entirely here, to have supper and to spend the night in a flat which he shared with his sister. This was in the Rue du Plat which flanked the Place Bellecour in the heart of Lyons, at least two miles away from the college. The Abbé thus lived in this respect a double life. After saying Mass early in some church or convent in the city, he would proceed to the Institution des Chartreux for his *petit déjeuner*. There he would spend the day teaching. *Déjeuner* he took with the Brethren and dealt with his large correspondence in his study there. But he had always to return for the evening meal with his sister and to spend the night in the fourth-floor flat at 5 Rue du Plat.

Abbé Couturier was not a successful schoolmaster. Conscientious, accurate, thorough, devoted, he could never acquire the tricks of the trade. He failed, at any rate with the smaller boys, to attract and sustain their interest and even to preserve good discipline. He was lacking in the dramatic sense, the passion for detailed fulfilment of instructions and the gift of timing which make a good teacher. Yet he was clearly as little cut out for parochial or any other regular pastoral ministry. So under obedience he continued faithfully with notable awkwardness and discomfort to carry this strangely ill-fitting cross for the larger part of his life. This uncongenial labour was, however, by no means unfruitful, quite apart from the great part it played in his own development. There is clear evidence that for older pupils who had a real thirst for knowledge of unknown worlds, the Abbé often proved a source of rich stimulus and inspiration. One of his former pupils was amazed to find how the master who in his large mathematics class had bored him to tears as a younger boy, opened windows of revelation for him in the small sixth form where the subject was the natural sciences.

> It was through him [writes one] that I learnt to know the immensity of time and the perspective opened by the fact of evolution on the divine work of creation—to see it as in perpetual generation through a process of expansive and fertile development. He was the first to teach me how to read the Bible; to find there not a cosmogony, but a hymn of praise addressed to him who created all things good and in process of ascension towards himself, a movement of gradual and graded advance and of slow interior enrichment. Thanks to him I have come to understand that the Bible is a drama of history opening with the first *Fiat* of creation but demanding the co-operation of human activity with the Divine. Thanks to him I learnt that the Book of Nature also manifests a divine design, the traces of which must be sought so as to enable us to share in the dialogue between the Creator and his creation.

The same former pupil, now a man of eminence in the life of the city, recalls that already in 1928 Abbé Couturier was deeply aware of the importance of the work and genius of Père Teilhard de Chardin, S.J. who, after the publication of his writings some thirty years later, is judged by minds of discrimination to be not only a great scientist but one of the ablest Christian apologists of our time. The Abbé especially valued and would recommend, with discreet though cordial comments, Père de Chardin's penetrating essay on the spiritual life, *Le Milieu Divin*,[5] which he would send in roneoscript to his friends.

The Abbé's colleagues were not alone in combining a critical attitude towards him as teacher with profound reverence for the priest. Boys have an acute intuition for reality and some of these in later years can recall their sense that they had before them a man of God, poor, self-denying, recollected, disinterested, a priest of true and transparent holiness. The tones of his voice saying the hymn *Veni, Sancte Spiritus* are not forgotten.

Neither boys nor masters, however, could have realized that God was silently preparing this schoolmaster for a more comprehensive vocation. Nor did his later collaborators in the field of ecumenism often recall the nature of their leader's earlier training ground. Yet there remained of the mathematician and scientist in the apostle of unity not only a marked lucidity and precision of mind with a few characteristic expressions, e.g. 'method of limitation', 'convergent appeal', 'parallelaboration', savouring of a mental discipline of a kind rare in the ecumenical field; but along with these a saving sense that the quest of Christian unity is something more than a primary ecclesiastical duty—that it has a larger significance in the fulfilment of God's design for his creation as a whole.

After ten years there supervened the blessing of a great and transforming friendship with a fellow-citizen of Lyons, M. Victor Carlhian, a layman six years older than himself. But before we speak of this friend and of his influence, we must try to give some idea of what it means, at least to one with a very lively historical sense and imagination, to have been born and for the most part bred, a Christian of the city of Lyons.

NOTES

[1] Half a century later, the future cardinal, Archbishop Mercier, on his way to his new diocese of Malines, was to spend—in the room that had belonged to the Founder—a memorable and fruitful day in prayer, developing his vision of the apostolic priesthood. Cardinal Mercier used strongly to recommend Père Antoine Chevrier's great book, *Le véritable disciple*, as a devotional companion to his clergy. Until he died he treasured the copper crucifix that had belonged to Père Chevrier.

[2] The Mission-Priests of St Vincent de Paul: known in England as Vincentians. At this date the Brothers of the Christian Schools, who had taught Paul Couturier in El Biar, had replaced the Vincentians at this college, which still bore its old name.

[3] The grandmother seems to have been dominant and the severity of the family standards may well have been enhanced owing to her origins; she was

the daughter of a distinguished painter, M. Lepage and a Jewess, Mlle Blum, converted by her husband before their marriage.

⁴ Issue of March 1935, pp. 141–53.

⁵ Now volume IV of Père de Chardin's collected works, as published in France; then only in private circulation. The first of these, *Le Phénomène humain* was published by Collins in an English translation (with preface by Sir Julian Huxley) in 1959 as *The Phenomenon of Man*, and was followed in 1960 by *Le milieu divin* which retained its original French title for the English translation.

2

A CITIZEN OF NO MEAN CITY

HERE are cities in which it is possible to grow up without being deeply affected by their character and tradition. Lyons is by no means one of these. Its unusual geographical situation, its general history and, above all, its unique Christian tradition render this impossible. To show traces of having been to a high degree, consciously as well as unconsciously, influenced by a rich environment, if it goes along with a real independence, is a mark of sensitiveness and of strength, not a sign of weakness. Paul Couturier grew up profoundly Lyonnais. He loved every stone of his city and was eager to share the treasures of his heritage with others.

Lyons is a great city. Its site has played its part in ensuring this. It is the city of the two rivers and the two mountains. The great rivers, the impetuous Rhône and the tranquil Saône, which traverse it and meet at its extremity, have done much to carve the face and mould the soul of the city. And the two mountains, the one called Croix Rousse, the other a cluster of three hills, St Just, St Irenaeus and Fourvière, have been watchers over an age-long conflict between nature and man—his struggle to make full use of the possibilities provided by the confluence of the rivers. Of these two mountains the one which embraces Fourvière (*Forum vetus*) formerly the stronghold of the Roman Legion, stands on the right bank of the western river, the Saône; the other, Croix Rousse, whose southern slopes had been from earliest days the merchants' quarters, stands between the two rivers. Bridges were soon thrown from the land at its base over the river Saône. But there followed a period of enormous labours in damming and drainage, comparable to those expended in

28

Holland, so as to make use of this land between the rivers. A further four hundred years of effort were needed before a stone bridge could be thrown over the Rhône. The large growth of the city on the left bank of the Rhône belongs only to the last century and a half; and it is hardly more than a century since the peninsula which forms the heart of Lyons had its last dangerous inundation. So citizens of Lyons are very much aware of the untameable character of their rivers, and the thought of them has mingled intimately with their joys and sorrows. In ages of prosperity what manifestations of civic jubilation there have been on the river Saône! Whereas memories of times of violence and distress include the murderous cry, 'Au Rhône! au Rhône!'

Nor should we forget that for many centuries the rivers here were a frontier and rampart of France. There are still alive those who have been taught by their elders to think of the banks of the Rhône as *côté empire* (the left) over against *côté royaume* (the right). Yet whatever power claimed it from century to century, Lyons has always maintained a certain cosmopolitan independence. The confluence of its rivers has provided a highway for cultural and commercial currents of great importance in history.

Indeed if the bare events of its more or less exterior history were recorded, how momentous they are! The valley of the Rhône opens a way to the Orient as well as to the Mediterranean. Greek merchants must have found their way here before the year 43 B.C. when the Romans created this city of Lugdunum, a station of the first importance for imperial communication and commerce, which they were to establish as the capital of 'the Gauls'. When in A.D. 142 Polycarp, the bishop of Smyrna in Asia Minor, was asked to supply a bishop for this distant spot, the city had already been founded for two centuries, counted some 200,000 inhabitants and was the most cosmopolitan city of the west. The six names known to us of the forty-eight martyrs of Lyons and Vienne who perished so soon after their aged bishop, Pothinus, had died of the strain of persecution, indicate that they represent a variety of ages, classes and races. Moreover it was against the background of the assembly in this city of the sixty Gallic tribes that these dire events took place.

29

So Lyons from the first takes a leading part in the history of Gaul and is known to all the civilized world. From the earliest days, as now, it was said, 'No one is a foreigner in Lyons!' And from the beginning almost, though confronted in this earliest phase with the utmost hostility, the Church in Lugdunum clearly exercised a profound influence. The letter of the Christians of Lyons and Vienne to their brethren of Asia describing the passion and death of their fellow-citizens,[1] reveals the countenance of a brotherhood that by its strength of character and by its qualities both natural and supernatural is likely to win ascendancy. During the episcopate of Irenaeus which follows and under his wise direction it does so grow in stature. This first great theologian of the Church left the Christianity of Lyons marked by four abiding traits. First, faithfulness to Rome; second, a sense of the duty of preserving the unity of the Church of Christ; third, devotion to the blessed Virgin Mary; fourth, a sense of missionary responsibility. Irenaeus was recognized as a saint and so were twelve of the twenty-one persons who succeeded to the See of Lyons before the end of the fifth century. The twenty-first of these, St Patient, ministered effectively to the Burgundian royal family, especially to the princess Clotilda who married in 493 the Frankish king, Clovis, so that the first child of the Church to ascend the French throne derives from Lyons. The triumph of the Christian faith radiating from Lyons was the fruit of a Christian tradition which in the best sense was that of Christian humanism, counting amongst its sons Sidonius Apollinarius, distinguished (before he became Bishop of Clermont) as a poet and likewise as prefect of Rome, and Gregory of Tours, the famous historian of the Franks, as well as his uncle, St Nizier, the bishop who, twenty years before the reform of St Gregory the Great was teaching the church at Lyons rules for the performance of the liturgical chant.

In short, Lyons was already a great centre of learning and devotion when, towards the close of the eighth century, it was threatened with devastation by the Saracen invaders. Though these Arabs respected its strength, Charles Martel, reconquering the neighbouring regions from the pagan marauders, despoiled Lyons, so that darkness prevailed over the city for half a century during which Lyons had no bishop.

The task of reconstructing the city was entrusted by the Emperor Charlemagne to his friend, Bishop Leidrad, who must be counted second founder of the See. It was he who introduced the Lyons rite, that is to say, the Roman rite as performed in the palace of Charlemagne, a rite which is still preserved at Lyons in its Carolingian simplicity. Bishop Leidrad also founded a celebrated college which trained many distinguished scholars and became the place of refuge for other theologians, including St Anselm of Canterbury, who composed several of his works here. The archbishopric became the centre of an immense diocese and its authority both spiritual and temporal was constantly on the increase. In 1079 Pope Gregory VII established the authority of the See of Lyons over the provinces of Rouen, Tours and Sens.

By the time of the Crusades, when Christendom in turn took the offensive against the Arabs who had seized the Holy Sepulchre, Lyons had become an independent principality of great strength comprising territory taken from both the French Kingdom and the Holy Roman Empire. At its heart lay the fortified cloister around the Cathedral of St John. The valley of the Rhône was one of the chief routes of the crusading armies. Indeed the passage of the army of Philip Augustus and Richard Coeur de Lion led to the collapse of the old Pont de la Guillotière across the Rhône. This way too came St Louis, King of France, on his journey to the Holy Land, stopping to worship at the shrine of Fourvière. In 1270 his mortal remains were brought back the same way. By this time Lyons has won the description of 'second Rome'.

She has already had five popes taking refuge within her walls between 1095 and 1132. Two popes are to be crowned there within a century after this: and before that has come to pass, two 'ecumenical councils' have taken place here, the former convoked by Innocent IV in 1245, the second by Gregory X in 1274.

The council of 1274 was held in the Cathedral soon after the building of the major part of it which began in 1110. Five hundred bishops attended and sixty abbots. The gathering included Peter of

Tarentaise, formerly Archbishop of Lyons and later to become Pope Innocent V. St Bonaventura, the soul of the great assembly, died at Lyons soon after its close. St Thomas Aquinas who had been due to take part, died on the way there. At this council the union of the Churches of the East and of the West (Eastern Orthodox and Roman Catholic) was proclaimed. Though this union, like that decreed at the Council of Florence nearly two centuries later, was to last a very short time, it left great memories—symbolized by the two crosses (the Greek and the Latin) formerly placed behind the high altar of the cathedral.[2] It is surely significant that this great issue should have been treated at Lyons. It is only one of a number of events since the days when St Irenaeus pacified a quarrel between East and West, which seem to have indicated a special vocation for Lyons in this field.

In 1320 after three centuries during which its archbishop was also temporal head of an almost independent principality, the city became part of the Kingdom of France. In 1419 under the patronage of Charles VII, still Dauphin of France, and 1463 under that of Louis XI, came the beginnings of the great fairs, now held yearly, which were so to increase the fame and wealth of Lyons. It was indeed not until after it had enjoyed a century of great commercial prosperity that the French king, Francis I, led his army through the city of Lyons on its way to Italy. Within five years there began the wars of religion between Catholic and Protestant; this led to a terrible spoliation of a city whose sympathies were acutely divided. Since the days when Irenaeus wrote his great book against heresies, Lyons has always harboured earnest groups of dissentients,[3] some of them of a much nobler type than those whose beliefs that great theologian described.

We must observe incidentally that though his teaching was to flourish in the Waldensian Church most vigorously elsewhere than in Lyons, Peter Waldo (1181–1217) was a Lyonnais and his disciples were first known as the 'Poor men of Lyons'. Frequently the Church of Lyons has cherished prophetic and critical spirits within its fold. Such was Jean Gerson, the greatest spirit of the Conciliar Movement, who, driven from the post of Chancellor of the University of the

Sorbonne in Paris, during his last ten years bent his great powers to teaching the catechism to the children of the parish of St Paul. Such also was Frédéric Ozanam, founder of the Society of St Vincent de Paul. In modern times there have been Marius Gonin and other great spirits of the *Chronique Sociale de France* and of the *Semaine Sociale* initiated in Lyons in 1904.

After the wars of religion there came a second period of restoration of the churches and sanctuaries of Lyons. Another century or more of great commercial prosperity followed, due to the possession by Lyons of a monopoly in the manufacture of silk. It was to be closed by terrible bloodshed during the Revolution at the hands first of the Republicans and then of their opponents. The city was regarded as no longer existing by the time both factions had done their worst. It was then that Jacquard perfected his great invention with regard to the process of weaving, an invention which brought a wonderful recovery and an age of still greater prosperity. Such are some principal moments in the city's exterior history.

More important are events in the realm of the spirit, a realm just as concrete if less spectacular. The story as told so far has made clear the city's great influence in earlier centuries. It was during the seventeenth century that Lyons found itself a great centre of the religious renaissance brought about by the Counter-Reformation. In 1616 St Francis de Sales established at Bellecour, very close to where Paul Couturier was to live, the second convent of the order of the Visitation which he had founded. He died there in the gardener's cottage six years later and the spirit of gentleness and of true devotion which he exhaled left its deep imprint upon the Christians of Lyons. This was pre-eminently a period of religious foundations. A dozen religious communities were founded here within ten years of the arrival of the Sisters of the Visitation. Even in the century that followed, which has been called the least Christian in the history of France, this tradition of devotion and good works maintained itself. There was notable church building and at least one religious foundation. At the time of the Revolution there were more than a hundred places of Christian worship in Lyons. Many of these, specially beautiful and rich in sacred historic associations, were particularly dear to Abbé Couturier—the church of St Nizier, a lovely renais-sance building on the site of the first place of Christian worship in Lyons, the church where Paul Couturier as a boy had made his first communion; the Basilica of Ainay dedicated to St Martin, a splendid Romanesque building of the eleventh century, parts of which go back to the sixth century, the church where Abbé Couturier most often said his daily Mass; the cathedral, a building in which Romanesque and Gothic styles are so harmoniously blended, whose exquisite stained glass has survived the cathedral's drastic spoliation at the hands both of religious dissidents and political revolutionaries, and which was the place of his ordination.

Yet it would be a mistake to think of Paul Couturier as viewing Lyons simply as a beautiful city rich in sacred associations. There is no doubt that for him it was *par excellence* the city evangelical, the city of Mary and of the beloved disciple, St John, the city through whose history flowed the stream of apostolic faith and life direct from Ephesus, the home of the fourth evangelist.

Such is the Lyonnese sentiment and conviction about its own religious heritage and trust. To grasp this the reader must lift up his eyes, as the eyes of a priest were raised each day from 5 Rue du Plat, to the hill of Fourvière on the other side of the Saône. His glance must rest upon the shrine so finely situated there, that wonderful compound of splendour and ugliness, of the mystic and the common-place, the Basilica whence the Mother of the Saviour gazes serenely over her city.

It seems that there had been a shrine erected here to the Mother of Jesus from about the middle of the ninth century when the Roman forum was demolished. In the twelfth century a larger building was set by its side and dedicated to St Thomas of Canterbury, who in exile had taken refuge in Lyons; of this only a small chapel remains. It was in the middle of the seventeenth century that in gratitude for the protection of the city from the plague which was decimating Europe, the little primitive oratory of our Lady gave place to a larger building, whither every year a civic procession mounted to offer, in fulfilment of a solemn pact, a wax candle and a golden sovereign (*escu d'or*). In the eighteenth century there was a further pact and a gilded chapel was added. This, closed in the Revolution, Pope Pius VII came himself to reopen in 1805. In the century that followed many founders of religious communities dedicated themselves here. The Curé d'Ars brought a parochial pilgrimage and later secured that the dedication in 1836 of his parish to Mary Immaculate should be specially commemorated at Fourvière. In 1872 the present great Basilica began to rise at the side of the older buildings and it was completed and consecrated in the year 1896.

This was but the most recent monument of the great heritage of Lyons, the memorial of a pact many times renewed, a pledge of future faithfulness. Whenever the city has been in peril through sickness or the menace of war, request has been made by the representatives of the city for the intercession of Mary. So it had been once more in 1870 when the Prussian armies were at Dijon. Three times they had received orders to march on Lyons, but somehow circumstances prevented it. On 8 October, in the name of the city, Archbishop Ginoulhiac had made a vow to the Virgin Mother to build a church worthier of her name if her prayers should keep off the invader. The great Basilica of Fourvière is the generous if somewhat flamboyant fulfilment of this promise.

Devotion to the Blessed Virgin Mary is certainly the heart of the spiritual life of Lyons. It can be traced back at least as far as St Irenaeus. It flourished in the Middle Ages when St Bernard thought it right to rebuke the canons for observing 8 December as the feast of her conception.[4] It finds annual re-affirmation in the inscription registered in letters of light on the hill of Fourvière on the evening of this festival: LYON À MARIE, a device suggested by the far older custom still practised of setting lights in every window from one end of Lyons to the other; or again in the ceremony of 8 September when the archbishop in honour of St Mary's birthday, renewing the consecration of the city, blesses the crowds from the hilltop. Apart from these occasions of public homage the devotion of the people of Lyons to our Lady is reserved, strong and simple. There are here no legends demanding credulity, no miraculous images to be venerated. Though the city abounds in statues of the Virgin, there is something different here from the ordinary western

35

cult of the Madonna; a sobriety and strength of devotion reminiscent of early ages of Christianity. Despite the wider racial variety of its population in our times, the religion of Lyons has kept its character. Loyalty to the Roman See, missionary enthusiasm, desire for Christian unity, devotion to the Mother of God. It is Christianity as Johannine in its emphasis as it must have been at the beginning. Indeed by reason of its increased ardour for social justice it has become even more so. There is for instance a small house in the gardens that lead to the summit of Fourvière where lived a family eminently Christian and typically Lyonnais named Jaricot. Pauline-Marie Jaricot (1799–1862)—whose name was dear to Abbé Couturier —not content with being the founder of the society of the Propagation of the Faith, the greatest missionary society of the Roman Catholic Church, merits by her heroism and suffering the title of patroness of Christian socialism; and her brother, Abbé Philéas Jaricot, another soul of fire, laboured devotedly in these ways as well as in his parish—especially for the reform of hospitals.

In this world of ours, fashioned and ruled by God, the conception of Chance has but a slender and shadowy reality. In the interplay of time and space and freedom everything has its setting, its connexions, and convergences conditioned by Providence. It is not by accident that the city of St Pothinus, St Blandina, St Irenaeus, of Peter Waldo, Jean Gerson, of Ozanam, of the Jaricots, of Antoine Chevrier, was the birthplace of the society of the Propagation of the Faith, the French capital of the Catholic social movement and also the spring from which flows the Week of Universal Prayer for Christian Unity. From St John and St Polycarp to Paul Irénée Couturier and Marius Gonin we find burning continuously a single flame which derives, by way of the apostolic home in Asia Minor, from the empty tomb of the crucified Saviour.

NOTES

[1] Perhaps the loveliest jewel of the literature of the sub-apostolic age. Eusebius, *Historia Ecclesiastica* V. 1.55.

² They now stand against the wall on either side of the presbytery. For another explanation of their existence, see Archdale A. King, *The Liturgies of the Primatial Sees*, London: Longmans, 1957, p. 21.

³ This was a theme dear to Huysmans. See R. Baldick, *Vie de J. K. Huysmans*, Paris: Denvel, 1958.

⁴ See p. 173.

3

A TRANSFORMING FRIENDSHIP

———

O N one for whom the communion of saints was a living and practical experience,[1] the city of Lyons itself must have had an ever-growing influence. But during the Abbé's youth the range of this influence was limited. Until he reached the age of 39, owing to parentage and education, the dominating influences on his life were marked by a cautious and restrictive conservatism. The providential meeting in 1920 with a mind of a very different cast immensely enriched the Abbé's spirit; indeed in so far as this can happen to one immovably anchored in the faith, this friendship thoroughly re-orientated his outlook, so that he was able to enter far more deeply into the whole Catholic heritage of Lyons.

Between 1920 and 1938 the Abbé was for a month every summer the guest of M. Victor Carlhian on his family estate at Saint-Ours, Isère, a lovely and sequestered home in mountainous country within sight of the Grande Chartreuse, the monastery founded by St Bruno himself. The Abbé first went there to give lessons to one of M. Carlhian's daughters. But during these visits he was to learn lessons more momentous than those given to his pupil. There developed between host and guest a deep, unalterable friendship, and one with rich consequences for both.

Conditions seemed unpropitious for such a friendship. The priest was six years younger than the layman, but he was already a man of great singleness of mind and formed convictions. The layman was a personality of outstanding originality and force. Their appearances were in as vivid contrast as were their ruling ideas. The priest was frail, in countenance diaphanous but of insignificant stature; the layman robust, square-built and sturdy, with piercing glance and memorable beard. He looked like a farmer, but he was owner and director of a large gilding firm in Lyons. The priest, moulded by conventional Catholic education, had been subjected to extreme right-wing influences in politics, his warm heart cramped under the strait-jacket of 'correct opinions'; whereas the layman was one whose conception of the Christian life had been enlarged by the sociology of Leo XIII (*Rerum novarum*), by the *Sillon*,² the democratic movement which for a time had rallied much that was noblest in the aspiration of French youth, by a first-class mathematical and philosophical training, and by the influence of such men as Blondel, Fonsegrive, Laberthonnière, Bergson, Chevalier, Pouget, Remillieux and Teilhard de Chardin; but one who possessed, despite immense reading, the discretion of a sage rooted in the humility of a child. Each however recognized in the other one who lived by the light of Christ and in him they found one another.

M. Carlhian was very conscious of the transformation in his friend that occurred during these years. But in his modesty he attributed this drawing of the priest 'by charity towards greater light' almost entirely to the influence of a Jesuit, Père Albert Valensin. It is true that the retreats given by the latter and attended by Abbé Couturier now for several years, made their great contribution to the Abbé's spiritual development. Père Valensin's influence, through his retreats even more than through his writings, was one of the best apostolic forces of the period between the wars, rescuing many priests lost in the wastes of philanthropic humanism or liberalism or Pharisaism—an orthodoxy correct in the letter, but void of the Gospel. A disciple of Blondel as well as a son of St Ignatius Loyola, Père Valensin knew well how to interpret in terms of contemporary life the Ignatian *Spiritual Exercises* and to use them as a means of preparation for a life of action grounded in contemplation. But deep though this priestly influence went, the long conversations and daily contact with his host during the months spent at Saint-Ours were of greater moment for the liberation from spiritual bondage of M. Carlhian's guest and chaplain.

There is evidence that it was chiefly through Victor Carlhian that Paul Couturier learnt to recognize fully the all-embracing truth of the primacy of charity, a truth which he already carried unconsciously in his heart: and together with this came a new conception of progress towards the Truth, a conception no longer static but dynamic, a sense not only of the cosmos as in process of continuous creation, but of mankind as having the work of caring for the Seed entrusted to it and of labouring for its development. For all this, as his friend insists, no Damascus road conversion was required. He needed only to be true to himself and to the new light given him. Henceforth he was guarded against *intégrisme*[3] by the sense that progress in the attainment of truth is to be found, but its finding is conditioned by faith in the primacy of charity. The quest of Christian unity can no longer be thought of as a reversion to the past, but rather as an integration, to be attained in the future, of all Christian values. His rooted habit of spontaneous obedience and fidelity to the light was the secret of this transformation, as it will also prove to be of his gradual discovery of God's special purpose for his life.

Meanwhile the Abbé was to spend twelve years of apprenticeship in the school of charity. It was Père Valensin who in 1923 led him to take an active part in caring for the Russian émigrés. Largely as the result of the Bolshevik revolution, there were some 10,000 of these in Lyons or its suburbs. He thus got to know intimately Orthodox priests and archpriests of the Russian colony as well as their flocks; and through them certain exiled members of the Russian hierarchy, in particular Metropolitan Eulogius of Paris, who must be introduced more fully later. This ministry to the Russians brought him to see the need of wider Christian unity. 'As always happens', he adds in a biographical note made in 1938, 'the Russian question led me to the Anglican question'.

There is no doubt that the door of entry into his apostolate of Christian unity was devotion to the destitute and suffering. But this work of the Abbé for the Russians was pre-eminently a work of friendship. From the first he had known instinctively that charity consists not in giving presents or even in giving service but in opening one's heart: indeed less in giving than in receiving. He knew how easy it is to wound the extreme sensitiveness of men who, unable to forget their former importance, have been reduced to abject poverty and misery. A number of letters received by the Abbé from such folk—letters of appeal, of gratitude, of poignant self-disclosure, letters even of lofty spiritual counsel—reveal this work in progress. The Abbé secures work, food, warmth, or education fees for these unfortunates, but above all wins their trust and accepts their precious friendship. Such work is to the last degree exacting and full of disappointments. But the Abbé found it difficult to accept the relevance here of a theologian-friend's reminder that 'discretion is a divine attribute', being convinced that trust and self-forgetfulness are necessary conditions of love. It must have been much later that the Abbé got to know, to love well and to recommend the teaching of Charles de Foucauld as expounded and lived by Père Voillaume and the Little Brothers of Jesus. But his approach to the Russians very closely resembled that of the Little Brothers to their children in lands where they are undernourished or depressed. Only we must remember that this work of caring for exiled Russians, so absorbing in its requirements, is the spare-time work of a professional schoolmaster-priest.

What a safety-valve his friendship must have been for their confidences, often highly dramatized in form! The diseased, the workless, the student aspiring but hungry, families on the rocks whether of penury or threatened disruption—the correspondence introduces us to all these. And with what gratitude and affection he was rewarded! The tributes of these include inferior ikons, little books, sketches, bric-à-brac of all sorts: and once a model mailboat in full sail, christened 'the cathedral'—the work of a tramp who had secured refuge with the Sisters of the Poor—found its way to the fourth floor of 5 Rue du Plat.

And how much the Abbé will have enjoyed such a letter as this, received just before his departure for his holiday in the country, a letter from an old man who can quote the Apocalypse, Pascal and Dostoevsky and whose wisdom finds sometimes almost lyrical expression!

Touch the earth. For he who touches the earth, you know, renews his strength.[4] Besides he who touches the earth at the same time finds contact with the eternal life of nature. Away then into the woods and fields to contemplate and ponder the splendid rays of sunshine, the mysterious noises of the forest, the joyous cry of the birds—a treat for sages and children alike! . . .

There are two means of being happy in this world below: 1. To be successful in human affairs, that is to say, to possess power, glory, wealth, etc. . . . or 2. to despise these as futile things which can satisfy only those people who, like children, have no idea of the true value of things. The contemplation of the eternal life of nature disposes one always to seek happiness along the second way, the way of wisdom. But unhappily everyone is in perpetual hesitation as to which way to take—especially Russian refugees!

There are letters too from Russian priests so often in dire distress. Thus long before meeting the representatives of the Eastern Orthodox Church in the field of ecumenical endeavour, we find the Abbé doing what he can to discover how best to provide for its children and their pastors in their temporal needs. We may well quote the letter of Archpriest Lucas Golod, written just before his departure from the district:

> I should like to express my gratitude for all the help you give to my fellow-countrymen and to express the keen desire and hope that your interest in our poor refugees will not cease. Christian charity will reunite us all around our one and only Master and Shepherd, Christ our God.

This task of caring for the Russian refugees, great work as it was of friendship in Christ, led inevitably in a soul so humble and so receptive as that of Paul Couturier to the discovery of the liturgical, theological and spiritual riches of Eastern Orthodoxy. And more and more he came to feel in the very core of his being the horror of the rupture which had for nearly a thousand years separated such fellow-Christians from what was for him the living centre of Catholicity, a breach for which they were not to be held responsible. There were deep heart-searchings about this, and problems too which required quiet counsel and prayerful pondering with a view to their resolution. The place of succour that clearly suggested itself to a mind so disquieted was the Benedictine Priory of Amay-sur-

Meuse in Belgium, the home of the Monks of Unity. So thither the Abbé went in July 1932, preceded by a letter of recommendation from his friend, Commandant François Paris, a former French interpreter of the Russian army and a generous supporter of the monastery.

The Abbé's stay at Amay was a stage of deepest importance in the gradual discovery of his vocation: and the influence of the Monks of Unity endured fruitfully throughout his life. So something must be said of the origins of this spiritual family and of its history during the momentous years spent in its first home at Amay.

NOTES

[1] On this characteristic of the Christian life of Lyons from the first, see G. Jouassard, 'Le rôle des Chrétiens comme intercesseurs auprès de Dieu dans la Chrétienté lyonnaise au 2me siecle', *Revue des sciences religieuses*, 1956, No. 3, pp. 217–29.

[2] Founded by a student, Marc Sangnier in 1894, the aim of its members was first 'to Christianize themselves', then to 'Christianize democracy'. Its condemnation by Pope Pius X in 1910 was the most regrettable act of his pontificate. The acceptance of this by the officers of the movement was exemplary. 'It had been for me a school of action', said M. Carlhian, 'before becoming a school of obedience.' He had been president of the *Sillon* in Lyons.

[3] The extremists on the right-wing after the condemnation of Modernism by Pope Pius X in 1907 took the name of *Intégriste*, though Cardinal Innitzer of Vienna called them 'Super-Catholics'.

[4] The two seem to have been conversing about the two kinds of bows required in the Eastern Orthodox worship, the lesser (ἡ μικρὰ μετάνοια) an inclination from the hips, the greater (ἡ μεγάλη μετάνοια) involving a prostration or at least a touching of the ground.

4

THE MONKS OF UNITY

THE Benedictine Priory of the Monks of Unity at Amay-sur-Meuse in Belgium had been established in 1925 by Dom Lambert Beauduin, monk of the Abbey of Mont César, Louvain, who had been for the last five years Professor of Fundamental Theology at the Benedictine College of St Anselm in Rome. The foundation had the warm support of Cardinal Mercier, the Archbishop of Malines. But it was His Holiness Pope Pius XI who had made this great venture possible. In a letter addressed in 1924 to the Abbot Primate of the Benedictine congregations, Dom Fidelis von Stotzingen, the Pope had entrusted a primary place in the work for Christian unity to the sons of St Benedict, requiring that each congregation of the Order should have a monastery dedicated to this great end. The foundation of the monastery at Amay in the following year was the first concrete realization of this appeal. It was an immediate and generous response, and has been immensely fruitful. But it was not until 1959—thirty-five years later—that the Benedictine abbots, meeting in Rome, decided to carry out the proposal made by Pius XI. The prospect of the coming ecumenical council had no doubt stimulated this resolution. But it seems very probable that the courage and faithfulness of the Monks of Unity and in particular the sacrificial labours and the even more heroic obedience of their founder, Dom Lambert Beauduin, have done more than yet can be realized to make possible the opening of the new chapter in the history of the Universal Church of which such decisions as these are the first fruits.

There can have been few that realized that the seed-thought of this great idea which Pius XI so wisely developed, had been sown by this monk himself. Yet there is evidence that a memorandum prepared by Dom Lambert Beauduin containing some of the main points of the Pope's letter had with the encouragement of Cardinal Mercier been sent to His Holiness in November of the previous year. Pius XI who, in Poland after the end of the first great war, had encountered the flood of Russian emigrants, thus witnessing the vitality of Russian Orthodox faith and the riches of their tradition, had from his accession shown that his heart was set on union between Western and Eastern Christians. But it seems clear that this letter so far-sighted, so clear in its directions yet lying so long almost unheeded, had been influenced by the great Belgian monk whose vision, singularly penetrating, realistic and well-balanced though it was, proved always far in advance of his generation. It is good to know that three months before his death on 11 January 1960, Dom Lambert Beauduin had news of the decision made by the abbots in council at Rome that in each land there should be a monastery consecrated specially to labour for Christian unity and associated in this work with his own foundation at Chevetogne.

Such a wholly supernatural triumph of prophetic Christian vision is won only by prayer, suffering, patience and, above all, by the obedience of faith. When Abbé Couturier came to visit the monastery of Amay-sur-Meuse, the founder of the Monks of Unity had already gone into exile. He was living a hidden life of great humility and austerity in the monastery of En-Calcat near Toulouse. But the spirit of Dom Lambert reigned in the hearts of his spiritual family. So did also that of his dear friend, their great Archbishop, Cardinal Mercier. Some words about the friendship of these two great Christians will help to explain the fact of the expulsion of the founder from his monastery in the previous year 1931 and his twenty-one years of exile.

Cardinal Mercier was nominated Archbishop of Malines in 1906. In 1909 that city was the scene of the national Congress of Catholic Activities and it was there that a young monk from Mont César, engaged at that monastery in the teaching of theology, drew the attention of his archbishop and less immediately that of the Christian world in general by creating the celebrated Liturgical Movement. The movement, which was in deep harmony with the mind of Pope Pius X as expressed in a document (*motu proprio*) issued in 1903, the first year of his reign, was cordially encouraged by Archbishop Mercier. The Archbishop's immense pastoral ardour was a strong bond between him and Dom Lambert Beauduin, for it was a kindred passion that had moved Dom Lambert, formerly a factory chaplain, to espouse the sacrificial life of his monastery and thus made possible for him the discovery and exploration of the treasures of the Liturgy.

But the Archbishop and the monk had other things in common. Their great longing for Christian unity was a link just as profound. The supernatural insight and vision which made them akin was matched on the natural level by a tenacity, a warrior spirit, intense patriotism, certain common hatreds, e.g. of the German tendency to heavy pomposity and bullying, together with a vivid sense of humour. They shared these qualities also with another treasure that both possessed in common, their love for their spiritual director, perhaps the greatest Irishman of this century, Dom Columba Marmion, later to be translated from Mont César to become abbot of Maredsous.[1]

Of these three great men, Cardinal Mercier's nobility and courage were acclaimed during his life-time in every land, and because of his fearless defiance of the enemy in the 1914–18 war, he has a unique place of honour in the hearts of English-speaking people. Abbot Marmion through his writings has been hailed as a source of wisdom and light by an ever-growing multitude of souls. The greatness of Dom Lambert Beauduin—'perhaps the greatest figure of the Church in the first half of the twentieth century' (Louis Bouyer)—was hidden during his life-time even from some of his disciples and friends. He was one of those who influence the minds that have the greatest influence on others.[2]

When in the years 1921 to 1925, in response to pressure from Lord Halifax and the Lazarist priest 'Monsieur' Portal,[3] Cardinal Mercier invited to his palace at Malines theologians, Anglican and Roman Catholic, to participate in the famous Conversations of Malines, it was Dom Beauduin, at that time Professor at the Benedictine college of St Anselm in Rome, who was asked to give counsel and help on matters of special difficulty. In particular Dom Lambert Beauduin had been asked by the Cardinal to compose a memorandum on the subject of the *Pallium*, the significance of which had troubled his Anglican visitors. This resulted in the famous study, 'The Church of England united not absorbed', which so enchanted the Cardinal that he read it to his guests on his own responsibility at the fourth conference without revealing the name of the author. Dom Lambert's connexion with the conversations led later to a trial of exceptional acuteness for the newly founded monastery. This was not due, as is usually imagined, to Lord Halifax's inclusion in the Record of the *Conversations*, published in 1930, of this confidential contribution provided by Dom Lambert. It was Dom Lambert's alleged proposal for the continuation by correspondence of the Conversations of Malines, closed after the death of Cardinal Mercier, which led to his denunciation at Rome and which proved a major cause of his long and fruitful exile. It was not until 1951 that Dom Lambert could return to live in his own monastic family, now established at Chevetogne, where he lived until his death in January 1960, surrounded by the veneration and affection of all and recognized more and more clearly as having been the friend and helper of the whole Church of God. The misjudgement of ecclesiastical authority had been wonderfully overruled, for it had set Dom Beauduin free for his great work as creator of the Liturgical Movement in western Europe and for a most fruitful ministry as *pastor pastorum* in France. But all these manifold labours were the labours of one whom his old friend, His Holiness Pope John XXIII did well to recognize[4] as pre-eminently a *monk*—and a monk of great eminence: moreover all were controlled and sustained explicitly by the power of a single motive, the desire to fulfil the Saviour's supplication 'that all may be one'.

It is not surprising then that though the founder was himself in exile in France, where he and the Abbé were to come later to know and reverence one another, the spirit of Dom Lambert Beauduin pervaded the monastery. And while the guest from Lyons was to make other inspiring friendships there, his first concern was to ponder a booklet by Dom Beauduin, later to become his (the Abbé's) bedside book, in which the founder's conception of the task of the Monks of Unity was vividly and lucidly described. This task involves the cultivation in Christians of a loyally Roman spirit in combination with an oriental and Orthodox soul, the latter to be developed by the study of the Fathers, by the study and practice of ancient oriental liturgies, by travel, by personal contacts and monastic hospitality. The common origin of Benedictine and of oriental monasticism[5] creates a natural point of contact between Latins and Greco-Slavs, so much the more since the monastic life holds a place in the life of the Greek and Russian Churches of which Latins have little idea. The booklet is a notable call to penitence, to labour and to patience, not least in its description of catholicity:

> *sentire cum ecclesia*: a spirit universal, ecumenical, strange to all the narrowness of misconceived nationalism, transcending all racial barriers—the true spirit of that universal Church which Christ substituted for the nationalist synagogue.

All this was closely akin to the 'Testament of Cardinal Mercier',[6] another sacred treasure which, along with the booklet of Dom Beauduin, some Russian ikons and some batches of the incomparable journal of the Monks of Unity, *Irénikon*, the Abbé took back in his bag to Lyons. This Testament ran:

> In order to unite with one another, we must love one another; in order to love one another, we must know one another; in order to know one another, we must go and meet one another.

These words sank as deep into his heart as did the challenging words of Dom Beauduin. So did the memory and the whole spirit of the monastery with its Latin and Byzantine chapels and liturgies and the irenic and contemplative temper of its life. At the end of his month's retreat the Abbé left Amay with the desire to become an oblate of the monastery, in order to bind fast the tie of spiritual kinship of which he was conscious, with those through whom he had been given the sense of his vocation. It was through the Monks of Unity, we may even say, that the Abbé had found himself—as yet, it is true, with only a slender idea of the ways along which the Spirit of

God would lead him, but with perception sufficient to know that this was his spiritual home. On returning to Lyons, he wrote:

> I am very happy to have become a member of the Benedictine family of Amay; I have found there that of which I dreamed: the Benedictine peace of which I had heard: the Benedictine spirituality in which the supernatural is in such harmonious accord with nature: the love of the East, of its spiritual and intellectual treasure: a devotion well-informed and unshakeable to the cause of Unity. . . . (30 August 1932.)

A year later in the month's holiday which he took as chaplain to his friends, the Carlhians, in the mountain country of the Isère, there took place Abbé Couturier's reception as oblate. The Prior, Father Belpaire, received this letter from him:

Pax　　　　　17 August 1933

My Very Dear Father,

I write to you as a son since now I belong to the Priory of Amay as its oblate. . . . I had hoped to make my profession as external oblate on the day of the Assumption. This has not been possible. It was on Sunday the 13th that I came down far from our village in the woods to Saint-Ours. After shriving me, the aged curé received me as oblate in his lovely church, empty at that moment. I seemed to feel the great Benedictine peace.

Here am I henceforth associated very closely to your joys, sufferings, prayers, merits and labours. Here I will pray far away from you all, for all of you, and I will endeavour inspired by the spirit of Amay to be a sort of small, very small advance-post in the jungle [*brousse*] of France and of Lyons.

As my oblate's name I have taken Benoît [Benedict], that of the patriarch, and Irénée [Irenaeus]. Irenaeus was not a Benedictine, but he had the spirit of St Benedict. He [St Irenaeus] is the patron of the Russian chapel at Lyons, and his name is that of the society to which I belong, of priests of the diocese: and finally Irenaeus is the East come to Lyons: it means peace, Irénikon, Amay. . . .

Paul Couturier
Benoît-Irénée O.S.B.

The correspondence of this period shows him living by the 'grace of Amay', sharing its joys and trials. He assists in his prayers at the ordination of Father Basil and Father Athanasius, rejoicing that provision was thus made for both Byzantine and Latin chapels. He congratulates Dom Clément Lialine, the young Russian theologian, on his making his solemn vows and their friendship is deepened by correspondence.

At Amay the great soul of their visitor had impressed all who had made contact with him. Dom Belpaire (Canon Belpaire who had sacrificed a brilliant career to give himself up entirely to the apostolate of the East), Dom Clément Lialine, offspring of an ancient Russian family soon to be renowned as the able editor of *Irénikon*, and the other monks of Amay including, a little later and in another country, Dom Beauduin himself—all fell under his spell. But if the Abbé was, as he said so delightfully, *tanquam oblatus*, the spiritual son of the monastery, he was also the *enfant terrible*. There were times when his boldness would cause alarm and he would need to be cautioned for the monastery's sake. Yet soon his friends at Amay would be saying: 'There is nothing happening in the cause of Unity greater than what is going on at Lyons.' Certainly the seed had fallen in fruitful ground.

There was another priest who came for a few days on a short visit to the Monks of Unity at Amay while Abbé Couturier was there. It was a young Dominican, aged 28, Père Yves Congar, O.P., and the motive of his visit was the same as that of the Abbé. Each of these two great labourers for Christian Unity (who were to renew their acquaintance several times in after years) was to begin, soon afterwards and at the same time, his fruitful apostolate. It was in the next year or two that Father Congar, on the one hand, composed his first great work *Chrétiens désunis*,[7] and that, on the other hand, the January Week of Prayer for Christian Unity, clothed with a new life, was being launched into the world by Abbé Couturier. Père Congar's weapons so faithfully used have been chiefly those of the reasoning mind and of the richly stored intellect. Abbé Couturier was convinced that it is necessary first of all to touch the hearts of men in order that souls may have a chance of mutual understanding. There is a deep accord between the one labour and the other. One is reminded that Cardinal Mercier, like Père Congar a great disciple of

St Thomas Aquinas, in defending the Malines Conversations, recalled the insistence of the Council of Trent before its definition of Christian justification is given, that with a view to its reception *hearts* must first be prepared to hear the word of God: '*Praeparate corda vestra Domino*'.[8] The Cardinal thus illustrates the harmony between the two kinds of apostolate, making clear the profound need for Christians of the work of Abbé Couturier whom Père Congar himself so fitly honoured as the father of spiritual ecumenism. So also before the recitation of the Creed worshippers in the Eastern Orthodox liturgies are summoned to charity:

> Let us love one another that with one mind we may confess the Father, the Son and the Holy Spirit. . . .

NOTES

[1] Columba Marmion (1858–1923), Irish by birth, though he lived as a monk in Belgium from 1886 till his death thirty-seven years later, remained very much an Irishman. He was abbot of Maredsous from 1909 to 1923, and an unusually gifted spiritual writer and director. His teaching is based on St Paul interpreted with the aid of the patristic and liturgical tradition of Benedictine monasticism.

[2] It is now recognized that the inspiration for the famous letter *Patriotism and Endurance* which Cardinal Mercier addressed to his people in Christmas 1914 came largely from Dom Lambert Beauduin in his cell at Mont César.

[3] It was thus that Abbé Fernand Portal was known in student circles in Paris, to which he ministered most fruitfully during his latter years.

[4] *Telegram received from His Holiness on the day of the funeral:* Sa Sainteté ayant gardé très vivant Souvenir Dom Lambert Beauduin apprend avec peine décès zélé artisan renouveau liturgique contemporain. Recommandant tout coeur divine miséricorde âme excellent religieux envoie moines Chevetogne gage divins réconforts. Paternelle bénédiction apostolique.   *Cardinal Tardini.*

[5] St Benedict himself in his Rule speaks of 'our holy father, St Basil', and of his rule with great reverence (*Regula* LXXIII).

[6] It was, no doubt, Dom Beauduin who concisely summarized the ecumenical wisdom of his friend, the cardinal, in these words which came to be known as Mercier's 'Testament'. The pamphlet quoted above is *L'Œuvre des moines Bénédictins d'Amay-sur-Meuse*, 2nd ed., Amay, 1926.

[7] Yves M. J. Congar, O.P., *Chrétiens désunis*, Paris. Editions du Cerf, 1937: English trs. (*Divided Christendom*), 1939; see note 1, p. 122.

[8] Conc. Trent XI. C.6 quoting I Sam 7.3.

5

CRUSADES OF PRAYER
FOR UNITY

————◆————

ABBÉ Couturier returned from Amay determined to propagate at Lyons the devotion known as the Octave of Prayer for Christian Unity. In seeking to bring about the dedication of Christians throughout the world to prayer for Christian unity, neither he nor the founders of the Octave were the first in the field. It is clearly right for us to consider the antecedents, the genesis and the development of this idea.

Prayer for unity has always been offered by the Church of Christ who himself on the night of his betrayal prayed that we may all be one. In the Eucharist, wherever the Roman rite is said, prayer is made regularly that our Lord will grant to his Church 'that peace and unity which is according to his will'. The liturgies of the East all contain prayers to the same end. In the Anglican Communion, and in those increasingly numerous Methodist churches which use the prayers of the Book of Common Prayer, God is constantly besought 'to inspire continually the universal Church with the spirit of truth, unity, and concord'. The Churches of the Reformation, especially the most venerable of all, the *Unitas Fratrum* or Moravian Brethren, pray constantly for unity, though the unity sought for by these Churches has been predominantly invisible unity in the domain of the Spirit.

Besides such liturgical prayer there have sprung up organized movements of prayer which may be regarded as preludes to the crusades of prayer for unity, as they have been in a sense analogous to them. Amongst these may be recalled the great movement of united prayer for the Holy Spirit and Revival which passed from Scotland to America and swept back thence to England, Holland, Switzerland and America finding prophetic expression in the work of the New England Congregationalist, Jonathan Edwards (1705–58), *An Humble Attempt to Promote Explicit Agreement and Visible Union of God's people in Extraordinary Prayer, for the Revival of Religion and the Advancement of Christ's Kingdom on Earth, Pursuant to Scripture Promises and Prophecies concerning the Last Time.* To this wide-spread movement which lasted throughout the latter part of the eighteenth century can be traced the great outburst of missionary activity in Britain and America in the beginning of the nineteenth. It had outstanding results in drawing together Christians of different denominations in that missionary and evangelistic activity which did so much to bring about the ecumenism of our own times. The mantle of Jonathan Edwards fell on James Haldane Stewart, Rector of St Bride's, Liverpool, whose book, *Hints for a General Union of Christians for Prayer for the outpouring of the Holy Spirit* (1821) was even more widely influential. His invitation to Christians to set aside the first Monday of the year for prayer for the outpouring of the Spirit may well have suggested to the Evangelical Alliance its New Year Week of Prayer. To 'The World Evangelical Alliance' as it is now called we may be indebted for the currency of the term 'ecumenical' which its founders used frequently. But its Week of Prayer with its 'call to prayer to Christians all over the world' is probably its most significant achievement.

Perhaps it is owing to the influence of this that a number of organizations have set aside special days or weeks for united prayer with a view to their several objectives. Amongst these St Andrew's Day, now widely observed in many denominations as a Day of Prayer for Missions, is associated with the inspiring memory of Bishop George Howard Wilkinson of St Andrews, Primus of the Scottish Episcopal Church. In 1901 Bishop Wilkinson had joined with Dr William Milligan and other Presbyterian leaders in securing the setting aside of 13 October as a special day of prayer for union amongst the Churches of Scotland. But it was his last words, spoken to the Executive of the Representative Church Council of the Scottish Episcopal Church at Edinburgh, 11 December 1907, which made the greatest impression. He bade Christians, when the Church is in any special need, to speak of it together to God 'as a child would tell its mother all its needs. The acknowledgement of God will ensure that God will bless the work.' The Bishop died before the meeting could be closed.

The Calls to Prayer issued by the World Student Christian Federation and by the Y.M.C.A. and Y.W.C.A. have laid increasing stress on prayer for Christian unity. But though all these movements have laid trails in the direction of unity and wonderfully prepared the way, the impulse to pray explicitly for the reunion visible as well as invisible of Christendom came largely, though not entirely, from the leaders of the Roman Catholic and of the Anglican communions and first from the initiative of individual Roman Catholics or Anglo-Catholics.

The first proposal for a union for prayer for unity came from a Roman Catholic 'convert' from evangelicalism,[1] the Hon. and Rev. Augustus Spencer better known afterwards as the Passionist Father, Ignatius (carefully to be distinguished from 'Father' Ignatius of Llanthony). On a visit to Oxford he proposed to Newman and Pusey a union for prayer for unity such as he had been instrumental in inaugurating amongst French and German Christians. Pusey saw difficulties: amongst others that he had rejected such a proposal from the Low Church side, i.e. from James Haldane Stewart of Liverpool. But with the encouragement of Keble and Newman, he sought to find a plan for a union of prayer which might meet with the approval of the bishops. Though the bishops gave little encouragement, Newman sketched a Plan of Prayer for Union which furnished the idea of the prayers circulated in 1845 by Pusey, Keble and Marriott for use at three Hours of the day: 1. for the unity of the Church, 2. for the conversion of sinners, 3. for the advancement and perseverance of the faithful; these are still in constant use by several Anglican communities after the offices of Terce, Sext and None respectively, and by a multitude of individuals.

The honoured and beloved name of Ambrose Phillips de Lisle, a distinguished layman who left the Church of England for Rome in pre-Tractarian days and later founded the Trappist monastery of Mount St Bernard in Leicestershire, is closely connected with the Association for the Promotion of the Unity of Christendom (A.P.U.C.), which was the first society actually founded to pray for unity. Its formation was provoked by de Lisle's famous pamphlet, *The Future Unity of Christendom*, highly praised by Newman and itself developing the theme of a notable writing of Cardinal Wiseman, his *Letter to Lord Shrewsbury*. The good feelings[2] engendered by de Lisle's pamphlet with its hope of corporate reunion led, after conversation between Bishop Forbes of Brechin and Dr F. G. Lee on the Anglican side, and de Lisle and A. W. Pugin on the Roman side, to the foundation of the A.P.U.C. in the same year 1857 and this with the 'distinct approval' of Cardinal Wiseman. The Association united in its membership Anglicans, Roman Catholics and Orthodox and had for its sole object daily intercession for visible unity through the use of the 'Our Father' and the prayer for unity from the Roman Missal. Unfortunately it had many enemies and when Cardinal Wiseman's health failed, the charge of English affairs came more and more into the hands of the chief of these, the ex-Anglican Dr Manning. When in 1864 the Holy Office issued a decree forbidding Roman Catholics to become or remain members, though this contained a misrepresentation known by him to be based on mistranslation,[3] Manning did his best to prevent the withdrawal of the decree and to get the condemnation of the Association confirmed at Rome. It was the victory of the English Ultramontane Roman Catholics, Manning, Talbot, Ward and others over such minds as Wiseman, Newman and de Lisle that first made Anglican reunionists look for understanding to the Continent rather than to members of the Roman Church in England. For it is to be remembered that what Rome had believed itself to be condemning was not a union of prayer for Christian unity, but a union which put forward (as the charter of A.P.U.C. in English carefully refrained from doing) the assertion that the three great bodies concerned, the Roman Catholic, the Greek Orthodox and the Anglican each had 'an equal right to claim the title Catholic'.[4]

Three years later in 1867 came the first Lambeth Conference. From this time onwards the bishops of the Anglican Communion have never met in conference at Lambeth without pressing the need of prayer for reunion. In 1878 they recommended the observance of a special season for this round about Ascension Day. The scope of this idea was enlarged in 1894 owing to the labours of a great Methodist worker for reunion, Henry (later Sir Henry) Lunn. This young Methodist minister of catholic outlook who was also medical doctor, missionary, journalist and tourist agent, created with the aid of his *Review of the Churches* a series of notable Home Reunion Conferences at Grindelwald from which appeal was made to the Archbishop of Canterbury to invite Christians of his own and other Communions to join in prayer if possible on Whit Sunday, for unity amongst Christians. The Archbishop (Edward W. Benson) issued such an invitation for Whit Sunday 1894 and 1895. In the latter year, in obedience to the command of Pope Leo XIII, the Roman Catholic Church in England also offered special prayers for unity on the same Sunday. But already the Pope had himself enjoined upon Catholics throughout the world the first octave or novena of prayer for Christian Unity to be observed from the feast of the Ascension to Pentecost and in 1897 he established this in perpetuity.

What is the relation between this week of prayer enjoined by the Pope for the reconciliation of the 'separated brethren' and that which the Abbé Couturier was so wonderfully to enlarge? To get a clear idea of this we must return again to the great figures of Lord Halifax and Abbé Portal, meeting them at an earlier point in their friendship.

It was in 1890 that this friendship was formed through their providential meeting on the island of Madeira. Halifax's clearly Catholic spirit and faith and his glowing enthusiasm for unity roused in Portal the desire to know and to make known the Church of England. After the two had exchanged a number of visits, the idea was born of a direct approach to Rome to secure consideration of the subject of Anglican Orders. Soon the diplomatic activities of Lord Halifax and the literary labours of Abbé Portal led to representations being made to Rome at the highest level. Leo XIII, despite great friendliness to Portal, showed at first a signal lack of understanding of the English mind and religious situation. His encyclical *Ad Anglos* of April 1895 rather naïvely appeals to the English people *in toto* to return to its true home in the Church of Rome. Later in the year, however, he felt constrained to appoint a commission of six theologians to go into the matter of Anglican Orders. Three of the commission at least seem to have been at one time convinced that the Orders were valid, but a further commission of cardinals had to adjudicate upon the question, and here the influence of Cardinal Vaughan who was naturally opposed to any yielding on the point, triumphed. (Vaughan had sensibly enough urged upon Halifax that the first question discussed should be the doctrinal question of the claim of Rome itself, and perhaps his subsequent hostility to proceedings was augmented by the small attention paid to his wishes.) So the high hopes of the two friends were dimmed by the issue in 1896 of the Bull *Apostolicae Curae* which refused to recede from the uncompromising attitude over this matter that Rome had taken up from the time of the Reformation. The next year in the encyclical *Divinum illud munus* the Pope established the Ascensiontide novena of prayer for unity. It is thus the Papacy itself which took the initiative with regard to the observance of a week of prayer for Christian unity. This novena is still observed between Ascension Day and Pentecost in Rome and in many other places, but except in Rome less officially than the Week of Universal Prayer.

Lord Halifax and Abbé Portal were undaunted by this disappointment. For one thing the official *Responsio* of the Anglican archbishops to the bull of condemnation set forth the Catholic position of the Church of England with regard to the priesthood, the Real Presence and the Sacrifice in the Holy Eucharist in terms more explicit than had ever before been used by such authority. Lord Halifax for the next quarter of a century, with the aid of Abbé Portal, continued quietly to prepare men's minds for a further step towards that reunion in the eventual attainment of which he never lost faith. When Halifax was already 82 years of age, the second great venture of these two friends in quest of unity which led to the famous Malines Conversations, was made possible by the issue by the

Lambeth Conference of 1920 of the *Appeal to all Christian People* and by the cordial reply sent by Cardinal Mercier, in whose archiepiscopal palace the Conversations were held.

II

It was in 1908, half-way between these two ventures, that under Anglican auspices was founded, in circumstances to be described later, the second crusade of prayer for Christian unity long known as the Church Unity Octave, which we have seen Abbé Couturier setting out to use at Lyons.

It is difficult not to associate this week, the 18–25 January, with Cardinal Mercier and Lord Halifax: the 'year's mind' of the former comes on the sixth, that of the latter on the second day of this week. Lord Halifax's presence at Cardinal Mercier's deathbed while he was expected to appear at a great Reunion meeting in London, along with the Cardinal's touching gift to Halifax on his deathbed of his ring, was unforgettable. And the death of Lord Halifax in this week eight years later, soon after his last trumpet-call for reunion, must also be closely connected with this week of prayer in the minds of many who observe it. Moreover as we shall see, a suggestion from Lord Halifax led the first step to be taken towards the creation of the Octave.

Cardinal Mercier's death in 1926 virtually brought the Conversations of Malines to a close. The fifth Conversation had been due to open on 25 January. The final one, felt by all to be a winding-up, came later under his successor, Cardinal van Roey. Malines, it has been well said, 'sums up nearly a century of endeavour to put into practice the ecumenical ideals of the Oxford Movement'. The cutting-short of the Conversations through the death of the host gave them the appearance of failure. But a torch had been lit, the torch of irenic charity whose light has been shining since in many small gatherings between the Roman and other Churches. It is a 'light that has waxed rather than waned', and perhaps few Roman Catholics and still fewer Anglicans doubt any longer that it was kindled by the Holy Spirit.

As Cardinal Mercier lay dying, his friend, Dom Lambert

Beauduin, prior of the new foundation which had been sanctioned that autumn at the Pope's request by the Benedictine abbots gathered at St Anselm in Rome, was taking possession of the buildings at Amay-sur-Meuse under the patronage of the Archbishop of Malines. The Monks of Unity, who are thus a living memorial to Cardinal Mercier, also come gratefully to the minds of those who pray for unity that week.

It was, we have noticed, half-way between the first venture of Halifax and Portal for unity and the second venture of a quarter of a century later which we have just been describing, that the January *Octave* for church unity came into being. The seeds from which it grew had been sown earlier, with Lord Halifax's approval, on St Peter's day in the first year of this century. On that day the Reverend Spencer Jones, an Anglican country clergyman, preached a sermon at St Matthew's, Westminster, in a series arranged by the Association for the Promotion of the Unity of Christendom, a society which continued bravely until 1921, despite its having been deprived unjustly as we have seen of its Roman Catholic members.[5] After the sermon Lord Halifax came into the vestry and said 'Now you must publish that!' On returning home the preacher found the sermon growing into the book, published two years later with a preface by Lord Halifax under the title *England and the Holy See* (Longmans, 1902). The book was a lucid, able expression of the point of view of the minority within the Anglo-Catholic party of the Church of England known as Papalists, and it is still worth reading. It created a minor sensation, being reviewed in every country in Europe. It also led to a correspondence between its author and a priest of the Protestant Episcopal Church of America, the Reverend Lewis Thomas Wattson. The latter was in October 1908 to become the Reverend Paul James Francis, S.A., first Father General of the Franciscan friars of the Atonement. Until, with this community which he had founded as an Anglican, he joined the Roman Catholic Church, Wattson, at the same time as Spencer Jones and in a similar manner, had been attempting to blaze a way through a forest of Protestant prejudice in America. The two priests became friends and, despite a marked difference in character and gifts, along with the change of ecclesiastical allegiance on the part of one, remained so all their lives. Together they wrote *The Prince of the Apostles* (Graymoor, 1907).

In November of the same year Spencer Jones provided what Wattson thereafter called 'the seed-thought of the Octave'. He wrote to Wattson suggesting that St Peter's day each year, 29 June, might be observed as a day for preaching sermons on the prerogatives of St Peter and on the Holy See as the centre of unity. This suggested to the zealous American a more effective scheme. 'After prayer and consideration', Father Wattson recorded, 'the thought of the Church Unity Octave came to me strongly, and I wrote that I intended to begin . . . eight days of prayer for the reunion of Christendom from the feast of the Chair of St Peter at Rome to that of the Conversion of St Paul 18–25 January inclusive, instead of 29 June.' The purpose of this Octave was thus primarily for the reunion of Christendom on a papal basis. It was observed by both priests for the first time in the following January (1908). On 13 October of that year in the chapel of Graymoor the American apostle of unity and all his flock were received into the Roman Catholic Church.

There is a notable contrast between these two friends and their ways of seeking reunion, though both were so firmly united by their faith in prayer and their grateful devotion to Rome. The English scholar-athlete of Oxford University, near relative of John Keble, had known Dr Pusey and had visited Cardinal Newman; he had something in him of the reserve of the Tractarian fathers and had chosen the quiet life of a country parish priest, being specially eminent in the art of catechizing children. The generous heart of the American rejoiced in publicity and in all the streamlined techniques of the Catholicism of his land. The Fathers of the Atonement inherit his devotion, his prodigious energy and his gift for propaganda. Their zeal for the spread of the observance of the Octave is in principle indistinguishable from their eagerness to win 'converts' to their own Church. This enthusiastic devotion has won the approval of the highest authority. In 1909 Pius X approved the observance of the Octave. In 1916 Benedict XV extended its observance to the whole Roman Catholic Church. Pius XII in 1946 augmented the indulgences affixed to the observance of the Octave which requires the recitation of special prayers for the return of all Christians to submission to the Roman See and prayer for the intentions of the Supreme Pontiff.

Of the co-initiators of the Octave, Wattson died on 8 February 1940 and Spencer Jones on 28 January 1943. From the first modest Anglican efforts in the chapel of our Lady of the Angels, Graymoor, and in the ancient parish church of St David, Moreton-in-the-Marsh, they had lived to see the week they had chosen very widely observed as a time of prayer for unity. It was only Spencer Jones who lived to recognize that, at the hands of another apostle of unity, the dear friend of his old age, Paul Couturier, the Octave had been baptized into a larger and a more evangelical life.[6]

NOTES

[1] The Hon. and Rev. Augustus Spencer was attracted to the Roman Church by Ambrose Phillips (later Ambrose Phillips de Lisle) whose father had hoped that Mr Spencer might win his son back to the Church of England. Doubtless Spencer's former evangelical background made him at one time encourage unions of prayer, though he afterwards distrusted that method.

[2] The pamphlet was, however, criticized by Cardinal Wiseman as full of errors. Its phraseology is certainly unfortunate. *Vide* W. Ward, *Life and times of Cardinal Wiseman* vol. II, London. Longmans, 1897, p. 485ff.

[3] The English version of the Basis of the Association (of which there were more or less free translations in French and Latin) of set purpose and in order to avoid controversy, spoke merely of uniting in prayer all who *claimed* to belong to Christ's Holy Catholic Church, i.e. Roman Catholics, Anglicans and Orthodox. The Latin, and still more unhappily the French, failed to translate this faithfully. 'Had the English version, which was corrected and edited by de Lisle, been literally adhered to, it is probable that the Holy Office might have taken a very different view of the Association' (E. S. Purcell, *Life and Letters of Ambrose de Lisle* vol. I, p. 373; cited by H. R. T. Brandreth, *Doctor Lee of Lambeth*, London: S.P.C.K. 1951, p. 101).

[4] Father Bernard Leeming, S.J., in his book *The Churches and the Church*, London: Darton, Longman and Todd, 1960, p. 51, writes that Cardinal Wiseman, 'far from being friendly to A.P.U.C., had sent a report on the subject to Rome'. He refers to Ward, *op. cit.* vol. II, pp. 479-91. The Report

printed there is entitled 'Report on the "Union Party" in the Anglican body'. It does not mention the A.P.U.C. *The Union Review*, which it describes, was a journal edited by certain members of the A.P.U.C. It was welcomed at first by Phillips, who was prone to excessive optimism, but was disapproved later, when it opened its columns to 'factious Catholic priests'. Phillips himself had received, and deservedly, more than one reproof from the Cardinal for his romantic schemes of reunion and his ill-considered language in propagating them. But he knew how to accept rebuke. Hence 'Wiseman, who so long as his position was not misrepresented, always had a sympathy with the Association, offered to present to Rome a memorial from its members, to the effect that its nature and aims had been misunderstood.' This was after its condemnation. See Ward, *op. cit.* vol. II, p. 489.

⁵ Père Maurice Villain, S.M., has written: 'Who can say if in the secret weavings of Providence the *Church Unity Octave* of which Spencer Jones was one of the promoters, is not a daughter of that *Association for the Promotion of the Unity of Christendom* for the organization of which Phillips (de Lisle) laboured so hard, and if the Conversations of Malines are not related to those projects of theological conversations (*colloques*) about which eighty years before the squire of Grace-Dieu (Ambrose Phillips de Lisle) talked with Bloxam?' See the admirable article by Père Villian called 'Un Promoteur de la "Corporate Reunion" ' in volume II of *L'Église et les Églises 1054–1954*, a collection of essays offered to Dom Lambert Beauduin, O.S.B. on the occasion of his eightieth birthday (Editions de Chevetogne, 1954). The historical facts correspond with Père Villain's divinations. Lord Halifax in his youth had known Phillips (de Lisle); Father Spencer Jones venerated him.

⁶ Since the last war there has been a growing change for the better in the relations between Anglicans and English Roman Catholics. It has been due to the Roman Catholic religious orders, especially the Dominicans. They realized that it is the method and still more the spirit of the Malines Conversations despite the mistakes made by the pioneers which will bring about the reunion of Christendom. Under obedience they have been pursuing the same course in our land. Recent events have produced a wholly new spirit of friendliness. In some cases this has led to the formation of groups for the discussion of religious topics such as have long existed among religious. Many secular priests now show wonderful understanding towards us. French Catholic understanding—and our continued need of it—is evident in *Lumiere et Vie* XII, no. 64, devoted to the Anglican Communion. This contains a kindhearted but woefully misleading article by the present Archbishop of Westminster.

6

THE PSYCHOLOGY
OF THE OCTAVE

IF it was from Amay and its home of Benedictine peace that Paul Couturier had brought the idea of propagating the Church Unity Octave, it was in the milieu—Catholic, Orthodox, Protestant—of cosmopolitan Lyons that the idea had first to triumph. So it was evident that it could not long flow in a mould similar to that framed by its initiators. There were to be some trial flights and a good deal of costing reflection and searching experiment before it could find its new life and its fresh name. But two things should be observed. First, Abbé Couturier never hesitated to make clear, even to the sternest critics of the Octave, that it was to this that the Week of Universal Prayer owed its origin. For example he writes much later to Pastor Rosendal of the Swedish Church:

> The origin of this movement is in fact the Octave of the Atone-ment pure and simple, which you have seen in *The Lamp* [Father Wattson's magazine], but I have shown how it must be broadened and decentralized, and how Providence blesses this broadening and this purely evangelical concentration.

Secondly, as a Roman Catholic, he could not see why the Octave in its old form should not serve a good purpose amongst papalists in his own and other Churches. Thus he writes to the English initiator of the Octave, the Reverend Spencer Jones:

> You know how much I desire the increasing success of the Church Unity Octave which is your work; and it is a magnificent

work. I pray for this success. But [he continues], I have the profound conviction of the absolute necessity of the *Universal Prayer*. May God bless both of these movements for his glory alone.

The attitude of the Abbé here[1] recalls the shrewd and gentle charity of our Lord towards those who 'find the old wine better' (Luke 5.39). Indeed, as regards the original Jones-Wattson Octave, Christians have surely the right and the duty to ask God, for his glory, to extend belief in what we believe to be truth and justice, even if we are humbly aware that we see through a glass darkly. To use a crude metaphor, it is wholesome and natural in rowing to hope that one's own boat will win, especially if one fancies that other crews have some of them, consciously or unconsciously, broken the rules! A Christian does thus hope and desire whether in explicit prayers or in the half-conscious yearnings of his heart that the divine truth which he sees so clearly and which seems to be obscured elsewhere, shall prevail in the Church of the future. But he cannot ask Christians who do not share his doctrinal premises to join him in offering these prayers. Nor in any case is it in prayers for unity *framed to express a particular doctrinal standpoint*, however dear this be to him, that any Christian will find the deepest satisfaction and expansion of his being. Prayer is not like that, or rather it finds its depths in a simpler abandonment of our will in union with that of our Saviour.

Be that as it may, it was abundantly clear to Abbé Couturier that the vast majority of Christians found the papal basis of the Octave an insuperable obstacle to participation; and he set himself to seek a way and a formula in which all might join in praying for unity without any wounding of denominational loyalties. He found this implicit in the Roman Missal where the Church asks in almost every Eucharist that our Lord who prayed on the eve of his Passion that all may be one, will grant to his Church 'that peace and unity which is according to [his] will'. It was necessary for the intention of the Octave—an intention clearly identical with that of Christ, since it uses this prayer from the Missal, albeit with Petrine versicle and response implying the papalist viewpoint—to be expressed in a form to which every Christian in whatever religious tradition or stage of development could subscribe. The Abbé came therefore to ask all to join in prayer 'that God will give the visible unity of his Kingdom such as Christ wishes and through whatever means he wishes'. (There are several slight variations from year to year in the wording of this form, but it remains in substance the same.) The Octave of prayer which by reason of the very character of its devotions as well as of its accompanying propaganda has been eschewed by the large majority of Eastern Orthodox, Anglicans and all other Protestants[2] was thus renamed to become the *Week of Universal Prayer of Christians for Christian Unity.*

The success of this change was immediate. Already in 1938 the flood of supplication evoked in the Week exceeded its founder's hopes.

> It is an immense current [he wrote to Pastor Rosendal] in which are mingled several streams including the primitive waters, those of the Atonement. But the current is strong enough now to draw in these without harming the river of the Universal Prayer. . . . Have you not, as I have, the unshakeable conviction that God is *waiting* for this Universal Prayer, modulated according to different spiritualities, springing forth at this one sorrowful point of Christian divisions just in order that all Christians through prayers sincere and loyal may receive from him the gift of their recovered unity?

The first stage at Lyons was the setting aside for this purpose not of seven days, but of three—a *Triduum for the return to unity, 20–22 January 1933.* The folders announcing this run as follows:

CHURCH OF ST FRANCIS DE SALES
Solemn Triduum of Prayers and Instructions
given by
R. P. ALBERT VALENSIN, S.J.
For the return of separated Christians
to
The unity of the Church

Friday 20 January and Saturday 21 January
at 8.15 p.m. sharp
Under the Presidency of
Mgr ROUCHE, vicar general

Sunday 22 January at 3 p.m. sharp
Under the Presidency of
His Eminence Cardinal MAURIN
Liturgical vocal music in Latin and Russian alternately

It was a comparatively small undertaking, but a description which survives shows its high quality and the rightness of its fresh approach to the people of Lyons. Père Valensin, who directed devotions, emphasized the necessity of fraternal prayer to express and render fruitful the charity which must be displayed on each side. Thus little by little would be dissolved the misunderstandings accumulated by a separation of several centuries on the road which leads to the cradle of Christ. And so the hope of unity founded on the truth of the living Christ, perpetuated in his Church, will be neither illusion nor mere sentiment nor compromise. It is a unity as much visible in corporate fellowship as hidden—that is to say from any eyes but those of God—within the mystic Christ which our prayer and our hope must be relentlessly seeking.

> This unity was once a reality in Lyons. . . . The two crosses behind the high altar of the Cathedral recall the days at the close of the Council of 1274 when the arches rang with the double rendering of Gloria and Creed in Latin and Greek.

In this triduum the alternate singing of the Latin and Slav choirs seemed to recall that exhilarating but fleeting moment of reunion in the thirteenth century. At the same time there was held in the city an exhibition of Greek and Russian ikons to strengthen the impression given in church of the Eastern Orthodox religious approach.

Simplicity, prudence, humility: these were the notes of this small beginning, so notable for its refusal of one-sided apologetic and for the liberty given to free and authentic expression of the Christian mentality of both East and West.

Next year 1934 the triduum has become a *solemn octave of prayer*, 18–25 January. Every evening at the convent of *Adoration Réparatrice* there was a sermon, and afterwards prayers which the congregation might follow in a booklet called *For the union of nations in the Unity of the Church*. On Sunday at the Cathedral a Jesuit Father gave an address, and once more there was Russian as well as Western liturgical music.

In 1935 the word Octave was used for the last time. There was already to be heard the new note of penitence for the *intolerable scandal* of disunion, a note so characteristic of the Couturier approach; and the intimation that Christians of other Communions were adding their prayers. Mention was made of Anglican communities, in particular of the Benedictines of Nashdom. During the week instructions were given on the Papacy, on Orthodoxy Greek and Russian, on Anglicanism, on Protestantism and on Judaism. The question of the 'causes of the separation of the East and its persistence' and that of the 'proper means for recovering its unity with Rome' were also treated.

But the great event of the week was the service of Sunday in the Cathedral with the sermon of Père Salet, S.J. The crowd exceeded the limits of the space available. There were present hundreds of Russian Orthodox, with their archpriest, Victor Pouchkine, by whom was seated Père Nedtochine who ministered to Russian Catholics in Lyons. The Abbé had invited the Orthodox, with the sanction of their Metropolitan Eulogius, at the same time securing that at each of the three Orthodox chapels in Lyons as well as in the Russian Catholic chapel there should be a sermon on unity and a *moleben* (service of intercession) for this end.

Père Salet took as his text that used by St Bonaventura in preaching at the Council of Lyons held in the same building in 1274: 'Lift up thyself, O Sion, and gaze towards the east; behold thy children that had departed, return to thee' (Baruch 5.5).

'But what help can it be', he said, 'to tell citizens of Lyons this ancient story of seven hundred years ago, since the aftermath has been so gloomy?' The preacher insisted that whatever has been the failure in the past, there was now something more, and something indispensable, to be said: There was need for the initiative of the Church to be supported by—something lacking in the Middle Ages —the great orchestra of the Spirit provided by the people of Christ. There must be preparation on the part of the bulk of the Church in prayer and longing for reconciliation, if the complementary treasures of truth from East and West are to find their unity in Christ. There was much in all this that was new to Latin minds and profoundly consoling to their Orthodox brethren.

Sad to say, the presence of the Eastern Orthodox in the Cathedral on that Sunday, 21 January 1935 received unfavourable comment, so that the Abbé was temporarily estranged from some of his friends and supporters. The suffering that this brought him was the occasion and, at least in part, the cause for his giving utterance to a larger truth, a word of God which had been burning its way into his soul.

NOTES

[1] Compare also his article, 'Rapprochement between Christians in the XXth century', *Reunion*, V, No. 36, 1946, p. 187: see pp. 127, 131.

[2] For this use of the word Protestant to include Eastern Orthodox and Anglicans, cf. Professor H. S. Alivisatos of Athens University: 'The Orthodox Church in many respects and ways can be regarded as the first Protestant Church, having repudiated certain things against which the Protestant world protested some centuries later' (*Ecumenical Review*, XII, No. 1, October 1959, p. 10).

7

FIRST UTTERANCES TO THE CHRISTIAN WORLD

———◆———

Lux vitae caritas.[1] Light came in the darkness: and its source was charity. Darkness for the moment had seemed in charge. The Octave, Abbé Couturier saw, ought to give the impression of unanimity in prayer offered by all Christians. The facts even at Lyons had been sadly different. If in the Cathedral this year there had been, in the large attendance of the Orthodox, an augury of a new and better state of things ahead, this had been sadly misunderstood. Moreover their presence had been due to special conditions. The sanction of their own Metropolitan Eulogius had enabled the Russians to co-operate in freedom and without any loss of self-respect. It was indeed the letter which the Abbé had received from the Metropolitan Eulogius which clarified his notion of what was wrong in the contemporary state of affairs and of what was needed to remedy it.

Who was Metropolitan Eulogius? A prelate to whose statesmanship, clear vision, courage and firmness of character the Russian Christian dispersion in the west of Europe is most deeply indebted. But the debt is shared by all Christians of the West. A great person and as great a personality! His vivid Memoirs,[2] which by his instruction were published the year after his death in August 1946, give by the chapter headings his biography in a nutshell: 'Rector of the Seminary', 'Bishop', 'Member of the Second Duma', 'Member of the Third Duma' (the Duma corresponds to the House of Commons, to membership of which Bishop Eulogius was elected by free voting),

'Bishop of Holm', 'Archbishop of Volhynia', 'Metropolitan exarch of the Ecumenical Patriarch for Russian churches in Western Europe'. Clearly Providence was preparing him for the difficult and important position recorded in the last of these headings, a position which he occupied for the last quarter of a century, 1920–46, of his long life. Another point in his preparation was that, as Bishop of Holm, in 1912 he became a moving spirit in the Russian Society of the Friends of the Anglican Church inaugurated in St Petersburg in 1912. It was by invitation of this Society that in 1912 Father F. W. Puller of the Society of St John the Evangelist—'a charming old man, my dear friend', says the Archbishop—went to Russia and gave lectures on 'The Continuity of the Church of England', and in 1914 Father Walter Frere of the Community of the Resurrection, later Bishop of Truro, delivered in St Petersburg his lectures on *English Church Ways*[3] and *The Life of the Anglican Church*.[4]

Metropolitan Eulogius's earlier ministry was exercised largely in the extreme west of the Russian Empire, in a belt of territory which for hundreds of years had been a battleground between Orthodoxy from the east and Roman Catholicism from the west: a struggle partly political, Roman Catholicism standing for the Polish striving for independence, Orthodoxy identified with the claims of Russia. The young prelate managed to rise above the political passions which surged around him, and in Volhynia and Galicia Orthodoxy prospered under his administration. He was a leading member of the famous Sobor (church council) of 1917, called after the Revolution and carried out under the barrage of the struggle in which the Communists broke the last resistance of the Liberals. Here he was responsible for two valuable forward-looking proposals—the first, for the provision of shorter services for the ordinary churches, the very long ceremonial to be preserved only in the monasteries: the second, for the translation of the Liturgy into Russian from the Church Slavonic which dates from the evangelization of the Slavs in the ninth century. Both proposals were most regrettably defeated.

After the new patriarchal order had been established, Eulogius was one of the six hierarchs elected to the Patriarchal Holy Synod charged with the reorganization of church life, canonical and liturgical. When final disorder rent the country, especially the stormy west, he was imprisoned for a time by the Poles and Roman Catholic authorities and eventually escaped to Western Europe. There in 1921, contact between Moscow and the West becoming more and more difficult, he was named by Patriarch Tikhon Metropolitan for Western Europe, and at once took up his official residence on the ground-floor of a clergy-house by the side of the Russian cathedral in the Rue Daru. Henceforward he played the chief part in securing that the Russian Church in exile should recover its own full life, both by nourishing that life through his ministry and by enabling Eastern Orthodoxy to shed its transfiguring influence freely on Western civilization: an influence analogous to that of the French Catholic dispersion in the time of the French Revolution, which in England prepared the way for the Oxford Movement, but even more enriching. The greatest factor in Russian Orthodox influence in the West has been the Academy of St Sergius in Paris, of which Metropolitan Eulogius was the father-founder. He showed great courage in deciding to purchase the property in the Rue de Crimée, and, as its Rector, showed great wisdom in its guidance. His participation from their very beginning in the discussions which led to the formation of the World Council of Churches, made him a leading influence in the ecumenical movement. This was a remarkable spiritual achievement in one who remained to the end temperamentally a Russian of the old régime.

> Yes [he exclaimed towards the end] to live in one's own country, to work for it, to get back there! Our Russian Church was and is a national Church and for my part, I cannot conquer flesh and blood. I can't live in the supreme Christian ideal. . . . I'm sorry, but there it is!

The impression made on the Metropolitan by meeting a priest of the Roman Catholic Church with so profound and disinterested a love and veneration for the Eastern Orthodox Church, as had Abbé Couturier, was deep and abiding.

These two met only once—in October 1934, but there was established a profound mutual understanding between them rooted in their common priesthood and in their deep veneration for the saints of each other's Churches. The Archbishop wrote:[5]

> I realized in my conversation [with the Abbé] that there are Catholics who venerate our saints in the same way as they do those of their own Church. They are right. For men like St Seraphim, St Francis of Assisi and many others have accomplished in their own lives the union of the Churches. Are they not citizens of the same Church, a Church holy and universal? On the heights of their spiritual lives have they not passed beyond the walls that separate us, *walls which*, according to the grand saying of Metropolitan Platon of Kiev, *do not mount up as far as heaven*?

This saying had become deeply engraved in the Abbé's soul, as time showed. And in the meantime he felt sure that he would find sympathy when he asked the Metropolitan, as has been indicated, for the co-operation of the Orthodox clergy and people in the observance of the Octave at Lyons. He deeply valued the Archbishop's reply which proved a guiding-thread in his reflection on those problems. The Archbishop wrote:

12 Rue Daru, Paris
5 December 1934

Reverend Father,

> In reply to your letter of the 16 November on the subject of the Octave of prayer for the unity of the Churches, I have great pleasure in intimating to you that I join very gladly in this Octave of prayer in the spirit of the holy Orthodox Church: that is to say in praying for the union of the holy Churches of God, while safeguarding the fullness of their honours and rights—in the spirit proper to Orthodoxy with regard to reciprocal independence, liberty and equality in apostolic brotherhood, recalling the words inspired by God in the third Ecumenical Council on the subject of the liberty which has been given us through the blood of our Saviour Jesus Christ, liberator of the human race (8th canon of the Council). . . .

The letter is emphatic, but very precise in its delineation of the exact limits within which the Orthodox can accept an invitation to prayer in common. Any compromise in matters of faith—the

Orthodox conscience is as convinced of this as is the Catholic—must be sternly avoided. No wonder the Abbé asked permission to quote from this in a forthcoming article with which at the age of 54 he began his career as an author.

This first article touched so courageously on such delicate points that it did not find its way easily into circulation. It was sent from one editorial office to another by professional theologians clearly interested, but hesitant. Critics could not realize that, in order to get the separated brethren to pray thus at the same time as Catholics for unity, it was necessary first to do away with their fundamental objection to what they called the Catholic 'totalitarianism' or the 'monopoly' of Catholics. Fortunately the editor of the *Revue apologétique*, Abbé Edouard Dumoutet, had the courage to accept the article, though he was aware of its audacity and of its vital potentialities. So in the year 1935 in the December number of this journal appeared an article entitled 'For the Unity of Christians: Psychology of the Octave of prayer of 18–25 January'.[6]

Among the points made were these. The thirst for reality in these days has had the happy consequence for men of rediscovering their heritage of a common humanity and for Christians of rediscovering their heritage of a common faith. But this great wave from the depths on coming to the surface is found dashing itself against particularism—particular types of rationalism as well as diverse groupings of Christians, resulting for the former in a movement of narrowing and exasperation, amongst the latter in the pained sense that they are menaced by destructive forces of confusion. There is thus a tension in every Christian communion between loyalty to the faith inherited and aspiration towards unity. The Octave of prayer is bent on mastering this paradox by finding the spiritual solution. In view of denominational susceptibility ought not such a week of devotion to be styled simply 'For Christian Unity'?

It is of urgent importance to face up to the fact of *sin* which is at the origin of such divisions. That is the first duty of Catholics. It has been seldom of late that we have heard a priest, discussing in public the causes of schism, who had the courage to speak of the guilt of the Catholic Church. What an Innocent III did not hesitate to do when he denounced the sins of Crusaders,[7] nor an Adrian VI nor the Fathers of the Council of Trent blaming the clergy and particularly their leaders for the occurence of the Reformation—this has become in recent centuries an unheard-of audacity. There is a singular fear of giving scandal to the weak. But as the result of ignorance of history or of receiving only a truncated sketch of it, a Catholic is no longer able to control his spiritual pride. After recalling some[8] of the dark moments for which a Catholic must crave pardon, the Abbé goes on:

> If only since the separation there had been compensation—an immense, intense, inexhaustible expiation by means of humble prayer and penitence! But no, up to this moment there is no great general movement, no new style of crusade in which the countless army of the faithful, the cross of reunion on their breast, take for their weapons humiliation for admitted sin ('in all and all men, for all and all men, we are guilty of all', said Dostoevsky),—humiliation, prayer and penitence.

Humility, prayer, penitence: these are the keynotes for the Octave. Hence its golden rule:

> We understand this Octave as a convergence towards Christ of the prayers of each Christian confession in full liberty and independence; but as excluding anything far or near which could harm the spiritual independence or liberty of any. To keep the Octave is to make spiritual preparation for the Reunion desired by the very manner of praying for it.

When it will come we know not. But its coming would be hastened if everywhere there should arise some dozens of pioneers of the type of Halifax and Mercier, on condition always that their work were accompanied by the desire and prayer of all, for lack of which the Councils of Lyons and of Florence came to nothing.

The reintegration of the Church will be the crowning achievement of the divine Wisdom, its magnificence excelling the splendours of the Church in primitive times. It will be seen that the genius of each group of Christians, separated up to now, is complementary to rather than opposed to that of others. Enriched, thanks to the convergent humility, prayer and penitence of all, by treasures from every quarter, the Church will come to express better than ever, though always from beneath the mist of the created, the infinite splendour of the Incarnate Word. So will come to an end the intolerable scandal already nine centuries old—the disunion of the disciples of Christ, so real a stone of stumbling both for the unbeliever in quest of the Gospel and for the pagan who observes the rivalry visible even amid heroic missionary devotion.

The author forestalls the objection that his attitude is prejudicial to the rights of the Papacy by imagining the objector as one who charges him with inconsistency, calling attention to the Abbé's own description in the Anglican review *Laudate* of 'the successor of St Peter' as 'the one and only visible centre of unity', etc. . . .[9] No, there is no inconsistency here. It is just because he believes his to be the one and only true Church of God, that the Catholic will be the first to give an example of humility, sympathy and charity in the truest sense of the word. Yet the author relies rather on the witness of Eastern Orthodox theologians (notorious for their intransigence in the ecumenical field) as proof that the paradox of ecumenism involves no 'relativism' in the sphere of belief. He has quoted Metropolitan Eulogius. He now quotes at length a still more trenchant utterance of Dr Sergius Bulgakov on Christian reunion, on the ecumenical problem in its impact on the Orthodox conscience:

> The ecumenical instinct of the Church as it seeks the road of Unity is accompanied by a conscience ever more acute and more refined of doctrinal differences between one communion and another along with an increasing sense of their profound unity in Christ.

The Protestant and the Anglican find themselves facing this same crux of conflicting loyalties.

In this situation which humanly speaking is an *impasse*, we can only throw ourselves into the arms of God. Loyalty to his Church to which he owes the best that he has and is, the Christian knows to be the life of his life. Yet by reason of his loyalty to the one Christ he cannot, he sees, pray that his Church shall remain ever in every point what she has been. How then can he be sure of keeping faith with her? There is only one solution—an act of complete *abandon* and absolute trust in the infinite Goodness and the infinite Power of the risen Christ.

The love of Christ alone can resolve this agonizing antinomy. And after all how many other antinomies arise in the soul of every believer which cannot be resolved save by this confident dive into the love of him, the omniscient, the all-powerful?

> By dint of this, in a region fresh and lofty, reached by this transcending of self, we recover the gentle peace of Christ, a peace now found sweeter, more penetrating and more secret, radiant with the light of Mount Tabor. Where is the Spirit leading us? We know not. He breathes where he wills! . . . We only know that it is he who leads and that suffices us.

To resume, the Octave which is not of specifically Catholic origin and which Catholics must not monopolize, rests upon three psychological pillars:

> 1. A *confiteor* sustained by all in humility, prayer and penitence which are independent but convergent.
> 2. The necessarily ecumenical aim of this convergence. It is unity with all in Christ that each group is seeking.
> 3. The scrupulous conservation of the radical independence of the theological traditions concerned, despite this common ecumenicity.
> This may be called the Triangle of the Octave which has for its goal a general Reunion about which we know nothing else except that God desires it since Christ has prayed for Unity.

There are two ingredients still to be added before the Abbé can give full and clear expression to his thought and thus perfect that ecumenical weapon of prayer which he is here in process of forging or reshaping. It needs first to be made clear that the *prayer for unity must coincide with that of Christ himself*. And secondly, the potentially universal brotherhood that is ours in Christ rooted in or to be realized in *baptism* must find its place in the foundations. It was perhaps the enlargement of his spiritual horizon apparent in the call for the next Week of Prayer, that of January 1936, which enabled him to draw the spiritual chart of Christendom more satisfactorily.

The character of the Week showed clearly the influence of the article. The word 'Octave' has disappeared. It is styled simply 'For the Unity of Christians'. On the back of the leaflets we read:

> A unique fact in Christian history—in these days vast spiritual forces of prayer, proceeding from all Christian confessions, converge in a common immense distress over the separation of Christians.

Here the horizons are enlarged: Israel and Islam are introduced as destined also to be gathered in by the one Christ. The redemption of mankind is thus seen to be a single problem. The reunion of all Christians is the way that leads to the union of all men in Christ.

This new note first heard in 1936 but to be sustained henceforth, is an essential part of the heritage of Abbé Couturier. We may well owe it humanly speaking to the formation of a new friendship with a great servant of Christ, Abbé Jules Monchanin. This man of God, whom to have met is a source of thanksgiving and praise to so many in Europe as well as in India, while owing much to Abbé Couturier, repaid the debt by making him realize far more vividly the universal and cosmic aspects of Christology. Of these, glimpsed first in the scientific panorama of Père Teilhard de Chardin's philosophy, he had found the classical delineation in Eastern Orthodox liturgy and theology. We must stop one moment to speak of this friend who, with Victor Carlhian, Professor Richard, p.S.S., Père Valensin, S.J., Abbé Remillieux, all great influences on Monchanin likewise, must along with the Monks of Unity be counted amongst the greatest human influences in the life of Paul Couturier.

Jules Monchanin, born in 1895 at Fleurie, Rhône, read theology at the Grand Séminaire of Francheville and at the University of Lyons. He was ordained priest in 1922 and his second curacy was in a suburb of Lyons. Appointed theological counsellor of the Group of Medical and Biological Studies and a member of the Society of Philosophy at Lyons, he was intimately associated with the intellectual and artistic life of that city between 1925 and 1938. In many ways he was brought very close to Abbé Couturier, with whom in any case there would have been the closest spiritual concord. There was their common interest in the suffering Russian Orthodox community. There was Jules Monchanin's active assistance in the magnificent work of Abbé Remillieux, Couturier's dear friend, in his foundation of the famous working-class parish in Lyons of Notre Dame-St Alban. There was Abbé Couturier's constant recourse to Professor Louis Richard, his own theological adviser-in-chief, who at the seminary had been Monchanin's teacher and guide and remained to the end a wise influence upon his former pupil, and a beloved friend. Perhaps the strongest human bond was the devotion that both evinced to that astonishing layman, Victor Carlhian, whose encyclopaedic mind and passion for truth made him as stimulating a friend to the younger as he had already proved himself to the older priest. Though Monchanin was twelve years younger than Couturier and eighteen years younger than Carlhian, the young priest's extraordinary maturity made the relationships rather different from what would have been expected. Even with Professor Richard, though he had no more attentive pupil, from the day when in a class-discussion on 'What do you ask of theology?' he had received the reply 'To be *unified*', instruction often gave place to dialogue. There was indeed in Monchanin a great deal that needed unification, despite his early maturity. The range of his interests and the accuracy of his information in the field of science and of philosophy and of the arts classical and contemporary were phenomenal. But his erudition was most marked in the study of the oriental religions in which he had had a passionate interest from boyhood; and along with this went a deep love for the works of the great Christian mystics, especially those whose advance to God is along the negative or apophatic way.

In 1939 at the age of 44 he found himself free to fulfil his dream of going to India and of giving his service to Christ under an Indian bishop. Though asthmatic and very delicate—'only just enough body to carry his spirit'—his ministry there has proved abidingly fruitful. He ministered in various villages of Tiruchirapalli with ever fuller understanding of native language and thought and life until in

1950 he was allowed with Dom le Saux to found the hermitage at Kulitalai where he was able to lead the contemplative life in a manner which combined the principles and doctrine of true Christian mysticism with a sanely developed version of what is best in Indian asceticism. In India he made a very deep impression, the fruits of which have yet to be clearly estimated. In Europe his influence was greatest perhaps through the Personalist movement of his friend, Mounier, a younger man who both taught and learnt from Monchanin and who regarded the sacrificial life of the latter as giving daily sustenance to himself, his work and his family. Flown back from India to Paris for a serious operation, Jules Monchanin died there in hospital in 1957.

> For us people of Lyons [writes Cardinal Gerlier, Archbishop of Lyons] he will take his place for ever among the great figures— apostles and pioneers, such as our dear Church of Lyons is accustomed to offer the Universal Church. In the wake of a Remillieux and of a Couturier, to speak only of the dead, he will give lustre, in the memory of the faithful and of others too, to this last half-century of the Catholic life of Lyons and of the world. May his prayer in heaven raise up amongst us many priests who resemble him.[10]

In the coming week of prayer (1936) it was on 'Israel and Christianity' that Abbé Monchanin was to speak. He might well have spoken on 'Islam and Christianity' also, as he would do in 1939. For he had already begun, almost without knowing it, to inspire the missionary vision of a sisterhood who would offer themselves for a sacrificial life of contemplation amongst Moslems in Morocco. But, needless to say, Abbé Couturier's horizons and those of his younger friend, had not widened only to include Israel and Islam. It was easier for the people of Lyons to see the relevance, in a call for prayer for Christian unity, of these two great sects which despite blindness and heresy, share so large a part of the Christian heritage than to see the necessarily total range of the call. In the eyes of both priests there were no limits to the dominion of the cosmic Christ who prays that all shall be one. But both were convinced that the way along which he calls is a narrow way. The witness of Monchanin himself is unequivocal:

> The highest Hindu mystics aspire to pass beyond the level of phenomena, including the *avatars* (incarnations), to immerse themselves in the abysses of an Absolute too transcendent to receive a name. The Christian mystics—an Evagrius, a pseudo-Dionysius, an Eckhart, a Ruysbroeck, a St John of the Cross do not plunge into the modeless Godhead save by imitation of the naughted Christ who introduces them into an eternity which does not absorb but transfigures time, the universe and souls. . . . My twelve years of residence in India, my contacts with the Hindus have only intensified and deepened in me this vision of total salvation through the Christ, a Saviour as universal as he is unique.[11]

NOTES

[1] This is the motto of the College of St John, Johannesburg, a college once under the care of the Community of the Resurrection, Mirfield. The Abbé loved this motto and chose it as a title for an article on *émulation spirituelle* in a special number of *Catholicité* devoted to reunion, published in January 1946.

[2] Eulogius, *Souvenirs* (in Russian), ed. T. Manouchina, Paris: Y.M.C.A., 1947. See review by Dom D. T. Strotman, O.S.B. in *Irénikon* XXIV (1951), pp. 285–7, and D. A. Lowrie, *Saint Sergius in Paris*, London: S.P.C.K., 1954.

[3] London: John Murray, 1914.

[4] Published in Russian, Paris: Y.M.C.A.

[5] *Souvenirs*, p. 576.

[6] 'Pour l'unité des Chrétiens: psychologie de l'Octave de prière du 18 au 25 Janvier', *Revue apologétique*, 1935, pp. 684–703.

[7] *Op. cit.*: 'The bitter memory of the Fourth and Fifth Crusades is still a thorn in the heart of the Christian East'.

[8] *Op. cit.*: These include 'the iron ages of the tenth and eleventh centuries when the passionate intrigues of warriors have too often raised to the throne of Peter worthless popes, even a young debauchee eighteen years old, John XII; the fifteenth and sixteenth centuries, ages of the pagan renaissance which includes the wretched Alexander VI. If Peter had remained his true self, if the divine had not ceased to shine through the human personality, would Christendom have known these two ruptures?' (the first between East and West, the second between Catholic and Protestant).

[9] *Laudate* XIII, No. 49, March 1935.

[10] See E. Duperray, *L'Abbé Jules Monchanin* (Coll. Eglise Vivante), Tournai-Paris: Casterman, 1960; reviewed by their friend, R. P. Maillet in *Revue Nouvelle* XXXI (June 1960). (A large part of this book appeared in the journal *Église Vivante* X/1.) Also: J. Monchanin, *De l'Esthétique à la Mystique*, Tournai-Paris: Casterman, 1955; J. Monchanin, in collaboration with Dom le Saux, O.S.B., *Ermites du Saccidânanda* (Coll. Eglise Vivante), Tournai-Paris: Casterman, 1956.

[11] Article on Monchanin by E. Duperray in *Ecclesia* No. 122.

8

RESTATEMENTS

THERE had been two circulars sent out for this week of prayer of January 1936. The Abbé had sent one to the Jews to invite them to the lecture by Abbé Monchanin on 'Israel and Christianity'; the second to Protestants, demanding outright their collaboration. The letter runs:

> The root of the problem is to manage to elicit ecumenical prayer from all the Christian groups, prayer that reflects our deep suffering over the horrible sin of disunion. We have all sinned. We ought all to humble ourselves, to pray without ceasing and to demand indefatigably the miracle of total reunion. We certainly shall not see this coming to pass, but our urgent duty is to make ready for it, however distant it may be. Our Christ, our common Lord, awaits the unanimous prayer of all Christian groups that he may reunite them when and in what manner he wills.

The Abbé goes on to solicit all the prayers that can be mustered for this great object with a request that this prayer shall be intensified during the week of 18–25 January. So straightforward and openhearted a request could not but evoke an answer. Numerous Protestants participated in the days of prayer at the church of St Bonaventura; and their response was soon to be followed by one from the official summit of French Protestantism.

Amongst the Catholics, who constitute the great majority of Christians in Lyons, the week was a greater success than ever. This year *Le Nouvelliste*, the great daily newspaper of the Lyons of those days, excelled itself by producing a page full of photographs telling of Christian unity, including one of an ikon of St Peter (his keys carried modestly and his cheeks bedewed with tears) and others of monuments representing the great Christian confessions, likenesses of Paul Wattson and Spencer Jones and views of Amay and Nashdom.

The Abbé—who never himself appears by name in the preparatory literature of the week which, single-handed, he compiled from year to year with such tireless labour—noted in the *Semaine religieuse de Lyon* the qualities which marked this year's observance of the week of prayer for unity. These were: 1. the awakening to a realization of our common guilt; 2. the emphasis on the true nature of the apostolate as contrasted with proselytism; 3. the indication that the object of this prayer is a miracle, the mode of which is a secret of God—for this there must be prayer, intense, persevering and common amongst all Christians, to render them sensitive to the action of the Holy Spirit; 4. finally the realization that the prayer for unity must be necessarily ecumenical. Neither Catholic prayer nor Orthodox nor Anglican nor Protestant will suffice. We must have them all and all together. Already millions of souls have prayed and will go on praying. Soon they will be joined by millions more.

And elsewhere he wrote:

> The time for the work of theologians and of hierarchies has not yet come. What has come and is a matter of urgency is the work of psychological purification (*assainissement*) by prayer, by goodness, by reciprocal appreciation on the part of individuals in terms of all their values human and Christian—all the tender fruits of charity.

The article referred to earlier on the psychology of the Octave was a phenomenal success. In a short time it won for the support of the Week of Prayer friends from every quarter. Evidence of this is to be found in the immense correspondence which was to become one of the Abbé's heavy burdens. Yet he was already at work on another study of the same subject, in part a new version of the first, in part complementary to it. This appeared in 1937 in the November and December issue of the same journal, the *Revue apologétique*, under the title 'The Universal Prayer of Christians for Christian Unity'.[1]

The general drift of this is the same as that of the first. But there is a greater depth and richness in this second essay and it is better

83

constructed. It contains the message that it is the Abbé's vocation to proclaim, a message which will through the years be deepened, developed, in some points better formulated, but will not be essentially changed. At this stage we will be content with quoting fragments only, while indicating their general setting.

First the author here states his life-long conviction that the ideal of the unity of Christendom is an attainable ideal: the hope for it is, as had been the longing of Israel for its Messiah, a sure and certain hope. This certainty is rooted in the prayer of our Lord in John 17.9–26. Further it is clear, from that prayer itself and from the character of the primitive Church developed in the light of it, that the unity of Christians must be a visible unity. This is a necessary consequence of the Incarnation itself.

> If the Word has become visible in the humanity of the person of Christ, his visibility ought to perpetuate itself and to extend to the whole stature of this Christ, since, mystically but really, Christ continues and extends himself by his universalization in each man in whom he lives. The internal law of the organism of the mystical Body demands an affirmation of unity in the realm of the sensible. If this was not bound to be so, if Christians ought normally to live in separate groups, one would have to say that Matter has conquered Love. The essence of love is to unify, to make one. If all Christians love Christ, they must in consequence love one another; that is to say, they must together all make one, as they each and all make one with Christ. Since each one is a visible continuation of Christ—does not *Christianus* mean 'another Christ'?—they ought also all to be visibly one.

> Never, it seems, in modern times has there been right through the whole of divided Christendom so clear a vision, so true a desire, so profound a conviction as to a visible Christian unity, never so acute a suffering for the breach of this same unity. A wide-spread outpouring of the Holy Spirit is in process of descending on all Christians. Christendom, broken, rent in pieces by the internal oppositions of differing confessions, is gathering itself together. It realizes in the recesses of its conscience, in the growing depth caused by painful self-examination, the horrible sin of separation, aggravated by its dreadful consequences, a sin for which all are

accountable, for there are no broad and lasting separations where, psychologically, all the wrongs are on one side. Christendom lives amid a humanity shaken by spasms of egoism, of nationalism, of revolution, of worrying fears of a possible world-war. Towards it there rise from this human mass appeals for Peace and Unity—towards this Christendom which knows that it is only Love which pacifies and in so doing unifies, and knows that it is only Christians who possess this great effective message of all-embracing, living Love. But how can they give this message, since they live it so badly; since they who call themselves Christians, are so divided? Humanity in danger of death remains in its agony. It awaits the union of all Christians. This is the tragic element in the modern Christian conscience.

Action must clearly be taken. And at the height of the ideal of Unity (at once realizable and transcendant) there is but one action adequate, and this 'the authentic source and effective support of all other endeavours after unity, the action of Prayer'. In every Christian soul it is living faith in the divine person of Christ, our common Saviour, which will set prayer in motion. But each will pray within his own confession (Church) and in integral loyalty to it, for it is here that he has learnt to love and to pray to Christ—Christ has his martyrs in every confession. Thus all find themselves by reason of their very fervour situated in a kindred psychological dilemma which springs from the agonizing fact of their separations, torn between the faithfulness pledged by a believer to his Church and the necessity of praying for Christian unity. For to pray for unity is to be ready for some change in one's own Church: the Protestant to give up his position of independent critic; the Anglo-Catholic to surrender his wide ranges of liturgical liberty; the Roman Catholic to meet the shock of the invasion of his spiritual home by multitudes culturally different from himself; the Orthodox to face the great issues of the Renaissance and the Reformation.

Abbé Couturier brings as witness with regard to the antinomy which besets the Christian of our day another stout witness: this time not from the ranks of Eastern Orthodoxy, but from those of Protestantism. It is Karl Barth who is now quoted at length to this effect as was Sergius Bulgakov in the 1935 article. It is interesting to note how the Abbé's conviction as to this crucial point quite independently reached, is thus corroborated by the insight of two of the tougher and most influential Christian leaders, men very dissimilar in their cast of thought and alike only in wisdom and devotion to Christ. The point was as clearly seen by several eminent Roman Catholic theologians, e.g. Dom Lambert Beauduin as well as by Anglicans, e.g. Professor Goudge. It is the very antithesis of the 'false irenism' condemned by Pope Pius XII in the encyclical *Humani Generis*.

In an article on 'The Church and the Churches' in *Oecumenica* (III, 1936, pp. 137–55), Barth had made clear his own conviction as to the inacceptability of '*Inter-confessionalisme*' (interdenominationalism):

> We do not exist above the differences which separate the Churches, but right in the middle of them; we cannot believe *this* and say that *that* is also Christian. Those who pretend to soar above these differences are in fact spectators of God and of themselves. They listen to nothing but their own words. . . . The duty of reuniting the Churches coincides, essentially and of necessity, with the concrete and practical task of listening to Christ which is the presupposition of all ecclesiastical action. How are we to listen otherwise than concretely, precisely in the Church to which we belong, in which we have been baptized and led to the faith and to which we have ties of obligation? . . . Let us repeat [he continues] Jesus Christ, the Mediator between God and Man, is the Unity of the Church, this Unity which comprises a multiplicity of parishes, of gifts, of persons; but which excludes a multitude of Churches. The duty of the Church is to be One Church. . . . We cannot leave on one side the demands of Christ. If we listen to the voice of the Good Shepherd the question of the Unity of the Church cannot help being a burning one. . . . The union of Churches is a duty and a command which the Lord addresses to the Church, if we truly believe that Jesus is the Unity of the Church and that in the multiplicity of Churches lies our unhappiness. . . . The union of the Churches is not a manufactured article; one discovers and finds it through obedience to Christ in whom unity is already accomplished. . . . The union of the Churches is too great a thing to be

the result of a movement, even of the best of movements. . . .
The first and last word of this practical problem (confronted as we
are by the Church, One by right, Multiple in practice) should be
prayer for pardon and sanctification addressed to the Lord of the
Church.

Karl Barth's whole article, quoted by Abbé Couturier, contains a
vivid description of the antinomy which the Abbé had sketched, and
the same conclusion is reached—the duty of prayer. But here we
find a different approach—that of *listening to Christ*. It is the conviction that God, Christ and the Church are *one* but that each Christian
must obey God in his own Church, that unites Karl Barth (here at
his best) with Sergius Bulgakov and Paul Couturier and with many
a Roman Catholic and Anglican theologian.

Here then is the *impasse* which calls for action. And prayer is the
action to which we are obliged. How are we to pray for unity?
There are two competing solutions. That of a prayer which rises
from the heart of the believer and passes through his intelligence,
that is through the concepts dictated by the faith of his Church,
before rejoining through this Church the Prayer of Christ at the
Last Supper; or that of a prayer which goes direct from the heart of
the faithful to the Heart of Christ praying.

The first way may be formulated thus:

> O Lord, may all come to this blessed Faith which nourishes my
> soul: may all enter into this sanctuary of the Father which you
> have made me to know, into this form of the Christian life which is
> the inner joy of my being. I know that my brother separated from
> my beliefs will pray to you in the same way in his own Christian
> confession—that we pray for Unity while opposing one another
> even in your presence, in our very prayer itself. . . . *Fiat voluntas
> tua.*

How easily this form of prayer may hold consciously or unconsciously a hidden bitterness ready to pour itself into the least breach
in our spiritual life and, in the form of controversy and polemics,
into our relations with our Christian brothers! There is a dangerous
slant in this prayer which may even find vent in our praying that for

the sake of the preservation of our faith as it is, union may come not after due preparation by reunions *en masse* but immediately by 'the conquest of successive units'. . . . 'The realization of this request would bring with it an immeasurable loss.'

It would indeed be a mistake to think of Christian unity as to be achieved thus, by a series of individual conversions. Unity so made quickly slows down to a speed which hardly covers its losses. (Newman's example, the Abbé remarks elsewhere, is a classic example. Despite his outstanding worth and sanctity, hardly anyone followed him.[2]) If *per impossibile* this method of reunion were to succeed, it would, by reason of its slow progressive assimilation, act as a dissolvent of the riches of the different cultures which are designed to form one great harmony of different complementary elements, symphonizing one with another. The Creator calls all the riches of his creation to make one great symphony in Christ. This call expresses itself in the individual, conscious of possessing through Providence such a cultural heritage, in the legitimate joy he feels in bringing his contribution, his own note. This joy ought to remain his. All ought to welcome and esteem his gift, if they wish as they should, to enter into the mind of the Creator.

No one, it is true, can deny the right and duty of individual conversion to a soul which believes itself to be no longer in the right way. These conversions are like short-cuts and footpaths. If they are sincere and organic—the only kind which have true religious value —it is ordained that they should be very rare. Then they will be acts of high nobility and everyone will respect and bow to them. Corporate reunion remains the normal way to unity. As great mountain roads which mount gradually higher and higher by wide bends, so the way of 'corporate reunion' unfolds in its slow progress —the persevering preparation of the mind of the public as well as of that of the hierarchy. Later, much later, will come a day, the day marked out by Providence, when with the sanction of their religious leaders, the hearts of the faithful will seal, each by his own act, this reunion which is the common object of their inmost desire. The works of God are slow and proceed by making use of the psychological laws of our souls.

The second way, which is one in harmony with this divine principle of freedom, could be called 'the solution of love' or 'the Gospel solution'. It is an act of abandonment into the hands of Christ after this manner:

> Saviour, under the intolerable weight of this affliction—the division of Christians—my heart fails me. I have trust in thee who hast conquered the world. . . . My confidence in thee (begotten of love) is limitless and justly so, for thou art omnipotent: it casts me into thy heart where I find thy prayer, 'Father, may they be one, that the world may know that thou hast sent me. May they be consummated in unity.' My prayer, the prayer of a sinner is thine own prayer which alone gives me peace. When and how will unity come to be? What are the obstacles to be surmounted? That is thy concern: my faith only bids me pray with thee, in thee, that thy unity may come, that unity which thou hast not ceased to desire, that which thou seekest and preparest, that which thou wouldest have realized long ago, if all, myself among them, had been as crystal between that which from creation, through the Christian, seeks to rise towards thee and that which from thee, through him again, seeks to descend to the world.

Any temptation to doctrinal 'confusionism' (failure in doctrinal integrity) is avoided in this prayer, for it rises above, without obscuring, the barriers which divide, making us all rest together in the Heart of Christ. The Abbé later will emphasize the *disponibilité*[3] which belongs to souls reaching this level—the disposition most desirable for progress towards Christian unity. But he also guards, on the practical level, against any charge of 'confusionism', recalling the law of *parallelaboration* which was so dear to him.

> There is no sort of necessity (and it would do real harm since ritual confusionism is already one step towards religious indifferentism) for this convergence to take bodily form in a gathering of heterogeneous Christian crowds to take part, whether officially or not, in the same religious ceremonies. In the complete separation of their various places of worship, in the full independence of their beliefs, their rites, their spiritual traditions, families of Christians separated from one another will send up together from their heart,

just as each will do secretly in his private prayer, a single appeal—that raised to the Father by Christ before going to his Passion.

Yet this universal prayer must not be confined to an élite, the inhabitants of monasteries and the frequenters of retreat-houses, but must be the very breath of the whole mystical Body, rising periodically in a great cry which will form

> an act of reparation, collective, simultaneous and as far as may be, visible. . . . Over against the ugliness of their separations, this simultaneity will enable Christians to offer to their non-Christian brethren and to all creation, the moving visible beauty of their unity in spiritual effort, a prelude and a pledge of that unity in Christ, the beauty of which will transcend any harmonization of efforts merely human.

The crux of the problem is that, as we draw close to Christ (a problem of personal sanctification), we learn to behold our separated brethren in the Heart of Christ who welcomes and loves them perhaps more than he does ourselves. There comes into being gradually an intercommunication of souls, produced by the Spirit in and through Christ in the organic life of his mystical Body which includes those baptized by implicit as well as those baptized by explicit desire. Herein the Christian's prayer contains unifying power in proportion as he himself is near to God, that is to say stripped of self. It is not enough to say that one possesses the Faith.

> Following the ineffable prescience of God [says St Augustine] many are without who seem to be within, and many are within who seem to be without. Those who are within in a manner, so to speak, hidden, represent also the enclosed garden, the sealed fountain of which Scripture speaks. They too have the benefits of the inexhaustible Charity in this world and of life eternal in the other.[4]

This real supernatural communication has as its natural seat the solidarity of mankind, their real interconnexion as members of the one immeasurable human species.

> Even the stifled aspirations to repentance, the failures to make reparation, the hollow appeals which criminal souls fling to Christ by their very crimes (misguided quests for happiness), the exulta-

tion of gratitude, the sweet joy of souls who are in peace, the whole inner life of every man presses itself into my own spiritual life. Their prayer passes vitally into my own prayer. I have only to give my assent to this. And to do better, as we must always strive to do, I have to become profoundly conscious of this current deriving from the depths of humanity and flowing through me Godwards, registering my conscious acceptance of all by impressing on it my moral personality.

The author then quotes (from the *Cantique de Palmyre*) the poet Paul Claudel as one whose 'intuition has penetrated far into these depths of the Mystical Body':

Not one of our brothers, even should he wish it, is capable of being lost to us, and in the coldest miser, in the heart of the prostitute, and of the most degraded drunkard, there is an immortal soul which is devoutly intent in aspiration and which, shut out from the day, practises adoration by night. I hear them speak when we speak and weep when I kneel to pray. I accept everything. I take them all. I understand them all, there is not one of them whom I do not need, with whom I can dispense. There are many stars in the sky and their number is inexhaustible, and, nevertheless, there is not one of them which I do not need for the praise of God. There are many living stars and yet we can with difficulty see some few shining while the others toss in chaos and in the whirlpools of a dark mire; there are many souls, but not one with which I am not in communion through that sacred point in it which says '*Pater Noster*'.

We are all dependent upon one another—consciously or unconsciously. My prayer for unity comes from my heart, filters through the circulation of the mystical Body as does my brother's prayer though he may be far removed from me by the content of his beliefs. But if he is nearer God than I, it is in his prayer that my poor prayer will find its greatest efficacy, its most rapid flight to the Eternal.

There will be no need to say 'I pray for so and so: I pray for someone else unknown'. Nor yet to say 'I pray instead of the one or the other'. What will matter most is to say 'I let the other pray in me: I open to him with love the path of my soul. May the way of my prayer be freely open to him: *via orationis.*' So at the altar, in the Holy Mass, at the choir Office, in silent prayer, with me and in me are praying my brethren, Protestant, Anglican, Orthodox. And just as truly, I am and I pass into the loyal and sincere prayer of the Divine Liturgy and the Offices of convinced Orthodox believers, into the public and private prayer of fervent Anglicans, into the fervent Protestant commemorations of the Holy Supper.

We seem to have here an unveiling, unconscious rather than conscious, of a personal experience of universal prayer which marks the writer as a practised intercessor as well as a contemplative. To a level of prayer so costing only souls of some degree of interiority will attain, souls consecrated to God by a special vocation, whether in the cloister or in normal life. The character of the spirituality here disclosed is as far as possible from being narrowly ecclesiastical. Indeed it will remind some readers of the writings of Charles Williams, whose insight on this point is even more penetrating than that of Claudel. Others it will remind of the Abbé's friend, Jules Monchanin:

> In the same way [said the latter] that there is an inherence of each (Christian) soul in the circumincession of the Holy Trinity, so likewise there is an interiority of souls one with regard to the other. . . . We are not separated for we are living in the one and only love. . . . And when the veil falls, we shall understand that our souls interpenetrate one another (*sont intérieures les unes aux autres*), that we have been created, chosen one for another by him who gathers us together and whose promises do not fail.

The outlook of both these friends is profoundly Trinitarian and may well be coloured by a great love of the Eastern Orthodox liturgy saturated as that is by a profound sense of *sobornost*—of unity through the Spirit, as when the deacon cries:

> Having prayed for the unity of the faith and the communion of the Holy Ghost, let us commend ourselves and one another and all our life to Christ our God.

The occurrence of such a passage here in this article is an augury of the eagerness Abbé Couturier will show to support any attempts in communions other than his own towards the restoration of the religious and monastic life and indeed towards every deepening anywhere of the life in Christ.

The great hope that breathes through the whole writing finds more concise expression in an article published ten years later.[5] There we find him prophesying that under the influence of this Christocentric prayer,

> Each Christian group, Catholics among them, will deepen its life, will make the best of its talents, will reform what needs reforming in it, will mount towards our Lord until the walls of separation are left behind. Then all, recognizing in their brethren that Christ whom they adore, will see him as he is, one, undivided in his love, his life and his thought. Then it will be found that dogmatic unity has come, the full allegiance of all souls to the one mind of Christ. Union will be proclaimed by the voice of church leaders—by the voice of Peter: perhaps it will be done in a vast ecumenical Council.

Already the writer perceives the first gleams of dawn:

> Division, mutual persecution, tolerance of one another, indifference or inertia—these have been the various stages in the gloomy history of the Church in relation to Unity. But now in spite of a few sad, but happily spasmodic, outbreaks of persecution among Christians of the present day, we have come to a period of mutual esteem, of comprehension, and of brotherhood founded on that which really unites us. In a word, we have come to a time of 'spiritual emulation'.

These last words name a principle which was to be fruitful in his work for Christ, and is a note of the new age which, thanks to his oblation and that of other hidden servants of Christ, God has given us.

NOTES

[1] English translation in *Reunion* II, 1937, pp. 455–69; III, 1938, pp. 3–16.

[2] Cf. the words of Newman in a letter to Phillips de Lisle (1857): 'I believe that it is important for Catholicism that individual conversions should not develop and that these verities remain in the Anglican Church: they will be a

leaven in the mass. I mean to say, they will do more for us staying where they are than in being converted.' (Quoted in J. de Bivort de la Saudée, *Anglicans et Catholiques* vol. I, Paris: Plon, 1949, p. 7.

[3] A word *disponibility* perhaps needs to be coined in English to express the meaning of the vivid French word. It seems to signify freedom from attachment as well as docility and suppleness.

[4] Augustine, *De baptismo contra Donatistas* V, 27: Migne XLIII, 196.

[5] In English translation: *Reunion* V, 1947, pp. 227–31. This article seems to contain a revised version of some paragraphs from the earlier article, along with other matter.

9

THE TRACTS

IN the two articles described a new prophetic message had been
given its first full utterance. But in this form and reprinted, as it
soon needed to be, in the form of leaflets this message would find its
way only to a limited public, and that composed of Christian intellectuals. It needed to be given clearer, more concrete and more
careful expression. This was the work of the next fifteen years, a
many-sided and laborious work. Christians of Lyons must first
become fully possessed of the message. And this must mean the
development there of a pattern of witness and worship which could
serve as a model for the observance of this week in other regions.
The Abbé at once set about this task. He hoped that the week would
become an annual event as significant, as dear to Christians of Lyons
and as widely influential for Christian unity as the *Semaine Sociale*,
inaugurated there in 1904, had been for Christian social progress.
The outbreak of war prevented the complete fulfilment of the Abbé's
hopes. But realize that all this was the spare-time work of a delicate,
middle-aged, priest-schoolmaster in a minor position, one without
connexions or influence, and you will see that the establishment of
this week in Lyons and its swift propagation throughout the Christian world is a signal fruit of faith: a convincing evidence of the
truth of his own belief in the power belonging to action rooted in
faithful prayer offered in full harmony with the will of God.

At the base of all his propagandist activity lay what he rejoiced in
calling by an English name, the *Tracts*. It was his admiration for the
Oxford Movement that suggested this word.[1] Perhaps it is a good
thing that he was never confronted with any of Pusey's or Newman's

Tracts for the Times, as formidable in size as they are uncouth in form. The Lyons 'Tracts' are leaflets in which a great deal of information, reflection and counsel is condensed clearly in a very small space. They are like the Oxford Tracts only in being the fruit of much labour, devotion and thought. Months of work and pondering were given to their concoction, while texts from the Liturgy and the Bible and cuttings from journals along with notes of his own meditation were collected as potentially valuable for his purpose. This procedure went on at the same time as his planning of the programmes for the Week and later with that of the meetings of priests and ministers. But there was one great difference in method. With regard to both of the latter undertakings the Abbé was eager to take counsel. But the contents of the Tract was a secret known only to himself and to God, at least until the first submission of it to the ecclesiastical Censor. Professor Louis Richard, the Censor, proved all that could have been desired: a true theologian, a devoted friend but one who *ipso officio* had to have the interests of the 'weaker brethren' at heart. The field of Christian unity, in any case difficult enough for theologians, is for censors exceedingly delicate ground. The Abbé had occasionally to struggle single-handed to procure what he felt to be an integral presentation of his message; and always for these engagements he secured the help of a veritable barrage of prayer.

The Abbé learnt much through his visits to the Séminaire Universitaire, the residence of the Censor and of his brethren, all priests of the company of 'Priests of St Sulpice' which for over a century had laboured in the training of priests in Lyons. We have already met Professor Richard as teacher and friend of Jules Monchanin. An open-minded, experienced, wise priest, he was now professor of dogmatics in the Faculté Catholique of the University of Lyons and a notable source of inspiration for students, especially in the seminary where he was *'directeur spirituel'*. He combined a rich and forceful humanity, a passionate love of the Church and a keen and learned grasp of orthodox doctrine with a profound sense of the supernatural dignity of the life in Christ—the priestly life in particular—deriving from the great founders of the *'école française'* of

Lyons: the Cathedral of St John Baptist and on the hill
the basilica of Notre Dame de Fourvière (1894)

St Martin d'Ainay (1107), where the Abbé most often said Mass

Christian spirituality, Bérulle, Condren, Olier, who are the fore-
fathers of the family of St Sulpice. During the period of his own
training—which occurred during the crisis over modernism—Louis
Richard had suffered much from a narrowly scholastic fashion of
teaching dogmatic theology, while he himself conceived of dogma as
the foundation and food of spiritual life. So he had a hatred at once of
text-book theology and of the doctrinal ambiguity of liberalism. At
the same time he had an immense respect for the working of God in
other minds and a horror of substituting his own insight for theirs.
He was aware of the immense value of the vocation and gift of the
Abbé and was confident that he had to do with one whose training
in the exact sciences would lead him to respect a like precision in the
field of theology. There is a deep concord between these two minds
as to the meaning of the mystery of redemption which Professor
Richard has so magnificently expounded, especially in the great
book which he completed just before his death.[2] He wrote:

> In him (Jesus Christ) all the attributes of God shine forth:
> holiness, wisdom and justice. But he is essentially the mystery of
> the gratuitous love of God made man, Mediator of grace and of
> divine pardon while being at the same time inseparably Head of
> Humanity in its return to God; consequently mediator both of the
> love which makes reparation for sin and of filial adoration to the
> glory of God.

Professor Richard was not only a large-hearted and trustworthy
guardian of the faith. He had also a shrewd, humorous sense of the
climate of contemporary Catholic opinion, of its fears and suspicions
which it might be wasteful or even harmful to provoke—a valuable
safeguard for regulating the public utterance of one whose vision
was far in advance of many of his fellow-churchmen.

The Tracts vary in size. Those of the first three years are the
largest and contain from four to twenty-four pages. During the war
when paper was scarce, they were reduced to small folders containing sufficient matter to enable clergy to conduct a service of prayer.
But along with these there appeared in smaller supply pamphlets
expounding the spiritual orientation of the week or providing factual

information. Sometimes these publications include a drawing or a woodcut. So things went on until 1948. From the next year onward Abbé Couturier had neither physical nor financial resources sufficient to keep pace in the same fashion with the growing circulation. Henceforth the contents of the Tract, now reduced to a small-size leaflet containing only twenty pages, remains substantially the same each year—a paragraph of spirituality, intentions of prayer, liturgy, hymns; on the cover a small reproduction of the poster, the work in alternate years of Catholic or Protestant artists. There have by this time come into being reviews and journals devoted to Christian unity, an ecumenical press; so all that is needed is the clear call to prayer.

It is in 1939 that we first get in the Tract the new title, 'The Universal Prayer of Christians for Christian Unity'. It is here that attention is drawn to the need of recovering the right relation between the values of Truth and Charity.

> It is no good dreaming that there will come *first* a realization of the unity of minds in Truth and *then* union of hearts in Charity. Truth is not to be apprehended save by a soul prepared to receive it, a soul already dedicated to it through a glimpse, however obscure, of desire and of love. Charity is the herald of Truth. The Word began by the charity and the humility of the Incarnation in order that in the form of the Servant [*esclave*] he might win the hearts of men: the only means which he judged capable of obtaining the attention of their minds in freedom. Christians in their separation have no other model for their common work of mutual understanding, for all, Catholics included, are surrounded with darkness and ignorance of one another. For example the work of reconciliation with the East requires as one of its conditions that Latins 'shall abandon the errors of vision inrooted in the majority on the subject of the doctrines and institutions of oriental Christians'.[3]
>
> It is clear enough that the unity desired by Christ is an organic unity such as will grasp and gather into his heart the soul of mankind in its entirety. The unity of Christians will then necessarily bring with it, athwart a great cultural diversity which it will

harmonize, a unity of thought, of faith, of creed, since in all Christians it is the unique thought of their one Saviour which will develop itself. *But that is the end and not the beginning.* There are ages which are given to controversy: excellent minds, scholars, geniuses like Leibnitz and Bossuet have been engaged thus and have expended their energies in this way: and always they have come up against the *humanly impossible.* But now at last we are to start from the beginning. God alone is the master of the impossible. The whole fabric of Christendom must be shaken to its very depths by the universal prayer of Christians: it must experience a supernatural shock which will break down all its prejudices, rectify its super-ficial and false ideas, cause hearts to grow into one another and finally unite minds in the eternal light of the one Christ. It will be a sort of second Pentecost descending on Christians 'unanimous in prayer'.

The Tract of 1940 is remarkable for its size. As the world plunged into the darkness and chaos of the war, Pius XII published his first encyclical, *Summi Pontificatus.* This background gave the Abbé his theme, the relation between 'Peace and Christian unity'. He shows God at work in the heart of the world drama:

We have absolute certainty that the events of this world's history, as much the highest and most tragic in which nations confront one another as the smallest and most trivial which are the stuff of our ordinary life, are charged with the divine. They are literally *signs.* Only the practised eye of an upright [*droit*] soul, attentive to discern reality under appearances, projecting upon it the pure light which makes everything transparent, can discern the divine element hidden in the heart of each event.

Though the war is a horrible sin,

there is one aspect of things left too much in the shade: that of the intimate connexion between war and the disruption of Christen-dom.

We are given the messages of the Archbishops of Canterbury and York in face of war, and a manifesto of the Protestant students of China and Japan, resolved to maintain their spiritual links with their brethren in Christ, despite the storm. But the chief place is given, as is clearly right, to the first utterance of the new Pope who, not forgetting the cause of unity, speaks here not only to his own flock but with special attention to his separated 'brethren', a call which, as we shall see, Abbé Couturier took special care should be heard responsively by his own non-Catholic friends.

In the Tract of 1941 we get the first intimation, often to be reiterated, that the problem of unity is primarily the question of a *right orientation of the interior life.*

> Where the sin of all has passed, breaking and separating as it goes, in order that grace superabundant may find its way in reparation, there is need for a great number of souls in every Christian group to open themselves wide to welcome it. Then like 'burning and shining lamps' (John 5.35) countless Christ-bearers (*Christophoroi*) will shed across the mass of Christians such a unifying tension of the spirit that there will shine forth before the eyes of all a universal Christophany (manifestation of Christ). The intensification of the Christian life will have recovered unity in the faith while preserving the legitimate and fruitful diversity of families of the spirit, of cultures and of races.

Here for the first time in the Tracts we get the idea of *Spiritual Emulation.*

> It is for all Christians to embark upon holy, brotherly emulation in humble, penitent prayer and the deepening of the spiritual life.

In 1943 a supplementary tract on green paper tells us about the *Invisible Monastery.* This is

> *the commonwealth of souls whom the Spirit has been able to make conscious—and intimately so, because they have tried truly to open themselves to his flame and thus to his light—of the sorrowful state of separation among Christians.*

This causes them to experience a '*permanent suffering which issues in habitual prayer and penitence*'. These words were clearly destined to go far, finding their echo in souls consecrated to Christian unity, those who the whole year long keep the fires of this prayer burning.[4]

The same idea recurs in the Tract of 1944 in a passage on 'the place of the Prayer of Christ in our life'.

This prayer of Christ and the spirit of this prayer ought to animate, quicken and possess the soul of any Christian who approaches his Saviour, whether in the solitude of his mental prayer or in his sacramental life or in his participation in the eucharistic feast. If every Thursday evening, the night of Holy Thursday, an ever-increasing multitude of Christians of every confession would form as it were an immense net embracing the earth like a vast invisible monastery in which all should be absorbed in prayer to Christ for Unity, would we not have here the dawn of Christian Unity? Is it not this attitude of spiritual emulation, sincere, profound, ardent, which the Father awaits for the realization of the visible unity of the body of the Church, for the accomplishment of the miracles necessary, for the reunion within his visible Church of all those who love him and have been visibly marked by the seal of baptism?

The Tract of 1946 adorned by a design from 'Rib' (Abbé Ribes, then a seminarist at the Grand Séminaire of Francheville) over the words 'The walls of separation do not rise as far as heaven', gives us another variation on the theme of spiritual emulation. It is by the progressive revivification of each Christian group that we shall advance towards a kindred grasp of the message revealed by God and will finally attain dogmatic unity. Underneath the declaration of his own 'faith in the Roman Church which proclaims itself to be the One Church, a truth consequent necessarily upon the fact of its Apostolicity', the Abbé has printed Pastor Rosendal's dictum, 'No one has the right to pray for the defeat of another Church and the triumph of his own.' Unity will not mean the triumph of a Church, not even of the Mother-Church, but the triumph of the Love of Christ. It is absolutely necessary that every Church should attain a new depth of life. Hence the list of intentions given for the days of the week is centred on the *sanctification* of each group of Christians. 'Spiritual emulation leads us to note with joyous hearts all the signs of religious renewal, wherever they occur'; it also makes us sensitive to the sins of Christians towards one another in the course of history and makes us specially ashamed of our mutual persecutions.

A spiritual transformation must take place everywhere. The sundering memory of the shedding of blood must be dissolved in unifying penitence for that bloodshed.

Here is introduced for the first time the idea that Catholics ought to do reparation for the massacre of St Bartholomew's day and for the Revocation of the Edict of Nantes—crimes of which Christians of Huguenot descent still carry the scars. But to this pre-occupation of the writer we must return in a later chapter.

A pamphlet of 1947 contains 'Texts from the Bible for each day of the Week of Christian Unity', which the preface tells us were chosen by a Protestant pastor.

Then in the last years of his life from 1949–53 for reasons we have explained—the author's illness, the immensely increased demand for the Tracts, the advent of an ecumenical press—there is published a small condensed Tract, small enough in weight for cheap postage at commercial rates, the form and outline of which are always the same. It is in three parts: *The Problem, The Intentions, Prayers and Liturgy*.[5]

I. THE PROBLEM

A FIRST FACT

According to the last statistics provided by U.N.O. which appeared in 1952, there are living on the earth two milliards four hundred millions of men, one half of whom live in Asia. Nominally four hundred and twenty-two millions are Catholics, a hundred and sixty-one millions are Orthodox, five hundred and fifty-two millions are Protestant, fifty millions are Anglican. We have then a Christian world of seven hundred and eighty-five millions divided into four groups over against sixteen hundred and fifteen millions of non-Christians.

Results: Rivalry or opposition or at least divergences in the proclamation of the Gospel in missionary countries; and hence astonishment or bewilderment or hesitation amongst the populations evangelized. The surprise of unbelievers in so-called Christian countries. Suffering on the part of those who are seeking the truth. Weakening of the supereminent spiritual power of Christianity in the world. Ugliness and disharmony intruded into the work of Christ by the separations among Christians. Lack of the visible adoration of the Trinity by the Body of baptized Christians: that is to say, mutilation of the work of God. Check to the anxious longing of the whole creation for the manifestation of the sons of God.

A SECOND FACT

We are face to face with a new historical phenomenon, unique in the history of Christianity: from all the Christian groups there arise, independent but parallel to one another, immense spiritual forces of intercession, all converging in a single immeasurable distress over the separation of Christians, and a single intense desire:

> *For the coming of the visible Unity of the Kingdom of God*
> *—Unity such as Christ desires*
> *by whatsoever means he shall choose.*

A CERTAINTY

Conceived in the movement of hearts which turn towards their one Saviour Jesus, how could the union of all Christians fail to be achieved one day in the perfect atonement of Unity? There is certainly no question here of Unity sold at reduced prices, based on a least common multiple of faith! but rather of the Unity for which Christ prayed and continues to pray eternally; for any other unity would be a treachery such as all Christians reject with horror.

Here are inserted the words which constituted the title of the 1947 poster which had caused a considerable stir:

ALL CHRISTIANS BEFORE THE CROSS

Listen to the silent prayer which he addressed and ceases not to address to his Father, the prayer for Unity, prayer offered at the Supper: 'That they may be One as we are One that the world may believe' (John 17).

They understand that the supplication of Christ requires that Christians shall unite themselves with their whole soul to the prayer of their Redeemer.

They recall that their prayer will be vain and Pharisaical if they do not begin by all together asking pardon from Christ for all the injustices, outrages, deeds of violence and bloody persecution which in the course of history they have wrought one against another.

They know also that this petition made to Christ for pardon, collective and fraternal as it is, would not be sincere if they did not begin by asking humbly for pardon one from another before Christ in agony upon the Cross of our redemption.

As for Christians of France, both Catholics and Protestants recognize that they have much to forgive one another.

French Catholics in particular ought to realize that Protestants cannot forget facts like the St Bartholomew massacre and the revocation of the Edict of Nantes. The preponderant part played here by political passions and the ways of a past epoch should not prevent them from feeling before Christ crucified a pang of sorrowful regret for those events. And in perfect harmony with the spirit of our Mother, holy Church, they will find great peace in expressing this regret.

This first part always closes with spiritual notes commenting on one or other of Abbé Couturier's favourite ideas. In 1953 their theme is the attitude of the blessed Virgin, commended as the pattern of the obedient soul: these lines were amongst the last that the Abbé wrote before his death on the eve of Lady Day, 24 March of the same year.

Let all Christians come to their Saviour with an open soul, attentive to the divine call, in humble abandonment, the attitude of the humble Virgin Mary! Her answer to the angel is the archetype of the creature's response to its Creator: 'Behold the servant of the Lord. Be it unto me according to his Word.' When the disposition of the Virgin's soul shall be that of Christian souls, when the answer of the Virgin Mary shall resound silently in our souls, the souls of all Christians, this immense silent cry, guided and dominated by the voice of the Virgin, will be unfurled before the throne of the Eternal in a single irresistible supplication. And once anew, by the action of the Holy Spirit, Unity will come to pass.

II. THE INTENTIONS

There follows the formula of prayer for the sanctification of every group of Christians. We have seen in what context in 1946 these headings were first suggested—in close contiguity to the Abbé's own declaration of faith in the Roman Church as the one and only Church of Christ. They were explained and vindicated in an article in the Review *Catholicité* (1946), for which the Abbé secured a large circulation; they are thus introduced in the Tract:

Those who, over and above the general intention of the Week of Unity

UNITY OF ALL CHRISTIANS SUCH AS CHRIST DESIRES
FOR HIS CHURCH

should desire a particular intention for each day, might feel drawn to use the following intentions:
18 January: Unity of all Christians
19 January: Sanctification of Catholics
20 January: Sanctification of Orthodox
21 January: Sanctification of Anglicans
22 January: Sanctification of Lutherans
23 January: Sanctification of Calvinists
24 January: Sanctification of all other Protestants
25 January: Unity of all men in the charity and truth of Christ
or the following:
18 January: Unity of all Christians
19 January: Sanctification of Catholics
20 January: Sanctification of Orthodox
21 January: Sanctification of Anglicans
22 January: Sanctification of all Protestants
23 January: Sanctification of Jews
24 January: Sanctification of all non-Christians
25 January: Unity of all men in the charity and truth of Christ

There were protests against the second list of intentions from persons who wished the Week to 'stay Christian'. But the Abbé was conscious that the Church includes the whole human race, indeed all creation. Reunion will never be accomplished without an all-inclusive love. Besides, Jewish, Moslem and Hindu friends would be reading the Tracts and must see that they are not forgotten by a priest of God who has Jewish blood, who passed formative years of his boyhood amongst Moslems and whose most understanding friend, Jules Monchanin, is living his priestly life as a Hindu among Hindus.

From time to time there was a particular intention recommended in relation to current events, for example (after the Assembly of Amsterdam [1948] which signalled its birth), for the World Council of Churches; in 1952 for the third world-conference of Faith and Order. In the same way, if he had lived longer, the ninth centenary of the separation of East and West and the second assembly of the World Council of Churches at Evanston, falling in the same year, 1954, would both have been remembered. Nor is there any doubt that the Tracts of the last few years would have concentrated on evoking prayer with regard to three great events and for God's guidance for all those responsible for the preparations required. The announcement by the late Pope to the cardinals, made on the last day of the January week of 1959, that he proposed to call an Ecumenical Council was the fulfilment of the Abbé's ardent prayer. He would have called for thanksgiving, penitence and fervent inter- cession from all Christians. The Assembly of the World Council of Churches which met in New Delhi in December 1961, with as its theme 'Christ the Light of the World', he would have presented as constituting a like call to the universal prayer of Christians. And he would have called attention to the crucial step taken there—the integration of the World Council of Churches and the International Missionary Council. He might well have quoted Bishop Stephen Neill:

> It could be no more than an ingenious piece of ecclesiastical carpentry. Our hope is that it may be a rebirth, a coming together of things that ought never to have been separated, and so a means by which the power of God can be released for the service of all men through the Church.[6]

III. PRAYERS AND LITURGY

This last section of the Tract is intended to help the clergy in providing acts of worship during the Week of Unity. It includes a number of prayers ancient and modern, hymns with music provided by various composers, Catholic and Protestant, or borrowed from good collections. Though it is since those days that the psalm-chants of Père Gélineau, S.J., inspired by the present-day folk music of our Lord's own kinsfolk after the flesh, have become a sort of ecumenical plainsong, it was Abbé Couturier who in our interconfessional gatherings provided the conditions for their diffusion which has been accomplished even more by Protestants than by Catholics.

The antiphon of Pope Benedict XV—'Thou art Peter and upon this rock will I build my church'—(placed before the collect for peace taken from the Roman Missal) is never omitted from any Tract.

The Litany (*invocations*) which goes back with certain variations to 1939, when it appeared in the Congo in a version completely travestied and full of words hurtful to the separated brethren, is now widely used and deserves to be recorded. It is in three parts.

1. For the little importance we have accorded to that word coming from thy divine Heart: 'I have other sheep which are not of this fold, them also must I bring and they shall hear my voice';
Forgive us, Lord.

For our controversies sometimes full of irony, of narrowness of spirit or of exaggeration with regard to our non-Catholic Christian brethren, for our intransigence and our severe judgements;
Forgive us, O Lord.

For all acts of culpable violence wrought by us Catholics against our Protestant brethren;
Forgive us, O Lord.

For all unjustified restrictive measures taken against them;
Forgive us, O Lord.

For all attitudes of pride and self-sufficiency that we may have shown towards our Orthodox brethren and for all our failures of understanding with regard to them;
Forgive us, O Lord.

For our bad examples in conduct which have retarded, diminished or destroyed the effect of grace in the souls of men;
Forgive us, O Lord.

For forgetting to offer prayer, frequent, fervent, fraternal on their behalf;

Forgive us, O Lord.

2. Across the frontiers of language, race and nation;
   Unite us, O Jesus.

   Above our ignorances, our prejudices, our instinctive antipathies;
   Unite us, O Jesus.

3. O God, for the increase of thy glory;
   Gather thy scattered people.

   O God, for the triumph of good and of truth;
   Gather thy scattered people.

   O God, that there may be but one fold and one Shepherd;
   Gather thy scattered people.

   O God, to confound the pride of Satan and his hosts;
   Gather thy scattered people.

   O God, that peace may at last reign in the world;
   Gather thy scattered people.

   O God, to bring fulness of joy to the heart of thy Son;
   Gather thy scattered people.

It must be remembered in reading the Tracts that for some years not only the composition and writing of these, but the addressing, preparation for mail and posting of them was the spare-time work of an ageing, invalid schoolmaster with large professional claims upon his time and energy, besides an ever more voluminous correspondence which his work for unity entailed. For all this labour done in loneliness and often in disabling cold he had the most grotesquely inadequate material equipment. Even the weighing-machine he used, borrowed from the school science laboratory and failing to register by the metric system, involved him in complicated mathematical calculations. By the time he carried the packets off to the post on his way from the Institution des Chartreux to supper at his sister's flat, he had given by hard office-work some initial testimony to the sincerity of the earlier long sacrificial prayer the ardour of which permeates the pages of the Tracts.

NOTES

1 Abbé Couturier never suspected that the idea of the Tracts, suggested originally by Hurrell Froude, owed something to the influence of *L'Avenir*, the organ of the great prophet-journalist of La Chênaie, Abbé Félicité Lammenais: see Christopher Dawson, *The Spirit of the Oxford Movement*, London: Sheed and Ward, 1933, pp. 58–64.

2 L. Richard, *Le Mystère de la Rédemption*, Tournai: Desclée & Cie, 1956.

3 Pius XI, *Allocutio*, 18th December, 1924.

4 See later, pp. 277, 292–3, 327 and Appendix B.

5 I find that in the last two years of the Abbé's life, the editing of the Tracts was done by Père Villain, S.M. He gives no indication of this in his book on Abbé Couturier.

6 Stephen Neill, 'The Missionary Movement and the Ecumenical Movement', *History's Lessons for Tomorrow's Mission*, Geneva: W.S.C.F., 1960.

10

THE WEEK OF PRAYER
IN LYONS

ALONG with the preparation of the Tracts went on another task
of which we have spoken—the effort to provide at Lyons a
pattern of witness and worship which might serve as a model for the
observance of this week in other cities and lands. For this there was
clearly need of official authorization and of powerful support from
priests and theologians both secular and religious.

For stable authorization everything would depend upon the
choice made by His Holiness to fill the vacant throne of the archbishopric of Lyons which carries with it the ecclesiastical 'primacy
of the Gauls'. The choice when it was announced in July 1937 was
not unexpected and was everywhere cordially welcomed. We, who
have not already known him as Bishop of Tarbes and Lourdes, must
be introduced to Pierre Gerlier.

A collateral descendant of St Catherine of Genoa, it is by no
means for that reason only that the choice of Gerlier would have
been one after Baron von Hügel's heart. The mystical, the intellectual and the institutional elements of religion are in Pierre Gerlier in
almost perfect equilibrium. Born in 1880 at Versailles, son of a high
government official, he did brilliantly at school and university and
became a leading figure amongst lawyers. The subject of his thesis
for his doctorate of law, 'Points with regard to usury in labour con-
tracts', indicates a pre-occupation with social justice. But all this
time he was doing valuable work as an inspirer or collaborator in
Catholic youth movements. More and more he felt himself drawn to

give himself entirely to full-time apostolic work and at the age of
33 he was knocking at the door of the Sulpician Grand Séminaire of
Issy with a view to being trained for the priesthood. In the following
year, 1914, came the war. He left the seminary, became adjutant of
his infantry regiment, was badly wounded and to the great benefit,
both spiritual and social, of his companions in captivity, was taken
prisoner by the Germans. After the war he returned to his seminary
and was ordained priest in 1921. He was appointed sub-director of
diocesan activities in Paris—and of this a large variety of folk soon
became aware: drapery assistants, clerks from banks, exchanges or
insurance offices, and men and women workers in the state sanitary
system, all incorporated now into their appropriate Catholic unions,
not to speak of members of the already existing parochial guilds.
This was equally true with regard to representatives of the Press,
for Gerlier was charged to look after relations between this and the
Church. But to the regret of Paris this lasted only four years, for in
1925 he was made Bishop of the diocese of Tarbes and Lourdes. This
diocese profited by his almost miraculous power of administration,
as well as through his presidency at the National Marial Congress
of 1930, at the seventy-fifth anniversary of the Apparitions in 1933,
on the occasion of the canonization of Bernadette, at the great
pilgrimage of *anciens combattants* and at the triumphal Triduum of
1935 when Cardinal Pacelli (later Pope Pius XII) represented His
Holiness. It meant much to countless Christians to hear his straightforward apostolic counsels as to the one remedy for the ills of society,
'the sincere renovation of private life and public life according to the
mind of Christ'.

Robust Christianity along with commonsense, clarity and cen-
trality. Any Englishman, especially in the Cardinal's radiant
presence, might readily think of him as just the man for Canterbury.
He would hesitate when he heard that Pierre Gerlier attributed all
his success to loyalty to his motto *Per Mariam ad Jesum*. A practical
mystic and leader of men, valiant defender of the faith, he seems
almost to have been predestined to be father-in-God to the people of
Lyons, a city where a real and efficacious consciousness of the social
claims of Christ is closely allied to the veneration of his Virgin-

Mother. Certainly no other could have more acceptably and more fruitfully shouldered the great burdens that now awaited him. And the happiness of Christians in Lyons over this was increased when less than four months after his enthronement, their archbishop was raised to the cardinalate.

There was no delay in the receiving by Abbé Couturier of authorization from his father-in-God. Cardinal Gerlier was a man of great vision with a special faculty for encouraging, using and protecting inspired initiative in others. We have seen this in the case of Abbé Monchanin, the encouragement of whose Indian adventure meant a heavy sacrifice for the diocese. He was a most steadfast, understanding and wise friend; and the patronage of one whose holiness and charm were combined with the powerful gifts of a trained barrister, stood the Abbé in good stead in time of difficulty. Their relationship was a delightful one. Exemplary and truly filial obedience on the Abbé's part, an affectionate blend of reverence and judicious humour on the Cardinal's part. 'Here comes my executioner!' he would say, as the Abbé arrived to win his approval for some new scheme, needing official sanction, which might perhaps require firm fatherly support or revision in view of probable criticism.

The Abbé needed not only authorization, but also competent speakers for the Week of Unity, a need not so easily satisfied in days when the subject of ecumenism was a tiresome by-way not much frequented by theologians. However, a great many priests, taught and influenced at their seminaries by Abbé Portal, were already at work, men imbued with that inspiring teacher's own deep interest in this crucial question. Wider still and deeper was the influence of the Monks of Unity of Amay through their prayer, through their excellent journal *Irénikon* and through their founder himself who, though *in terra aliena* acting as a chaplain to a small convent near Paris, exercised thence a wide-reaching apostolate.

Père Congar's book, *Divided Christendom*,[1] appeared only at the end of 1937; and *Catholicism* by Père de Lubac, S.J., a book full of patristic insight with regard to the mystery of the one Church, not until the

Notre Dame des Dombes, scene of many interconfessional gatherings

LESMURSDELASÉPARATION
NEMONTENTPASJUSQU'AUCIEL

See p. 72. (*In the original, the initial letters of the text are in red.*)

A nous tous, chrétiens,

l'Humilité

ouvrira les routes barrées

See pp. 314, 324. (*In the original, 'l'Humilité', the kneeling figure and the trees beyond the wall are in green.*)

next year. The Abbé had only his own long articles to use as an introduction explaining the object of the conferences, when he wrote to invite theologians to Lyons to speak during the Week. However for the most part, thus invited, come they did! Though there were some excuses and hesitations and one or two misfires, many came and came again and also did much to spread the light on return to their own homes.

After a beginning had been made, as we have seen, in the first three years, 1933–5, on apologetic themes, such subjects were chosen as would bring sympathetically to light the positive Christian values in which separated Christian confessions rejoiced and such as would suggest the possibility of a richer synthesis of Catholic values within the one reintegrated Church of the future centred (as he hoped) at Rome. There had been many memorable pronouncements and writings in the past on the causes of division. It was time to emphasize the unity that is already ours. There are therefore chosen one by one, three comprehensive yet profoundly theological main themes, one for each year, themes whose positive non-controversial aspects might be expounded from different angles. Thus we have in 1937 *The Kingdom of God*, in 1938 *The Mystical Body*, in 1939 *The Sacrifice of Christ*.

The programme of 1937 is particularly interesting:

Catholic Synthesis of the Kingdom of God	P. Salet S.J.
Self-Government in the Kingdom of God (with special reference to Anglicanism)	P. de Pierrefeu S.J.
The Virgin in the Kingdom of God	Dom Th. Becquet O.S.B.
The Russian Vision of the Kingdom of God	Dom Th. Becquet O.S.B.
Greek Orthodoxy: the Kingdom of the Pantocrator	P. Broussaleux, A.A.
Israel, Prophet and Prefiguration of the Kingdom of God	P. Ferrand of the Fathers of Sion
Elements in Islam of a Kingdom of God	Abbé Monchanin
Invisible Membership of the Church	Mgr Besson, Bishop of Fribourg

Many of these addresses, breaking such new ground must have

made a great impression, but perhaps none more so than the meditation on Islam by Abbé Jules Monchanin. Père Villain, who was at
Lyons throughout the week, remembers nothing more vividly than
that.

> What economy of words, what richness of phraseology was used
> to evoke from the Koran, illustrated by images of the desert and of
> the white Moslem city, the vision of a theocracy: a theocracy para-
> Christian, and God grant it, pre-Christian!

Two lectures by laymen added great interest. One by Jean
Guitton—then a young man of promise, now the distinguished
writer and professor in philosophy of the Sorbonne—on 'Lord
Halifax' whom he had known as a visitor to his venerable friend,
Père Pouget, the Lazarist teacher and biblical scholar whose harsh
repression by church authority and other sufferings bravely borne
have done so much to liberate the splendid biblical movement in the
Roman Church of our day.[2] The other by Jacques Zeiller on 'The
Kingdom of God and Unity on earth in the first Christian Age'. Jean
Guitton also gave a radio message on 'Sympathy, the condition of
Unity'.

The printed programme closed with a characteristic note, indicating a principle dear to the Abbé: 'No tickets and no seat-
reservation: no paid seats', a point hotly contested by the cathedral
sacristan; who managed in the end to insist on a collection, since as
he wrote dourly to the Abbé, 'The Master blessed the poor woman
who put her mite in the *gazophylacium*!'

In 1938 the theme of the *Mystical Body* included amongst its
expounders Père Mersch S.J., the theologian whose great work *Le
Corps Mystique du Christ*[3] has associated the revived interest in this
Pauline conception so closely with his name. Professor Louis
Richard p.S.S. and Père Maurice Villain S.M. were also collaborating
in this week. There were also three radio messages one after
another, by the Protestant Pastor Rivet (*The Right Hand of Fellow-
ship*), by the Eastern Orthodox Dr G. Lodizhensky (*Modern Christian
Martyrdoms, prelude to Christian Unity*) and by the Roman Catholic
Professor Flacelière (*Catholic Universalism in St Paul*).

In 1939 the theme of *The Sacrifice of Christ, Mystery of Unity* had amongst its expositors Père Aupiais, Superior of 'Missions Africaines' and Père Yves Congar O.P., the great ecumenist whom we have already met at Amay-sur-Meuse.

It was my great privilege to be at Lyons during this week, just a year after my profession in the Community of the Resurrection at Mirfield. My venerated teacher and dear friend during the last few years of my earlier ministry, Professor Sergius Bulgakov, Dean of the Eastern Orthodox Academy of St Sergius in Paris, had asked the Superior of our community whether I could come and under his supervision enlarge my knowledge of Orthodoxy. His request came about the same time as one from Abbé Couturier asking that one of us who could speak French should come and give in a broadcast from Lyons a message from the Superior (as a member of the Church of England) alongside members of other Churches, in the Week of Unity of 1939. Father Talbot, our Superior, accepted both invitations, told me I was to go both to Paris to study Orthodoxy and to Lyons to speak in his name, and then went off to visit the houses of the community in South Africa.

The three months I spent in France between the Eastern Orthodox Christmas (our own Epiphany) and Easter week have left me with many enriching memories. I had already got to know and to love the Abbé in circumstances to be described later. I was now to see him at work in his own city: self-spending, self-effacing, militantly irenic, a living proof of the unitive power of the Sacrifice of Christ. After the joy of sharing at the Russian Academy of St Sergius in Paris the latter part of Eastern Orthodox Christmas celebrations, there followed for me the great adventure of a visit to the city of Lyons which we guessed had already become, through Abbé Couturier, the birthplace of spiritual ecumenism.

On the Saturday evening of my arrival came a dinner party at the home of M. and Mme Carlhian where several of the visiting speakers were entertained, including Mgr Bruno de Solages, Rector of the Catholic University of Toulouse, by whom I was placed at table, to find myself as deeply impressed by his conversation as later by his preaching. He has since proved the most powerful critic of the

Intégristes (rigid traditionalists in theology) and of their distinguished leader, Père Garrigou-Lagrange, O.P., who himself in another
field has deserved equally well of the Church by his insistence on the
place of contemplation in the normal life of the Christian. Mgr de
Solages said that night things I have remembered to my profit, but
perhaps nothing so worthy of record as his remark during the
course of that later controversy,

> If Père Teilhard de Chardin had not existed, he would have had to
> be invented!

It was only later that I came to realize the eminence of the bluff, kind
businessman who was our host that night, but his and Mme
Carlhian's warm hospitality was already a great factor in the work
at Lyons for Unity.

For that first night and that night only I was billeted at the
Presbytère of Abbé Remillieux, curé of the church of Notre Dame-St
Alban in a suburb of Lyons. I am always thankful that I met that
great priest and in his own home. Along with Abbé Couturier and
the young German curate of the parish we talked late into the night.

From their seminary days Laurent Remillieux and Paul Couturier
had been devoted friends, despite their contrasting temperaments
and characters. Remillieux was a whirlwind of sacrificial energy
which was squandered prodigally as much outside on a mass of noble
ventures and undertakings on behalf of Christians in general as
within his own parish. His was a spirit as creative as it was incapable
of self-limitation. He had made his own church the first working-
model for those seeking to develop the liturgical life of a parish.
Twenty years later with Dom Lambert Beauduin's inspiration a
similar scheme was put forward in the *Centre Pastoral Liturgique* in
Paris. Unfortunately the liturgical life of the parish of Notre Dame-St
Alban at Lyons was frequently put out of gear owing to the curé's
sense of the urgent need to scurry about Europe preaching the duty
of Christians to work and pray for peace.

The Abbé Couturier whose own energies had to be so carefully
husbanded and whose limitations had through self-knowledge with
deep humility become a strength, found in Abbé Remillieux a most

helpful fellow-labourer. They were allied in a kindred vision of God's design for his Church and for his world, as well as of the obstacles that threatened it, though Abbé Couturier had learned better, partly through very weakness, the necessity of putting first things first.

Already on 3 July 1937 Abbé Remillieux had written to his friend:

> If we meet soon and have an hour at our disposal, I will let you know the whole tragedy (on the psychological plane) of everything relating to the problem of peace. To unite Christians and to avoid an infernal conflict are, in my opinion, the two urgent tasks for which it would be worth giving one's life.

Hence the presence when I stayed with him of a young German curate whom the Nazis, on his return to Germany, put into a concentration camp. And hence our host's sermon at the parish Mass next morning which dwelt on the eminent value of Lord Halifax, great statesman and great churchman, as a harbinger of true peace. (I was never quite sure whether he did not conflate two distinct persons, father and son, both of them certainly great Christians: Lord Halifax, the British Foreign Secretary at the time who had recently gone with Neville Chamberlain to talk to Hitler—his climbing into the aeroplane whither he had come spiritually fortified from the *messe anglo-catholique* was vividly described!—and his father, the Anglican sponsor of the Malines Conversations!)

I was taken after breakfast to the baptism of a distinguished Jewish lawyer from Paris; then on to preach at the Anglican church (in those days immoderately Protestant in its set-out). I left truncated Mattins before its close in order to be in time to give the Anglican message in the Unity Broadcast.

To have to give one's first broadcast in another language is anxious work. But the Abbé's presence along with his meticulous care for detailed preparation and rehearsal, infused peace into the proceedings. There were four of us by his invitation giving messages. Mgr Lavarenne, President at Lyons of the Propagation of the Faith, represented the Roman Church; Professor Zander of the Academy of

St Sergius, Paris, the Eastern Orthodox; Pastor Ribagnac the French Reformed Churches; and myself (on my Superior's behalf) the Church of England. We were allowed seven and a half minutes each for our messages which were afterwards printed in *Oecumenica*.

I stayed on in Lyons for the rest of that week and for most of the next, enjoying for the first time the gracious hospitality of the Séminaire Universitaire on the hill St Just, half-way up towards Mont Fourvière. So I had the immense privilege, frequently renewed since, of growing to know a group of the company of priests of St Sulpice, those inspiring fathers and fosterers of so much that is best in the life of the priesthood in France. For an Anglican priest for whom the teaching of Bérulle, Condren and Olier has been a source of inspiration, it was a special happiness to be in contact with a living stream of their spirituality. It was from such priests of St Sulpice that Abbé Couturier had learned Christian doctrine and it was these in particular who were by their sympathy, appreciation and counsel to provide his most valuable aid. It was a wonderful background against which to enjoy participation in the further events of the week. From time to time the Abbé would arrive to take me off to meet some of his friends. There was the privilege of a visit with him to the sons of the venerable Père Chevrier at the Prado, unforgettable monstrance of gospel poverty, and that of dining with Père Aupiais and others of the 'Missions Africaines'. Or with Professor and Mme Zander I was taken to see some monument or church that Abbé Couturier loved in Lyons, or on pilgrimage to the shrine of the patron saint of parish priests, St Jean-Marie Vianney, the curé of Ars.

This year the Chapelle d'Adoration Réparatrice proving too small, the conferences were moved to the Church of St Francis de Sales and to the ancient Basilica (dedicated to St Martin) of Ainay. I shall never forget the sermon of my venerable friend, Professor Richard on 'The Sacrifice of the Mass in the worship of the separated brethren' or the closing address of Mgr de Solages at the cathedral on the 'Mass as Prayer for Unity'. The cathedral that week was also the scene of another celebration of the Byzantine liturgy, concelebrated by four priests, a Greek, a Slav, a Ruthenian and a Melchite: the Cardinal read the Creed in Greek and the Seminary of the Missions of Syria provided the choir, brief explanatory comments on the worship being given by the Abbé from the pulpit.

On another day of the week Jean Guitton gave a talk to a full hall on 'The Great Figure of Cardinal Mercier'. One might have observed that truly the irenic spirit of Mercier seemed to prevail in Lyons. I had no idea that there was any opposition there to the proceedings of the Week. But there was a great deal. For instance there was in circulation a four-page tract produced by Catholic opponents, containing the words:

> Obedience is the distinctive mark of the children of God. Those who do not obey [the supreme head, the Pope, successor of Peter] belong to the party of the great rebel who dared to say '*Non serviam:* I will not serve.'

And a leaflet announced that a man

> converted through St Thérèse of the child Jesus, cast off by his orthodox parents and despoiled of all his fortune, but splendidly serene amid tribulations, would give an address at the Salle Blanchon!

The war cut short the further development of the week at Lyons. The preparatory scheme for January 1940 shows that the title was to have been *The Bible, Bond of Unity*. Assistance was requested from Cardinal Tisserant, Dom Bernard Capelle, Mgr Mulla (The Bible and Islam), Archimandrite Alexis Kiréewsky, once a monk of Mt Athos. Abbé Gratieux, formerly pupil of Abbé Portal and now noted for his work on the great Russian lay-theologian Khomiakov, was to speak on 'The Gospel in Russian Piety', Abbé Nédoncelle on 'The Bible in the Religious Formation of the Anglican Soul', Père Villain on 'The Bible in Stone of the Middle Ages'. But the cataclysm of the preceding September blew such fine prospects to the winds. When January 1940 arrived, there was one address only in the week, 'The Unity of Mankind, mirage or hope?', by Père Salet, S.J., and a celebration of the Byzantine liturgy. In 1941 nothing. In the next four years a couple of speakers mustered from Lyons itself. In 1946 several speakers of whom one was a layman. And in that year also at the Salle Rameau choirs from the Catholic, the Orthodox and the Protestant churches gave a combined concert on the theme 'Noel,

Feast of Christendom' with addresses from a Roman bishop, an Orthodox priest and a Protestant pastor who together led those present in the saying of the 'Our Father'. Henceforward, though there was no lack of distinguished theologians accepting his invitation, the Abbé found it no longer possible to group the subjects round a single theme.

How generously from the first men and women invited to help in the Week gave themselves to serve the vision the Abbé had shown them! This was specially true of the speakers. There was, for example, Père Emile Mersch, S.J. He wrote:

> I am happy that my journey to Lyons is giving me plenty of work and the opportunity to speak of the subject which is so near to my heart [the Mystical Body]. Other addresses? As many as you wish! The audience to whom I'll get over best will be *scholasticats* [houses of studies] and seminaries rather than Sisters. But of course I don't exclude them. Several times a day—there's no difficulty about that. But a possible half-hour or hour of recollection before the chief engagements would be very desirable.[4]

No visiting theologian was ever closer in mind and heart to Paul Couturier. One of his Brethren wrote of Père Mersch:

> His entire life was dominated by the profound conviction of the real ontological union between each Christian and the Incarnate Word, and of each Christian with all other Christians in Christ.[5]

Through all these years (1937–53) there was devoted service given by the Christians of Lyons itself. The Faculty of Theology of the Catholic University of Lyons and the Seminaire Universitaire, the Jesuit Scholasticat (House of Studies) of Fourvière and the Marist Scholasticat of Saint-Foy, the Dominican hostel of the Holy Name of Jesus gave their support, providing valuable speakers from among the professors and welcome help from among their students. There were artists, Catholic and Protestant, willing to design posters or illustrate tracts, and musicians and poets likewise to compose hymns of unity. The Abbé was always eager to bring home to artists how greatly they could help by using their gifts in the cause of Christian Unity, and during the war he wrote an inspiring appeal to artists to this effect, printing it in the second number of his *Pages Documentaires sur l'Unité Chrétienne*—over his own signature, P. Couturier.[6]

The designs made for the cover of the Tracts were usually enlarged to form the poster for the Week. The Abbé knew what he wanted: something fresh and striking which would challenge the mind of the ordinary Christian. The old-fashioned conventional ecclesiastical art, known unfairly as 'Saint Sulpice', he would not countenance. But modern art, he believed, soon went beyond the limit of the ordinary Christian's receptivity. The designs he actually published sometimes had a wide success which surprised his advisers. The distribution of posters met unexpected setbacks. It was much easier to get the authorization of Catholic authority for a design than it was to get Protestant pastors to hang up anything containing the words *cum permissu superiorum*. So there had to be two brews: one containing these words so important for Catholic viewers; the others for Protestants free from such a blemish. Finally a third set of posters was added devoid of any *illustration* for the sake of the old guard, both Catholic and Protestant, who found the Abbé's choice too modern.

In Mgr Lavarenne, president in Lyons of the Propagation of the Faith, he found a mind thoroughly awake with regard to the relations between Missions and Christian unity and a friend devoted to his cause. This meant valuable financial help when things were most difficult and articles in the press in thorough harmony with the Tracts. In the last years when sickness disabled the Abbé, the offices of the Propagation of the Faith kindly undertook most of the work of sending out literature.

At the Seminaire Universitaire where I was staying in 1939, the Abbé came to *déjeuner* one day during the Week. Meals there were ordinarily taken in silence on that day. But the Father Superior from the high table where he sat with Abbé Couturier at his side, surrounded by theologians and professors, gave out to the assembled company of these and the students of the seminary that though it was the Week of Universal Prayer for Christian Unity, we were free to talk because we were very happy to have 'the *Soul* of the week with us'. It was wholly unexpected and perhaps the only moment when the all but unknown yet most alert conductor of proceedings during the Week—watchfully regulating every detail, he was indeed its life and soul—was drawn out of his hiddenness. During the public events of the Week there was scarcely ever any clue as to who was their director. He would arrive first, check quietly points of importance, then sit in a corner or, if seating was short, remain standing throughout. He would have arranged for the speaker to be introduced and thanked by someone well qualified. Only when all was over would he communicate his own gratitude which, whether by word of mouth or by letter, was bestowed with a warmth and grace, intimate, rewarding, and not easily forgotten.

NOTES

[1] Y. M. J. Congar, O.P., *Chrétiens désunis* (Paris: Éditions du Cerf); translated into English by M. A. Bousfield, O.P., omitting *inter alia* the dedication 'to the great soul of Cardinal Mercier and to all who took part in the Conversations of Malines. *In memoriam, in spem*' (*Divided Christendom: a Catholic study of the problem of reunion*, London: Bles, 1939).

[2] See Jean Guitton, *Monsieur Pouget*, Paris: Gallimard, 1954, and *Dialogues avec M. Pouget*, Paris: Grasset, 1954; the latter translated as *Abbé Pouget Dialogues*, London: Burns and Oates, 1959.

[3] E. Mersch, *Le Corps Mystique du Christ*, 2 vols, Louvain: Museum Lessianum, 1933; 2nd ed., 1936—trans., *The Whole Christ: the historical development of the doctrine of the mystical body in Scripture and tradition*, Milwaukee: Bruce Publishing Co., 1938.

[4] Cardinal Gerlier being prevented from giving the closing sermon of the Week, Père Mersch preached *impromptu*. He was killed during the war when ministering to the wounded during an aerial bombardment of Lens. His death occurred on the feast of Corpus Christi, 23 May 1940. The incident reminds us that the Blessed Sacrament in the early ages of the Church was known as the Mystical Body of Christ. There was found on his prie-dieu the day after his death a note just written full of the eucharistic spirit that breathes through the letter we have quoted: 'There's need of men detached from themselves, living to give everything. *Sit mihi velle et nolle tecum, nec aliud*; a positive will to find my joy, my motive power (*entrain*) there. *Ita Pater*. Yes, yes, active.'

[5] J. Levie S.J., 'Le Père Emile Mersch (1890–1940)', *Nouvelle Revue Théologique*, March–April 1945, pp. 64–68.

[6] A large part of this is printed in Villain, *L'Abbé*, Appendix II, pp. 335f., but it deserves republication separately.

II

THE GROWTH OF THE
MUSTARD TREE

———————

THE spread of the Week of Universal Prayer and of the spirit
that influenced it was largely the result of the influence of
individuals quickened by contact with enthusiasts at Lyons, but
there was one exception. The Reformed Churches of France sought
at once to assess the significance of this appeal for prayer proceeding
from a Roman Catholic priest who seemed to rise above denominational claims or interests. As early as April 1936, through the
initiative of Pastor A. N. Bertrand, they discussed this and made
clear their support as follows:

> The National Synod, learning that an effort of intercession for
> the Unity of the Church will be made on the 4th Sunday after
> Christmas by numerous groups of Orthodox, Anglicans and Roman
> Catholics;
> (a) welcomes this initiative with joy;
> (b) suggests that pastors should on that Sunday direct worship
> with the intention of Christian unity and with special attention to
> joining the prayers of the Reformed Churches of France with those
> of other fractions of the Universal Church.

Other great cities were soon found following the example of
Lyons. The earliest to do so were Strasbourg, Marseilles, Toulouse
and Lille; and these influenced smaller towns in the neighbourhood.

Strasbourg came first. Two of its citizens were moved by the
Abbé himself, not without the aid of the hospitality of his friends. It

was on a lovely Sunday evening in May 1937, in a garden belonging to M. Carlhian close to St Alban's church, at an interconfessional week-end party organized by the curé, Abbé Remillieux, that M. Schmidt, a lawyer of Strasbourg, and his wife first met the Abbé. He told them and the Protestant pastor of Belfort, M. Marchand, about the proceedings of the January Week of Prayer at Lyons and how well things had gone. The Abbé had to leave; but hearts had been moved, so that conversation continued until at M. Marchand's request those who remained had shared in the singing of the Creed and in the saying of the Lord's Prayer. Returning to Strasbourg the Schmidts founded an ecumenical circle where the Abbé's brochure on Universal Prayer was studied and preparations were made to observe the Week of January 1938.

Strasbourg is, like Lyons, one of the great crossroads of civilization, by reason of its rivers, its rich religious traditions and the contest between French and Germans for its possession. Christians there responded well when in January 1938 Père Congar O.P., came down from Le Saulchoir and he and Père Lorson S.J. gave instructions on the theme of Christian Unity, prayers being conducted for this end, as at Lyons, both in chapels and churches: broadcasts also were given both by a priest and by a pastor. Sad instances of Roman Catholic proselytism cast a shadow on the circle, but a couple of visits from the Abbé who gave counsel with real frankness and sympathy restored its equilibrium. Once again in 1939 Protestants and Orthodox as well as Catholics observed the Week, welcoming instructions on the Bible from Dom Clément Lialine O.S.B. of Amay and from M. Raymond Chasles.

After the war, during which Strasbourg suffered grievously, it was *Una Sancta*, the Society founded by Father Max Metzger, the German apostle of unity,[1] which revived the flame. The University of Strasbourg, established under state control with both a Catholic and a Protestant professorate working side by side, has played its part in keeping this alive.

It is surely a significant thing that the streams of irenic devotion flowing from these two great apostles of Christian Unity, Couturier and Metzger, of France and Germany respectively, should so mingle in Strasbourg, the home of the Council of Europe and of so much secular endeavour both political and cultural for unity and peace. Providence ordained that during the years that Christians in Germany were isolated under Nazi oppression, Max Metzger should be exercising in that land a ministry similar in aim and in spirit to that which Paul Couturier exercised in Western Europe and thence by his writing throughout the free nations of the world. I had always been impressed by the likeness of these two apostles in character and calling, even before this conviction was confirmed by the mysterious and unexpected arrival in my mail of a batch of brochures, each containing in the German language brief accounts, first of Abbé Couturier (this a translation of one by myself) and secondly of Max Metzger (by an author unknown to me), each with a drawing of its subject. Both of these priests throughout their lives travailed in labour and prayer for Christian Unity and offered their lives for that end. Both because of their resolute loyalty to the same supranational ideal were imprisoned by the Nazi power in Eastertide of the same year, 1944. 'Bruder Paulus' (as he was known to his friends) was executed on 17 April, 1944 on the charge of high treason against the Reich and the Führer of his nation, dying bravely a martyr for his faith. Paul Couturier who was in prison for two months, was released to endure the long-drawn-out martyrdom of suffering in sickness amid suspicion and harsh antagonism and the growing weight of labour, before his death nearly nine years later. Both were greatly in debt to the monks of St Benedict. Both expressed in challenging and unforgettable words their hope of a forthcoming great and truly ecumenical Council of the whole Church.[2] Both had the same absolute devotion realistic and undeviating to the Church of Rome. Both were convinced that penitent humility is the great need of ecclesiastical authority. Max Metzger said after his condemnation,

> I have offered my life for the peace of the world and the unity of Christ's Church. God has accepted it and I am glad.

The testimony of his death differs from that of the French priest only in that the oblation is specially orientated in love towards his

German Protestant brethren: the Abbé's intention is, as we shall see, more explicitly universal in its scope. But he would have found himself absolutely at one with Father Metzger's last will and testament:

> . . . I confess before Almighty God that I desire to die in the Holy Catholic faith as a true son of the One Church of Christ whose unity I believe to be represented and guaranteed according to the will of God by the Holy Father in Rome. According to my firm belief, the above statement is not endangered by the fact that I feel myself as closely united to my believing and conscientious Protestant brothers in Christ Jesus through Baptism and our common experience in the same Lord, as to the brethren with whom I can share the fellowship of the Holy Sacrament.

The two witnesses were perhaps closer still to one another at the opening of their ecumenical ministry. Metzger in founding the *Una Sancta* Brotherhood as 'a fellowship for prayer and work for reunion amongst Christ's disciples everywhere', sent out widely, as did Couturier in the same year, 1938, a 'Call to Prayer in the sense of the high-priestly prayer of our Lord in St John 17 *that they may all be one*'. He spoke of the Unity of Christendom as 'the last will and testament of Jesus Christ', bidding the members of his brotherhood to

> undertake to pray, using the Lord's Prayer common to all Christians, and also the high-priestly prayer of Christ for the coming of the Kingdom of Christ on earth and for its unity in faith and love.

The two streams have mingled and now are one. Dom Th. Sartory of the Benedictine abbey of Niederaltaich, leader of *Una Sancta*, speaks of Abbé Couturier 'much venerated in Germany' as a primary source of the inspiration of his work and does all he can to extend the 'invisible monastery'.[3]

In other parts of France the spread of the Week of Prayer was greatly helped by the admirable *Association Chrétienne de Professeurs*, usually known as *L'Amitié*. This interconfessional society groups together Christian teachers of the universities and of the state schools with the aim of mutual spiritual support and of the deepen-

ing of the life of the Spirit. It found in Abbé Couturier's way something closely in accord with its own high ideal of fellowship and has
been an invaluable aid in promoting his work, especially in the cities
where its branch meetings are held. The Association is most widely
known through its magazine *L'Amitié*, which title gives the name
most frequently used for the society itself. There is a double motto
for the Guild expressing its inspiration at once Christian and human:
'*Ut unum sint sicut tu in me et ego in te*' and *For friends by friends*. Abbé
Couturier loved this society and wrote of it cordially:

> Introducing the ecumenical ideal into professional life through
> the warmth of sympathy—that 'little name of charity'—this
> association has its place midway between individual *rapprochements*
> and ecumenical ones. This is a truly unionist method, uniting
> together a few individuals to be organized, as so many cells, into a
> living body.[4]

It is the founder of *L'Amitié*, Professeur Miroglio, a Protestant
who every year at Le Havre invites a priest and a pastor to give
addresses and to direct listeners in united prayers. A group of the
Association was active in initiating the observance of the Week in
Bordeaux. Anyone who is able to look through a series of numbers of
its fascinating magazine, *L'Amitié*, will see how loyal its members
are to their friend, Abbé Couturier and how deeply they have been
influenced by his spirit. Why, one wonders again and again, is there
not a similar family of Christian teachers—schoolmasters and mis-
tresses, and the staffs of universities and training colleges—in our
own country!

At Toulouse, 'the intellectual capital of the South', it was, as has
often happened elsewhere, a seminary student who in 1939 took the
first step. Jean Lafargue shared tracts received from the Abbé with
his fellow-students, was drawn in their company to pray for unity
and found encouragement to do so from the Superior. Soon it was
the Cardinal Archbishop, Mgr Saliège himself, who took the lead. It
was recalled that the theme of his address at his enthronement had
been the words of the high-priestly prayer 'that they may all be one'.
The onset of the almost total paralysis which soon disabled the

Archbishop in everything but mind, soul and will did not dim in him this fundamental longing. Nor did it prevent him from being the chief French leader of spiritual resistance against Nazism. It seemed not only to deepen his sympathy and understanding, but to heighten his gaiety, his courage and the lucidity of his pregnant style. He wrote:

> The prayer of Christ that they may all be one does not cease to be in action. It is present. It is today, it will continue tomorrow. The Father hears it. The Holy Spirit is active there. It is true—men have a long way to go and divine action is in the habit of proceeding slowly. Grace which prepares the way goes slowly.
>
> It is certain that a Catholic who lives his faith, who lives charity, by his prayer becomes a ferment of unity. 'By this shall all men know that ye are my disciples if ye love one another.' The true disciples of Christ are marked by this sign. Irresistible attraction of love, of charity.
>
> It is necessary, it is but honest to recognize doctrinal positions which separate Christians as well as those which draw us together. Unity based upon equivocation would be only confusion.
>
> The deepening of their grasp of one truth often brings a mind to accept other truths. There is a link of kinship between truths of the same order. Our acts are richer than our ideas.
>
> You know Christ. If you wish to know him more perfectly, pray to him in confident humility and live that which you know of him.
>
> To pray that our separated brethren grow in fervour is then to pray for unity. The same is true of the prayer that Catholics may live in Christian integrity.
>
> Holiness gives birth to anxiety in souls that witness it. It disturbs their little combinations, their systems of compromise, their view on the sense and value of life.
>
> Prayer for unity—indeed yes. Life for unity, even better. Prayer of a day, a week, a moment. Life is of every day, hour, instant.
>
> For Christian unity there have been lives offered: and the offerings have been accepted.[5]
>
> For Christian unity from certain monasteries there rises to the Saviour prayer as incessant as the desire it expresses.
>
> Christian unity will not arrive tomorrow. Much depends upon Catholics preparing for it by their prayer, by their life.[6]

The Abbé recognized here and in other utterances of the Cardinal a standpoint so close to his, that he got permission to reproduce this message and to distribute copies.

In 1945 the theme for the Week of Universal Prayer at Toulouse was 'The religious soul of the nations and Christian unity'. Père Villain was asked to give the addresses. There was present also a Hindu teacher who, in the presence of the Archbishop, gave an exposition of 'The Meaning of Christ for the Hindu Soul'. Though the subject was marginal in relation to the theme of the Week, it had great value for the Abbé who dreamed, like his friend, Abbé Monchanin, of a doctrinal and liturgical approach to the most deeply religious continent, free from everything in the Latin-Greek idiom of our Christian heritage which renders our faith incomprehensible to Indians.

The Bishop of Montauban that year asked Père Villain to repeat in his cathedral the addresses given at Toulouse. The Bishop planned to start in his seminary conversations between a priest and a pastor conducted in public before a select audience of their colleagues. Abbé Couturier could not approve of such a programme, a scheme which must clearly stimulate controversy and one the penetration of which by a spirit of prayer it would be hard to secure, though this would be a primary condition of its doing any good. When in 1949 the Cardinal Archbishop of Toulouse included ecumenism in the programme of the addresses to which the bishops who are the *protecteurs* of the Catholic faculties of the University of Toulouse are invited, he asked Père Villain to deal with this subject and to do so in the spiritual perspectives adopted by Abbé Couturier.

It is not surprising that Lille soon made the ecumenism of Abbé Couturier its own. The record of Lille excels even that of Lyons as a source of inspiration and leadership in the kindred field of the social expression of Christ's Gospel. It is perhaps because for many years there had been at Lille a Dominican Centre of Oriental Studies under the care of Père Dumont, O.P., that the city had long shown signs of possessing a keen ecumenical conscience. In 1943 Cardinal Liénart forestalled the directions from Rome given in the Instruction *Ecclesia*

Catholica of 1949 by establishing a diocesan committee of Christian unity. The report of the committee in speaking of the observance of the Week of Prayer reproduces the general intention of the Lyons Tract, 'The Unity of all Christians such as Christ has willed it for his Church'. But there have been splendid new developments in the conduct of the week as developed at Lille. These include a solemn assembly in the great hall of the University presided over by the Cardinal himself assisted by a Protestant pastor and an archpriest of the Eastern Orthodox Church with a speech from each of these as well as choral music from each religious tradition represented.

Christians of Lille having such leadership, there is no wonder that it is the Christian Unity circle founded there by Abbé Emile Meura which has made the widest impression upon Christians in France, England and Italy.[7] But it is through the initiative of many different kinds of person, including persons almost unknown, that parish after parish, city after city, has caught fire and is found observing the Week in a manner which recalls the doings at Lyons. The influence of the Tract is felt everywhere and is not least remarkable in places where previously the Octave with its more specialized intention has been observed. The most fruitful work of all for the spread of Universal Prayer for Christian Unity has been done through visits to seminaries and 'scholasticats' (houses of studies). To influence a priest, it has been observed, is an exercise in multiplication. Under the incentive of Abbé Couturier's encouragement, Père Maurice Villain found himself engaged more and more widely in this most fruitful and enjoyable part of his great apostolate. During the war and the years immediately following he visited more than sixty seminaries. In this way he has been able to inspire the hearts and minds not only of many future priests, but of their tutors and not infrequently of their bishops with a sense of the call to Universal Prayer and, along with the knowledge of its chief instrument the Week of Unity, with a wider vision of the task of spiritual ecumenism.

NOTES

[1] The facts recorded in this chapter about Metzger are taken from the brief but admirable book by Lilian Stevenson, *Max Josef Metzger, Priest and Martyr*, London: S.P.C.K., 1952

[2] See in Stevenson Metzger's noble letter from prison to Pope Pius XII: cf. pp. 44–55.

[3] See his article 'L'esprit de l'oecuménisme en Allemagne', *Istina*, 1960, no. 1, especially pp. 17, 19.

[4] *Rapprochements entre les Chrétiens au XXme siècle* (Le Puy: Editions X. Mappus, 1945): English translation in *Reunion* V, No. 36, 1946, pp. 169–89.

[5] The Cardinal's motto inscribed in his coat of arms under the Cross was *Sub umbra illius*.

He summarized in conversation his own story in words the beauty of which, his biographer tells us, he did not suspect:

'I loved speaking. And God has taken my tongue.

I loved walking. And God has taken my legs.

He may take everything. I have given him everything.'

See Jean Guitton, *Le Cardinal Saliège* (Paris: Grasset, 1957), a worthy biography of a great leader, pastor and saint.

[6] Before the Abbé had it printed separately, these sentences were part of a message printed in *La Croix*, 19 January 1943. It was no doubt a jewel due to Abbé Couturier's campaign to win the alliance of the press for the promotion of universal prayer. Cf. pp. 82, 145, 239f. A later utterance of Mgr Saliège is characteristic: 'I believe in the sincerity and in the value of the desire for unity. For this desire to become efficacious, I believe in the value and the necessity of prayer.'

[7] Abbé Meura is now French representative on the staff of *L'Osservatore Romano* and lives in Rome. But he continues to guide the Lille circle of Prayer for Christian Unity.

THE INFLUENCE OF THE WEEK
IN THE ORTHODOX CHURCHES

THE monastery of Nashdom has been thought of by many
Anglicans as an institution having as its unique aim the
furthering of reunion between the Church of England and the
Church of Rome. If this were the whole truth, it would be, granted
that the light of conscience leads us in that direction, no mean thing.
But church historians of the future will have a more balanced story
to tell.[1] Nashdom has certainly a vital part to play in our story, and I
think it may help to correct perspectives if it is introduced at this
point.

On the feast of St John the Evangelist, 1928, there arrived at the
Abbey doors, not without due notice, a noteworthy and impressive
visitor clothes in *cappa magna*, mitre and *pallium*.[2] He was solemnly
received by Father Abbot and his monks, and conducted to the
chapel where all sang the *Te Deum*. The visitor was Bishop Tikhon,
the bishop in Berlin of the Russian Orthodox in Exile. His Lordship
in the chapel proceeded to address the community on the need for
unity amongst Christians. After Vespers, with the permission of the
Russian Metropolitan Anthony as well as of the Father Abbot,
Bishop Tikhon clothed his Russian attendant with the habit of a
Benedictine oblate. Next morning the bishop attended at the throne
the Latin Mass of the Holy Innocents and took his leave in the afternoon, leaving behind him a very pleasant memory of courtesy and
goodwill. The Russian oblate stayed on for two months to learn
more of the life and discipline of the Rule.[3]

English Christians are much indebted to this Russian scholar who came to England from Lyons over thirty years ago, and who has since become a familiar figure in the ecclesiastical landscape of our growing cosmopolitan society. His story is a deeply interesting one. Serge Bolshakoff, for this is the oblate's name, was born in St Petersburg in 1901, and in that city he underwent training as an engineer. During the civil war he left Russia and went to Esthonia. There in 1924 at Tartu University he founded a religious society for members of the Orthodox Church called the 'Logos Circle'. Its members graduated, left that university and settled, many of them, in other countries. The former rule which involved periodic meetings and discussions, as well as active participation in parish and diocesan life, proved impracticable and demanded revision. At a meeting in Paris in 1927 Bolshakoff was charged to write a new rule and constitution. With this in mind, after a brief visit to the Monks of Unity at Amay, he went to stay at the Cistercian monastery of La Trappe des Dombes, where he read with care the rules and statutes of many Catholic religious orders and fraternities. A rule was needed at once clear and supple in character. He did his best to provide such a rule, basing it on that of Franciscan tertiaries and sending it to Bishop Tikhon of Berlin, the Visitor of the Logos Circle, for his approbation. Bolshakoff's connexion with the Trappist monastery at which he devised this rule, was specially fruitful, because it was there that he met Abbé Couturier, whom later, at the Abbé's request, he was to supply with the names and addresses of bishops and other leading personalities of the Eastern Orthodox dispersion.

Meanwhile Serge Bolshakoff had decided to carry further his investigation of the divers forms of the religious life by visiting the Anglican Benedictines of Nashdom, of whom he had heard. Fresh from the massive buildings of La Trappe des Dombes, of which we shall have reason to speak later, he was surprised to find himself in England ringing the bell of a commodious country house built in what, in Russia, is known as the Imperial style—that style characteristic of the Napoleonic empire, which is princely rather than monastic. Indeed the community had occupied this fine building only since 1926. It had belonged to Prince Alexis Dolgoruky, a

Russian diplomatist who had married a wealthy English lady, Miss Fanny Wilson. The house had been built for them by the renowned and versatile British architect, Sir Edwin Lutyens. The Dolgoruky family is the noblest of Russian families, descending from Rurik who founded the Russian state in 862 and having given its name to many distinguished statesmen and soldiers; and the name of their house, Nash-dom, is the Russian for 'our house'.

That evening the young stranger was presented to the Abbot, Dom Denys Prideaux, a priest eminent in prayer, of vast learning and much spiritual shrewdness, and one tried by long endurance. It was he who had brought the community into being after the débâcle of Caldey. Their conversation,[4] as Bolshakoff recalls it, seems to me of special interest. He was first questioned as to his impressions of Nashdom, to which he could only reply that it seemed to him perfect after the Latin pattern—'I could hardly believe I was not in a Roman monastery.' He was then asked whether he thought union between the Anglican and the Eastern Orthodox Church was a possibility. He pointed out to his host the marked diversity of Anglican opinions as to its desirability.

> Many Anglicans consider the Anglican Church akin to those on the Continent. Some even deny the need of the Apostolic Succession and do not attach to the episcopal office any more meaning than do the continental Protestants to that of their Superintendents and Moderators.

The Abbot replied:

> Such people do exist amongst the extreme evangelicals, but they must not be taken too seriously. We are not unanimous on this point. But look how many Anglican priests signed the Declaration of Faith, sent to the Patriarch of Constantinople, admitting practically everything you consider essential.[5]

Bolshakoff was next asked as to prospects with regard to the reunion of Orthodoxy with the Roman Church.

> Are the Orthodox bishops to swallow papal infallibility or is the Pope to disclaim it?

This question is still more difficult to answer. The term *ex cathedra* is very vaguely defined. The monks of Amay say it is so because the Vatican Council of 1870 was forced to interrupt its session and leave unfinished a full and comprehensive scheme of the Church's constitution, elaborating only the part concerning the Pope. We must await the whole scheme. Then we may express our opinion. In any case the difference between us, the Orthodox and the Romans, is so great in the outlook, customs, way of life, tradition, etc., that no reunion is possible without a long and careful preparation. I think Amay does this work well.

The Abbot smiled once more.

I would like to see Nashdom doing the same.

At Nashdom, whence Bolshakoff paid his first visit to the Oxford home of the Cowley Fathers, his future home for so many years, he studied the statutes of Benedictine oblates and became convinced that the best way to preserve the 'Logos Circle' was to reorganize it as an independent confraternity of Benedictine oblates. Its aims were registered as the cultivation of the interior life, co-operation with the hierarchy, assistance to missions, Christian social reconstruction and, above all, the endeavour to promote Christian unity—

We could try to carry out in the Orthodox Church in our humble way a work similar to that of Amay.

With this in mind he went to Berlin to see Bishop Tikhon. There he had the good fortune to converse also with Metropolitan Anthony Khrapovitsky. This learned and holy prelate, formerly Metropolitan of Kiev, while being a great pillar of church tradition, seems to have lived on the summits of Russian culture. He had been specially close to Dostoevsky[6] and had also known Tolstoy, Soloviev and Rozanov. He scrutinized and approved the young man's design, advised him, as one called to work for closer relations with Western Christianity, to make England his base and Anglicans his first study.

Thus it was with the sanction of Metropolitan Anthony that before the year closed, Bishop Tikhon, as we have described, received in Nashdom chapel the vow of Serge Bolshakoff to observe the Rule of the 'Orthodox Confraternity of St Benedict' for life and, in the presence of the Abbot and his monks, clothed him in a habit similar to that worn by Benedictine secular oblates. This is less astonishing than it might seem. Though Benedictine monks no longer exist in the Orthodox Churches, St Benedict is there venerated and his feast observed; his ikons are familiar and his Rule is known and prized. Of all the Latin rules it is the nearest and the most comprehensible to the Orthodox mentality, permitting the Orthodox to understand the Latin spirit close to its very source.

The Confraternity thus inaugurated, however much it may have been inspired with the spirit of St Benedict, was a society of men pledged to observe its rule living in the world. They were bound not only to say a form of the Divine Office and to live strictly the life prescribed by the Church, but also to be active for the Church, special emphasis being laid on work for Christian unity. It is not surprising that the January Octave, still operative in its original papalist form, seemed to Bolshakoff a useful instrument for this work. He was soon in close connexion with its American founder, Father Paul Wattson, visiting the brothers of his community at the St Benedict Labre Home at Shoreham and the sisters in Bermondsey.

It was true that he was also in close touch with Abbé Couturier and sought to collaborate with him. In all his propaganda for the Octave, Bolshakoff included a statement repudiating as an Orthodox Christian the papalist note of the Octave. But though he did invaluable service to the Abbé in providing him with introductions within both the Orthodox and the Anglican worlds, it was not until too late that he learned to prize the wisdom that had led Abbé Couturier completely to reconstitute the Octave as the Week of Universal Prayer. Bolshakoff prized the new wine, but not sufficiently to refrain from mixing it with the old.

For a time the promotion of the Octave by the secretary of the Orthodox Confraternity of St Benedict was a great success. Many bishops commended the observance, including those of the Russian episcopal synod of the Karlovtzy jurisdiction[7] and the leading prelates of the Esthonian and Rumanian Churches. But the Octave movement alarmed those more keenly averse to *rapprochement* with the Roman Church, and efforts were made to compromise it. It was said repeatedly that the Octave, as promoted by the Confraternity, could be only a fraudulent device to implant the original papalist Octave, concealing for a time its purport. So in 1937 Archbishop Tikhon found himself driven by the strength of the opposition to resign from the Presidency of the Confraternity. The observance of the Octave within the Orthodox Churches soon came to an end, and the Orthodox Confraternity of St Benedict is no more.

The real services rendered by Serge Bolshakoff to the cause of Christian unity, are, as he has himself come to understand, of a different kind. He has been a source of countless life-giving contacts, and he has been, in the ecumenical field, a source of much invaluable information. For many years he was secretary of the International Academy of Christian Sociologists, a society open to all Christians validly baptized and professing the Nicene faith. This society concerned itself with studying social problems in the light of the great papal encyclicals, *Rerum Novarum* and *Quadragesimo Anno*, thus providing a general sociological programme for Christians. His work as secretary for this society partly explains Bolshakoff's amazing range of acquaintances, amongst churchmen of almost every communion, in the ecumenical, scholastic and literary fields. He has always been generous in using this to promote the noble ends for which he lives. So he has been a liaison officer of considerable value between the Eastern Orthodox, the Roman Catholic and the Anglican Churches. Having something of the mentality of the *Strannik*, the Russian peasant pilgrim, he has been a constant traveller and has become the most notable journalist of inter-church travel in our days. His range of acquaintance is constantly enriched, and his memoirs, when they come to see the light, will be of real importance.

Of those whose names and addresses were provided by Bolshakoff to the Abbé with a view to promoting in the Orthodox Church the Universal Week of Prayer for Christian Unity, Metropolitan Eulogius of Paris, as we have seen, gave invaluable support. And from him, as Exarch for the Eastern Orthodox in Western Europe, came authorization to the Archpriest Behr in London, as well as to the Archpriest Popoff in Lyons to invite prayer *in the spirit of Abbé Couturier*. Archimandrite Kirik of the Monastic Republic of Mount Athos in northern Greece, wrote to the Abbé, acknowledging gratefully his article (on 'Universal Prayer') 'so full of the love of God', and said that he would make it known to the Council of Russian Archbishops when they meet in 1935. From Tikhon, whom we have already met, now Archbishop of Berlin and Germany, came in December 1934 a letter expressing his cordial approval of such universal prayer as necessary in face of atheism which has caused such suffering to Russia. Later he published a Russian translation of the Abbé's article.

There followed letters of approval from His Holiness, Benjamin, Patriarch of Constantinople (Christmas 1939); from Gavrilo, Archbishop of Petch and Metropolitan of Belgrade and of Karlovtzy; from Professor Alivisatos of the University of Athens, author of the celebrated book on Anglican Orders;[8] from the Metropolitan of Imbros and Tenedos (1940); from another Archimandrite of Mount Athos, in charge of the 'cellule' of St Michael the Archangel; from the Greek Archimandrite Timothy P. Thelemis of Jerusalem. There is a large correspondence with Pavlovsky, founder of the University of Harbin in Manchuria. What must it have meant to that university for the library of which the Abbé is found begging books from his friends, to have received a visit, suggested by the Abbé Couturier, from the inspiring Père Albert Valensin, S.J., who was travelling in China, giving his renowned Ignatian retreats?

There is no doubt that the Abbé Couturier's influence on the Eastern Orthodox was considerable. But its fruits were disappointing. It is the paradox of Eastern Orthodoxy that, while it claims to hold intact the imperishable treasure of unity, its adherents have been themselves, at least until lately, too divided to give effective witness on this point. It is true that their dividedness, being canonical rather than dogmatic, is of a less painful kind than that which divides one communion from another in the West. They conceive of it as not really separating them from one another, as being temporal, even where not connected with political misunderstandings; as proceeding from the inertia of ecclesiastical machinery rather than having to do with faith and spiritual life. That this is not a full and final account of the matter anyone can discern who will take care to compare, for instance, the teaching of different schools of Orthodox theologians on the constitution of the Church. From time to time the Orthodox themselves have realized with distress how their divisions blemish their offering of true glory (*orthē doxa*) to the one and only God.

It was not, however, until 1961 that the reproach that the unity of the Eastern Orthodox is theoretical rather than real was given a general answer by the epoch-making event of the conference on the Isle of Rhodes. All but one of the Orthodox Churches were represented in the gathering convened there by the Ecumenical Patriarch of Constantinople. Here the Church of the Seven (General) Councils, as the Eastern Church has been called, achieved the nearest approach to a general council for many centuries—in fact since its largest element, the Slav majority of the Orthodox world, came to the faith. The purpose of the meeting was chiefly, as the official message states, 'to manifest our unity'. This desire had been roused, no doubt, in great measure by the papal gesture—the summoning of the Second Vatican Council by the late Pope John XXIII 'in order that Christendom may be edified by the dazzling spectacle of this gathering of the members of the Catholic Church in charity'. It was also certainly furthered by knowledge of the World Council of Churches and of the efforts there after unity in Christ; unity which the Eastern Orthodox claim to be Christ's gift to the Church, a gift which Eastern Orthodoxy has never lost.

In France in 1943 there was needed the influence, albeit indirect, of Abbé Couturier, before steps were taken by leaders of the three groups into which the Orthodox were divided, to give co-operative witness as to their unity in the one Church of God. In that year there was founded the *Comité Interorthodoxe d'Action Oecuménique*. It was sanctioned by Metropolitan Eulogius (exarch for Western Europe of the Ecumenical Patriarch of Constantinople), Metropolitan Seraphim (representative of the Karlovtzy jurisdiction), and Archimandrite Athanasius, who represented the jurisdiction of Moscow. There were also enrolled in the *Comité* representatives of the other Orthodox Churches which had centres in Paris—Greek, Rumanian and Ukrainian.

The chief work of this council was to promote in the different Orthodox Churches in France the observance of the Week of Prayer. This it succeeded in doing, for reasons we shall give, for some years only. The service on Sunday, 23 June 1944, which launched this observance, marked indeed a memorable and inspiring moment of recovery. The Divine Liturgy had been celebrated in Paris earlier that day with special prayers for unity by Metropolitan Eulogius at the cathedral in the Rue Daru. But the 'Grand Reunion of Prayer' was at the Rumanian church in the Rue Jean de Beauvais. This was attended by many Catholic and Protestant clergy and theologians, as well as by Orthodox members of the different national Churches in the three jurisdictions. The Rumanian Archimandrite welcomed all present to share in an act of faith and an act of love—'an act of faith with regard to the divine mission and an act of love towards the separated brethren in Christ: a twofold act which will mark this day as a great day in Orthodox history'. Then, after prayers entitled 'Prayers for increasing peace and charity among Christians', sung in six languages, Greek, Latin, Slavonic, French, Rumanian, and Ukrainian, Metropolitan Eulogius addressed the congregation in Russian, translated into French by Professor Leo Zander.

Beloved brothers and sisters in Christ, I would like to introduce these few words of welcome by the Easter refrain, 'This is the day which God hath made: let us rejoice and be glad in it.' Blessed are the initiators of this feast of Orthodox unity, who have given us the opportunity of praying together for the holy cause of the unity of the Church of Christ.

Protestants and Anglicans had already for some time taken the initiative in drawing nearer to one another. And now we have Roman Catholics likewise taking part in this movement of prayer. I rejoice to see them today amongst us. Abbé Couturier of Lyons, that indefatigable apostle of this great cause, gives us a great example of perseverance and of charity. But before we approach other confessions, we Orthodox must be united amongst ourselves. We speak too often of 'the Churches'—Greek, Russian, Rumanian,

Serbian or Bulgarian, as if they were separate organisms which have no unity amongst themselves. And yet we must state and proclaim with a loud voice that truth of which this gathering is a visible proof, that the Christian East, despite all its administrative divisions, forms but one single Catholic and Orthodox Church.

Then Professor Pierre Kovalevsky mounted the pulpit and spoke of the Week of Prayer and of its intention—the return to the Unity desired by Christ, by the means desired by him. He described the whole movement connected with the Week as centred on Lyons, with Abbé Couturier, an apostle of unity, as its animator, 'zealously, inexhaustibly co-ordinating all its efforts'. (For this phrase, he was sternly rebuked by the Abbé when he read the report of the meeting!)

We Orthodox meet one another too rarely. We are dispersed throughout the world. We have no centre at which we can gather. Nevertheless the history of the Catholic Orthodox Church can be gathered in these few words: 'the Miracle of Unity'. For more than a thousand years, the Christian East has lived without a general council and without one single administrative authority. The national Churches have had no mutual relations during long periods. Groups of believers were separated from their brethren for centuries. Yet anywhere and always, seen in the most isolated parts of the Christian world, the Catholic Orthodox Church, conducted by the Holy Spirit, her only guide and pilot, has preserved the unity of Faith and Grace. . . . A Greek, a Russian, an Arab, a Rumanian Orthodox have the same belief and the same liturgical life, have recourse to the same Sacraments; and in 1944 the Catholic Orthodox Church is as much 'one and indivisible' as it was a thousand years ago.

The speaker closed by prophesying that it is Orthodoxy that will give unity to the whole Christian world. He gave as a symbol of this the providential location of this service of prayer. He found it deeply significant that this first reunion of the Orthodox of different nationalities should be taking place on neutral soil—in Paris, the city of St Geneviève and of St Denis, equally venerated in the West and in the East, after Orthodox pilgrimages to the tombs of each; in an

ancient Roman Catholic church dating from the epoch when relations between East and West were still close, a church founded by
Jean Dormans, Bishop of Lisieux (city of religious peace), a church
actually administered by Rumanians, the only Orthodox people of
the Latin race capable of serving as a bond between the two parts of
Christianity.

Such a conjuration into action of the latent unity of the Orthodox
Churches as occurred that day does not seem to have been repeated
in Paris, though the *Institute of Christian Unity* emerged from it and
lived to publish a brochure containing a full account of the service,
together with the *Litany for Peace amongst Christians* from the *Rituel
byzantin*.

Perhaps the most abiding and fruitful work done through the
Comité Interorthodoxe was that its Secretary General, Professor Kovalevsky, was charged by its President, Metropolitan Eulogius, with
the duty of co-ordinating the various enterprises that should be
undertaken in relation to the Week of Unity and with the task of
collaborating closely with the headquarters at Lyons, i.e. with Abbé
Couturier.

It is probable that the Abbé never had a more understanding,
faithful, and useful friend and disciple than the Eastern Orthodox
scholar, Pierre Kovalevsky. Other friends have names more illus-
trious, but true modesty, with an eagerness to put himself unspar-
ingly at the disposal of others, has kept Kovalevsky to some extent
in the background. Born in 1901 at St Petersburg of a distinguished
Russian family, he received his education at the Lycée Réformé in
that city. His studies were continued in Paris at the Sorbonne, at the
School of Oriental Languages, and at the Russian University of Law.
An unexpected, providential contact made in 1922 with a conference
of Catholics and Protestants into which he stumbled on a holiday
walk turned him into a keen ecumenist. Since that time he has been
in relation with the French Student Christian Movement, and in
1923 was one of the founders of the Russian Student Christian
Movement and has been its delegate at conferences in Britain and in
Geneva. He also accompanied the Metropolitans Eulogius and
Anthony and Bishop Benjamin to London for the commemoration of

Nicaea in 1925, and took part in the subsequent official conversations between Orthodox and Anglican theologians.

M. Kovalevsky is one of a number of Eastern Orthodox theologians who have found their spiritual home in the West through Benedictinism, in one or other of its presentations in 'black' Benedictine, Cistercian or Trappist monasteries. In particular, since 1934 he has been closely in touch with the monastery of Amay-Chevetogne, which he has visited regularly since 1938, rejoicing there in the worship of the Byzantine church.

Here comment is needed. Such an Orthodox Christian has a hatred for 'uniatism'—the Roman Catholic policy of using the eastern rite when, in any region, this seems most likely to advance its dominion. An Orthodox Christian feels that this procedure shows a failure to realize the deep relation between worship and life—as if one were to attempt to put on a new skin with the ease with which one might put on a new suit of clothes. On the philosophical level indeed uniatism may seem to indicate a kind of ritualistic nominalism, as contrasted with the realism of Eastern Orthodoxy. But the discerning Orthodox recognizes exceptions, and most of all with regard to the use of the Eastern Orthodox rite under Catholic obedience in the Byzantine chapel at Chevetogne. Here the background of the worship is a really profound attempt to enter into the life of Orthodoxy. A pledge of this is that the community of the Monks of Unity is divided into two groups, the Latin and the Eastern; one of which practises only the Western rite, the other, only the Eastern, without alternation or confusion between the two, while the liturgical life of each group is grounded in a kindred theological life.

In the Abbé Couturier, oblate of this community, M. Kovalevsky found a priest who, while he represented all that he most admired in the Western tradition, yet most truly loved and venerated the Eastern Orthodox Church. The Abbé, on his side, was immensely encouraged to find, on his exodus from prison in 1944, this gifted and radiant scholar, astonishingly youthful in spirit, though mature in experience, commissioned by Metropolitan Eulogius to promote harmony between Catholic endeavours in the cause of reunion and those of the Eastern Orthodox Church. This arrangement was especially agreeable to Couturier because, for some time, he had been estranged from his Russian friends in Lyons. These were now divided into three congregations. There were first those subject to the jurisdiction of Metropolitan Anthony, the loyalists of the former Russian régime which now had its centre at Karlovtzy: secondly there were those subject to the Abbé's friend, Metropolitan Eulogius. Thirdly, there was now the chapel where the Orthodox rite was performed under Roman obedience. The Abbé refused to associate himself specially with any one of these. And there was a further difficulty. At one time even charitable activity of a material kind on the part of Catholics for the relief of the Orthodox became suspect in the eyes of the latter. This grew out of a Roman Catholic concept of the One Church which led certain Roman officials to ignore the hierarchical structure of the Eastern Orthodox Churches and to treat their children insistently as if they were strayed children of their own. There is no doubt that it was widely held amongst Roman Catholics that the Revolution in Russia was a providential chastisement for Orthodox obstinacy, giving the true Church its opportunity to recover such exiles into her own bosom. This is perhaps a necessary corollary of the Bellarminian doctrine of the Church. It may be a sign that something has gone wrong with doctrine on a wide scale! I am sure it is. But the memory of similar conduct which blemishes the records of the Church of England should teach us that such notions and attitudes are not incompatible with a robust Christian piety.

But now came a new opportunity of fruitful collaboration in the field of Catholic-Orthodox relations. And this went on to the very end of the Abbé's life, as the fascinating correspondence between him and Kovalevsky records. It includes arrangements for ecumenical broadcasts in Lyons and in Paris; and for participation in the interconfessional gatherings at the monastery of La Trappe des Dombes. It discusses the preparation of tracts and posters, on which Kovalevsky is the Orthodox adviser. Information is exchanged about the keeping of the Week in the different spheres known to each. Arrangements are made for lectures to be given by Kovalevsky at

Lyons, sometimes for interconfessional circles, now for Catholic priests at 5 Rue du Plat, now for a meeting organized by a Russian parish. Then Professor Kovalevsky takes a foremost part in the most considerable venture of the Abbé in the field of journalistic activity. This was made possible by Abbé Catrice of Lille and his journal, *Catholicité*, several numbers of which are devoted to the subject of ecumenism. It was in *Catholicité* that Couturier first proclaimed his great idea as to the duty of moral reparation on the part of Catholics for the massacres of St Bartholomew's Day.[9] He develops here his theme of the need of reciprocal reparation on the part of Christians for the wrongs committed by one Church against another, which was to become one of his governing ideas. The theme is one very congenial to Russian religious mentality. But Abbé Catrice was a man whose interests were more of a political cast; so after some years he ceased to welcome the collaboration of these fervent ecumenists.

In 1946 at the death of Metropolitan Eulogius, difficulties became even graver in the relations between the different Russian congregations. But while these misunderstandings isolated Abbé Couturier from the Orthodox neighbours at Lyons whom he loved so well, providence had brought him into touch with various eminent personages of the Eastern Orthodox Church who lived at greater distances. One or two of these were less congenial than the sages and the unfortunate ne'er-do-wells whom, in earlier years, he had so happily befriended and from whom he had learned so much in the poor quarters of Lyons. But some, like Pierre Kovalevsky, became very dear to him, and part of his life.

In Paris, however, Eastern Orthodox leaders grew to feel cautious about the observance of the Week of Prayer for Christian Unity, even in the form into which it had developed in Couturier's hands. It still lay between two Western Catholic feasts, the first of which (18 January—the feast of St Peter's Chair at Rome, only recently removed from the Calendar) signified the triumph of St Peter's See at Rome, the second (25 January) recalling the Conversion of St Paul. It had been chosen as a 'universal' week without any consultation of the East. In view of this, still wishing in deference to their

Western brethren to co-operate in their prayers for unity, the Orthodox Theological Institute in Paris selected another date, closely following the Week of Unity, but devoted to three great Fathers of the Universal Church revered both in the East and in the West—namely, 11 February, the Feast of St Basil the Great, St Gregory the Theologian (St Gregory Nazianzen) and St John Chrysostom. On this day it holds an ecumenical gathering to which representatives of other Churches are invited. So though the spirit of Abbé Couturier has been influential in these circles, devotion has developed there a new form more congenial to the Orthodox mind.

Within the last few years, since the abolition of the Feast of St Peter's Chair at Rome from the Roman Catholic Calendar, readiness on the part of the Orthodox to observe the Week of Prayer has revived. In the Near East, especially, it is ever more widely observed in certain centres, e.g. in Egypt and Lebanon. But the most important event of recent times was the holding during the Week of Prayer in 1962 of a service in the Armenian church at Istanbul, where the Ecumenical Patriarch of Constantinople took part with the Armenian Patriarch in a common act of worship. A few weeks later, this visit was returned and a joint service according to the Armenian rite was held in a Greek Orthodox church in the same city. On both occasions the churches were packed to overflowing. So there seems some reason now to hope for larger participation in the observance of the Week on the part of the Orthodox and of the other ancient Eastern Churches. In January 1963 it was admirably observed in Athens and in other centres in Greece.

NOTES

[1] Peter F. Anson, *The Call of the Cloister*, London: S.P.C.K., 1955, p. 191: 'The community welcomes any work which can prepare the reunion of Christendom, and especially closer relations between the Church of England and the Holy See of Rome.'

[2] This description of the visitor's attire comes from 'Notes from the Abbey' in *Laudate* VII, No. 25, 1929, p. 1. No doubt the bishop wore, along with his *mandias* and his crown, his *homophorion*—*not* a *pallium !* But Anglicans have been

charged by Eastern Orthodox critics with inability to clothe or describe even their own faith except in Latin dress!

[3] *Ibid.*

[4] The Abbot, who was a great linguist, spoke and read Russian and Armenian, as well as half a dozen other languages.

[5] In May 1922 priests to the number of 3,175 had signed this Declaration consisting of ten articles affirming adherence to the faith of the undivided Church.

[6] Anthony Khrapovitsky as a young man is said to be portrayed for us in the character of Alyosha in Dostoevsky's great novel, *The Brothers Karamazov*.

[7] The governing body of the Russian Church in Exile, established in 1922.

[8] Athens, 1940 (in Greek).

[9] P. Couturier, 'A propos de la Saint Barthélemy', *Catholicité*, Nos. 8–10, 1947, pp. 42–45.

13

OTHER ORTHODOX FRIENDS

WE must now speak of some further friends in the Eastern Orthodox Churches which Providence brought to Abbé Couturier at a time when circumstances had made relations with the Russian Orthodox of Lyons particularly difficult. Though a loyal member of the Eastern Orthodox Church, Dr Georgy Lodizhensky, Secretary General of *Pro Deo*, was a man of political rather than religious importance. The International Commission, *Pro Deo*, which he served in Geneva, was founded there in 1933. Composed of Christians of all confessions it has been well described as a 'defensive crusade against the Anti-God'. Humiliated by the failure of Christianity in face of the persecution which had been overwhelming believers in Soviet Russia during the last fifteen years, Christians, Orthodox, Protestant and Catholic joined in that year to form this Commission. Its principal aims were stated as being to gain information about the activity of the Anti-God in Russia and elsewhere; to make this known to the public by conferences and exhibitions; to evoke Christian action with a view to checking this evil. Its bureau was at Geneva, staffed by an Orthodox, a Catholic and a Protestant who were to convoke a plenary meeting twice a year. It possessed national commissions in Switzerland, Germany and Yugo-Slavia of which in France the association 'Dieu-Patrie-Famille', a centre of anti-Marxist action and information, was said to be the counterpart.

In September 1937 the lecture at the plenary meeting was given by Dr Lodizhensky himself. In reply to the resolution reached by the world-congress of the Anti-God held at Prague the year before to form 'a united front of the anti-religious' he chose as his theme the desirability of a 'United front of Christians'. The Abbé was invited, but being too short of money could not attend. He was glad, however, to discover in the copy of the lecture sent him phrases that showed clearly the influence of the Tracts: for example, commendation was given to 'the method so simple yet so efficacious, of spiritual emulation'.

Next year, 1938, however, it was Abbé Couturier himself who lectured at the plenary meeting on 13 September, a service which was to be repaid by Dr Lodizhensky providing at Lyons the Orthodox message in the Unity Broadcast of January 1939. This meeting at Geneva gave the Abbé an opportunity of real importance for speaking of the greatest weapon in the armoury of God. His message despite its simplicity may well have surprised some of the councillors in this Christian Areopagus of the metropolis of Protestantism.

The points he made are these. There is no more effective way of fighting *Pro Deo* than prayer itself. We are too confident in our own poor human efforts. For us *laborare* comes before *orare* because we are lacking in faith. Without prayer any other kind of effort is useless. Therefore we must all pray. Yet before the offering by all Christians of prayer *Pro Deo*, or at least along with this, isn't it urgent to pray for the recovery of unity amongst ourselves? This union in prayer will once more display before the eyes of unbelievers and atheists the fact of Christ living amongst us. It was with a view to rendering prayer of this kind a reality evident to all that the January week of universal prayer for Christian unity was founded.

Paul Couturier cannot have found this circle a congenial one. He eschewed any negative presentation of the quest for Christian unity, still more the presentation of Christianity itself as a system to *counter* error or falsehood. Such an attitude not only endangers Christian endeavour, but impoverishes and narrows its meaning. Perhaps it did not surprise him that some years later Dr Lodizhensky thought it expedient to join Metropolitan Anastasius in America: the latter, who had recently visited Geneva, had found himself compromised owing to his relations with political enemies of the Union of Soviet Socialist Republics.

Another exiled son of Holy Russia whose hopes were orientated in a political rather than a religious direction, was Professor Michel Zyzykine, a friend of Serge Bolshakoff. He had been formerly professor of international law at the University of Moscow and became later professor of canon law and Christian sociology in the University of Warsaw. At the Abbé's request he had striven to win from Archbishop Denis, the Orthodox Metropolitan of Warsaw, his support of the January Week of Prayer. Unfortunately Professor Zyzykine had referred to Metropolitan Eulogius as a promoter of this. The latter's changes of allegiance—to and fro, between subordination to Constantinople and subordination to Moscow—made his patronage of such a movement cast a shadow upon it in Archbishop Denis's eyes.

On his side the Abbé was more successful in his attempts to help Zyzykine to become known in the West as an author. To him was entrusted the task of securing the publication in France of a French translation of Zyzykine's work, *The Church and International Law*. The author had hoped that its publication would precede his visit to Oxford for the 'Life and Work' conference of 1937. But the book was highly seasoned, idealizing as it does the rule of the Tsars and including a panegyric of the Holy Alliance. The publishers demanded a complete revision of the work to prevent its wounding a Catholic conscience. Paul Couturier accomplished this work with immense tact and care. In this he was assisted by a Russian student, while M. Jules Patouillet, formerly director of the French Institute at Petrograd, secured correctness in the technical terminology. The book did not appear until 1940 by which time the author had endured the horrors of the siege of Warsaw (which he regarded, somewhat surprisingly, as just retribution upon Poland for its persecution of Russians). But two years earlier on his way back from the Oxford conference he had been the Abbé's guest at Lyons, an 'enchanting city', his visit to which remained, he wrote, a beautiful dream in his memory evoking abiding gratitude.

In its November–December number of 1935 the Review of the Monks of Unity, *Irénikon*, published a brief article entitled 'Ways towards the Unity of the Church', signed by Nicolas Arsenev. The author calls upon the charity of the Catholic Church to consent to take its share in bearing the cross which the Orthodox Church has carried since the Bolshevik persecution. He declares:

> The Cross of Christ is the way of unity, because participation in his sufferings, the carrying of his cross, is done by his *whole Body* which is the Church. . . . The principle of disunion between the Churches lies in a different comprehension of the mystical reality of the Church. In uniting to carry the cross of Christ we open wide, even for those who know nothing of it, the possibility of becoming conscious of this reality.

Arsenev notes with joy that Cardinal Mercier, Cardinal Innitzer and Dr Lang, Archbishop of Canterbury, had each one by one entered upon this way; and he expresses his ardent desire that the Roman Church should through the Holy See take the lead in preaching to the whole Christian world this active participation in the sufferings of the Russian Church.

The Abbé underlined the passage quoted as one with which he found himself in deep agreement and sent to Professor Arsenev a copy of his newly printed article on *The Psychology of the Octave*. Thus opened a long and affectionate correspondence between himself and one of the most attractive, learned and forceful personalities of the Russian Church of our times.

Nicolas Arsenev, in 1935 already verging on his fifties, was born at Stockholm, the son of a Russian diplomat of ancient and noble family. His school and university education was at Moscow, but he completed his studies at the German universities of Munich, Freiburg and Berlin, returning afterwards to the University of Moscow as lecturer in the history of western-European literature. At the outbreak of war in 1914 he gave up teaching to work with the Russian Red Cross. On his resumption of teaching he suffered at the hands of the Bolsheviks the fate of many of his profession and was twice imprisoned. On his release he was elected professor at the University of Saratov. But in 1920 he was compelled to leave his native country and found refuge in Germany where he lectured in the University of

Königsberg. He taught also in the Latvian University of Riga and in that of Warsaw and represented the Orthodox Church of Poland at the ecumenical conferences of Lausanne, Lambeth and Edinburgh. His subjects included Comparative Religious History, Patristics and Mysticism, and along with his vast knowledge of literature, both religious and secular, Western and Russian, he was a member of the Academy of Christian Sociologists.

In his early youth Nicolas Arsenev, whose memory is prodigious, had concentrated on the study of the Bible and of the mystical literature of the Western as well as of the Eastern Church. Thus all his work as a scholar has been specially directed to the sphere of mysticism. And his writings have had as their special aim his desire of making Eastern orthodoxy comprehensible to the West. Yet his book on 'the realism of the primitive Christian message' as reflected in modern trends of thought throughout present-day Christianity, *We beheld his Glory*, shows clearly his disposition and capacity for seeking always what unites rather than what divides from Christians of other communions.

If Paul Couturier has been the father of spiritual ecumenism working outside or rather transcending the official organizations which pursue unity, Nicolas Arsenev has been perhaps more than any other the prophet that seeks from within their ranks to render their members conscious of the one thing needful—an evergrowing consciousness of God whose overwhelming, all-transfiguring victory over sin and division is already won in the glorious resurrection of the crucified Saviour. The realism (his favourite word *realismus* demands his book *We beheld his Glory* fully to elucidate what it means for him) of the Gospel of the risen Christ, the triumphant sense of objectivity which empowers it, is a phenomenon of which anyone who has been in the presence of Nicolas Arsenev has unforgettable first-hand evidence. One incident may be related to illustrate the humble, radiant realism of his faith. Abbé Couturier had this incident described to him by Dr Lodizhensky.

After the Bolshevik revolution Nicolas Arsenev was, like almost all theologians, the object of persecution, and had to flee from his country with two of his colleagues, professors of the University of

Moscow. The flight was spectacular. They had to pass through the lines of the Red Army under very dangerous conditions. With great difficulty a peasant was persuaded to lend his wagon and to serve as guide through the marshes and forests. Arsenev's two companions and the peasant were terrified, expecting each instant to be arrested and shot. He alone remained cool. He settled himself on the seat in front with his back to the horse and began to describe the lives of the saints whom he most admired. First he himself and then his listeners were so gripped by the story that they completely forgot the danger of the flight and gained the impression of being in a world wherein the Reds were powerless. They were thoroughly astonished to find themselves safe and sound at the end of their journey and declared that these hours, the most tragic perhaps in their lives, would remain nevertheless in their memory as the fullest of serenity and happiness.

The first service the Abbé rendered Professor Arsenev was to suggest and to secure the publication in the *Revue apologétique* of a dissertation on 'The Meaning of the Eucharist in the Orthodox Church', which he was to contribute to the Faith and Order Conference of Edinburgh 1937.[1] Then his acceptance of the Abbé's invitation to take part in the programme of the Week of January 1938, led the Abbé to plan for Arsenev, whose letters revealed a spirit truly aflame for unity, a journey which would give him the opportunity of lighting similar fires elsewhere. The route proposed lay through Rome, Lyons, Geneva, Maria Laach, Le Saulchoir, Amay and England. Unfortunately illness delayed his starting and finally the journey was reduced to include only Italy, France and Switzerland. Even so, what imagination and devotion the Abbé displayed in arranging everything!—not only introductions needed supplying, but lodgings had to be arranged and the financial wherewithal for the tour to be provided. Arsenev's stay at Rome with the Benedictine fathers of the Greek college as his hosts and with Lord Halifax's friend, Father Pierce, to guide him, was particularly happy and rewarding. But it cannot have been fuller of incident than his thirty-six hours at Lyons where he spoke at the seminary of the African Mission at the request of the Superior on the evening of his arrival and next day no less than four times—to the personnel of the *Chronique Sociale*, to the Historic and Scientific Research Group, to the Jesuit fathers of Fourvière and to the Philosophical Society of Lyons. Between the morning and evening of this full day he had and used the opportunity to entrance the guests invited by M. and Mme Carlhian with his wonderful gift of conversation.

On from Lyons he went to Geneva and Strasbourg, where he gave a public lecture on 'The Religious Life of the Orthodox Church' and another to the ecumenical circle on the 'Union of the Churches'. Mme Schmidt wrote thence to the Abbé,

> Yes, the visit of M. Arsenev has been blessed by God. Everybody was delighted. A Protestant theologian wrote to me, 'M. Arsenev is thoroughly Protestant; I could have signed everything he said!' A professor of the Catholic University rejoiced to find in M. Arsenev a mind thoroughly Catholic. This proves that M. Arsenev has the mind of Christ, the evangelical spirit, and can thus do an enormous amount for the *rapprochement* of minds and their fraternal understanding of one another.

With regard to the whole journey Nicolas Arsenev gave his impression thus:

> I believe that my journey has perhaps had a certain value. In any case the work of spiritual *rapprochement* in the Churches is a great and holy work. In putting all our efforts into the hands of Christ Jesus our Saviour, we entrust to him the success and development of the work.

It was in the Abbé's spiritual home, the monastery of the Monks of Unity, that many years later I was to meet his Russian friend. It was a joy to speak with him there also of my own Community of the Resurrection and of its home at Mirfield of which he had happy memories and of its co-founder, Bishop Walter Frere whom he honoured and loved. A realistic grasp of the objectivity of the Resurrection of Jesus Christ and of the life of the Redeemed as life here and now in the Risen Christ—there lies his hope for the closer union of the Anglican Church with the Orthodox Churches of the East with whom he finds it has so much in common.[2] For Nicolas

Arsenev, as is true of every Christian in proportion to the integrity of his faith, the mystical *is* the real.[3]

The next Russian visitor to find his way to Lyons to see the Abbé was Leo Zander, professor of the Orthodox Academy of St Sergius in Paris where he lectures in philosophy. He is an acute philosopher, a fine teacher, an indefatigable traveller, a most valuable pillar of the Student Christian Movement, a brilliant photographer, a distinguished ecumenist and an incomparable friend. Towards one man in particular, the late Dr Sergius Bulgakov, his attitude is that of a devoted disciple as well as of a loyal friend. There has been within my experience no intellectual discipleship more generous and more fruitful than that of Leo Zander towards this great sage whose many-sided contribution to the stock of Christian wisdom we are perhaps only just beginning fully to appreciate—a progress largely due to this humble though not uncritical admirer.

This visit of Zander to Lyons was but the beginning of another attachment just as firm and perhaps even more filial, for the Professor speaks of the Abbé always as his 'dear Father Paul' in a tone of endearment in which a Russian Orthodox habitually speaks of his *staretz* or spiritual father.

Next year, 1938, Professor Zander accompanied by Mme Zander and myself came from Paris to Lyons to give the Eastern Orthodox message over the radio for the January Week of Unity. We were met at the station by Père Villain, S.M., and taken to the Hôtel d'Angleterre where, after tea, our messages were rehearsed. The professor's message was ideal in character and length and expression, for he is a brilliant linguist as well as a capable and experienced ecumenist. We met more intimately some days later when the Abbé took us to Ars where we attended Mass offered by him before the shrine of the saintly curé. On the way the Abbé developed an idea, to which he was much attached, that of the parallel between the curé of Ars, St Jean-Marie Vianney and the famous Russian hermit of the forests, St Seraphim of Sarov. Both were resplendent with the glory of the Beatitudes, living tabernacles of the Spirit of God; both were prolific in miracles and attracted crowds; both, whatever confessional barriers separate them, find union, each with the other, in God, in charity. Their portraits should come side by side on the panels of a diptych, as a symbol of the union longed for by both Orthodox and Catholic souls. Could no historian be found to show the way? Mme Zander, a writer of real distinction, has since been doing her best in her own literary medium. But so far it is only her portrait in miniature of St Seraphim of Sarov that has appeared.[4] Meanwhile St Jean-Marie Vianney has a secure place in the iconostasis of the Zander's home.

Though the war separated the Zanders from Lyons, Professor Zander continued generously to serve the cause of spiritual ecumenism both among the students at the college of St Sergius and in the addresses he gave to students in other lands. His excellent, but hotly criticized, book on the ecumenical movement, *Vision and Action* (Victor Gollancz 1952) has passages certainly full of the spirit of Abbé Couturier. There he speaks of Abbé Couturier as one

> whose lovable personality and intellectual power attract all hearts and minds and contribute largely to the success of his work. . . . His mission is wholly welcome.

But he goes on to criticize his teaching from a fresh angle.

> If the prayer of Catholics, Orthodox, Protestants is to be united in Christ's High-Priestly prayer, it must be 'apophatic'—must be prayer for a miracle, for a mystery, for the fulfilment of God's will, but certainly not for some concrete form of Church unity which we all conceive differently. 'May the visible unity of the Kingdom of God come in the form that Christ wills, by the ways that are pleasing to Christ'—such is Father Couturier's prayer. He calls it *survol*—flight over confessional limitations, remarking that to fly over means neither to deny nor to forget.

Yet we are to pray for visible unity.

> But when Catholics, believing that the one Pope is the vicar of Christ on earth, pray for the visible unity of the Church, they are not likely to rise above (*survoler*) this basic Roman dogma and to renounce the idea of the Pope heading the Christian world as a whole. Consequently joint prayer for the unity of Christendom

conceals a possible ambiguity of the most serious kind and this must not be overlooked. The ambiguity is not inevitable, for at great spiritual heights where the air is rarified and the pull of earth is scarcely felt, we may be able to pray for unity as such, apart from the confessional interpretations; but this is psychologically difficult and scarcely compatible with the hope that unity will be given us during this earthly historical aeon.

He goes on to say that the work of Couturier seems to

do more for increasing holiness within the Church than for furthering inter-church unity.

This is a mistake unworthy of an Eastern Orthodox writer. It is a virtual denial of the teaching of our Lord in the Gospel: John 8.31f.; 14.15–23. But such reflections of Professor Zander do not represent his whole mind. When he and Mme Zander (author of *The Social Implications of the Holy Trinity*) wrote their *témoignage* to Abbé Couturier, he rose above such sterile rationalism as behoves a child of the Orthodox Church.

The true organ of the *rapprochement* of Christians is not the reason, but the heart. The heart clear-sighted and understanding, the heart which has its own manner of thinking, the heart which according to the Hesychast doctrine, is the very foundation of Christian reason. Otherwise it is sterile, intellectual.[5]

Certainly it is to such a height, or to put it another way, to such a depth of humility, that Paul Couturier calls Christians. The air on the top of Mount Carmel may well be rarified. But it is rather the Mount of the Beatitudes that all Christians are called to ascend. And here no prayer is valid save such as seeks to unite itself with our Lord; our prayer, prayer which, though offered by sinners, has no ambiguity other than that of Gethsemane: prayer 'apophatic' indeed in that it loses itself in consciousness of the divine mystery and demands unity as a miracle of God's grace.

Towards the end of the Abbé's life relations with his Russian Orthodox neighbours in Lyons could be resumed. There was no longer danger of becoming implicated in their internal discussions. He specially valued his friendship with Father Abraham, now Archimandrite Abraham of Rozay-en-Brie, who recalls him with deep gratitude.

> I knew very well, revered and loved the never-to-be-forgotten Abbé Couturier. . . . I met him (October 1948) in the house of a close friend of his, Mme Khorvat, niece of the well-known Kiev archbishop and theologian, Anthony Khrapovitsky.[6] Owing to various circumstances we were deprived of the hall where I celebrated our Holy Services. We asked Abbé Couturier to help us find another place. . . . He could only procure us the possibility of celebrating Christmas and Epiphany in the building of a Catholic lay-organization. He was so good as to come and tell me personally of this possibility. After Christmas service I went to the Maison des Chartreux to thank him. He had a room there where he received visitors and sometimes passed the night. It was on this occasion that he took down from the wall a beautiful reproduction in colour of an ancient Byzantine mosaic of the apostle Paul painted by a well-known Russian artist and gave it to me, saying, 'This picture, maybe, would be better in your hands than in mine.' On the back of it he wrote: 'Remembrance of a great Russian friend—to dear Father Abraham. Russian Christmas 7 January 1949.' This picture even now hangs above my writing-table. . . .

The friendship was strengthened during the Week of Christian Unity in 1949 which was led in such an inspired way by Abbé Couturier. The whole week was

> consecrated to the mutual relations of Catholics and Protestants in the spirit of self-effacing delicate love towards these 'separated brethren'.

Both Father Couturier and Father Abraham shared in close friendship with ministers of the Reformed Churches in the neighbourhood.

> At Easter, the greatest feast of the Orthodox Church, I celebrated Mass in the lateral, bigger hall of the Reformed Church. Abbé Couturier approved this, taking a large interest in the success of my church services.

On Easter Monday I found a postcard in my letter-box left by Abbé Couturier who had failed to find me at home. At the back of this English postcard containing a picture of the Holy Women at the Tomb after the Resurrection, there was written: 'Souvenir from a friend in England transmitted to a friend from the East'. Thus in the light of the Resurrection he united the representatives of the three Christian confessions. I treasure this card in my prayer book.

When I had arranged a permanent chapel in my lodging, Father Couturier came to see me and asked me to show him the Reservation of the Holy Sacraments on my temporary communion-table. With a prayer he deeply bowed and proposed we should say together the 'Our Father', he in French, I in old Slavonic. He ended our prayer by saying: 'Christ is here at this altar.'

Twice Abbé Couturier arranged for Father Abraham to take a rest in the Trappist monastery of Notre Dame des Dombes.

The brothers opened their doors and hearts wide to me. One of the brothers, a Slav, was even dispensed of the vow of silence. We took many walks together through the vast estate of the monastery in open-hearted conversation despite our divided confessions. . . . When he heard the details of my visit Abbé Couturier laughed and said: 'You upset all the rules of the monastery!'

(It seems that the Abbot had yielded out of pure love to the insistent request of this Slav brother.)

Reading in a review that Abbé Couturier had been made an honorary Archimandrite, Father Abraham wrote at once to congratulate him. He was already very ill. In reply he sent the book he had edited, *Christian Unity and Religious Toleration*.[7] A bookmarker at the place of Couturier's own article contained the words of the Russian bishop which he so loved—'The walls of separation do not rise as far as heaven', and his card with the words: 'Profound gratitude, brotherly homage, prayer.'

Those were Abbé Couturier's last words to me. When news of his death reached me I held a funeral service—*panihida*—and always pray for him during Mass.

NOTES

[1] See *Revue apologétique* LXIV, 1937, pp. 702–17.

[2] See his article on 'The possibility of a united Christendom from the Eastern standpoint' in *The Union of Christendom* (ed. Bishop K. Mackenzie), London: S.P.C.K., 1938, pp. 381–403, especially 396–402.

[3] This is true notwithstanding the fact that the terms *mystical* and *mysticism* may be repugnant to him.

[4] V. Zander, *Vie de St Seraphim de Sarov*, Paris: Publications Russes, 1953.

[5] *Paul Couturier, apôtre de l'Unité chrétienne: Témoignages*, Lyons: E. Vitte, 1954, p. 105.

[6] See p. 135.

[7] See pp. 274ff.

14

FIRST CONTACTS WITH ANGLICANS

I T was Serge Bolshakoff, his helper in relations with the Eastern Orthodox, who first made Abbé Couturier known to members of the Church of England. He did so by introducing the Abbé to the two communities at whose homes he had stayed: to the community of the Benedictine monks at Nashdom and to the Society of St John the Evangelist at Oxford. The relationship for several years between these and the Abbé was one of correspondence only. In 1934 the Abbé wrote to thank the second Abbot of Nashdom, Dom Martin Collett, for his hospitality to a student from Lyons, Jean Carlhian, the son of the dear friend whom we have already met. At the same time he enquired about the community's attitude with regard to the Octave. There was an enthusiastic reply, showing eagerness to share with the Christians of Lyons in prayer for Unity and promising that steps would be taken to secure the same response from Anglican communities of sisters to whom the monks of Nashdom ministered. At the same time Father Fynes-Clinton, chairman of the Church Unity Council was asked to make himself known to the Abbé and to his Cardinal Archbishop by sending them copies of the Council's literature. At Lyons Cardinal Maurin as well as Abbé Couturier received these overtures graciously. So there was good news to be communicated in the Anglican chairman's next yearly bulletin about the Octave—though this required to be done with as much discretion as he could muster, there being those at Westminster Cathedral who guarded anxiously against any approach to the repetition of what seemed to them the gross improprieties, or at least the grave irregularities, of Malines.

The Church Unity Octave Council founded by Father Fynes-Clinton in 1921 was the legitimate descendant of the pioneer Association for the Promotion of the Unity of Christendom, already discussed, founded in 1857 which, though the prohibition as regards Roman Catholic membership was secured by Manning in 1864, continued until it was replaced by this new society. The Church Unity Octave was, we have seen, in itself the outcome of a sermon preached for this society by the Rev. Spencer Jones on St Peter's day 1900 which had grown into his book *England and the Holy See* published two years later. The friendship, resulting from perusal of this book, between the American priest, the Rev. Lewis Thomas (later Father Paul) Wattson, and the author led to the observance of the Octave simultaneously in England and America in January 1908. The Council for promoting Catholic Unity was founded in 1920. And there were many other repercussions from that sermon: for example, the Confraternity of Unity founded in New York in 1926 and equipped with its English secretariat at St Saviour's, Hoxton in 1929;[1] the Catholic League, the Society for promoting Catholic Unity and the Sodality of the Precious Blood. In all these Father Fynes-Clinton counted for much. In fact he was a leader of the whole group often known as the Anglican Papalists. He would have described them as followers of the Tractarians who had faithfully developed their teaching with regard to the Catholic nature of the Church of England: drawing the important distinction between the action of the English State at the Reformation and the Church of England's retention, despite the limitations forced upon her, of the essentials of Catholic Faith and Order, they saw and taught clearly that reunion with the Apostolic See must constitute the goal of the Catholic Movement.

There were in the background other leaders greater no doubt than Father Fynes-Clinton, but he was the most accessible. The greatest figure until his death in 1943 was the Rev. Spencer Jones. Lord Halifax was the more active leader until 1934, the year of his death. There were various bishops overseas who were counted as patrons, the Bishop of Zanzibar in particular. Though his attitude towards the Papacy made clear in his great book, *The Fulness of Christ*, was a vitally different one, yet owing to his dramatic gesture of proposing a message of greeting to the Pope from the Anglo-Catholic Congress of 1923, Frank Weston, Bishop of Zanzibar, was a special hero for Papalists. The monastery of Nashdom is regarded by Papalists as a stronghold and sanctuary of Catholic truth.

We are beginning to see that Anglican Papalists have been unfairly judged. Abbé Couturier saw this clearly. They are accused by English Roman Catholics of failure in logic and by many of their fellow Anglicans of disloyalty. There may be Anglican Papalists who are a law unto themselves and who ignore the force of the ordination pledges and are thus disloyal to our Church and to its bishops. There may well be an Anglo-Roman underworld as there have been Protestant and Modernist underworlds and, for all I know, an Inferno of 'Moderation'. But the true Anglican Papalists are not of this calibre. They are a small group with a long lineage in our Church,[2] and many are of the salt of the earth. Their particular standpoint many of them have recognized as involving a call to a life of reparation. Contrary to average opinion this small group is notable for its intellectual power as well as for its holiness. Perhaps the books of Anglican theology of this century that have been most widely read abroad have been books by Papalists—Spencer Jones' *England and the Holy See* and Gregory Dix's *The Shape of the Liturgy*; Dr S. H. Scott's great work, *Eastern Churches and the Papacy*, is used by scholars in most parts of the world.

To other Anglicans their position seems neither disloyal to our Church nor, given their convictions, contrary to the logic of charity, but rather sadly disproportioned. We believe that our own Anglican heritage possesses certain Christian values in trust and that these would be jeopardized if we were to submit to Rome as she now is. It is true that Archbishop Laud's judgement that first 'Rome must be other than she is' can be too lightly echoed. It must go along with a deep penitent acknowledgement of our original debt to Rome for sending us the Gospel, with eager readiness to recognize our kinship and our continual indebtedness—we are all debtors to her for her strong moral witness over many issues, her never-ceasing prayer, her guardianship of supernatural truth. There is also need on our part of penitence and of a spirit of reparation. We have acquiesced in having been separated from her for what were in the first place (at best) dynastic reasons. And since Rome showed her fierce resentment, we must confess that we have done nothing by filial and long-suffering courtesy and consideration, to win her to a new disposition —'I was sick and in prison and ye visited me not.' But Anglicans too have borne their share of this cross. For example, the great renaissance of biblical studies in the Roman Church owes much to the labours of our scholars.

> The brunt of the attack especially in the realm of biblical criticism and of Christian origins, has been borne by non-Catholic scholars, amongst whom the names of Anglicans have held and still hold a high place.[3]

For the bearing of this burden there was necessary the costing atmosphere of intellectual freedom found in our Church. This in an earlier age Newman also may have needed in order to reach his fruitful conception of doctrinal development, a conception to which modern Roman theology owes much.[4] The fear of modernism and of liberalism seems in Anglo-Romans often to obscure their sense of the value of such freedom for members of the Christian Church.

Abbé Couturier esteemed as friends many leading Papalists. He discerned their special vocation and their spiritual value, being well aware as to the character of the relationship of this group with the Church of England in general. It is they who were the means of introducing the Abbé to Anglicans. Though other Anglicans came to share his view-point more fully, these remained among his intimate friends to the end of his life.

Their character was first made known to him by two pilgrimages to Lyons. The first was that of the novice-master of the Anglican Benedictine community of Nashdom, Dom Benedict Ley, who came to Lyons in Ascensiontide 1936. Of this 'pilgrimage of penitence and prayer' we have his vivid description in *Laudate*, the journal published from his monastery.[5] Here was an Anglican specially ready to be of one heart and mind with the Abbé. The son of an Anglican vicarage and entirely convinced of the catholicity of his own Church, a strain in him, derived from Roman Catholic ancestors, made him specially averse to English religious insularity and made him feel close to frustration until he found his vocation and his home in the Benedictine family of Nashdom. There he drank copiously of the river of French spirituality, nourishing his soul particularly on the works of St Francis de Sales. In the writings of this great Doctor of the Church he found not only principles for the instruction of novices but the germ of an attitude towards ecumenism which was more fully developed in the teaching of Abbé Couturier. In the article to which I have referred he quotes the great bishop's words to St Jeanne Chantal:

> When shall we be all bathed in sweetness and gentleness towards our neighbour? When shall we see the souls of our neighbours in the sacred heart of our Saviour? Alas! anyone who looks at him elsewhere, is in danger of loving him without purity or constancy or equality. But seen there, who would not love him? Who would not bear with him? Who would not suffer his imperfections? . . . For he is there, this neighbour—in the bosom and heart of the divine Saviour. He is there as one much beloved—so lovable that the lover dies for love of him.

The English disciple continues:

> The true and only fruitful method of approaching those Christians who are separated from visible communion with us is to see them in the heart of our Lord. Any other outlook, more especially one that seems to deny them any light or life, cannot but be sterile and harmful. The proselytizing spirit which adopts such a negative attitude, has much to answer for before the throne of God. It prolongs the present state of separation between those who should be visibly one, and it makes no positive contribution to its conclusion. The true positive outlook which is to see our separated brethren in the heart of Christ, can only come from an intense interior life; and in all work for Reunion as in any other apostolate, the cultivation of our own inner life is of primary importance.

The writer has clearly been not only with St Francis de Sales, but with Paul Couturier of Lyons.

Lyons is the place where St Francis de Sales died, in the gardener's cottage of the nuns of the Visitation, not far from the Place Bellecour where Abbé Couturier lived. It is not surprising, however, that on his way there Dom Benedict Ley visited first Annecy, the saintly bishop's home, where his remains and those of St Jeanne de Chantal are enshrined in the basilica dedicated to him.

> It was a great happiness to me to pray at his tomb and to commend the intention of my pilgrimage to his intercession. His spiritual writings have had and still have a great influence in England; for apart from their intrinsic merit and appeal to that liberty of spirit so akin to our national outlook, there is also his daily prayer for our country, attested by St Jeanne de Chantal, 'that God would take hold of it and lead it back to its cradle'.

The visit to Lyons was a feast of graces. The Abbé spared no pains to introduce his English friend, who seemed to understand everything except the actual spoken words of the French language which he was still less capable of speaking, to the persons, the communities and the shrines which would mean most to him. One day was spent with Père Albert Valensin, S.J.[6] at Châtelard, a Jesuit retreat-house outside Lyons. Here as at Annecy and later at Paray-le-Monial a visit was made to a convent of St Francis de Sales's order of the Visitation. There were visits also to the Trappist monastery of Notre Dame des Dombes, to the Congregation of Adoration Réparatrice, to a modern congregation of active women Religious, the subject of one of the prophecies of the Curé d'Ars; to the cathedral of St John for the Pontifical High Mass sung by Cardinal Maurin according to the Lyons rite; to the shrine of St Pothinus (first bishop of Lyons) and of the martyrs of Lyons, his children.

Most treasured memory of all was the excursion to Ars. There after attending Mass said before the shrine of the saint, first by Abbé Couturier and then by the Jesuit father who accompanied them, the venerable curé of the village, Mgr Convert, showed them the presbytery where his famous predecessor led his life of poverty and spiritual conflict. Dom Benedict wrote:

> By such an experience [as that of this visit to Ars] one's values are, as it were, automatically adjusted. The things of earth, the trials and difficulties of this poor human 'here and now', lose their sharpness and impressiveness. . . . [In the light of the Eternal], God and our life in him are shown as alone being of abiding worth; all else seems as dross.

A letter afterwards from Mgr Convert to Nashdom showed how deeply the English pilgrim had impressed him, whereas the aged priest had struck his visitor as closely resembling, as indeed in some ways he did, his great predecessor, the patron saint of parish priests.

From Lyons to Paray-le-Monial, the famous centre of devotion to the Sacred Heart of our Saviour. Here in the chapel of the Visitation convent, the scene of the apparitions of our Lord to St Margaret Mary, the Anglican monk was allowed an interview with two English-speaking nuns who gave him literature concerning the Holy Hour and a small relic of St Margaret Marie Alacoque. In the afternoon he called at the Jesuit house of Blessed Claude de la Colombière, the director of St Margaret Marie. Blessed Claude was in London as chaplain to the Duchess of York, Mary of Modena (wife of the future King James II, herself therefore a future Queen Mary) when Thomas Goodwin, friend and confidant of Oliver Cromwell, was also in that city. It was the Protestant Thomas Goodwin who wrote the first book ever written on the theme of the Heart of Jesus. Hence French Christians, Jansenists in particular, who disliked this devotion said that the alleged apparitions at Paray were to be explained as deriving really from the English Puritan. This was nonsense; but there are likenesses between the teaching of Thomas Goodwin and the spirituality of Paray-le-Monial. The latter at its best recalls the teaching of the founder of the order of the Visitation, St Francis de Sales, who devised for the nuns a coat of arms containing the pierced Heart of Jesus. Is it possible that devotion to the Heart of Jesus, the Prince of Peace, might become a bond between the severed segments of Christendom rather than a barrier? Only if it could be purified, through closer conformity to Holy Scripture, from the sentimentalism found in some of its more regrettable forms. Thus purged and enlarged it might not only recall, but continue and harmonize the devotion of Christians from many lands and Churches, to whom this conception was dear—St John Chrysostom, St Gertrude, Mother Julian of Norwich, Nicolas Cabasilas, Thomas Goodwin, Charles Wesley, Father Benson of Cowley, Arthur Smallwood and many others, as well as that of Paray-le-Monial. It would not lose its reference to the Passion, but would gain a note of triumph, if dedicated chiefly towards the pierced heart of the *glorified* Saviour who lives enthroned with the Father to make intercession for us.

None of the Abbé's friendships with Anglicans whom he met in the flesh, went deeper than this with the first Anglican he knew, the one whom he delighted to call his 'guardian angel'. A spirit so gentle, so guileless, so full of devotion for the great cause and of zeal in its pursuit was not only one whom Abbé Couturier could instinctively trust, but one whom he could, despite the barrier of language, by the aid of his own experience help to find more fully the glory of his own vocation. Many other priests and laity of our Church were to have the privilege of being entertained at Lyons and of being taken to La Trappe des Dombes and to Ars. Many were to learn thereby to find new ranges of grace and truth in the Church of Rome. But to none perhaps from England did friendship with the Abbé mean so specially, as it did to Dom Benedict, a discovery of the freedom of catholicism, a freedom already relished in the writings of St Francis de Sales, but here found in its full development in relation to divided Christendom—the freedom of complete obedience to God indwelling his Church, the price of which is the Cross. To Dom Benedict the Abbé was to give his crucifix containing a fragment of the Cross. It must have meant even more to one for long so vigorous in seeking unity, but in his latter years condemned by ruined health to that yet more fruitful labour—to what the world most falsely calls the useless inactivity of the Cross.

The Rev. H. M. Fynes-Clinton and the Rev. Gregory Dix came

four months later to Lyons. The former, Chairman and acting President of the Church Unity Octave Council, was Vicar of St Magnus the Martyr in the City of London and was to be the Abbé's first host in England. His goodness and great courtesy made him exempt from incurring generally the profound dislike felt by many Anglicans for the Anglo-Romans. He devoted the best energies of his life to Reunion. He founded the Anglican and Eastern Churches Association in 1906 and his unceasing labours on behalf of the Eastern Orthodox were recognized in honours conferred upon him by the Serbian and Russian Churches. But his chief interest lay in the restoration of canonical relations between the Church of England and the Holy See. He enjoyed close and intimate friendship with many whose names are inseparable from the movement, including in particular Lord Halifax and Athelstan Riley. He remained Chairman of the Church Unity Octave Council until 1958 and he died in the next, his eighty-fourth, year. His funeral Mass in the church of St Magnus the Martyr, a church designed by Christopher Wren which he had restored to use and transformed since his arrival there as rector in 1922, took place on 8 December 1959. This day had long been kept as the feast of the Immaculate Conception with special solemnity, being the annual festival of the parish Fraternity of our Lady de Salve Regina, a guild established in 1343 and refounded by the rector in 1922. The vast congregation included the Greek Orthodox Bishop of Apamea.

The young companion, the Rev. (later Dom) Gregory Dix, whom he brought with him to Lyons, has been one of God's best gifts to the Church of England in this century. It would be difficult to do justice to his charm, brilliance and versatility. By the time of his coming to Lyons in 1936 he had already done many notable things. He had coxed the Merton College boat at Oxford when it was second on the river. He had studied history there during the day, and the early Fathers while others slept. He had acted as marshal to a judge in the intervals of studying theology at Wells. He had been tutor at Keble College, Oxford and had been nominated as consultant at the British Museum on the subject of Greek papyri. Becoming an oblate of the Benedictine monastery of Nashdom he had ministered as a missionary on the African Gold Coast (now the independent state of Ghana), where he was confessor to the King and Queen. Invalided back thence in 1928, he spent the next eight years at Nashdom still as an oblate, deepening his knowledge of liturgiology. He had already seen the basic importance of the *Apostolic Tradition* of St Hippolytus of Rome, his critical edition of which was to appear in the following year. Later he became a monk of Nashdom, serving the whole Church by his theological writings at once erudite and sparkling, the Church of England in particular by his piquant and often wise counsel, a host of friends by his inimitable wit and refreshing sympathy and many souls by his prayerful understanding. He died in May 1952 at the early age of 50. His conversation was unforgettable, a marvellous blend of the paradoxical, the plausible and the profound. I sometimes felt that one had there Sir Thomas More, Erasmus and Dean Colet all rolled into one, not without an occasional touch of Rabelais.

The two Anglicans found an eager and sympathetic gathering prepared for them. Father Fynes-Clinton read a paper in French on the situation of contemporary Anglicanism, after which Father Gregory Dix, who was more at home in the language, discoursed freely on the history of the separation of the Churches in the sixteenth century. The former's paper was exceedingly frank and well-proportioned, considering his avowed papalist position. It was later published in the *Revue apologétique*[7] where the Abbé's prefatory note shows that he was under no illusion as to the border-line character of the group, though he may at this stage (1936) have overrated their numbers. This note closes as follows:

> The Church of England, whose priests are all convinced of the validity of their ordination, includes:
>
> 1. An evangelical party, more or less committed to Protestantism in their thought: the Evangelical Church [*sic*]. They are also known as Low Church, a term considered as one of reproach even by those of this group.
>
> 2. The central or moderate Church, conformist.
>
> 3. The High Church, more conformist, more ritualistic in their tendencies.

4. Anglo-Catholicism, continuation of the Tractarian movement of Oxford inaugurated by Newman, Pusey and their friends.

5. The group that holds the large number who accept integrally, or all but entirely, the Roman Catholic life. They are sometimes or often called Romanizers. This epithet, directed as a reproach, they fully and joyously accept.

'Conformiste' in the Abbé's description of groups (2) and (3) signifies conformity to the 1662 Prayer Book. He esteemed group (1) highly, but had heard[8] that they did not say the Divine Office daily in its Anglican form—Mattins and Evensong—therefore they are not *'conformiste'*. Group (4) because of their strictness with regard to this, he used to describe as 'Anglicans of strict observance'. Those whom he knew of group (5) for the most part say the Roman Breviary: so they also are not called *'conformiste'*.

Those present must have been surprised by the respectful attitude of the Anglican visitors towards the decision of Pope Leo XIII with regard to Anglican Orders announced in the Bull *Apostolicae Curae* of 1896. It was characteristic of Dom Gregory to begin by insisting that if he had himself been Pope, for security's sake he would have given the same decision. From this starting-point it was easier to win understanding for the confidence in the validity of their ordinations possessed by Anglicans in their separation, separation which will, they hold, pass away as schisms in the early history of the Church have done without leaving any significant trace of their having involved exclusion from the Church. 'Conditional re-ordination would be acceptable if required,' as Anglican bishops had made clear at the Lambeth Conference of 1920. 'The only real remedy for disunion is corporate action' of an official kind.

Father Fynes-Clinton closed by saying:

> The schism has been corporate. Its remedy must be likewise corporate. Individual conversions effect almost nothing. Recourse to proselytism deepens the breach. Romanophiles (i.e. Anglican priests who work for the recovery of corporate unity) have to face much opposition and rejoice to do so. Objects of wide-spread mistrust, they are exposed to the disapproval of authorities, and as far as possible, they are refused posts of responsibility.

Their task is an arduous one, but full of promise; so he appeals strongly to the French for the help of their prayers. . . .

> Yet in our ardent longing for [visible] unity, for firm authority, for corporate energy in the struggle against our common enemies— for our normal share in the fulness of the ecumenical life of the Church—we believe that beneath the schisms, temporary and juridicial as it was, there exists a sacramental unity in the mystical, organic Body of Jesus Christ; and we discern in the Holy See the great remedy of which we have such need for the healing of the ills from which our Church suffers today—a centre and a source of unity which are of divine institution.[9]

A pilgrimage to Ars followed. Then two days in Paris during which both Anglicans gave their discourses again, first before a group of professors of the Catholic Institute, then for Dominican fathers at Le Saulchoir. They were also received by M. Dumoutet and the Sulpicians at Issy-les-Moulineaux and by Cardinal Verdier.

From their hotel in Paris grateful and happy letters travelled to Lyons. The older priest wrote:

> My very dear Père Couturier, it is quite impossible to express my thanks for all you did for us at Lyons and for all that you have arranged here [in Paris]. . . . We have been given an impression of the life of the Church, intimate and inspiring.

So were formed Abbé Couturier's first friendships with Anglican clergy. He had a great esteem and love for the English though thoroughly aware of our defects and faults. He loved their freedom, their moral stability, their moderation, their capacity for fellowship and their *pietas*. He was aware himself of owing much to Cardinal Newman. Like the eminent Abbé de Tourville whose letters have helped so many Anglicans, he believed that the Anglo-Saxon had certain natural gifts of suppleness, realism and resilience which are needed in the divine mission of the Church. Englishmen respond, like flowers in sunshine, to such appreciation from foreigners whose heritage is larger and less insular than our own. So there were awaiting Abbé Couturier friendships with English Christians of many kinds, from every variety of Anglican church setting. He encountered them within the heart of Christ where each in giving finds himself ready and eager humbly to receive. Anglicans who would have bored or even infuriated one another at home, when they met one another at Lyons in the Abbé's company, found a new value in each other's sight. The Papalist, the central churchman, the Evangelical, the common or garden Anglo-Catholic—he has helped us to find one another in the Christ of our baptism. He loved us each individually besides getting to know the qualities and limitations of the groups to which each belonged. He investigated the significance and situation of the latter by shrewd personal interrogation and by reading carefully the magazines and papers sent him from England. He knew more about the Church of England than any English Roman Catholic I have ever met with the exception of the Abbot of Downside, Dom Christopher Butler, and the Father Provincial of the English province of Dominicans, Father Henry St John, O.P.; incomparably more, I should guess, than Abbé Portal to whom he was conscious of owing so great a debt. He humbly confessed that he believed that he himself had a gift of divination for things Anglican. It was the fruit of industry rooted in disinterested charity; but there was also at work here and in other fields a pentecostal gift of understanding and communication which enables certain spirits to penetrate the minds and spirits of others. As regards his special love of England, it seems probable that it was because of this that he was to be arrested and put into prison by the German *Wehrmacht*. It is fitting that it was the British army that in liberating Lyons, released him from prison.

NOTE ON THE FEAST OF THE CONCEPTION

8 December : Conception of Virgin Mary [Book of Common Prayer 1662]

It was Dom Gregory Dix who brought home to Abbé Couturier that the Feast of the Conception of the Blessed Virgin Mary (8 December) which means so much in the Christian year at Lyons, is a bond between England, Lyons and the Christian East. The feast was known in the East from at latest the seventh century. Before the

Norman conquest it was brought back to England by pilgrims returning from Italy where Byzantine usages still widely prevailed. The first liturgical text known in the West is probably that found in the Anglo-Saxon pontifical of Exeter Cathedral. Its only possible rival is to be found in an archiepiscopal blessing in a benedictional of the cathedral of Canterbury. The ancient Anglo-Saxon calendars of Winchester Cathedral and Hyde Abbey record its observance. After the Norman conquest the new bishops tried to suppress it. Eadmer of Canterbury and Osbert of Westminster wrote in its defence. But perhaps its most influential propagator was their friend, Anselm Junior, the nephew of St Anselm. He became Abbot of Bury St Edmunds and established the feast there. The monks of Westminster followed suit and the matter was brought before the Council of London (1129) held by the Bishop of London, Gilbert 'the Universal'. The Bishop had been a canon of Lyons. For this and other reasons it is more than probable that it was English influence which led to the observance of the feast at Lyons. Over this the chapter of Lyons was defended by another English bishop, Nicolas of St Albans against the protest of St Bernard. See Gregory Dix, 'La Religion de St Augustin de Canterbury', *Revue apologétique* LXVI, 1938, pp. 147–63; also, Gregory Dix, *The Shape of the Liturgy*, London: Dacre Press, 1945, p. 585, and A. A. King, *Liturgies of the Primatial Sees*, pp. 68–69.

NOTES

[1] The Confraternity publishes the half-yearly journal *Reunion*.

[2] It needed the Révérend Professeur Maurice Nédoncelle to make me conscious of this. See his book, *Trois aspects du problème anglo-catholique au XVIIe siècle. Avec une analyse des XXXIX art. . . .*, Paris: Bloud et Gay, 1951.

[3] Henry St John, O.P., *Essays in Christian Unity*, London: Blackfriars, 1955, pp. 41f.

[4] The discovery that led Newman to become a Roman Catholic, led Renan to leave the Church.

[5] *Laudate* XIV, No. 55, September 1936, pp. 126–37.

[6] See p. 39.

[7] Volume LXIV, No. 616, January 1937, pp. 61–76.

[8] The Abbé knew something already of this first group because it was represented by the Church of England services in Lyons.

[9] *Art. cit.*, p. 76.

15

FIRST VISIT TO ENGLAND

———

IT was inevitable henceforth that every effort should be made to persuade Abbé Couturier to come to England. His hesitations—because of poverty, poor health, ignorance of the language—were waived. Nashdom would make itself responsible for financing the journey. His friends would take great care of his health; furthermore M. Guillermin, English master at the Institution des Chartreux and known to Father Fynes-Clinton, would be already on the English side of the Channel in September 1937, and thus could act as interpreter. So the Abbé considered the possibility of coming then.

There was the problem of ecclesiastical authorization. The archbishopric of Lyons was just then vacant. The *pro-vicaire capitulaire*, who held the reins, authorized Abbé Couturier to go at his own risk. In a statement *Curriculum vitae* later addressed to Cardinal Hinsley, Archbishop of Westminster, he writes:

> I prayed a great deal and I asked many prayers. I took counsel from a Jesuit father of Lyons and I adopted the following course: 1. To Anglicans I shall say: 'I am come to you on a journey of goodwill and to gain information;' 2. To any Catholics who enquire the motive of my journey, I shall reply: 'I am making a journey for religious studies;' 3. To priests and prelated enquiring: 'Have you notified our English hierarchy?' I will reply: 'This has seemed to me impossible, for your hierarchy cannot officially authorize me without the risk of compromising itself: later on it shall be seen to.' I must make clear that situations (2) and (3) never occurred.[1]

He left Lyons on Sunday evening 5 September 1937, arrived at Paris next morning, said Mass at the Basilica of Sacré Coeur on

175

Montmartre and made a pilgrimage to Lisieux to put his expedition under the patronage of the little Ste Thérèse. A hoped-for meeting with Dom Lambert Beauduin, Father Founder of Amay, proved impossible. But Dom Lambert wrote:

> Frankly I don't understand how one could be without bowels of compassion and love for these excellent Christians [his Anglican friends] who have such a love for our Lord. I feel you have the same sentiments and are distressed by so much misunderstanding and arrogance.

On the morning of the 7th he took the train from Paris to Dieppe, found M. Guillermin awaiting him at Newhaven and, with the aid of the latter, reached Victoria that evening safe and sound. They were met by Father Fynes-Clinton, Dom Benedict Ley, and a younger priest, Father Phyall.

Father Fynes-Clinton gave the visitors hospitality at St Ermin's Hotel, not far from St James's Park, where he himself had a comfortable apartment. He was a wonderful host and he arranged the visitors' programme. No one could have excelled him as a guide to the little world of Anglican Papalism. His aim was to put the Abbé in touch with the leaders of this movement. Needless to say it was the venerable English initiator of the older Octave who was first of all invited to lunch at St Ermin's. He, the Rev. Spencer Jones, had been in correspondence with the Abbé since 1935, and he was an exceedingly fragile old man of eighty, subject to agonizing heart attacks. But come what may, the pioneer of the older Octave wished to meet the artisan of the new, which was so greatly to increase the volume of prayer for Christian unity. And what must it have meant to Couturier to meet one who had done so much for the cause! Moreover this aged relative of John Keble, who had himself known Dr Pusey and Cardinal Newman, seemed a kind of last survivor of the Oxford Tractarians. The old man did not say much that day, but the two understood one another.

Father Spencer Jones had already accepted the Abbé's suggestion that he should prepare an article for the *Revue apologétique* on his conception of the approach to ecumenism. One instalment after another was arriving at Lyons—the article had developed into a book. In the same way the sermon preached in 1900 by the author at a church close to St Ermin's (St Matthew's, Westminster) had, at Lord Halifax's request for publication, led to the emergence of the book, *England and the Holy See*. The book inspired by the Abbé which, translated into French, appeared under the rather similar title *L'Eglise d'Angleterre et la Sainte-Siège*, is an entirely different book, not published in English.[2]

On Good Friday 1936 Abbé Couturier had written to the author:

> I am deeply grateful. I admire the fervour and the great love of Christ and of his Church which amidst terrible difficulties enables you to find time and strength to compose so fine a work for him. Your activity, though reduced by the necessities of age, has remained young and lively. The delays don't astonish me. What astonishes me is the result at which you arrive! The plan of the article delights me. It is dynamic in character—just what I desired. A revivification of life gone by: a psychological unrolling which grows in volume and precision and gathers in everything on its way.[3]

Another of Father Fynes-Clinton's friends, with whom the Abbé had already corresponded, was the Rev. Ivan Young, vicar of Kensworth near Dunstable, who was a member of the Church of England Council on Foreign Relations. In this capacity he travelled a good deal in Germany and Scandinavia and was a close friend of Pastor Rosendal, leader of the Catholic movement in the Swedish Lutheran Church, who had already become through correspondence a friend of Abbé Couturier. Father Young was also in touch with Karl Barth and Friedrich Heiler. He was a prominent member of the Fellowship of St Alban and St Sergius, a fellowship of Anglicans and Eastern Orthodox, and edited its journal *Sobornost*, as well as sharing with Father Gregory Dix the editorship of *The Pilot*, the monthly journal of Anglican Papalism. He found time also to contribute valuable articles on ecumenical questions to other journals and in particular supplied one at the Abbé's request for the *Revue apologétique* on the history of the Church of England since the Reformation.[4] It was through Father Young that Abbé Couturier came to know

Canon J. A. Douglas, a learned and able Anglican ecumenist who had the confidence of the Archbishop of Canterbury and who used his great knowledge of Eastern Orthodoxy to be a chief instrument in forwarding the *rapprochement* between the Church of England and the Orthodox Churches.

There were several gatherings at St Ermin's Hotel. Amongst those the Abbé met there, were Father Corbould, president of the Society for promoting Catholic Unity; Father Plowden Wardlaw, vicar of St Clement's, Cambridge, a lawyer-cleric with experience of both Roman and Anglican communions, who writes under the pseudonym of 'Father Clement' and 'Clemens Humilis': his small book *Catholic Reunion*[5] is a plea for a uniat patriarchate of Canterbury in union with Rome, along with the return to Catholic unity of German evangelical Christians; Father Silas Harris, author of *The First Ten Years*, an attempt 'to indicate the extent to which the Roman goal was perceived and acknowledged by the early Tractarians'.[6] The Abbé visited the latter in his parish of Egmanton where Father Harris had in 1929 revived an ancient pilgrimage of the Blessed Virgin, but he decided he could not visit Walsingham as a guest of Anglicans, because of the parallel Roman Catholic pilgrimage to the Blessed Virgin there. His visit might so easily lead to misunderstanding.

As a Catholic of Lyons, neighbour and friend of Joseph Folliet, Paul Couturier could not fail to be interested in the sociological manifestations of Anglo-Catholicism. He gained glimpses of this by visits to Patrick McLaughlin at St Anne's, Soho, and to the Rev. Nigel Scott. Father Scott was developing the great work started by the Rev. Basil Jellicoe who transfigured some of the worst slums of London by providing truly habitable yet inexpensive workmen's homes along with attractive centres of communication.

The Secretary of the Seven Years Association, Henry Brandreth, came up from Sheffield to greet the Abbé. This vigorous association of young lay-folk, pledged to a seven years' plan of obedience to the precepts of the Church, has been described as the *Action Catholique* of the Church of England. It has been effective in recovering in many quarters the sense of the meaning of churchmanship and the acceptance of its responsibilities, not least as regards the duty of full participation in the liturgical life of the Church and of prayer for her reunion and extension. The Abbé was invited to meet a delegation from the 'S.Y.A.' and its members proved appreciative and responsive to his call to prayer for unity. There was also a compact of mutual prayer. The delegates were to remember the Abbé and his intentions on the first Sunday of every month, when he would remember them in his Mass. Henry Brandreth found his interest in ecumenical work deepened by his first meeting with Abbé Couturier. He was soon to take Holy Orders, but not before he had begun compiling his bibliography of ecumenism which has been followed by other equally valuable books connected with the work for Christian unity.[7] When in 1939 the Week of Universal Prayer was organized in England by a Committee of Superiors of Religious Communities, Brandreth became its Secretary. In 1943 he became a priest of the Oratory of the Good Shepherd, and was a member of the Church of England Council on Foreign Relations from 1945 to 1949 when he became a consultant member of the World Conference on Faith and Order. That year he became Chaplain of St George's Church, Paris, whence he was able to co-operate more closely with the Abbé at Lyons. Already from his London parish he had twice taken groups of youngsters to Lyons to meet the Abbé (who despite his age and ill-health showed astonishing energy and still more remarkable capacity to understand boys, notwithstanding the barriers of age and language). From Paris he made a pilgrimage every year to Lyons until 1953, the year of the Abbé's death.

Most refreshing and full of happiness for the Abbé was his visit to Nashdom, the more so because of his appreciation of the exquisite architecture of Sir Edwyn Lutyens (including its Russian associations) in contrast by no means disharmonious with the simpler, profounder beauty of its content—the Benedictine worship and life of the monks. The life at Nashdom has been described by many Roman Catholics as an almost perfect replica of Benedictinism as it is found in their Church today.

As you gaze round the refectory or look down on the choir from the tribune, you feel that you have been transported to a baroque

179

abbey in Italy or else to a French monastery of the seventeenth or eighteenth centuries.[8]

In chapel the impeccable recitation of the Divine Office, the perfection of the plain chant and of the ceremonial all confirm the sense of stability and tradition that belongs to Benedictinism at its best. The Abbé, himself the oblate of a Benedictine monastery, could not but feel at home. Benedictinism gives us the worship and the life of undivided Christendom and in a real sense transcends its divisions. Nor was it inappropriate as a porch into the Anglican household, for we must not forget that the Church of England owes much that is best, most characteristic and most formative in it—for example in its own Divine Office of Mattins and Evensong—to the influence of the worship of Benedictine monks.

If the house has continental characteristics and the chapel has a baroque dignity and beauty, the garden and the Buckinghamshire woodland into which it merges are English enough. The garden gave opportunity for needed rest along with the development of his friendship with two Englishmen whom he had come to love—Dom Benedict Ley, the 'guardian angel' whom he had met again more than once in London; and, now a novice under Dom Benedict's care, the erudite and delightful Father Gregory Dix. And to these were added now another friend, the second Abbot of Nashdom (Abbot 1935–48), the Rev. Martin Collett, a man of great goodness, humour and ability of whom the community recorded in its minutes that he

> established its unsteady foundations, amplified its worship, established its finances on a sound basis, founded its first daughter house, and guided it safely through troublous years.[9]

Perhaps the Abbot was the most English of them all.

'The ambassador of the Pope', or so the monks charmingly spoke of the Abbé to one another, was invited to give them a *lecture spirituelle* in the chapel. He spoke of the Universal Prayer for Christian Unity and of their own responsibility as pioneers amongst Anglicans in the quest of Reunion. A rough draft remains of his talk:

> Suffering of being misunderstood . . . on both sides. Your name, your habit. . . .

Suffering joyous, because it is a liturgical gift,
   because it enlarges (suffering of separation)
   because it is in an atmosphere of *peace* and makes you plunge
   in Christ who is *Pax*.
So your *rôle unioniste* is defined by your very vocation: to radiate
Your Peace. But in this Peace of Christ the mind sees clear, and so
radiates light. . . .
   Peace which gives prudence. Peace luminous. *Pax et lumen*.

Dom Benedict Ley introduced the Abbé to over a dozen Religious
Communities of women. The visitor wrote:

> Every visit had the same programme: a talk, for friendship and
> to elicit information, with the Mother Superior: a look over
> the house: a little address on prayer for unity to the assembled
> community: prayer together. . . . Then I gave them my bless-
> ing.[10]

The outcome of the visit to the nearest religious house, that of
the Servants of Christ ('The House of Prayer', Burnham, founded
1897) was twofold. First came the offer by the Reverend Mother
Foundress, and acceptance by the Abbé, of the beautiful set of white
vestments, made in the workroom of the convent, which he so
greatly prized.

Secondly Mother Elizabeth put him in touch with Arthur Smallwood who had already been greatly helped by an article by the Abbé
printed in English translation in *Reunion*.[11] The friendship between
Abbé Couturier and Arthur Smallwood, like that between the Abbé
and another contemplative writer, Maisie Spens, to which we will
return, was entirely through correspondence. These friendships
were grounded in deep mutual understanding, providential in
character, and grew through prayer for one another and kindred
suffering.

Arthur Smallwood (1873–1938), son of an Anglican priest, was
educated at Repton and Corpus Christi, Oxford.[12] He entered the
Civil Service in 1896. He was employed till 1920 in a department of
the Admiralty whose most important work is the placing of con-
tracts for new ships. In 1912 he became Assistant Director of the

Contract Department and he held this post throughout the war.

During part of his early career an atheist, he had come back to religion by 1921 when there came a welcome change of work in appointment as Director of Greenwich Hospital. This included the care of the Royal Hospital School which had been established there for 200 years. The conditions at Greenwich were hopelessly out of date for the education of nearly 1,000 young boys. The recent gift to the hospital of the Holbrook Estate in Suffolk gave Smallwood the idea of transferring the school thither. But the funds available were insufficient. The donor of the estate was now resident in New Zealand. Smallwood went there to see him and made him keenly interested. The result was the promise of a legacy of nearly half a million pounds, thank-offering for the work of the Merchant Navy during the war of 1914–18. This enabled the Admiralty to undertake the building of the magnificent school of Smallwood's hopes. He had determined that though meant for poor boys, Holbrook should be as good as any public school and he directed his scheme accordingly. Questions were asked in Parliament with regard to its cost (in all £1,077,000) and Smallwood narrowly escaped having to face a Select Committee on the charge of extravagance. He himself explained his escape as due to Our Lady of Walsingham under whose inspiration the whole scheme was carried out and who, he said, was responsible for the gift to the nation of the great chapel dedicated to her. The chapel he had made large, having in mind the days when there would have to be room for all the boys whereas, for the time being, many must worship separately. This was a fine expression of his sure hope of coming unity.

Arthur Smallwood had found in Father William of Glasshampton whom he visited first in 1924, an inspiring and understanding friend and guide. During Father William's last illness he cared for him devotedly until he died on Easter morning 1937. (Smallwood and I met first at the funeral and spent the rest of the day together. It was then I first heard of Abbé Couturier whom he was never to see, but to whose article in *Reunion* he expressed 'deep indebtedness'. In less than six months they were in intimate correspondence which continued till Smallwood's death on 9 March 1938).

In September 1937 the Abbé received a letter expressing a mind and spirit truly at one with his own:

An Anglican layman, I suffer as many of us do, from the atmosphere of controversy in which we live. I feel that there ought to be a true method of *interior* approach towards the divine ideal of Reunion; a method not only ecclesiastical, but one which has its roots in the spiritual and which follows a spiritual path. Let us set on one side for a moment the subjects of controversy which ought not to be treated by those unqualified for this.

When I speak of approaching Reunion in a spiritual way, I have specially in mind the spirituality expressed in the doctrine of Cardinal Bérulle, of Père Condren, of Monsieur Olier and of St Jean Eudes. There are amongst us many souls unconsciously attracted towards this spirituality. They are convinced that in the questions relating to Reunion, controversy without prayer is sterile or worse than sterile, and that prayer alone can be fruitful.

The vocation of the Body of the baptized, according to this spirituality—does it not consist simply in manifesting in the different ages of the world by virtue of a true participation in the life of the Incarnate Word, the mysteries of his most holy life? And does not true religion consist simply in perpetuating in the Body of Christians the unique act of adoration of the eternal Father by the Incarnate Word?

If this is so, how much has the total life of Christians been estranged, in our days, from true religion, since Christendom became divided against itself! And in consequence, what a loss this theocentric spirit of adoration must have undergone! Preoccupied —one might almost say obsessed—by human efforts which are necessarily partial, we appear in general to forget that disunion is an evil, and the greatest of all evils, because while it lasts, God, one in three persons, is not and cannot be adored in visible unity by the Body of Christ. Nevertheless it is uniquely for this work of adoration by which alone true human dignity can be attained, that this Body has been created. How then is it possible to arrive at this Reunion if it be not by the exercise in this same Body of penitence, contrition and supernatural hope in God?

I speak only as a simple Anglican layman, and a great number of my compatriots would speak in the same way, being equally incapable of making a judgement in the great controversies which hold us isolated for a time, the length of which is unknown. Many of us are ignorant why they are born in exile. The majority alas, because of our odd and extremely insular temperament, persist in thinking of this isolation of the Church of England as a blessing.

And yet each knows that there is always at the heart of English religion, despite its afflictions, the same disposition, unchanged and unchangeable, of the adoring Heart of the Incarnate Word whence sprang, on the very eve of the Passion, the great prayer for the unity of all Christians. Up to now, how few of us, although they suffer from the countless troubles of our Church, are conscious of the cause of their suffering! And how difficult it is for those who are so conscious, to make known the hidden truth which they burn to see revealed! What can they do better than *adhere*, as the Oratorians would say, with patience, in prayer, to this same Heart.

Nevertheless Smallwood did make efforts to give expression to this unrecognized truth. He wrote two articles, both of which were sent to the Abbé and deeply appreciated by him. The first and briefer article[13] had been already privately printed before this correspondence began. Its second part, called 'The Holy Family of the Servants of God', the Abbé had translated into French and he procured its appearance in *La Vie Intellectuelle* (January 1939). The second and longer article, completed just before Smallwood's death, is called 'The Nature of Religious Unity'. It has never as far as I know been published in English. The Abbé had this also translated into French and secured its printing in two numbers of the *Nouvelle Revue Théologique* (September and December 1939). The brief introductory note supplied by himself to be printed before the earlier article, was enlarged to form the introduction of the second. The contents of these introductions were largely furnished by Mother Elizabeth who provided for the second an account of Arthur Smallwood's holy death.

When he heard of his death, the Abbé wrote to their mutual friend, Father Phyall:

This news was sorrowful for me, for I didn't even know that he was ill and I loved him as a friend. I knew him only through his works and best of all through an intimate correspondence. What a beautiful soul! I have just offered Mass for him—his name is inscribed now for ever in the memento which I bring every day to the altar. I consider him, now that he has come to Christ's presence, as one of the most fervent protectors of all those who work for Reunion. Personally I beg him to help me and I do so with confidence. I thought of seeing him on my visit to England. . . . I will go to his tomb.

The Abbé was moved by two sentences extracted from his writings which were printed on a Memorial card sent to his friends. They contain, he said, in his printed introduction to Smallwood's essay, the deepest note in the writer's soul:

> 'There will be in heaven the souls of those who in this life have preserved in complete purity of intention the faith which they have received.'
> 'They have always walked in the presence of God, have loved him, served him and obeyed him as well as they have known how to do so.'

During this first brief stay in England the Abbé had contact with Anglicans only through his friends of the extreme right-wing. He was thoroughly aware of this and confessedly desirous of making contact in due time with the other and more representative sections of the Church of England as tabulated in his note quoted above,[14] especially sections (2) and (3) which he describes respectively as '*conformiste*' and 'more *conformiste*', and (4) the larger group of Anglo-Catholics whom he came to describe as 'Anglicans of strict observance'. His contact with Father O'Brien, the Superior of Cowley to whom he made a brief visit from Nashdom, made him realize the strength of this latter section; how integral its grasp of the Anglican tradition, how great its sense of responsibility towards the Anglican Communion as a whole and how deep its understanding of the movement of prayer for unity initiated in Lyons.

Aware though he was of its varieties, he was convinced that there was real organic unity in the Church of England. It was about this time that he first set eyes on and listened to one to whom his heart went out in reverence and sympathy which was later to be movingly reciprocated—the Archbishop of Canterbury, Cosmo Gordon Lang. He was so moved by an address by the Archbishop[15] that next morning Father Fynes-Clinton received a note in which for the first time the Abbé expresses an idea which became very dear to him—that of a 'convergent call' to prayer:

> Ah! if a day could arrive in which at one and the same time a message from the Archbishop of Canterbury and a message from the successor of Peter might resound throughout the world, calling the immense crowds of Anglicans and Catholics to prayer that in solemn conclaves Christian unity may be welded once more. Wasn't it something of this kind of which the great Lord Halifax dreamed?

He is already clearly intent upon some approach to the Anglican Communion as a whole. By this explicit enlargement of aim his deep sympathy with, and high estimation of Anglican Papalists was not affected. They were his first Anglican friends and he had no doubt either of their integrity and thorough loyalty to the Church of England, or of their irreplaceable part in its work for Reunion. He would have subscribed to the words of Dom Bede Winslow O.S.B. of Ramsgate Abbey, editor of the *Eastern Churches' Quarterly*, a Roman Catholic theologian in close touch with many of these men as well as with Anglicans of other types:

> The members of this group . . . are often in the unenviable position of being looked at askance by either side. This is understandable, but it is a pity, for, from a theological point of view, they should play an important part, and if they receive sympathy and encouragement, their work could be valuable. At the present they suffer, for the most part, from the isolation of their position. They should be less taut and more pliable.[16]

Abbé Couturier helped them towards overcoming their isolation and tautness and towards a greater sense that they are already as Anglicans 'citizens of no mean city'.

The Rev. H. J. Carpenter, now Bishop of Oxford, at the same place and time, gave expression to a similar view, along with reflections concerning the Anglican Communion as a whole which give the judgement which I believe the Abbé to have already reached:

> Those who are commonly, whether for complimentary or un-complimentary reasons, called Papalists, have a part to play in the movement towards unity, but they do not in fact represent the main body of Anglicans, with whom the movement [towards unity], if it is to be realistic, must reckon. It would be on the long view—and the movement must take the long view—a disaster if some small segment of the English Church effected an isolated reunion with Rome, leaving the rest of the Anglican Communion embittered and certainly farther off from the goal than ever. There is a central body of Anglicans, including many who would reject the label of Anglo-Catholic, who believe that they understand and practise the basic principles of Catholic Christianity, which they believe also to be the basic principles of the community to which they belong. If I had to summarize their position, I should say that they believed in the necessity of a definite dogmatic faith, in the reality of sacramental grace and in the need for the organic continuity of the life of the Church through the ages, guaranteed in their own community as they believe, by the transmission of the apostolic ministry, though not by that alone. Their position is not the peculiarity of a party within Anglicanism, since it has been substantially expressed in the well-known Lambeth Quadrilateral, formally promulgated and more than once repeated by the body of Anglican bishops, viz. that the basis of the movement towards unity must be found in the Scriptures, the Creeds, the two great Sacraments of Baptism and the Holy Eucharist and the historic ministry.[17]

The Abbé left England with the conviction that this larger body of Anglicans should be called to share the eucharistic prayer of our Lord Jesus Christ for the unity of all who bear his Name and that they would hear the call. So the Lambeth Quadrilateral would be enriched by another principle which would change its quality from that of a statesmanlike ecclesiastical proposition to a call from God to Christians through the pierced Heart of his crucified Son, their ascended Saviour and Lord.

The Lambeth Fathers have now added this coping-stone to their draft of what they believe to be required for God's temple. Resolution 57 of the 1958 Lambeth Conference, with its acknowledgement of the name, the work, the spirit and the teaching of Abbé Couturier, indicates the acceptance by the Anglican Communion in all lands of the message which Paul Couturier laboured in life and death to give the world.[18]

NOTE ON ANGLICAN PAPALISTS

The 'premisses' of the position of Anglican Papalists as represented by the 'Church Unity Octave Council', reprinted every year in their bulletin or 'Call' with reference to the January Octave are these. [We add in square brackets comments in which we attempt to express what the Abbé Couturier, who received the 'Call' yearly, would have thought concerning them. These are based upon a study of his writings and letters and on experience of his views as expressed in discussion with theologians of his own unity circle of Catholic priests and Protestant pastors. While himself intransigent in his loyalty to the Catholic faith as defined by the Holy See, he was strongly averse to any manner of stating it which he felt to be unduly narrow.]

The Dogmatic Position of the Church Unity Octave Council is summarized in the following statements or Premisses: (as in previous 'Calls')

1. The conversion of the world depends upon the Visible Unity of the Church of God, for our Saviour prayed, 'That they all may be one . . . that the World may believe.'

[This prayer of St John ch.17 was the Abbé's spiritual home. He would therefore have welcomed this opening. He also held strongly that our Lord prays for unity that will be evidential and therefore *visible*. But he would perhaps have preferred a full quotation of John 17.21. For the words omitted, 'as thou, Father, art in me and I in thee, that they may be one in us', make clear that the unity desired is unity analogous to that of the divine being: unity spiritual and interior at root. The evidential value of visible unity, he was vividly aware, will depend upon its representing the free obedience of consentient Christian minds to the divinely given organs of Catholic truth. It will be in inverse proportion to the extent to which unanimity is secured only by methods of discipline and enforcement. The massive witness of the Roman Catholic Church is immensely impressive. But it will be even more so when Rome no longer allows the use of weapons savouring of compulsion, e.g. the regulations in force with regard to mixed marriages; the restrictions imposed upon Protestants in Spain; the '*Index Librorum Prohibitorum*', etc.]

2. He provided means for the maintenance of this unity by the appointment of a visible head of the visible Body: 'Thou art Peter and upon this Rock I will build my Church'.

[Abbé Couturier would have been as ready as was Pope Adrian VI and as are now many Roman Catholic theologians, to show awareness that the visible head has sometimes proved and might prove again the means of provoking division.]

History has shown what interpretation the Church has given to this text, for none has ever been the Church's acknowledged head upon earth save he who sits on Peter's throne. Separation from this centre has always led the separated into further schisms, while acknowledgement of it all must necessarily result in the healing of all divisions.

[How true this is, granted that the acknowledgement is freely given without sacrifice of principle; granted also a continual supply of such holy and wise popes as we have now and have had for the greater part of this century! But there are other possibilities, and the great men of the conciliar period of the fifteenth century despite their errors stood for vital Christian truths which the Eastern Orthodox Church knows by instinct, but which are only now being fully weighed by Catholic theologians.[19]]

3. The dogmatic decrees that concern the supremacy of St Peter's successor and his infallibility in Faith and Morals, while not capable of being rescinded even by the Pope himself, do nevertheless admit of elucidation and of further definition.

[This is well observed and was one of the Abbé's constant contentions in this field of doctrine.]

4. Further, it may be hoped that many vital and important matters left over by the Vatican Council, such as those concerning the mystical nature of the Church, will eventually be considered and issue in such definitions as may bring out the true balance of the doctrine concerning the relationship between the successor of St Peter and the rest of the Apostolic episcopate and the body of the faithful.

[This hope was so strong in the Abbé as to amount to certainty. If Pope Pius XII's great encyclical about the Church and the Mystical Body, *Mystici Corporis* (1951), was the earnest of its fulfilment, the substance of this came much closer in the utterances and manifest convictions of his successor, John XXIII.]

Apart from these *premisses* Papalism consists of a certain interpretation of the history of the Church of England. The gist of it is this.

She is an integral part of the Catholic Church and dependent for her very existence upon loyalty to Catholic principles. But a study of history shows clearly that the principles upon which the Church of England is founded include belief in the spiritual supremacy of the successor of St Peter. She was forcibly torn away from the unity of the Western Church by the tyrannical action of Henry VIII and Queen Elizabeth.[20] The petition of Convocation in 1559, the first really free assembly of this body since 1529, for the continuance of the old religion (that of Queen Mary's reign) is striking and not sufficiently considered. It was supported by both universities, but was unconstitutionally ignored. Article XXXVI concerning papal jurisdiction is (as Dr Pusey, Bishop Forbes, Sancta Clara the Jesuit and others have insisted) to be interpreted in the light of its title, *Of the Civil Magistrate*. It simply denies the jurisdiction of the Bishop of Rome in 'the Realm'. The Church though forced against her will into material schism, has never repudiated the spiritual primacy of the Pope. Her acceptance of the three creeds and the General Councils—even the Statute Law recognizes *four*, but the Homilies (commended in Article XXV) *six* councils—together with her appeal to the undivided Church is seen more and more to involve the recognition of the primacy of the Pope.

Immediately after the death of Elizabeth attempts began to be made by kings (the Stuarts), by bishops, divines and statesmen to bring about (under the Anglican hierarchy) corporate reunion with the Holy See on the basis of complete dogmatic agreement. These were frustrated, not by any reluctance of the Roman Mother to receive back her daughter into the family unity, but by the violence of Puritan opposition and the unreasoning prejudice which had grown up in consequence of the Spanish Armada.

[Surely not wholly unreasoning! The Roman Church herself has learnt much through the great demonstration of loyalty to Queen Elizabeth given by English Roman Catholics in the event of the Armada—loyalty rendered despite the mandate given by the bull *Regnans in Excelsis* for this queen's forcible dethronement.]

After the end of the Stuart dynasty all further attempts at corporate reunion were in abeyance for a time owing to the accession to the throne of the Dutch Calvinist, William III and the German Lutheran House of Hanover and owing to the political triumph of the Whig party. The desire for corporate reunion with Rome runs like a golden thread through the troubled eighteenth century until, early in the nineteenth century, it finds its expression in the Oxford Movement and the Catholic Revival. Anglican Papalists are the true successors of the Tractarian Fathers and, we must claim, the only true members of the Church of England.[21] The three-branch theory of the Church of England as an entirely independent, self-going concern—Catholic but anti-papal—is a quite modern idea which would have been unintelligible alike to the Catholic intelligentsia and to the Church of England herself during the first thousand years of her history, while today it is becoming increasingly untenable. It has led nowhere save to the dilution of Catholic principle with modernism and the substitution of mere ceremonial for dogmatic faith. It is becoming manifest that Anglo-Catholics must choose between Papalism and Pan-Protestant federation. There is no half-way house.

[This statement is taken from the Annual Call (to the Church Unity Octave) of 1945 as it is one of the best brief statements I have seen. I have inserted points derived from an article on the same subject by Dr S. H. Scott, *The Pilot* XI, May 1943, p. 117.]

There is much here that Abbé Couturier would have hailed as true, outlining aspects of our history which are not unfamiliar to French Catholics. Other ways of vindicating an Anglo-Catholic standpoint such as 'Northern Catholicism', 'Liberal Catholicism' and 'Non-papal Catholicism', which attracted English minds earlier in this century, seemed unimpressive to his mind, especially as proclaimed by Christians of a land which owes perhaps more than any other to the Petrine See. The great attraction which the Eastern Orthodox Church has for so many Catholic Anglicans he vividly understood. But he asked of those whose first hope of reunion lie in this direction, the question which Khomiakov and so many Eastern Orthodox theologians ask so surprisingly of their Anglican friends— whether charity does not begin nearer home.[22] The Abbé too was acutely aware also of the need of Eastern Orthodox Churches for their own sake to resolve the question which Eastern Orthodoxy holds in suspension, as to a visible centre of the Christian Church. Furthermore the Anglican Papalists themselves could not but remind him of the Russian Orthodox sage, Solovyev, whom he held to be one of the greatest prophets of ecumenism. Solovyev had sought in witnessing to the necessity and function of the Papacy to be in brotherly and sacramental union with the Western part of the universal Church while remaining a member of its Orthodox part: for he held that a sinful, human quarrel between leaders had not disturbed the real, divinely ordained unity of the Church embracing both its parts.[23]

Moreover Anglican Papalism at its best has faced honestly and in a Christian way the relation of the Anglican Church to English Roman Catholics. It holds strongly that the Catholic Church in England bifurcated in the sixteenth century; that the true Church of England in our times is not merely the Church of England by law established, but is the Catholic Church in our land *as a whole*, albeit at present outwardly divided; that the Roman Church in England is not an intruded schismatic body, but the other section, so to speak, of the pre-Reformation English Church. This section inherits the view held by the great majority of the ecclesiastical lawyers who accepted the full claims of Papal authority. Anglican Catholics have their own antecedents in the upholders of the conciliar movement of the fifteenth century and those who inherited their doctrine. These believed in certain powers inherent in local churches which may have to be exercised. They held that the Papacy is of the *bene esse*, or rather in a sense of the *esse* of the Church, but is not essential to her very existence and may in case of necessity be disobeyed. As the great Gerson wrote,

> The end of all laws not merely human but divine, is love which brings about unity. If therefore there be a case in which the observances of any law would dissolve unity and hinder the public safety, what sane man would say that it is desirable to observe it?

The claim, implied in all seriousness in some Anglican writing, and in common conversation flippantly by the harmful phrase 'the Italian Mission', that Anglicans are the sole descendants of the pre-Reformation Church, is insupportable, if not ridiculous. The weakest point in much Catholic Anglicanism has been its failure to understand and to esteem English Roman Catholicism. We must recognize that even if its heroic sanctity has been conditioned sometimes by misunderstanding, it has its own unique glory within the history of the Church of Christ in England. As the Rev. Dr T. M. Parker has put it,

> We can admit that the monks of Ampleforth are the true lineal descendants of those of Westminster, just as cheerfully as we assert with equal truth that Dr Lang is the ninety-third successor of St Augustine, . . . [thus imitating] the excellent good sense and humility of the Anglican formularies which make no claim to be those of the whole Church.[24]

I cannot help recalling in this connexion the words with which Père Congar O.P. summarizes the conclusion supplied by him to the recent book of essays *Le Concile et les Conciles*:

Thus the two poles, *Ecclesia* (*Concilium*) and *Papa* remain at the same time real and living in their distinction, but implicated the one in the other, according to the very structure which Christ has given to the people of the New Covenant that it may live in his truth and in his love.[25]

(Père Congar's thought on this subject has at its root the sense of the need of bringing into fuller light the latent harmony between the two sayings of our Lord, to be found the one in Matt. 16.18–19, the other in Matt. 18.15–18.)

NOTES

[1] There were real and justifiable misunderstandings on both sides of the Channel. Abbé Couturier had corresponded with Cardinal Hinsley before (in December 1935) he closed his article, printed in the *Revue apologétique*, by quoting the Archbishop of Westminster's gracious letter to the Secretary of the (Anglican) 'Council for promoting Catholic Unity'. He had no doubt whatever that Cardinal Hinsley would indemnify later his conduct in having come in such circumstances without official authorization, for during an interregnum the request would have caused embarrassment. Hence he sent the Archbishop of Westminster a full account of the programme followed in his first visit to England before making the second in 1938. This document, the *Curriculum Vitae*, was amicably received. Later in 1938 he made application in the regular way for a third visit through the now established Archbishop of Lyons, Cardinal Gerlier. Cardinal Hinsley's reply, a definite refusal of permission, was a grievous blow to the Abbé. The refusal seemed to him to be based on misunderstanding, if not on misinformation. But he accepted it without question or resentment. He never did act and never would have acted against the known will of Catholic authority, nor indeed without the impression that his action would be approved. He regretted any irregularity there might have been in this regard in the conduct of Abbé Portal. The Anglican Religious Communities are at one with Abbé Couturier here in his respect for authority and thus share his deep regret for the misunderstanding and its results.

[2] Spencer Jones, *L'Église d'Angleterre et le Saint-Siège*, Préface et traduction par Maurice Villain, Paris: Arthaud, 3rd ed. 1941. It is an old man's book, but I find it singularly impressive—'a very pure book', remarked a distinguished Dutch Religious. I am grateful for the introductions written by Père Villain, S.M. for the first and third French edition.

[3] In a tribute to the Rev. Spencer Jones, Father Vincent McNabb, O.P.,

speaks of him as 'a deep thinker and holy soul combining qualities both of the martyr and the prophet', and as one whose 'manifest yet humble priestliness fitted him for higher rank than the priesthood', but who 'sacrificed such a hope for the sake of truth and of his undying love of the Church of England. The thought and reasoned thesis of his books . . . was dominant in creating a movement which after giving us the Malines Conversations, is now giving us greater than these in the mutual talks and joint action of our religious leaders' (*The Pilot* XI, No. 117, May 1943, p. 36).

⁴ Volume LXVII, No. 635, October 1938, pp. 266–90.

⁵ Father Clement, M.A., *Catholic Reunion, an Anglican Plea*, Oxford: Blackwell, 1935. This is dedicated to the memory of Cardinal Mercier and Frank Weston, Bishop of Zanzibar.

⁶ This is Tractate I, second series, Oxford Movement Centenary Tractates (London: Talbot, 1934). In the first series (1933) Tractate I is also by the same author and is entitled *What do the Celtic Churches say?*

⁷ *Unity and Reunion, a bibliography* (1945); *Oecumenical Ideals of the Oxford Movement* (1947); *Episcopi Vagantes and the Anglican Church* (1947); *Outline Guide to the Study of Eastern Christendom* (1951); *Dr Lee of Lambeth* (1951).

⁸ P. F. Anson, *The Call of the Cloister*, pp. 188f.

⁹ Anson, p. 187.

¹⁰ *Curriculum Vitae.*

¹¹ *Reunion* I, No. 7, 1935, pp. 194–209.

¹² The greater part of the account that follows is taken from Abbé Couturier's own introduction to articles by Smallwood which the Abbé had translated into French and printed. I have also made use of two obituary notices—that by Sir Vincent Baddeley, *The Times*, 11 March 1938, and that by the Rev. A. Phyall, *Reunion* III, No. 17 (June 1938).

¹³ '*Ecce Quam Bonum* (Psalm 133), a plea for a union in prayer for unity of faith', by an Anglican Layman. This was privately printed by Godwin, Oxted, Surrey. It is undated.

¹⁴ See p. 170.

¹⁵ The occasion, place and theme of this seem at this date undiscoverable.

¹⁶ *Report of the Proceedings of the Church Unity Octave held at Blackfriars, Oxford, 1942*, Oxford: Blackwell, 1942, p. 35.

¹⁷ *Ibid.*, p. 38.

¹⁸ Resolution 57 runs:

'The Conference wishes to emphasize the importance of wide-spread prayer for the unity of all Christian people, and commends to all Anglicans the observance of the Week of Prayer for Christian Unity in the spirit of the late Abbé Couturier, who taught many to pray for the unity of Christ's people in the way he wills and by the means he chooses. It welcomes the remarkable growth of such prayer and commends the formation of local groups of

Christians of different traditions for the purpose of promoting prayer for Christian unity.'

[19] See *Le Concile et les Conciles*, Paris: editions du Cerf, 1960.

[20] Dr Gairdner's verdict with regard to this is usually quoted and is surely most impressive: 'It was only after an able and despotic king had proved himself stronger than the spiritual power of Rome that the people of England were divorced from their Roman allegiance, and there is abundant evidence that they were divorced from it against their will. . . . It was a contest not of the English people but of the king and his government with Rome. . . . The people evidently regarded the cause of the Church as the cause of liberty. That their freedom suffered grievously by the abolition of papal jurisdiction under Henry VIII. there can be no manner of doubt', James Gairdner, *Lollardy and the Reformation in England*, London: Macmillan, 1908, Bk I, ch. 1, pp. 5f.

[21] Abbé Couturier was never within even remote distance of believing this.

[22] Khomiakov to Birkbeck: 'England has never rejected the authority of the Roman doctrine. Why should those who admit the validity of the Pope's decree in the most vital part of faith—in the Symbol—reject it in secondary questions or matters of discipline?' The reference is to the *filioque* clause in the Nicene creed (Symbolon) accepted without question by Anglicans.

[23] On the significance of Solovyov's admission to Holy Communion by a Russian priest of the Uniat Church in Moscow, subject to the Roman See, see S. L. Frank, *A Solovyov Anthology*, London: SCM Press 1950: Appendix I, 'Was Solovyov a convert to Roman Catholicism?', pp. 249–52.

[24] T. M. Parker, 'Sirs, ye are brethren', *Reunion* III, No. 21, June 1939, pp. 165–76. To Dr Parker I owe the reference to Gerson, *De auferibilitate Papae* ii. 215. The former refers also to N. Figgis C.R., 'Councils and Unity', lecture in *Our Place in Christendom* (Longmans 1916). Father Figgis writes in many other places on the Caroline divines of the Church of England as being residuary legatees of the great theologians of the Conciliar Movement.

The Rev. T. M. Parker's article on which the last two paragraphs have been based, constituted a talk given to the Community of the Resurrection of which the distinguished historian, Father Figgis (died 1919), had been a member. The occasion was a conference with Anglican Papalists, which like a similar conference with Anglican Evangelicals, resulted from the visit of Abbé Couturier to us in July 1938. The Abbé made us realize acutely that our quest of Christian Unity must begin by finding the theological basis for the unity of the Church of England.

[25] *Le Concile et les Conciles*.

16

SECOND VISIT TO ENGLAND

O F this larger Anglican body of which we have been speaking, the part most easily accessible to Abbé Couturier was that which he had labelled (4) in his analysis.[1] From this part sprang the larger religious communities and to it belong the majority of Anglo-Catholic parishes. Moreover it has been held by shrewd students of our Church that

> It is owing to the intellectual and spiritual vitality of this strand within it that the Church of England has remained, to the extent it has, the home of traditional and orthodox Christianity and has done much to preserve that Christianity in the various Free Church bodies.[2]

He was already acquainted with Father O'Brien S.S.J.E., Superior of the Cowley Fathers. After his return to Lyons he received from Father O'Brien his fine pamphlet, *Christian Unity, the Problem for Anglicans*.[3] This speaks directly in terms of Catholic principles of the danger for Anglicans of the scheme of Church Union operating in South India, refers gratefully to the work of Abbé Couturier in releasing the movement of Prayer for Christian Unity from unnecessary dogmatic complications and shows a sense of deep responsibility with regard to the unity of Christians within the Church of England herself.

Moreover two influential Anglican visitors of the larger group of Anglo-Catholics found their way to Lyons in the spring of 1938. There was first Father Lucius Cary, S.S.J.E., who came on the way from Oxford to Palestine where he hoped to prepare conventual accommodation both for members of his own community and for sisters of the Convent of the Incarnation (Fairacres) in a property offered by its owners near to Ain Karim, the scene of the Visitation of the Blessed Virgin Mary to Elizabeth. Father Cary was a deeply impressive priest. He had a wide knowledge of the history of monasticism and the Religious Life and of the science of spiritual direction: he was also the unrivalled interpreter of the saintly leader and great theologian, Father Richard Meux Benson, the founder of the Society of Saint John the Evangelist.

Secondly there came from Yorkshire Bishop Rupert Mounsey of the Community of the Resurrection. Bishop Mounsey's career was an unusual one. He had already done eight years of great work as Bishop of Labuan and Sarawak (the Anglican diocese of the island of Borneo) when, at the age of 57, contrary to Western canon-law (which refuses such a possibility to a bishop), he humbly and inexorably demanded probation as to a call to the Religious Life in the Community of the Resurrection. Within this Community, after having been for some years assistant bishop of Truro, he was now assistant bishop of Bradford. He was a man of long experience, strong common sense and real prayerfulness. The Abbé recognized that he would be of great value in any relations that he might be led to seek with the Anglican episcopate. Bishop Mounsey was as a matter of fact to take an active part in the Lambeth Conference of 1948, and during his last years (he died in 1952 at the age of 84) he was the senior bishop of the Anglican communion. Each of these distinguished visitors, in his audience with Cardinal Gerlier, the new Archbishop of Lyons, supplicated that the Abbé might be encouraged to make a further visit to England.

So due authorization was provided, and on 11 July in the same year, 1938, the Abbé left Lyons for England once more. He did not set forth without earnestly soliciting prayers in many quarters, including the monastery of La Trappe des Dombes, the Convents of *Adoration réparatrice* at Lyons, of the Visitation at Annecy (the home of St Francis de Sales) and of the Carmelites of Vienne and Lisieux; as well as from intimate friends, Protestant as well as Catholic—Père Albert Valensin, M. Carlhian and Pastor Wilfred Monod. His sister's final characteristic and valuable counsel to her frail and ever-selfless brother was:

> All will go well, provided you don't get carried away, that is to say if you don't forget to reckon with your body, if you say your breviary in the morning and if you take sufficient sleep. Sleep is just as necessary as nourishment.

It is recorded that he returned in a pitiable state, having neither eaten nor slept, minding this most, I expect, because it would cause her anxiety.

He spent at least six weeks in England, unless—and this is improbable—Dr B. J. Kidd, Warden of Keble, misdated a letter to the Abbé.[4] He was met at Victoria by Dom Benedict Ley and Dom Robert Petitpierre and taken straight to Nashdom to spend some days with his old friends there. Then, with their encouragement, he proceeded to fulfil his long-formed resolution of breaking fresh ground by visits to the larger, more characteristically and representatively Anglican communities of Mirfield, Kelham, Cowley, and Wantage. These visits, like those that he had made the year before, were entirely private and unofficial.

Abbé Couturier came to us at Mirfield at a significant time in the history of the Community. On 2 April of that year, 1938, had died that great labourer for Christian unity who had shared in all the Conversations at Malines, Bishop Walter Frere, at one time Bishop of Truro, formerly our Superior for eighteen years, a great scholar, a great bishop and above all a great Religious, whom we count as our second founder.[5] His last participation in the community's corporate worship had been at my profession.[6] This had taken place on 13 January in the lower church which the community was using for their worship for some months, during which the nave of our great church of the Resurrection was being completed. Not long, however, after Bishop Frere's funeral on 6 April, the newly extended upper church was ready for use.

So on Wednesday 6 July the church of the Resurrection was dedicated by the Archbishop of York, Dr William Temple, in memory of the community's first founder, the Archbishop's revered friend, Charles Gore, Bishop of Worcester, Birmingham, Oxford—

> a prophet, a theologian, a pastor and one who hungered and thirsted after righteousness, whose activities constituted a great part in the Church's history in the half-century before.

Thus the Archbishop described him in his sermon; and there followed the great service of dedication, drawn up perfectly before his death by Bishop Frere, using for the last time his large store of liturgical knowledge. That day recollection of the majesty and mercy of the acts of God in Christ and in his saints and of his constant government filled our hearts with thankfulness:

> 'This day is salvation come to this house.'

The splendour of it all somewhat eclipsed that of our annual Commemoration Day three days later—the day on which our friends, companions of our Fraternity in particular, come of their goodness from the ends of the earth to see us. But we enjoyed the production given by students of our college in our 'Quarry-theatre' of Bernard Shaw's *St Joan* until a heavy downpour forbade its continuance. There followed twenty-four hours later the community's annual retreat, giving time much needed for thankful, penitent recollection of how much God had given us in the past, of how much he still would give if we should remain faithful. Then one evening in the following week arrived amongst us a frail, slight, priestly figure, full of the grace of God. It was Abbé Paul Irénée Couturier.

He addressed us first assembled in General Chapter on the place of prayer in the quest of Christian unity. His audience contained men of very varied sympathies. Our community has been called a microcosm of Christendom. It certainly has come near sometimes to being a microcosm of the Church of England. There were those amongst us, and one in episcopal orders, to whom anyone or anything belonging to the Roman Church was more than suspect, indeed almost certainly dangerous or diseased. There were others, equally loyal members of our Church, who were constitutionally more ultramontane in their cast of mind even than the Abbé himself. I remember standing in the garden later after supper talking to a hardened 'Protestant' brother and others of contrary views. We were all agreed for once. This priest from Lyons was a man of God and must be listened to with deepest respect. It was clear from this that he had moved not only our minds but our hearts.

At our request he talked once again in General Chapter and I think that it was probably he who suggested that we should ask him questions. There were some which arose from the community's connexion with the Malines Conversations in which both of our founders had taken part, questions which could hardly be avoided. They were answered in a way which made clear to us that there were Christian motives in Rome's reserves; and that we must distinguish carefully between the *'action officielle'* of the Holy See and the unauthorized presentations and interpretations of this which were often merely *'officieuse'*. He bade us recognize realistically and allow charitably for the human elements in the Church of God, entailing imperfection in every ecclesiastical system. But we were made aware of the immense range of Rome's responsibilities and of her need sometimes of going slower than some of her most ardent children would desire. The maternal visage of Rome began to reveal itself from behind the barriers of fear and prejudice owing to which her representatives had developed admittedly in recent centuries the mentality proper to the besieged.

Her interpreter spoke with the authority that proceeds from a combination of certain qualities rarely found together and which experience had not led us to associate with Roman Catholicism— humility, absolute conviction—rooted in prayer—of the truth of the dogmatic position of his Church, penitence for the faults of its members, openness of mind, disinterested goodwill and reverence for the grace and truth of Christ revealed in Christian traditions other than his own. He was himself in his gracious bearing a living ikon of catholicity. The slender, neat, black-robed figure with his transparent countenance, bright blue eyes, snow-white hair, animated and precise gesture and diction and loving address held our attention and won our affectionate respect and our deep trust.

The next day General Chapter had to give to important business. But as the most junior brother and with some knowledge of the French language, I could be spared to escort our guest to York. The

Superior, Father Talbot, had felt clear that he must see the Archbishop of York. So the Abbé and I passed together the first of many days so spent of which I treasure the memories. York Minster was seen on our way to Bishopthorpe, and there Canon Bell was our welcoming and helpful guide. The Abbé had an immense love of good architecture—the historian and the mathematician in him combined with the liturgist to enrich this delight. There was also here in evidence his delight in finding the Catholic faith and ways of devotion manifesting themselves beyond the Roman boundaries. Two treasures of the Minster held a special appeal for him. There was that part of the crypt in which are still to be found elements of the oldest building where St Paulinus ministered, a church dedicated to the *Divine Wisdom*—an ancient devotion of the Patristic Church which has had such surprising results in Russian Orthodox ikonography and theology and which finds unexpected expression in the West in that rich poem to the Blessed Virgin, the church of Notre Dame de Fourvière at Lyons. Secondly there was in the sacristy of the Minster the episcopal ring of Cardinal Mercier given by the Cardinal on his deathbed to Lord Halifax and by his son, the Earl of Halifax, set above the base of a fifteenth-century chalice and presented to the cathedral to be used on the feast of St Peter's Day and on the anniversaries of the deaths of Cardinal Mercier and of Lord Halifax.[7] How deeply conscious the Abbé was of his indebtedness to the patron of the Benedictines of Amay!

When we reached Bishopthorpe we were given tea by the Archbishop and Mrs Temple. There were present also the Rev. John Ramsbotham (later to become Bishop of Wakefield) and his wife. The Archbishop gave himself up to converse with the Abbé. Dr Temple saw at once the rightness and truth of Abbé Couturier's observations about the prayer of Christians for Unity. For the Archbishop the seventeenth chapter of St John's Gospel which he speaks of as our Lord's Eucharistic 'prayer of self-dedication' was also his much loved spiritual home.[8] So there was real and deep communion between him and his visitor. He was moved by the Abbé's request that with the Archbishop of Canterbury, he would call Anglicans everywhere to unite themselves with the prayer of Jesus 'that they may all be one'. After tea the Archbishop took Abbé Couturier and myself to see his chapel. Dr Temple prayed there aloud *ex tempore* for God's aid for Couturier and others working for unity, closing his prayer with words from John 17 and an informal blessing. He asked the Abbé to give us his blessing. The Abbé did this, after asking us to join him in the Lord's Prayer which he himself said in Latin.

The Archbishop had evidently intended to see whether he could procure the fulfilment of the Abbé's request in time for the next Week of Prayer for Christian Unity (January 1939). But circumstances made this difficult. He wrote on 18 December 1938:

> I recall with great pleasure your visit of summer last. I had hoped, directly the summer holiday was over, to tackle once more, and this time thoroughly, the subject which we discussed. But at that moment the international crisis was occupying everyone's mind and it took such a hold on me that I could scarcely keep up with everyday business and had no leisure for reflecting on this vital problem.
>
> It seems to me preferable to postpone it until after the next Octave rather than to start a new development on too small a scale. So I hope to take up the question again immediately after the January Octave with a view to make sure of the future.
>
> May I send you my warmest wishes for Christmas. As we come together before the crib, let us pray together for the full expression of the Unity which is already so real in our experience.

In the train on the way back from York to Mirfield Abbé Couturier opened what was for me a truly illuminating conversation. It followed upon each of us saying part of his divine office for the day. He told me something of what the Hours of the Breviary meant to him. There is a well-known scheme by which each of the lesser offices is linked chronologically to the Passion. This had been in his own practice elaborated, or rather more richly concretized, so as to inweave other mysteries of the Gospel along with great moments in apostolic experience, such as the first visit of the disciples to Jesus, our Lord's committal of his Mother to the care of the beloved disciple, the denial of St Peter, the conversion of St Paul, the vision of St Peter on the house-top at Joppa. These were blended

with the mysteries of the Incarnate Life; so that his constant appro-
priation of our union with our Lord, present in the soul through
Baptism and Communion and continuing his Prayer in us through
the Psalter, was humble and watchful as well as realistic in its grasp
of the mystery, 'Christ in us the hope of glory'. We talked of the
community's life and work past and future and of vocations to and
within it. The Abbé described how wherever he went, he came into
contact with persons strongly marked with signs of a vocation to
live for the quest of Christian unity whether through pastoral work
or teaching or prayer. I found in all that he said, strong confirmation
of my sense of such a vocation, which I had had for almost as long as
I can remember. We spoke of the tragedy of the separation of the
Church of England from Rome, and he recalled Newman's realization that it was not only England that needed Rome, but Rome that
needed England. A Christian family in separation tends always to
seek to justify *doctrinally* its own prejudices and proclivities which
become intensified and soured through isolation. So the more Christians of different confessions grow to know one another the better;
and this not only within our own country where the wounds of past
conflicts make understanding so difficult. I did not need persuading
that this hostility originated largely through the oppressive attitude
of the State, with which an established church was *ipso facto* identified, towards Roman Catholics in Ireland as well as England.

On our return the Superior, Father Talbot, wished to see me. He
asked me how things had gone and told me that he proposed to take
the unprecedented step of asking Abbé Couturier to give the community his blessing after Compline that night, together with any
counsel he felt guided to give us as regards prayer for unity.

It was with characteristic simplicity that Father Talbot had
accepted the word from God that came to us through Abbé
Couturier. In him Paul Couturier met the classic Anglican tradition
in its full strength. It has been said that Father Talbot

> was great in the same way as the best leaders of our country have
> been great, not as an autocrat by the imposition of self-will, but as
> the embodiment of the collective wisdom and affections of the
> society which he governed.

But he not only embodied; he also guarded, cherished, inspired and interpreted these for his brethren, leading them, when occasion required, courageously into the channels indicated by God.

This leading was done so naturally as sometimes almost to escape notice.

> [His] religion was so integrated with himself as almost to be taken for granted. . . . A deep wholly integrated godliness, the godliness of the Catholic Creeds and of the Fathers of Christian theology, had been his grandfather's, his father's, his mother's, his nurse's religion and the religion also of that fine old country priest who had prepared both his father and himself for Confirmation.

No doubt the influence of his wonderful godfather, Canon Scott Holland, perhaps the most eloquent, lovable and wise priest-theologian of our Church in this age and of that other dear and revered friend of his family, Baron Friedrich von Hügel, the Roman Catholic theologian, author of *The Mystical Element of Religion*, helped to fix in him as a young man a conviction as to the vital place of worship and prayer in the Christian life and to guard this watchfully. But reverence was of his very nature and he seemed to be exceptionally responsive to the 'numinous'. His close friendship with the Halifax family through his Oxford friend, the Hon. Edward Wood (son of Lord Halifax, the great Reunionist; himself later Viceroy of India, etc., and first Earl of Halifax) helped further to deprovincialize his essentially English mind. Let this friend—whose father, Lord Halifax, was a revered figure in the Abbé's pantheon and who himself loved to hear of Abbé Couturier's apostolate—himself give us a glimpse of the unique quality of friendship with Edward Keble Talbot that he had enjoyed for half a century. He wrote of 'Ted Talbot' that he was so constantly at home in both the seen and the unseen world that,

> It was scarcely possible to know him and not to be aware of this double domicile that was to him so real: and everything he touched of this world caught something of the glow that belonged to the other. . . . There was always the rich zest for life—what men and women were thinking; the currents of politics, literature and

music; *The Times* crossword; the mysteries of science; the procession of history; the glories of nature; the frank enjoyment of all the little things of daily life, a perfect sense of humour—so that, as it seemed, nothing came amiss to those large gifts of interest and comprehension. With that went a poise of judgement, as valuable as it is rare, that was fed by complete detachment from any of the smaller motives that so often lead astray. And behind and beneath everything, the conviction of the Divine Compassion and Power, working in ways past human understanding to bring the world to the pattern of the Kingdom of God.

Abbé Couturier later at our request summed up the message he had given at Mirfield in a letter to our Fraternity of the Resurrection. This was published in the next number of our *C.R. Chronicle* (No. 143, Michaelmas 1938). Extracts from this are given later. For the moment Father Talbot's impression shall be given, cited from a letter to Lyons written as soon as General Chapter was over:

> This visit has been for us a divine benediction. Assuredly your brotherly good will, your liberality (needless to say I don't mean liberalism!) and your spiritual confidence have impressed us in an unforgettable way. But it is above all the faith which animated your words, the supernatural grandeur of your hope and the integral catholicism which you were the means of unfolding before the eyes of our souls—all this, it seems to me, has shed on us a ray of divine charity. With all my heart I thank you in the name of my community.
>
> God grant that as the outcome of your inspired and inspiring call, we may offer ourselves in truth, in union with the desire of the Sacred Heart of Jesus to unite all Christians in himself, and that our prayer may be fulfilled by his grace, in the spirit of his own prayer —*ut omnes unum sint. Amen.*

Before he left Mirfield the next day, the Abbé had obtained Father Talbot's special co-operation in two ways. First he had asked him for a broadcast to be delivered, if possible by himself personally, if not, by a member of the Community of the Resurrection representing him, at Lyons in the coming January Week of Prayer. As the Superior was due to be absent visiting our Brethren in South Africa and Borneo, he asked me to represent him at Lyons. Secondly, Abbé Couturier arranged, with Father Talbot's assent, to form a spiritual bond of mutual intercession between the latter and the Father Abbot of the Trappist monastery of Notre Dame des Dombes, Père Alexandre. I have no doubt that this compact has been of great assistance to both, not least through releasing further supplies of divine grace at that crucial time when each laid down his high office. I can never recall the serenity and brotherly accessibility of Keble in those last years of freedom from office without thanking God also for Père Alexander whose loving interest in Father Talbot was very evident when I visited him in his cell at La Trappe des Dombes.

On hearing of Father Talbot's death in 1949 Abbé Couturier wrote to express his true sorrow over the loss.

> I had from him some splendid letters, and the little book on Talbot House. He had welcomed me in 1938 in such a brotherly way. It is thanks to him that I have known you. I owe him immense gratitude. . . . Naturally I pray each day for Father Talbot in my Memento [at Mass]; he is also in the prayer of my breviary. He is a true Anglican brother whom I will find again sooner or later, when I too have received, as he has done, the sacrament of complete stripping—death—which introduces us to his heavenly kingdom where we will proceed *de claritate in claritatem*, and that without end, since he is infinite with whom we have to do.

The visit of Abbé Couturier has borne fruit in the life of our community. It led, it might be said, not so much to an awakening or even a re-awakening of concern for Reunion, but to a taking stock of our heritage, of our opportunities and of our obligations in this field. Already we had entered into the labours of elder brethren departed. We have spoken of the participation of our founders, Bishop Gore and Bishop Frere, in the Conversations of Malines. Earlier and more constant have been our contacts with the Eastern Orthodox Church. Father Frere's first visit to Russia, followed by his lecture-tour in 1914, led on to the foundation in 1928, through the initiative and zeal of Dr Nicolas Zernov, the Russian lay-theologian, of the Anglican-Orthodox Fellowship of St Alban and St Sergius of which Bishop Frere was the first Anglican President. But it was the advent of Abbé Couturier which led to our realizing corporately the vital and essential place of work for unity in the Christian and Catholic life. Since then it has been accepted as the fourth of the four main ends of our life, the other three—the extension of the Kingdom of Christ, the preparation of men for the priesthood and the full restoration of the religious life to our Church—being seen to be organically connected with it. The existence of a permanent 'Christian Unity Committee' which on behalf of the General Chapter of our community deals with its ecumenical activities, is a sign of our increased concern for Christian Unity.

Since 1938 there has been contact with the Church of Rome as close and constant as that with the Eastern Orthodox Church. We have been in frequent touch with the Lutheran Church of Sweden, a relationship now being stabilized through the Fellowship of St Hilda and St Eric. Through Abbé Couturier we have been brought into fellowship with the first two religious communities to come to birth in the Calvinist Church: the Community of the Brethren of Taizé (near Cluny) and that of the Sisters of Grandchamp (in Switzerland) and have had the joy of watching them progress without losing their simplicity and prophetic depth towards a more catholic conception of Christianity. Through the Ecumenical Institute at Bossey, as well as in ways more direct, we have been associated with the World Council of Churches with regard to which the Abbé nourished such great hopes. We share his conviction, however, that unofficial contacts are the most important. Though in all these ways the influence of Abbé Couturier is found, it is no doubt in the depth of our conviction that worship and prayer hold the primary place in this work and that without them our efforts would be worse than wasted, that lies the chief mark of his influence.

In summer 1939 Bishop Mounsey wrote to the Abbé to say he hoped he had seen a paragraph in our *Chronicle* (No. 146, p. 5) which stressed the value of intimate and unofficial efforts for Reunion.

> . . . It is not only the best, it is the *only* really hopeful method for the present. When the authorities and their staff, in the Church of England and in the Church of Rome, understand the meaning of our efforts, I think that the way will be prepared for official action.

We cannot reverse this order. There is much more to be done for the education and instruction of Anglicans than you can imagine, I am sure. Things are not helped by the 'Romanizers' and are completely spoiled by our pan-Protestants. All this, I hope, will encourage you, my very dear friend, to go forward on your work.

Please remember me to my kind and charming friends at Lyons, especially H.E. the Cardinal, the Reverend Père Aupiais, M. Guillermin.

About the same time Father Shearburn (now Bishop of Rangoon) remarked in a letter to the Abbé: 'It is important not to admire and do nothing!' and continued by relating that the community had decided to invite some representatives of the Protestant wing of our Church

> to talk and pray and listen together for the guidance of the Holy Spirit 'after the example', so we said, 'of what happens in France at the Trappist monastery of Les Dombes'.

(The latter was now a regular meeting-place of the Pastor-Priest Circle founded by Abbé Couturier.) The visit of the Protestant theologians was followed at Mirfield the next year by that of representative Anglican Papalists. We have done our best ever since to continue holding such yearly conferences with Anglicans of standpoints different from our own. Indeed we have become more and more aware that the union of Christians of divergent doctrinal views in our own Church of England needs to be vindicated by a far more adequate theological synthesis than has yet been achieved, and that the elucidation of such a synthesis is at once part of our Church's vocation and its chief potential contribution to ecumenism.

These are but some of the good things which, under God, came to us with the aid of Abbé Couturier. His own joy in being with us is best expressed in his own words, taken from his letter written to the Fraternity of the Resurrection under the heading '*Erant Unanimes in Oratione*—These all with one accord continued steadfast in prayer'.[9]

> For the second time, after an interval of some months . . . I have been enabled to respond to the fraternal request of my Anglican friends, and to visit them, share in their life, and pray with them

for the end of that great sorrow, that great stumbling-block—the rupture of the visible Unity of Christendom, Christians divided among themselves. I have experienced again and again, during these two journeys, the inexpressible supernatural joy of the '*Cor Unum*' and '*Anima Una*' that rests upon the foundation of the same prayer, a close echo of the prayer of Christ after the Last Supper, our souls weighed down by the same burden, hurt by the same grief. Each time I felt more clearly that in prayer was the heart of the matter, the true way that opens out into the hidden union of the future, the restoration of all spiritual wealth to Christ's service in his visible Church, the visible extension of his Incarnation in time and space alike.

This joy and certainty I felt most keenly during the days I spent last July with my Anglican Brethren of the Community of the Resurrection at Mirfield. It is true that I was in one of the most vital centres of Anglicanism. The memories of Bishops Gore and Frere, living in their disciples; the tombs of these two great workers for Unity, whose names reflect (even as they helped to give light there themselves) the memorable name of the 'Malines Conversations'; an atmosphere of religion deep and stretching forth toward the joy of the Resurrection; missionary activity in distant lands, its influence marked even at home; keen minds at work; a place of study for priests-to-be; all these give to Mirfield a real attraction and charm. It is unforgettable.

What we experience, what we planned together at Mirfield—this I am glad to be able to tell you, brethren, unknown but beloved, of the Fraternity of the Resurrection.

Together we summoned up the memory of our examples, our pioneers: Cardinal Mercier, Bishops Gore and Frere, Lord Halifax, Abbé Portal. . . . Can we not ask their intercession, for they have entered into the peace and light of Christ? And there are others too, not perhaps to be named giants of Unity, but not to be forgotten. There are those, men and women, who have offered their lives for the Unity of Christendom, and whose sacrifice we know has been accepted a very little while after it has been made: a Protestant Pastor in France, a Trappist Nun near Rome, a Japanese Trappist Brother in a monastery in Japan. There are others too, Anglican and Catholic, whose offering we know, has been made. And straightaway God has accepted it, for suffering, sometimes unaccountable, has come to dwell in their lives as the divine answer, the living seal of God's acceptance. It is the nature of things that offerings like this call for wide and supernatural wisdom: a call, counsel, prayer to be shown the way. May each and all be alert to catch the voice of the Spirit!

Souls like this have attained to heroism in carrying out the great duty that lies before every Christian soul face to face with the division of Christians. They, the hidden martyrs of Unity, have understood the foul sin of all Christian separation. Without studying learned or accurate statistics, or seemingly so, they have known well that believers in Christ, his worshippers, his servants, yes, even his friends, live separate and apart; that there are Anglicans, Orthodox, Protestant, Catholics, and that our Lord never willed that to be, for he prayed to the Father, 'Father, that they may be one, even as we are one . . . that the love wherewith thou hast loved me, may be in them . . . that they may be perfected into one . . . that the world may know that thou didst send me' (John 17). They are not living back into the past. They live in the present. The facts—the sight of a visible Church broken, of Christ Incarnate broken by men, shattered to the limits of man's power—this is not to be borne, for in them lives the Spirit of Christ, the Spirit of the Holy Trinity, the unifying and simplifying expression of the Love of God in the heart of the Divine life. They have said to themselves that if every man understood, prayed, humbled himself, did penance, daily understood better and prayed more and humbled himself further—entered more deeply into the desert of penitence, then from the Christian multitude would rise a mighty cry, and God would hear in this sound of many voices his whole Christ. The noble, distant, perfect utterance of Good Friday, the unending perfect pleading of the Lamb of the Revelation, the cry of all the baptized, in fact or in desire, living here on earth—cry imperfect but essential; that there may find utterance the whole voice of Christ, the whole prayer of Christ. And the thought is a true thought.

Such a great might of prayer, humility and penitence would open the hands of God, held fast by our indifference, our lukewarmness in the face of the scandal of our divisions, whereby so often there die in the dark those valiant flames in unbelievers, who, without our ever knowing, had begun the search, along with tender first movements of the heathen at the first preaching of Christ in a pagan land. From the open hands of God would flow forth the rivers of God, the river of charity—sympathy, its first beginning; cherishing the gifts of God in each other; longing to understand one another; the will to enter into others' ways of thought; the acceptance of all sacrifices; and especially a self-forgetting movement of longing to accomplish our Lord's desire. Then the fruit would be ripe. Psychological unity, widespread over the Christian multitude, would lead on to unity in thought, already outlined along the road; union of thought would find its realization in conference (whatever form this might take) whereby the seal would be set on corporate reunions or reintegrations.

The souls that pray know in detail neither when nor how these things shall come about. But this troubles them very little, for they have boundless trust in Christ. They only know that all that he does will be both good and perfect. Their only care is to lift up from off the Christian multitude the great stone of disunity which holds back our Lord from manifesting himself to the world in the glory of his visible Unity.

The Abbé goes on to relate the spread in many lands and in many different Christian confessions of the annual visible revival of prayer for Christian Unity during the week from 18–25 January. He describes in particular the method for its observance urged by Dr Rosendal of the Swedish Lutheran Church, quoting a declaration by Dr Rosendal which had secured widespread co-operation amongst Christians of divers persuasions. Abbé Couturier closed his letter as follows:

ΧΡΙΣΤΟΣ ΑΝΕΣΤΗ[10]

There remains the expression of a longing, namely, to see growing and spreading in the heart of Anglicanism, from next January, a great wave of Octave prayers, having as their foundation these evangelical bases purely and simply [i.e. union with our Lord's own prayer after the Last Supper]. This movement would in no way aim at, or even have an undertone of opposition to, the actual movement in existence in Anglicanism. It would be parallel. No more—it would rather be fraternal, in a way that is not possible for all such undertakings one with another. It would gather together all those who, rightly or wrongly, are afraid or simply are not attracted to join in the existing Anglican Octave closely or from a distance, because they believe they cannot in conscience be members of it. In this way there would come into being in Anglicanism a great river with two streams of prayer for Unity, which would lead in perfect peace all Anglicans towards the ocean of the mercy of Christ, wherein they would find all other Christian souls, gathered from the vast Christian world, also rent asunder, but even now on the path of Unity. And perhaps we might hope for this new current of Octave prayers the warm encouragement of the authorities of the Anglican Church. . . .

As I take my leave of you, my dear friends of the Community of the Resurrection, let me pass on to you, that I may pray it with you, this great prayer that a Calvinist Pastor offered in France at a gathering of some pastors and Catholic priests:

Thee, O God, our heavenly Father we praise, and to thee we give thanks through our Lord Jesus Christ.

Thanks be to thee for the gift that thou hast given us of thy Son. Through him we serve thee and consecrate our lives to thy praise.

We thank thee for the unplumbed riches of thy grace, wherewith thou hast filled our souls.

We thank thee that thou hast destined us to eternal life, and that by the Resurrection of thy Son thou dost offer us the deification of our being.

We thank thee for that wonderful reality, the Communion of Saints.

We praise thee in that thy Spirit has led us to prayer.

Lord Jesus Christ, thou who hast built thy Church and who wilt perfect it in the day of thy glory, we give thanks unto thee. Thou hast willed that we should be the witnesses, the ambassadors of thy Kingdom.

We pray thee, Thrice-Holy God, have mercy on thy Church. She is in distress. Her divisions work ill. Be mindful of her, thou, her Head and her Redeemer. Grant her peace and unity. Fill the hearts of all with thy Spirit; grant that we may know our nothingness before thy greatness.

Ever manifest unto us more and more that greatness, so that all that is not thou, may appear unto us of no account and not worthy

213

to hold us back. Help us to see thee only; draw us into thee. May our hearts unite in thine.

O Lord, give unto thy Church all power that she may show unto the world of men thy divine greatness. Grant that we may communicate thy life to our brothers among men.

We pray thee for all who bear authority in thy Church, for ourselves, thy servants and thy ministers, children of thy love. We pray thee for all our brethren and all our sisters in Christendom. Come to our aid, Lord, and bless thine heritage.

We offer, O Lord, all these prayers, and all the prayers of thy Church through the Heart of Christ. Amen.

Abbé Couturier visited two other of the men's religious communities of the Church of England before he left this country. From Mirfield he went for the first time to visit the Society of the Sacred Mission at Kelham. This community was founded for the training of priest-missionaries, so an essential aspect of its life is its self-forgetful service of the students of its great theological college. At Mirfield, though the College of the Resurrection, whose students were absent when the Abbé was with us, is one of the Community's principal services to the Church, the religious life of the Community is independent of all its various works. The Abbé saw Kelham in a characteristic light when he accepted the opportunity of giving an informal talk to a crowd of students and Brethren. He had the even more unforgettable experience of visiting the aged founder, Father Herbert Kelly; '*le saint* Father Kelly', the Abbé later called him, though Father Kelly succeeded in confounding the conventional patterns of sanctity. Father Kelly with his great mind and genial spirit came 'perhaps nearer to combining in his life and teaching all that is best in Catholicism and Protestantism than any other Christian alive' (Dr Visser 't Hooft); and there was a prophetic bite in his conversation.

The Society of the Sacred Mission was of special interest to Abbé Couturier. He found there a Christian family nourished by Catholic tradition as well as by Scripture, whose convictions linked them with his Swiss and French Protestant friends. The Community was specially indebted through the influence of the Father Founder to

F. D. Maurice, of whom Abbé Couturier knew little, though their doctrinal standpoints are, in some respects, closely akin. There is the same catholic and comprehensive existentialism, swift to descry truth in unfamiliar disguises, and the same keen distrust of systematization. Father Kelly said of himself:

> I learnt everything first from Maurice: then I learnt it over again—several times! . . . I think what St Paul said of human religion is equally true of our schisms: 'the time of this ignorance God winked at, but now commands men everywhere to repent'. . . . I do not think men are ever wholly wrong, except in thinking they are wholly right.

The Society combined Maurice's evangelical catholicity with his deep regard for the mysteries of the Church. It is specially strict in its conformity to Anglican standards, but so far from being insular in its outlook, its doctrinal and spiritual diet includes elements from St Thomas Aquinas, Martin Luther, and St Ignatius Loyola. Father Gabriel Hebert, with insight derived from wide liturgical studies, has been able to give greater theological coherence to this standpoint. But it perhaps needed the judgement of independent minds like those of Père Tavard, O.P., Dr Hans Küng, and Dr Max Thurian (of Taizé) to convince us that there is a deep unity underlying what appears at first sight to be the eclectic theological outlook of the Society.

Abbé Couturier gained in that brief visit his introduction to several with whom friendship was cemented later by visits to Lyons. These included the eminent scholar, Father Gabriel Hebert, whose books he loved to propagate, and who helped him to understand better the Swedish Church, whose theology was at that time his, Father Hebert's, special interest; Brother George Every, the brilliant young lay-theologian whose learning and insight has helped to build a bridge between Lambeth, Geneva and Byzantium; Father Stephen Bedale, a distinguished figure in Convocation, who would later be Prior and Director of the Society: and Father Reginald Tribe, the great priest who was Director of the Society from 1925 to 1943.

Father Tribe was later to visit Abbé Couturier at Lyons and they became great friends, who learnt much from one another. Reginald Tribe represented Anglican liberal Catholicism (free from the liberalism which Newman hated) at its best. The son of a doctor, he was himself trained for that profession. Indeed he had already attained some reputation as a gynaecologist when in June 1910 at the age of 29 he first asked to be considered as a candidate for the Kelham Community. He had been aware of his vocation for some time and with this in mind had been attending lectures at King's College, London, where in 1911 he took a degree in philosophy and economics. He went to Kelham in 1912. His ordination followed soon after, and in the First World War he served as a doctor in the R.A.M.C. and later as an army chaplain. After his return to Kelham, he spent the next four years partly in Africa, partly on the staff of the college, and became director in 1925. He soon disengaged himself from the internal administration of the college, and became very mobile, travelling a good deal in Europe, Africa, Australia, and New Zealand, discerning possibilities for the work of the Society which were later realized, some of them after his death. His special concern was the social significance of the faith. His interest in the Christian Social Union goes back to his days as a layman. He had much to do with the Anglo-Catholic School of Sociology and its organ, *Christendom*. But this led him to Stockholm in 1925 and to espousal of the 'Life and Work' movement inspired by Archbishop Söderblom, which, in its turn, resulted in his becoming a valued member of the British Council of Churches and in his giving keen support not only to the 'Life and Work' side of its activity, but also to that in connexion with Faith and Order. He was very much in favour of the amalgamation of these two movements of ecumenical endeavour, and would have been a great figure at the Assembly at Amsterdam when this was achieved in 1948. He was a man of great serenity, of deep stability, and of eminent foresight and notable power of leadership at the same time. He was a Christian humanist who owed much for his formation as a man of prayer to a great director of souls, an assistant parish priest in London, G. C. Rawlinson.

I have always counted him as one who died for Christian Unity.

He was killed in London by a German bomb when attending a meeting of the Faith and Order Commission. The Secretary, with whom he was conversing, suffered scarcely any injury. I was interested later to find in a letter to him from Abbé Couturier (27 September 1941) these words:

> I understand your hesitation with regard to the idea of the 'offering of one's life'. I will speak of that in Tract 1942.
>
> But briefly note:
>
> 1. Such an offering has no value unless it is a response to a divine invitation. The limit of human initiative must be: 'Saviour, if it is acceptable to you that I offer you my life, I do so with all my soul.'
>
> 2. From God's side there is no cruelty. He is Master. He has set us on earth only to see if we can learn to give him back the whole of this creation which he has made for us, ourselves included. He doesn't kill. He permits one of these nothings which every moment threaten us, and which his Providence so often removes (acting on the unconscious, on the subconscious, and on the free will, by his grace) to follow its course and bring us to death. He acted thus for his Son, allowing free play to the wickedness of man.

(The Abbé turns from this subject to describe enthusiastically an interdenominational circle that has been formed at Lyons for 'Biblical Prayer on matters of common concern'. The circle has Anglican and Quacker [*sic*] members as well as Catholic and Reformed.)

From Kelham the Abbé went on to visit the Cowley Fathers at Oxford. To stay with the brethren of the Society of St John the Evangelist at the Mission House in Marston Street was regarded by Abbé Couturier as a very great privilege. Here in the original home of the community founded by Richard Meux Benson, Dr Pusey's beloved disciple at Christ Church, he was close indeed to the springs of the Oxford Movement to which, through Newman's teaching, he and his friends were deeply indebted. The Superior, Father William O'Brien, was a devoted spiritual son of the founder, who, along with a gentleness and a gift of understanding all his own, inherited Father Benson's austerity and warrior spirit, and gave a similar impression of reality, strength and holiness. Outside the community his greatest labour was devoted to the cause of Reunion which was very near his heart and always in his prayer. Few can have done so much as he did for the growth of the Week of Prayer for Christian Unity. Because his concern for this was so deep, he was adamant in his view that the foundations should be truly laid: and he worked very hard to uphold the faith of the Church and to oppose any schemes for unity which seemed to endanger her true life. This unyielding firmness hid from others who knew him only from his written articles the extent of his real charity and his intense longing for Reunion.[11]

Father O'Brien had prepared for his guest the special joy of meeting the last Anglican survivor of those who took part in the Conversations of Malines, Dr B. J. Kidd, Warden of Keble College. Some days after Dr Kidd had dined at Marston Street, the Abbé received the following letter:

Keble College
26 August 1938

Dear Monsieur l'Abbé Couturier,

It was a great pleasure to me to meet you on Sunday last, for your name had been familiar to me for several years. I was particularly glad to hear from your mouth that many bishops and priests in France hold dear the memory of Malines, and to learn also how remarkable a volume of prayer rises from all Christian hearts in all the churches for the reunion of Christendom. It is the same with us and we cannot doubt that if we all persevere in the prayer that our Lord's will may be done, the reunion desired will come about though we be no longer in the world to see it arrive. . . .

A visit was also arranged to the Bishop of Oxford, and it proved fruitful. Dr Kenneth Kirk[12] wrote afterwards:

You couldn't have experienced more joy in our meeting or have left afterwards with more hope in the future than I did myself. It was for me in particular a great joy, having lost by death my two dearest French friends, M. Portal and M. Bremond, to find another who shares with them that profound sense of the unity of all Christians which they possessed so strikingly, each in his own way. The bond which unites French and English in so many ways will not, it seems to me, be less effective in the sphere of religion than in secular matters.

218

Dr Kirk wrote at this time in his diocesan magazine:

> At last we have grasped that we ought to pray for the reunion of
> Christendom as ardently as we do for the conversion of sinners, for
> the redress of social injustice, for the peace of the world, etc.

A visit was made from Oxford by the Abbé, accompanied by
Father Sedding, S.S.J.E., to the mother house of the Community of
St Mary the Virgin at Wantage, the largest of the Anglican communities of women. The community founded in 1848, originally
with a view to educational work, has been occupied also in missionary work in India and Africa, as well as in our own land, where
it has specialized from the beginning in moral welfare work of
various kinds. There have been many other developments in its
work, one of these being the study of Plainsong under Dr Palmer.

The Sisters were delighted to welcome the visiting priest of the
French Church. Hearing that he wished to be present at Vespers,
they prepared for him, as they did for another French priest who
visited them frequently by reason of his appreciation of their plainsong. The scruples of the Abbé B. made it necessary for him to have
a seat in the cloister near the chapel door: so it was there that a seat
and books were made ready for Abbé Couturier. But he would have
none of this. In the absence of the sub-warden, he gained the Mother
Superior's permission to use his stall, and after Vespers, he gave the
Sisters a brief but moving address on prayer for Reunion and, in
particular, on the offering of lives for this end.

In the Mission House in Marston Street neighbouring clergy, as
well as brethren of the community, were given the opportunity of
meeting the Abbé and hearing him speak. Few of those present will
forget that evening at the close of which the Abbé, before giving, as
had been requested, his blessing to his hearers, asked all to stand and
give him theirs for his work for Christian unity.

At the same time Father O'Brien wrote to another community:

> I hope the Abbé Couturier will stay with you and talk to the
> Sisters. He is a really inspiring person and burning with charity.
> We want to arrange an interview for him with the Archbishop if
> possible.

As no introduction could count for more in the Church of England than one from Father O'Brien, whose words were as few as his judgement was weighty, it seems certain that it was he who brought the Abbé into touch with Dr Cosmo Gordon Lang, the Archbishop of Canterbury, a meeting which was to result in a friendship greatly prized by both. Abbé Couturier told me later that deeply impressed though he was by the greatness of Archbishop Temple and by his sympathetic understanding, he had been conscious of fellowship of a much deeper quality with Dr Lang. He certainly spoke to that priestly and pastoral heart of the Archbishop, the reality of which his grandeur of deportment often concealed from those around him. In after years the Archbishop described the Abbé to his friend, Maisie Spens, as one of those very rare personalities who visited him who were completely disinterested.

> He came, not because he was in favour of this or that plan, but simply because of the prayer and the will of our Lord. His union with our Lord was such that he could not help loving those who, to the degree possible to them, were doing their best to love him.

There are letters from the Archbishop which throw light on the friendship between the two men. The correspondence opens in the days when Dr Lang accepted the Abbé's suggestion of asking prayers for the newly elected pope, Pius XII. He sends in March 1939 assurance of his 'cordial esteem for your efforts on behalf of the spiritual unity of all Christian people'.

At the time of the capitulation of France, the Abbé thanks the Archbishop for having proposed that 14 June should be observed as a day of prayer for France, a proposal in which he was seconded by Cardinal Hinsley. The Archbishop's reply, written in his own hand, was contained in an envelope curiously addressed:

Abbé Couturier,

On . . . this Friday,

Lyons, France.

Abbé Couturier kept this envelope and himself annexed a note:

> There is here surely an allusion to Good Friday, to the Passion which France endured on that Friday 14 June, and more generally

to the Good Friday of long-drawn-out suffering which France continued to undergo. The hope of resurrection is on the horizon.

The content of the letter itself confirms the Abbé's interpretation of the curious lapse apparent in this address. After thanking him warmly for his splendid letter and speaking of the difficulty of correspondence in times of such distress, the Archbishop continues:

> But at least I may thank you warmly for the remembrance of your visit to me two years ago and for your words with reference to the appeal which I issued to my fellow-countrymen asking them to pray for France. Those prayers, as often happens, have been granted in a sense different to that expected or hoped for.
>
> The answer is perhaps that your country must pass through a sorrowful crucifixion until at the time ordained by God, he may bring about in her soul a resurrection. With all my best wishes . . .
>
> Cosmo Cantuar.

The Archbishop's announcement of his resignation drew a letter of sympathy from the Abbé. From the house assigned to him by the King at Kew, the Archbishop replied with great humility:

> 16th March 1942
>
> I am deeply touched by your words about myself and the decision I have taken to lay down—to give back to the Lord with a deep sense of penitence—the high office which he permitted me to hold. This decision has involved more than one sacrifice. I must learn to offer Mass in union with the supreme sacrifice of our Saviour. Indeed I shall look upon this as a fuller prayer for the unity of the Church of Christ: and it is good to think that I shall be united with you in this ministry.
>
> It would be a great pleasure to see you again. Meanwhile may God the Holy Spirit give you strength and courage to continue that intercession for the Unity of the Church which has been given you as a special vocation! And in your prayers may I still, unworthy though I am, find a place!

Later, though full of encouragement to the Abbé with regard to the memorandum he is preparing on his work for unity to be conveyed to His Holiness Pope Pius XII by Cardinal Gerlier, he excuses himself from writing words of commendation:

> I am now a private individual (not as you address me: Archbishop of Lambeth: I am only called Archbishop by courtesy, and the only title I can claim at present is that of peer—Lord Lang of Lambeth—which the King conferred on me). As a private person it would not do for me to address His Holiness: but I am touched by your suggestion nonetheless.

The last message, written by the Archbishop about three months before his death on 5 December 1945, is as cordial as ever:

> It isn't possible for me to read every word of all those articles, but I have read enough to appreciate the vigour, the imagination, and the zeal which they show for the great cause. Allow me to repeat my assurance that I am doing and will continue to do what you have asked of me and that I remember you and your collaborators in the great enterprise—indeed I do so continually in my prayers. May God give you health and strength, steadfast faith and hope in all you endeavour to do for what must be the greatest cause in the world.

The Abbé had one last visit to pay on his way to the channel port. It was to the community of Benedictine nuns at West Malling in Kent, whose vocation is to the worship of God in the enclosed contemplative life, with special intention for the unity of the Church. The letter from Father O'Brien, quoted above, was to the Lady Abbess of this community. Malling Abbey had been the home of Benedictine nuns from 1099 until the suppression of the monasteries in the sixteenth century. The members of the present community, which had been founded in 1906, began to live here in 1916. The south transept to the old monastic church forms the nuns' choir. The original monastic gatehouse with its adjacent 'pilgrim chapel' stands near the abbey gates, where, as laid down in St Benedict's rule, guests are to be 'received as Christ himself'. The Community is under the spiritual care of the Society of St John the Evangelist.

The present Lady Abbess writes:[13]

Yes, indeed, Abbé Couturier paid us a visit and stayed a night here. He spoke to us in chapel, and those of us who heard him still recall a most vivid impression of his slight figure and delicate, almost transparent, look; but also of the strong, impassioned way in which he spoke of Christian unity. Our chaplain interpreted for those of the community who did not know French, and more than once the Abbé repeated a phrase which he did not think had been sufficiently emphasized.

We were all struck by his evident sanctity, and by his burning zeal for unity, which seemed almost to consume him. He spoke of the need for prayer and for those who would offer themselves for the cause; and though we had for years been praying much for Christian unity, many of us felt we had been given a new insight and fresh inspiration by his words.

The Abbé came to Compline and also was present in the sanctuary during our Mass next morning. He watched everything with evident interest and spoke afterwards to our chaplain of how particularly interested he had been to see how we were communicated from the chalice, asking if it was only a few drops that we received, as it had seemed like kissing the chalice.

It was clearly fitting that Abbé Couturier's last night in England should be spent in St Mary's Abbey under the patronage of St Benedict.

NOTES

[1] See pp. 170f.

[2] Henry St John, O.P., *Essays in Christian Unity*, p. 32.

[3] Published London, Pax House: no date, but its inscription in the Abbé's copy suggests 1937.

[4] Père Villain says that he spent three weeks: *L'Abbé*, p. 130.

[5] After the elevation of our first founder, Bishop Gore, Frere proved the master-builder who upon the first foundations formed 'the little group of disciples of a great teacher' into a fully organized religious community, translating principles into a detailed order. See Peter Anson, *The Call of the Cloister*, pp. 129ff.

For Bishop Frere's work for Reunion see *Walter Howard Frere*, a memoir by C. S. Phillips and others (London: Faber and Faber, 1947) and Walter Frere, C.R., lately Bishop of Truro, *Recollections of Malines* (London: Centenary Press 1935).

⁶ We were from the same school, Charterhouse, which has bred a notably large number of Anglican Religious, this being due, I believe, to the prayers of Carthusian monks, living and departed, especially the Carthusian Martyrs. Before I arrived as postulant at Mirfield, I had co-operated with Bishop Frere in producing a book in honour of the fourth centenary of the martyrdoms: *The Passion and Martyrdom of the Holy English Carthusian Fathers* (ed. G. Curtis), London: Church Historical Society, 1935.

There are Carthusians of both the ancient and the post-Reformation families who will understand how the earthly loss of my guide and friend, Bishop Frere, connects itself in my mind with the arrival at Mirfield of another 'Carthusian', Abbé Couturier, from the Institution des Chartreux at Lyons which, like the English Charterhouse, replaced a Carthusian monastery. Abbé Couturier valued the book I have mentioned and had it translated into French, but the advent of war prevented its publication.

⁷ As we have noted, both of the latter occur during the January Week of Prayer for Unity.

⁸ 'After a stormy meeting', says the Rev. Professor Hodgson of Archbishop Temple, 'as he opened his Bible and began to read (from St John's Gospel) the whole atmosphere changed. There was no mistaking the fact that in heart and soul we were being lifted up into the realm where he habitually dwelt'— F. A. Iremonger, *William Temple*, London: O.U.P., 1948, p. 418.

⁹ *Chronicle of the Community of the Resurrection* No. 143 (Michaelmas 1938), pp. 1–8 (translated by V.S.).

¹⁰ In that year our quarterly *Chronicle* had on its cover the figure of the Paschal Lamb holding the flag of victory, surrounded by these two Greek words written in capitals, meaning 'Christ is risen'.

¹¹ W. O'Brien, *A Cowley Father's Letters*, London: Darton, Longman and Todd, 1962, pp. xiif.

¹² Bishop Kenneth Kirk was 52 years old at this time. He had been Regius Professor of Moral and Pastoral Theology in the University of Oxford for five years before he became bishop. A man of great charm and eloquence, his great work as a theologian had been the re-establishment of the science of moral theology in the Church of England. He had also written a notable work on Christian spirituality, *The Vision of God*. He died in 1954.

¹³ To the author, 3 October, 1963.

17

ABBÉ COUTURIER AND THE REFORMED CHURCHES

I. ERLENBACH. BIRTHPLACE OF THE FIRST INTERCONFESSIONAL CIRCLE

FROM the first days of the awakening of Abbé Couturier's ecumenical vocation, he had sought to improve the relations of Catholics with their Protestant brethren. In January 1936 he sent his article on the psychology of Prayer for Unity to the Protestant pastors of Lyons, together with a humble and penitent appeal for such prayer. He also privately invited M. Durand-Granier, President of the consistory of Lyons, to an exchange of views in a small conference. When they eventually met, the Abbé was accompanied by Abbé Jules Monchanin, and the President by the layman, Dr J. de Rougemont, chief surgeon of the Protestant infirmary of Croix-Rousse. M. Durand-Granier's attitude was one of hesitation and even of disapproval with regard to the Abbé's overtures. How can the priest of a Church that will have nothing to do with the assemblies of fellow-Christians at Stockholm and Lausanne seek to promote Christian unity? However, the meeting did lead to the introduction of the Abbé to Pastor Bertrand, an influential member of the national synod with results of immense ecumenical importance which have been already recorded.[1]

The first spiritual contact however with Protestants—an encounter of the kind longed for by Abbé Couturier—came about not in France, but in Switzerland. By a strange paradox it was the quest of Abbé Couturier for *images*, i.e. for symbolic representations useful for his mission, which brought him into intimate touch with Protestantism which has been suspicious of such aids to religion. He found in some Protestant magazine a reproduction of an excellent stained-glass window by Eugène Burnand on the Beatitudes. He wrote asking the pastor of Herzogenbuchsee, whose church contained this window, to send him a photograph of it. Berthold Zwicky —for this was the pastor's name—turned out to be second in command of an ecumenical brotherhood, the Fraternity of St John, founded and directed by Richard Bäumlin, pastor of Erlenbach. Its aim was to lay to heart the guilt of separation and to cultivate a right appreciation of all forms of the Christian faith, without endangering the love and service of one's own Church. This circle was longing to get into touch with brethren of the Roman Catholic Church.

The Abbé found an ambassador in his friend, Abbé Remillieux. Late at night on one of his missionary journeys for the propagation of peace, M. Remillieux found his way into the church of Herzogenbuchsee where he came upon Pastor Zwicky and Pastor Bäumlin engaged in intercession. This led to a compact of prayer between the Catholic priests and the Fraternity of St John and to a touching exchange of greetings between the Pastor of Erlenbach and his flock and the parish and curé of St Alban, Lyons. Erlenbach—which was the first parish to give itself to the Reformation—was to be the first to receive priests of the Roman Catholic Church.

A prelude to this event in Easter 1937 was the participation of Abbé Remillieux with episcopal encouragement in a retreat of thirty pastors. This 'retreat' had as its theme 'The Church of the Risen Lord, and its Mission'. The Roman priest's presence there after the 400 years of estrangement between Catholics and Protestants was accounted on both sides a great and joyous event. Its natural outcome was the formation of a wider ecumenical circle, a *fraternité* recruited half from the region of Berne, half from Lyons.

The first gathering took place in July 1937 at the monastery of La Trappe des Dombes (Ain), about thirty miles from Lyons. Viewed as a conference it was perhaps a little too overweighted on the Catholic side. There were only three pastors present—Messieurs

Bäumlin, Herber and Zwicky. On the Catholic side the four priests
—Abbés Couturier, Monchanin, Remillieux, and Professor Richard
were assisted by M. Carlhian, the old friend of Abbé Couturier who
was never absent, while health permitted, from meetings either of
this circle or of its successor. The discussions were on four subjects:
'The Redemptive Act of Christ: the Lord's Supper and the Mass',
introduced by Professor Richard; 'The Mystical Body', introduced
by Abbé Monchanin; 'Questions relating to Unity', from Abbé
Couturier, and 'Unity in our Prayer: the Canon of the Mass and the
Prayer of the Holy Supper', introduced by Abbé Remillieux. The
introductions had as their aim to arouse frank and brotherly conversation. But despite their eagerness to learn as well as to stimulate,
and their resolve in no wise to impose their own views, the Catholic
theologians showed themselves naturally more at home in such a
debate than did their Protestant guests whose life had been wholly
devoted to pastoral work in the depths of the country. Perhaps,
moreover, the monastic background to some extent overawed the
latter. There was the supernatural peace of the monastery—the *Pax
Dei*—which embraced even the guest-house; the *opus dei* solemnly
offered in the church—a firmament of constant adoration with the
Mass as its sun: the contemplative life of the monks proving its
fruitfulness around them. *Sanabo aquas has et non erit in eis mors;*[2] so ran
the motto of the abbey: and certainly an immense area around has
been transformed from unhealthy marsh into fruitful farmland. The
joyous childlike smile with which the silent monks greet visitors is a
vivid testimony that the notions about the Trappist monk's life as a
living death are the wildest nonsense. The monastery has recently
received from the state which expelled its sons in 1880, the Legion of
Honour in recognition of its courageous protection of Jews from
German violence. In 1963, the centenary of its foundation, Christians from many lands joined with those of France in thanksgiving
for the abbey's work for unity.[3] It is not surprising that it was not as
a conference that the first days spent by this circle at Les Dombes
were remembered by the pastors, but rather as a wonderfully peaceful and illuminating retreat, containing at the same time a challenge
to their convictions.

The charms of Erlenbach, a Swiss village in an exquisite natural setting, where the conference was held next year on Protestant terrain, were quite different. The villagers themselves seemed to welcome these unwonted visitors from another land and Church to the Christian hospitality of the enchanting parsonage of Pastor Bäumlin. 'What a fraternal and profoundly Christian welcome we received!' wrote Professor Richard, recalling with special gratitude the privilege of worship in common—Mass said morning by morning in the devout presence of the Protestant brethren in an oratory prepared for this purpose in the parsonage; and in the evenings Gospel readings interspersed with hymns and extempore prayer in the choir of the old village church. On this occasion the Protestant representatives were strengthened by two additions—Pastor Peter Barth, brother of Karl Barth, an eminent theologian, best known as the editor of the works of Calvin, and Otto Strasser, professor of ecclesiastical history in the universities of Berne and Neuchâtel. The subjects were treated more fully than at Les Dombes. They included 'The Knowledge of God according to Nature and Revelation' (P. Barth); 'Holy Scripture in the life of the Protestant Christian' (O. Strasser); 'The place of the Sacramental Life in the soul of the Catholic Christian' (J. Monchanin); 'The Pastoral Role of the Minister' (B. Zwicky). Here for the first time meditations were given alternately by Catholic and Protestant, and this was to become a feature of such gatherings. On this occasion they were given by Pastor Bäumlin and Abbé Couturier. Pastor Huber contributed a moving address in Latin. Excursions had been arranged with a view to recreation and also with a view to giving insight into the life of Protestant parishes. In thanking his host, the Abbé wrote:

> These days are among the richest in divine goodness that I have yet lived. I have understood what mutual enrichment God reserves for all Christians, when prayer, humility, and the Cross of Christ, have filled Christian souls.

It is soon realized in such meetings between Catholics and Protestants that the Church is a crucial subject in great need of investigation and exposition. So it formed the theme for the meeting at La Trappe des Dombes in the next year, 1939. This gathering had the great benefit of the help of Père Pierre Chaillet, S.J., a gifted ecclesiologist, then professor at the Jesuit college at Fourvière, who had just completed a great work which profoundly satisfied and influenced Abbé Couturier and which he never ceased to recommend to his friends—*L'Eglise est Une, Hommage à Möhler (1796–1838).*[4] The centenary of Möhler's death had recently been commemorated. Père Chaillet himself had written only the introduction and the essay on 'The Mystic Principle of Unity', but the conception of the book as a whole is his, and it is magnificent. The essay which probably meant most to the Abbé was that by Professor Tyskiewicz of the Russicum at Rome on 'The Theology of Möhler and the Philoslav theologians'; for there Solovyev is most appreciatively treated and judiciously criticized. The great father of ecumenical theology, Möhler died at the age of 42 without discovering Eastern Orthodoxy, but Solovyev had profited by knowledge of his work, and the death of the latter on Easter Day in the first year of this century, leaving a last great message on Christian Unity, always seemed to the Abbé to mark our century significantly as one that must devote itself to this quest.[5]

It was a major blessing for both Catholic and Protestant members of the Fraternity to be introduced at this time to the thought of Möhler, the great mind which brought German theology back to the Fathers of the Church, which so generously esteemed Protestant masters of theology and on whose work 'basically all of modern Catholic ecumenism is formulated'. Pastor Marchand wrote with regard to the commemorative volume,

> I experience a great joy in reading Père Chaillet's fine book. . . . I find myself here in full communion of thought and faith. These pages prolong the days at La Trappe which were so beautiful and so rich—one is profoundly grateful for them.

Then came the Second World War, for which Père Chaillet and Pastor Marchand were mobilized. These years of hardship and anxious separation were relieved from time to time for the French by affectionate messages and letters from across the Swiss border. When in 1942 permission was again given to cross the frontier, Professors Richard and Chaine, Abbé Remillieux and Père Villain made their way again to Erlenbach to find themselves welcomed in a home whose holy, hospitable, carefree bounty seemed a blessed dream after the misery and impoverishment of occupied France. The theme of discussion was various aspects of Christian life treated under the general heading of spirituality. This proved a final gathering, for this same year there came to the Lyons brethren an invitation to engage in interconfessional discussion with another group of Protestants nearer at hand. From this the barriers of German mentality and language would be absent. This second circle did not really find itself until 1946, two years after the liberation of France. When it did so, its members were conscious of owing a great deal to the Fraternity of Erlenbach. This second circle flourishes to this day most fruitfully. It has been helpfully joined from time to time by members of the former circle; and it has never forgotten its debt to the Fraternity of Erlenbach.

II. THE SECOND INTERCONFESSIONAL CIRCLE

Though specialists from the universities came willingly to their aid, the large majority of the Swiss Fraternity of St John were pre-eminently pastors rather than theologians. Moreover they were separated from the French by their German mentality and language. The French-speaking Swiss were more theological in their interests besides being closer to French Catholics by reason of their language and cultural heritage. The moving spirit in the second cell, which met first in September 1942 at the monastery of La Trappe des Dombes, was Pastor Jean de Saussure, well known as a preacher, especially through his ministry at the cathedral of Geneva, and as a theologian through his persuasive exposition of the new or revived Calvinism. M. de Saussure is a figure of great distinction, and his eloquence reminds us of the renowned pulpit orators of the past—a Bérulle or a Bossuet. His sending to Abbé Couturier of two of his books, *Believest thou this?* a commentary on the Apostles' creed, and

At the School of Calvin, a summary of the doctrine of the Reformer, led to a lively correspondence.

As a member of the Faith and Order Commission who had attended the conference at Edinburgh (1937) Pastor de Saussure had already had experience of interconfessional discussions; hence his optimism was more reserved than that of the Abbé. He agreed that the Christian faith contains positive elements which Catholics and Protestants hold in common, as well as a negative element on which there is disagreement. But there are also, he observed, certain positive convictions held by each side which are mutually exclusive. It is this third element which constitutes the cross of ecumenism. We must ask God to transform it by the mystery of the Resurrection—it is not human minds which can work out a synthesis. Yet in the meanwhile, pursued M. de Saussure, much is to be gained by making the nature of these conflicting convictions clear.

It was arranged that conferences should be limited to the number of twelve participants on each side. The Protestant group was to include professors from the Protestant theological faculties—Geneva, Lausanne, Montpellier—members of the World Council of Churches, pastors particularly of the 'Church and Liturgy' group, and brothers of the Protestant Community of Taizé of whom we shall speak later. On the Catholic side, while there would always be present a certain number of diocesan clergy, they would be supplemented by theological professors from the University of Lyons and by theologians from the religious communities—by Jesuits from Fourvière, Marists from Sainte-Foi, and Dominicans from various quarters.

Experience gained at Erlenbach had taught the Abbé the immense value, for such a conference, of prayer in common. The conferences were to be held alternately at the Trappist monastery of Les Dombes and at the Protestant Retreat House of Presinges near Geneva. In the former there was never any hesitation on the part of the Protestants: they would attend the Mass celebrated solemnly for the monastic family in its own church. In the latter, there being no Catholic church nearby, permission was asked by the Catholics from the diocesan bishop both to say Mass in the Protestant chapel and to attend the Protestant celebration of the Lord's Supper. The bishop refused permission for what seemed to him procedure dangerously equivocal in character. The Abbé through whom the request had been made, obeyed with simplicity, notifying his friends of this decision which grieved him as much as it did his Protestant hosts. A pastor wrote that such exaggerated fear, on the part of the prelates, of scandal, perversion or equivocation, always impresses Protestants as betraying serious weakness in the Church of Rome.

The main concern of this circle, too, which continues to flourish, has been the nature of the Church. Though anthropology, Christology, the nature of worship and other subjects have from time to time demanded attention, the subject of the first conference—the Church—has had a dominating place. In the Faith and Order Commission and in the World Council of Churches, the focus of attention has been largely the same.

The procedure followed did not alter from year to year. Each subject of the year's conference was presented by a speaker from either side. It was usually the discussion of the papers by the whole group which followed that gave the most memorable moments and led to the most valuable results. Sometimes these moments were those of illumination, enrichment and concord. Sometimes they were those when the clash of opinion reached the surd of utter opposition. None was more aware than the Abbé of the value of the latter. Mgr Chevrot in a memoir of Paul Couturier has recalled this vividly and gives an example:

> His gaze clear and grave did not permit one to suppose that he could be satisfied with a field of understanding gained at the price of illegitimate concessions. I remember particularly one of the meetings at La Trappe des Dombes where those engaged in discussion (both Catholic and Reformed) were comparing their respective positions on the subject of the Real Presence of Christ in the Eucharist. No one dreamt of hiding their only too obvious disagreements; but these were being expressed with a degree of discretion which betrayed anxiety not to jar on the convictions of those holding a contrary view. Suddenly Abbé Couturier who up to that moment had not spoken, pronounced a single phrase—no

more!—of a sharpness that seemed to verge on deliberate brutality. The clash of doctrines could not have been brought out more strongly, with the result that there followed a moment of silence. I made use of it to glance at the Abbé whose countenance remained perfectly tranquil and even exhibited a certain satisfaction. His intervention had indeed dispelled the fog. He was not a man who could imagine that agreement could even be purchased by the least sacrifice of the truth. He lived, spoke, acted only in the light!

How well I remember that moment! It was a moment at which the mathematician's love of clarity and precision evinced itself as one with the Christian's supernatural thirst for the living truth. Yet this is the man who said later to be a special target of the papal condemnation of 'false irenism' in the encyclical *Humani generis,* and—even more ridiculous if not so damaging!—to have been the mainspring of a new brand of ecumenical 'pietism'.

There were other times when it was the Abbé's presence alone that, because it radiated the charity of Christ, dispelled bitterness and recalled the peace of the Gospel. When discussions grew too vehement, he sometimes suggested a pause for silent prayer and the deferment of a subject until a later occasion.

He himself tabulated the results of his experience in the following 'axioms' which concern the psychological rather than the doctrinal aspects of ecumenism.

Result of ecumenical experiences (numerous interconfessional study-groups, spiritual gatherings for prayer, letters, confidences.)

Axiom 1. The Catholic Church is not alone in believing itself to be in the sole possession of the Truth.

Axiom 2. The psychological situation with respect to one's own faith and that of other communions is exactly similar.

Axiom 3. No one thinks of the return of others to the faith of his own Church; or it is equally true to say everyone thinks of it.

Axiom 4. At the stage of spiritual emulation everyone thinks of convergence towards a common point transcending difference.

Axiom 5. The law of transcendence (*dépassement*) or of sanctification by lifting up the whole faith of one's own communion is the law of all alike.

Axiom 6. Every Christian believes that the Christian of another type has strayed and ought to return to the Church, that is to say his own.

The Catholic says to others: Mine is the only Church from which you have been separated.

The Protestant: I have returned to the one and only Church, that of the apostles, from which you have been separated.

The Orthodox: I have preserved the true Church and you have created the Roman schism by earthly ambition or weakness.

The Anglican: I have returned to the one and only Church, that of the apostles and the fathers, from which you have been separated by earthly ambition.

How grand that it should be thus, for the glory of God! There remains only dynamism and loyalty; or more simply, spiritual emulation.

The words 'dynamism and loyalty' recall one of a pair of striking essays privately circulated in 1944 and 1945 which deal with doc-trinal and philosophical factors that govern these psychological phenomena. They are occasional utterances elicited by Protestant perplexities, but they show such originality and boldness and such a rich and varied range of perception that they are worthy of careful reading and meditation. One of these called 'Concerning the Bull *Unam Sanctam*' discusses the notorious decree of Pope Boniface VIII (1302) which speaks of the distinctive functions civil and ecclesias-tical of the powers temporal and spiritual and that mutual harmony and subordination in relation to one another, of which the natural relationship existent in man between body and soul is the image. The contrast between the earlier pronouncement and the later encyclical *Immortale Dei* of Leo XIII (1885), contrast due to the change from a medieval mentality to that of the late nineteenth century, is striking enough. In fact from the former standpoint the latter would be treated as heretical. Nevertheless there is a profound agreement. The co-ordination of the powers is so expounded by Leo XIII as to declare in terms appropriate to modern conditions the primacy of the spiritual power which Boniface VIII had claimed so crudely and in terms so soon obsolete. The problem of the Middle Ages has, owing to a change of mentality in the course of human progress, given place to an 'over-problem'. The co-existence within Christendom of different mentalities, shaped or coloured differently by reason of their confrontation with different problems which are often only the same problem at different stages of development, is to a large extent the source of doctrinal disagreement. Such a change of viewpoint also makes more difficult the doctrine of papal infallibility.

There is a wonderful description prophetic in spirit of the rich variety of method employed by the Lord of History whose is the long-suffering humility as well as the majestic initiative of Eternal love, in raising man to higher levels and in drawing the human race together towards that great symphony of praise which will finally crown his work of creation. The blind Lazarist, Père Pouget, who fought the battle for the scientific study of the Bible, has contributed ideas found here. So has his dear disciple, Professor Jean Guitton, who wrote Père Pouget's life and has laboured in his spirit. Père Teilhard de Chardin, of whom Père Monchanin, mutual friend of Père Teilhard and Abbé Couturier, was so great an admirer, has influenced the conception of evolution. The whole reveals a sense of history and a breadth of imaginative grasp of these questions entirely the Abbé's own. Here is a great soul, a rich stimulating mind at work—one which if it lacks technical theological training, is *living theologically* in a way which many trained theologians fail to do.

'Dynamism and Loyalty', which owes much to Jacques Chevalier,[6] deals with the response required of the individual in relation to such a manifold and mysterious reality. Christian certainty, our possession of the truth of faith, must have a dynamic quality. The writer draws attention to certain existentialist elements in Holy Scripture the realization of which are necessary for the health and fullness of Christian life. The parable of the talents, the metaphor of the racecourse used by St Paul, the pilgrim simile of St Peter, all imply this dynamic character of the Christian life. We must embark with courage upon this pilgrimage towards truth—'this pilgrimage which has no ending'. Intellectual research ought itself to be at the service of this interior quest (at work in prayerful meditation), always open to the operation of grace. On the other hand this dynamism must lose its value unless it operates in the way of loyalty. Loyalty, because of the failings of every form of Christianity including Catholicism, may in these days take strange forms, even the loss of faith. Catholicism itself in its sociological expression suffers from deficiencies. Would it be temerarious to say that the grave separations it has undergone in the course of the centuries have deprived it of cultural values necessary here and there for its fuller expansion? May it not need revivification in a certain number of its human elements, even in the clothing of its dogmas? If the forms of their clothing were more numerous, belonging to all the great legitimate systems of human thought, it is probable that unity would be very near and thus attained within the life of the Church. This seems to be the way which ecumenism is providentially follow-ing. All the Christian confessions, if they really wish to do so, can thus learn to ascend towards the Father without confusion of doc-trines and this ascent is a continual *rapprochement* which prepares the final osmosis within the one eternal Truth.[7]

In conclusion a word must be said about the *Journées du Châtelard*. At the close of the war years Père Villain had submitted to Abbé Couturier the idea of a gathering which would enable priests fired by the spirit of spiritual emulation to get to know one another so that they might share their experiences and together search prayer-fully for ways of approaching their non-Catholic brethren. The starting-point was to be reflection on the experience of the inter-confessional circles described above. Needless to say, the project had the Abbé's warm encouragement.

Thus arose the days for training in ecumenism known as the *Journées du Châtelard* because since the first years (1945–6), when they took place at Saint-Égrève near Grenoble, they have been held every year in the first week of July at Notre Dame du Châtelard, the name of the house of the Jesuit Fathers in a suburb of Lyons. More than 300 priests have attended these days of prayer, instruction and meditation, including visitors from Belgium, Holland, Switzerland, England, Germany and the Middle East, as well as from all over France.

NOTES

[1] See p. 123.

[2] The Authorized Version translates Elisha's words in healing with salt the unwholesome waters as 'Thus saith the Lord, I have healed these waters; there shall not be from thence any more death or barren land', II Kings 2.21.

[3] By gracious invitation of the Abbot, the author shared at the monastery itself in the joys of this commemoration; may he here express his deep gratitude.

[4] Paris: Bloud et Gay, 1939. Johann Adam Möhler was professor of church history at Tübingen, later at Munich. His work has been called 'the first major development of what might be called a theology of ecumenicism' (Tavard).

[5] Père Chaillet had also written the introduction to the French translation (from the German) by Dom Lilienfield, O.S.B., of Möhler's book *Unity in the Church*, published in the previous year (1938).

[6] Cf. Jacques Chevalier, 'Progress towards the Truth', which appeared in the small but influential journal *Le Van*, edited by M. Carlhian. The latter told me that M. Chevalier made a great impression on Abbé Couturier when he visited Lyons.

[7] The whole of the essay 'Dynamisme et Loyanté', and, under the title 'Problème et Surproblème', a large part of the study concerning the Bull *Unam Sanctam* are printed in *Oecuménisme spirituel*, ed. Villain, pp. 187–213.

18

THE ONSET OF DARKNESS

———

THE Abbé Couturier returned to France at the close of the
summer of 1938 in time to attend the gathering of Catholic
priests and Calvinist pastors at the Trappist monastery of Les
Dombes. After this he immersed himself in the preparations for the
Week of Prayer of January 1939. Its subject was to be the Sacrifice of
Christ and I was myself to have the privilege of being with him at
that time. I have already recorded my memories of this first visit of
mine to Lyons. How little I realized that before the Week of Prayer
that followed the curtain of war would have fallen between the Abbé
and his English friends!

Before this happened providence had allowed time for his teaching to be formulated, for his methods to be tried and for the foundations to be laid which however frail were to prove strong enough to
carry the burden of his testimony. Lyons had been entrusted with a
working-model for the observance of the Week of Prayer. From this
city the Tracts had gone forth into all lands. A large number of
distinguished theologians had taken part in the observance of the
Week at Lyons by giving oral instructions. The first circle of priests
and pastors had been meeting alternately in Catholic and Protestant
settings. The great network of friendships and of correspondence
was generating what the Abbé came to call the 'Invisible Monastery', the mystical fellowship of lives consecrated to sharing the
priestly prayer of Christ for unity. Especially fruitful had been the
visits to England where so many religious communities had fully
embraced his principles and aims. These principles were indeed soon
to be espoused by a large number of our bishops. Scandinavia was

238

beginning to feel his influence powerfully through Dr Rosendal. Perhaps no region had been more deeply affected than North Africa, in particular, Egypt, whose remarkable ecumenical history has still to be written. The Abbé's close friendship with the Protestant brothers of the Taizé community and with the Protestant sisterhood of Grandchamp ripened as the darkness fell. It was to be of primary importance in their development and is still bearing fruit.

After the actual outbreak of war in September 1939 communications were maintained with English and German friends through Switzerland until August 1940. Then came three and a half years of separation and darkness. The more one hears of conditions there, the more one comes to feel that nowhere during the war was life harder for those not actually fighting than in so-called unoccupied France, whose inhabitants were often close to starvation.

Before the darkness fell new hopes had dawned. The first of these was occasioned through the death of one great and holy pope, Pius XI, on 10 February 1939 and on 2 March through the election of another.

The decease of Pius XI called forth tributes throughout the world, largely by reason of his courageous struggle against the totalitarian powers. There followed anxious days of waiting while the conclave of cardinals made up its mind over the election of his successor. The interval was brief indeed. But this brief time of suspense is one of profound significance. There is in a predominantly Catholic country at such a time (as I experienced, then living in Paris) a strange feeling of stiffened spirits being liberated around one —*we* are having our share, hearts seem to say, through our representatives, in choosing the Sovereign Head of Christendom. But something else fresh, indeed unprecedented, was happening at this time even in countries far less closely connected with Rome. Prayer was being offered widely for the guidance of the Holy Spirit for the elective body.

It was chiefly the unknown priest of Lyons who had ensured this by letters to his friends in other lands. In England voices archiepiscopal and episcopal were raised. The *Platform*, the Journal of the Seven Years Association, issued its own call to prayer. Protestants in

Scandinavian countries found themselves called alike from press and pulpit to pray for the right choice in the election of the Pope. A highly-placed servant of the Swiss Government made the same demand. Metropolitan Eulogius asked the same of Orthodox Christians under his rule. The patriarch-prophet of the French Reformed Church, Wilfred Monod, wrote to the *Paris-Midi*—moved to do so, he explained, by a 'venerated Catholic priest'—to propose the observance by all of a minute of silence on the first day of the conclave.

The election of the Cardinal Secretary of State, Eugenio Pacelli, as pope followed more swiftly than had the election of any pope for more than three hundred years. He who was crowned as Pope Pius XII was already widely admired not only as a diplomatist and statesman of tried skill, long experience, and intrepid character, but also as one acutely aware of the evil of Christian disunity, particularly in its effect on the relations between Church and State.

The Pope's first utterances with their note of super-confessional universality, a note new in papal admonitions, brought the Abbé consolation and new hope. The Abbé writes:

> Amidst the terrible anguish of the hour, Peter shows magnificently his sense of how to play the part of Peter—how to show the world that the deepest meaning of his mission is to continue to be throughout the world the *Vicarius Christi Caritatis*.

> 'May the Almighty grant', said His Holiness in his Message to the World, 24 August, 1939, 'that this appeal of the Father of the Christian family, the servant of servants, who brings to mankind—unworthily indeed, but nevertheless really—the Person, the voice and the authority of Jesus Christ, shall find in the mind and in the hearts of men a ready and willing response.'

The first encyclical was issued on 20 October, shortly after the outbreak of war; entitled *Summi Pontificatus* and translated into English under the title *Darkness over all the Earth*, it was made the main theme of the Abbé's Tract for January 1940. At the same time he sent this encyclical, in the French translation which had already appeared, to his most influential friends in other Christian communions, asking for their frank comments on it. The Pope, to whom he would send their letters by grace of Cardinal Gerlier, would thus be furnished with evidence as to the impression his teaching was making upon those brethren who do not belong to the visible body of the Church to whom the Pope had specially addressed his affectionate greeting. The Abbé writes:

> I do not believe that any previous pontifical document has ever been so majestic and simple, nor that any has diffused so sweet and penetrating a light of the pure spirit of the Gospel, nor that in any there has been realized a concord so harmonious and so winning between the rights of truth and the duties of charity. Non-Catholic Christians are here for the first time in a pontifical document called 'brethren'—'separated brethren', it is true, but truly 'brethren'. Amid darkness and gloom this encyclical appears like the pillar of light for which hearts and minds were waiting.

The Abbé's letter, drawing attention to the Pope's noble admonition, evoked a large number of responses, mainly appreciative, from his friends in various communions. This will not surprise those who recall, read or reread, *Darkness over all the Earth*. There is no better introduction to the mind and spirit of 'the great neutral' who during his long reign of nearly twenty years was so deeply to influence the whole Christian world. Making clear from the first his belief that the peace of the world is bound up with the mystery of Christian Unity, the Pope raised his voice in the darkness not only to protest at the exorbitant claims and self-importance of modern states, but to demand consideration for the innocent multitudes condemned to suffer helplessly; and to proclaim that the only sound basis for peace treaties is the Natural Law implanted by God in the heart of man: the denial and rejection of this lies at the root of international conflicts. After reviewing the potentialities for good to be found in the basic social units of family and nation, he adds, 'Every nation has its own genius, its own qualities, springing from the hidden roots of its being'. But the renewal of the world so clearly needed can come, he observes, only through an interior spiritual and supernatural power, the exercise of which is assigned to the maternal office of the Church.

The reception of the encyclical by representatives of the Eastern Orthodox Church was a mixed one. In Paris the wells had been poisoned. An article in the journal *La Croix* had cited an instruction given by the Roman Catholic administrator apostolic of Moscow to military chaplains on how to deal with Eastern Orthodox soldiers who had recourse to their ministry: everything possible was to be done to 'convert' them. This prevented not only Professor Zander, always very sensitive with regard to such pastoral *léger de main*, but even the Metropolitan Eulogius from reading the Pope's message with clear eyes. However, Dr Nicolas Zernov, a Russian Orthodox theologian, writing from England in the name of the Fellowship of St Alban and St Sergius, praised the vigorous teaching with regard to the position of the Church in the modern world and the attitude assumed by the Pope towards the religious and moral agnosticism of our days. He specially values the treatment of the question of national character and language. He regrets, however—and in this he was by no means alone—the silence of the Pope with regard to the responsibility of Christians Catholic or non-Catholic for the disorder of the world when a challenging reprimand from such a source would do so much to restore fellowship in the Spirit.

The encyclical was received with appreciation by the Anglican men's religious communities of Nashdom, Kelham and Mirfield. The Abbot of Nashdom, who had send a message of homage at the Pope's enthronement, avowed himself especially touched by His Holiness' expression of gratitude for the good wishes of those who do not belong to the visible body of the Church and by the display of charity reflecting in its universality that of God himself. The Community of the Resurrection made the encyclical a subject of discussion at our Christmas General Chapter and as a result a letter in its name was drafted and approved expressing its deep sense of the value of the utterance. Recalling the recognition given by the Anglican representatives at the Conversations of Malines of the 'primacy of responsibility' accruing to the Pope for the welfare of Christendom, we promised to give respectful attention to any further instructions His Holiness should wish to issue on such great moral issues. We thanked him for his kind references to the separated brethren and for their inclusion in his prayers and apostolic benediction and promised the continuance of our prayers for His Holiness. We asked His Eminence the Archbishop of Lyons, Cardinal Gerlier, who was recording the effect of *Summi Pontificatus* on Christians of different confessions with a view to informing the Pope on his next visit to Rome, if he would be so kind as to offer His Holiness three recent works by members of our Community: *The Universal Church and the See of Rome* by Dr E. Symonds, C.R., *The Council of Trent and the Thirty-Nine Articles* by the same, and the newly published version of a recension of Dom Maurice Chauncy's *Passion and Martyrdom of the Holy English Carthusian Fathers*, edited by myself. The books carried the following dedication:

PATRI SANCTISSIMO
Communitas Resurrectionis
reverentiae pignus et caritatis
quod sit
et in piam memoriam
Josephi Mercier S.R.E. Cardinalis,
Caroli Gore et Walteri Howard Frere
Episcoporum Anglicanorum,
Caroli Vicecomitis Halifax
et pro studii testimonio
fideliter in illorum vestigiis ambulandi
omnemque in Christo veritatem exquirendi
UT OMNES UNUM SINT.
Mirfield, in Fest. Conv. B. Pauli Ap. MCMXL
"Cum tenebrae factae sunt
super universam terram."

Bishop Mounsey, one of our Prelate-Brethren, at that time assistant bishop of Bradford, wrote associating himself with this message of his brethren at Mirfield and observing that the encyclical 'strikes a fresh irenic note which gives great joy and great hope'. He regrets the failure of Anglicans in charity towards the Roman Church and the inability of Anglican church authorities to correct this failing. Dare he hope that Rome which speaks with such authority will influence the Roman Catholic clergy of England to show a more irenic spirit with regard to Anglicans?

Father Hebert of the Society of the Sacred Mission, Kelham, observed that whereas the various Christian groups until 1914 were under the protection of the bourgeois state which they regarded as their guardian, now being all on theological grounds opposed to the secular power, whether this be hostile or professedly friendly, they are turning more and more to the Pope as the leader of Christendom. Hence the warm interest shown in the accession of Pope Pius XII.

Theologians of the Lutheran Churches were likewise much edified by the encyclical. Pastor Rosendal wrote a glowing tribute from Sweden, impressed by the 'love and wisdom' of the Papal utterance, its 'audacity and clarity', its open-hearted generosity towards the whole of Christendom, the 'great knowledge' it betrays and its notable acquaintance with the life and thought of different parts of the world.

Leaders of the Calvinist Reformed Churches were the most enthusiastic of all, but at the same time offered the most valuable criticism. Pastor Wilfred Monod found the publication of this encyclical a blessed event in Christian history, preparing the way for 'the reintegration of Christianity on true spiritual foundations, the *Una Sancta* of the New Testament'.

Here again what has touched Pastor Monod's heart and those of his colleagues is the Pope's expression of regard for the 'separated brethren'—a spirit of charity which, he believes, if exercised on both sides might have prevented subsequent catastrophes involving the bitterness of present relations: such a spirit goes some way to vindicate for the author the right to style himself 'Sovereign Priest', 'Supreme Pastor', and 'universal Father'. The Christocentric character of the encyclical,[1] Pastor Jean de Saussure observes, placed as it is 'under the sign of Christ the King', appeals to the instinct of Protestants whose great pre-occupation in the Reformation was that Christ the King, obscured by the growth of secondary devotions, should come into his own again. The simplicity of style, the biblical character of its thought (sixty quotations from the Bible as against six from elsewhere) and the straightforward Christlike humanity of its address, reminiscent of the Saviour's 'compassion on the multitude' are also praised by Pastor Monod.

But from Protestants there are also stern criticisms. The conceptions of natural law and natural morality are distasteful to the Calvinist mind. Pastor Jean de Saussure finds in the document a failure to distinguish clearly between the Reformation and the Renaissance. If they were 'sisters' in their common return to antiquity, the first to Holy Scripture, the second to paganism, they soon showed themselves 'sisters at enmity', as in the conflicts between Erasmus and Luther. At the same time Pastor Strasser enquires with great courtesy but not without real concern: (1) Why the Pope ignores the action of other Churches against the Nazi and Communist dictatorships (not a word about the Oxford conference of 1937 or the courageous behaviour of Barth, Brunner and Niemöller towards the Nazis!); (2) Why the Pope protects the dictatorship of Franco, if dictatorship is contrary to the Bible; (3) Would the Pope who calls for unity be contented with anything short of submission from the 'separated brethren'? (4) Why is there not a single ray of penitence on the Roman side to relieve the sustained proclamation of the claims of the Catholic Church and its Head?

These are questions which Pope Pius XII could perhaps never have answered satisfactorily because he could never have heard them aright. His character was a consummate expression of the heroic priestly piety and rich human culture of the Counter-Reformation in all its depth and breadth. But the range of his vision was limited by the tradition he so perfectly developed. The Papacy of the Counter-Reformation had no use for councils except to perfect its monarchy by the affirmation of its sovereignty and infallibility. The successor to Pope Pius XII, John XXIII, showed himself as clearly aware of such questions as was Abbé Couturier himself and responded to them as generously as the Abbé could have hoped. Best of all the note of penitence for disunity as caused in part by the sins of Roman Catholics—a note silent in papal pronouncements since the reign of Adrian VI (1522-3)—is heard again in his utterances and in those of the present pope, Paul VI.[2]

These blessings when the Abbé died were still in the unknown future, to be purchased by his sacrificial prayer and that of the whole Church. Nevertheless there reigned at Rome during the fourteen remaining years of his life as Pope Pius XII one for whom he had as deep an admiration as he had had for the preceding pope, Pius XI, who during his long reign (1922–39) had so often insisted that every venture towards unity must begin by mutual knowledge and love. Though the high hopes he rested in Pius XII were disappointed, he never ceased to do everything he could to serve him filially for the glory of God and the union of Christians. He believed that in the Papacy our Lord had given us in and through the apostle Peter a necessary visible centre of unity, of pastoral responsibility and of universal love. This entailed that the Pope as chief Shepherd on earth must know his own and be known of them. He must know also the principles and methods of those of his flock who are working to fulfil our Lord's aim for unity. The Abbé's inspired conduct with regard to securing the prayers of the separated brethren over the election of the Pope and his communication to Pius XII of all that he could discover concerning their welcome of his first encyclical were significant instances of his devoted service of the Pope and of the Church through him. We must once again recall that he managed to accomplish these things in the margin of what was already a specially full life.

Eight years later when the World Council of Churches had been brought to birth at the Assembly of Amsterdam (1948) and ecumenism was presenting new problems at Rome, the Abbé sent to His Holiness a memoir concerning the experience of interconfessional gatherings he had gained since 1937. He gave details with regard to fifteen such meetings, recording the names of the participants Catholic and Protestant, the prayerful character and great fruitfulness of these gatherings, and the testimony of those present as to their value. He observed that at such conferences prayer in common was a necessary complement of work in common. Devotions used had included the Lord's Prayer, prayer to the Holy Spirit, hymns, biblical meditations and psalms.

The Abbé was also anxious that the Pope should become personally acquainted with some of the separated brethren and that these in turn, besides being introduced to the reigning occupant of the See of Peter, should have a real rather than a merely theoretic knowledge concerning the function of the Papacy and the system of Roman ecclesiastical government. So with a tact and thoroughness and consideration all his own the Abbé planned visits to Rome for his friends, Eastern Orthodox, Anglican, Calvinist, Lutheran, and in their favour begged the good offices of his Catholic brethren. Consequently Cardinal Gerlier, the Sulpician Fathers, the priests at the French church of St Louis in Rome, the Benedictine monks of the monastery of San Girolamo, the professors at the Gregorian university, the Superiors of several women's communities, and other friends proved their esteem and affection for the Abbé Couturier by their gracious hospitality and their eagerness to help the visitors to see all that was best in Rome and especially to secure audiences with His Holiness and with his trusted lieutenant, Mgr Montini.[3] There was for friends of the Abbé special facility of access to the latter, because Abbé Travia, Mgr Montini's assistant, ministered to the Dames de Nazareth, the community to which Mère Lepage, the aunt of Abbé Couturier, belonged.

I myself was to have in 1949 the privilege of such a visit to Rome. It was for me a time of great enrichment. There was the privilege of being received in special audience by His Holiness whose courtesy and understanding were unforgettable. This gave an opportunity of making clear the deep regard for the Papacy maintained by that majority of Anglo-Catholics whose point of view is that which was presented by the majority of our representatives at Malines and whose convictions prevent them from accepting as articles of faith the Roman dogmatic definitions of this and the last century. How many thousands of Anglicans would attest that the sixteenth-century repudiation by the Church of England, at a crisis in the nation's political history, of the Pope's civil jurisdiction in our land[4] and our doctrinal disagreements both then and later have not destroyed our regard for Rome! How much has remained amongst Anglican churchmen from James I[5] to the present day of the deep reverence accorded by tradition to the Apostolic See, together with a sense of its unique responsibility—and consequent moral authority—for the care of the welfare of Christendom as a whole![6]

Of greater significance were the visits of Roger Schutz and Max Thurian, the founder-brethren of the Calvinist community of Taizé near Cluny in Burgundy. The first of these visits was the result of the papal *Monitum* about attendance at ecumenical gatherings, forbidding, except to those with special papal dispensation, the attendance of Catholics at the Assembly of Amsterdam (1948) which was to give birth to the World Council of Churches. This document seemed to be a lapse from the irenic policy of the Papacy, as there had been Catholic observers present with papal sanction at the great conferences of 1937 at Oxford and Edinburgh. One of the Taizé Brethren had criticized the Roman change of attitude courteously but firmly in the Protestant review *Verbum Caro*: though allowing that the motive of the change was to avoid equivocation, the author said that such rigidity could not but give to Protestant minds the impression of weakness and fear. To the Abbé it seemed clear that there was misunderstanding on both sides which a visit of Brothers Roger and Max to the Vatican might resolve. The consequent visit, the first of many, was certainly fruitful. It influenced the Instruction, explaining the *Monitum*, issued at the end of the following year (1949) under the heading *Ecclesia Catholica*. In this for the first time the Roman Church, without abandoning that claim to be the one true Church which is an intrinsic element of its faith, recognizes the great fact of the ecumenical movement which it welcomes as having arisen under the inspiration of the grace of the Holy Spirit and as a cause of holy joy in the Lord. It further outlines the pastoral attitude to be taken towards this movement. It entrusts the duty of observing, promoting and prudently directing it to diocesan bishops, giving precise regulations regarding ecumenical conferences between Catholics and other Christians. It emphasizes the need in this request of Christian unity for holiness in the clergy and the faithful alike and above all for the special grace of humility.

Nevertheless though this document registered a real advance, its rigidity still dissatisfied Protestants. Hence a second visit of the Brothers of Taizé especially in view of the coming ecumenical conference at Lund which was to deal with the difficult problem of the final integration of 'Faith and Order' into the World Council of Churches. The Brethren had also in mind the widely-known possibility that the Pope intended to define the Assumption of the Virgin Mary as a necessary article of faith.

On this second visit before being received by the Pope the Brethren saw not only Mgr Montini, but Mgr Ottaviani, the Assessor of the Holy Office. He gave them to understand to their satisfaction that in principle the presence of Catholic theologians as unofficial observers at ecumenical gatherings was with safeguards permitted. It also transpired that prayer in common might include the Psalter and the Credo as well as the Lord's Prayer. When the Brethren spoke about the widespread abuses in devotion to the Blessed Virgin Mary which so shock Protestants, Mgr Ottaviani expressed sympathy but did not feel he could condemn the childish expressions of loving piety practised by the more immature races. The rationalist errors current in Protestant circles ought to be just as much a matter of concern to his visitors. When they visited Pius XII himself it was to be told that the Church through the almost unanimous voice of the episcopate required the dogmatic definition of the Assumption and that His Holiness felt it his duty to listen to the Church in whom the Spirit speaks. The Brethren were outspoken as to the disastrous estrangement which they believed this must involve for Protestants, just at the moment when some understanding on the subject of the Virgin Mary was in sight. Though the Pope pronounced that his decision was irrevocable, they felt certain that their journey had not been in vain. Indeed the friendship between the Community of Taizé and the leaders of the Roman Church has proved a source of much blessing to all who seek unity. But it is time that this Protestant family was properly introduced to the reader, especially as they constituted for Abbé Couturier a second beam of light in the darkness.

NOTES

1 The encyclical opens by the Pope dedicating his reign to the Sacred Heart of Jesus and declaring that his sole principle will be to proclaim the universal Kingship of Christ.

² Père Michalon, member of the Secretariat for the Unity of Christians, writes from Rome, where he is attending the second session of the Second Vatican Council: 'In 1947 Abbé Couturier had called Catholics to enter upon a course of penitence and repentance for the faults committed against their brethren; and he looked forward to the hour when the Pope would pronounce the *mea culpa*, in humility and love. Sixteen years have passed. His expectations have been surpassed: it is at the heart of the assembly of the whole Catholic episcopate, in full session of the Council, before the fully qualified representatives of the non-Catholic churches, that Paul VI, in the name of the Catholic Church, implores the pardon of God and of the brethren. By love and humility henceforth there is nothing for which we may not hope. May we not believe in the same spiritual attitude in all the Churches?' (26 October, 1963).

³ Now His Holiness Pope Paul VI. He was then the Pope's 'substitute' (*Sostituto*) in the office of Secretary of State.

⁴ It is sometimes forgotten that the last but one of the Thirty-nine Articles which contains the denial of 'the Bishop of Rome's jurisdiction in our land' is entitled *Of the Civil Magistrate*.

⁵ King James I said before Parliament, 'I acknowledge the Church of Rome as our Mother Church'. In his *Premonition to all Christian Monarchs* he wrote: 'Let (the Bishop of Rome) in God's name be *Primus Episcopus inter omnes Episcopos* and *Princeps Apostolorum*; so it be no otherwise but as Peter was *Princeps Apostolorum.*' When a pamphlet by Richard Montague defending the Real Presence, the necessity of Sacramental Absolution and the use of images was denounced as 'popish', he exclaimed, 'If this is to be a papist, so am I a papist.'

⁶ Cf. the summary of the Conversations at Malines: 'Thus the primacy of the Pope is not merely a primacy of honour, but it implies a duty of solicitude and of activity within the universal church for the general good, in such wise that the Pope should be in fact a centre of unity and a head which exercises authority over the whole. . . .'—G. K. A. Bell (ed.), *Documents on Christian Unity* (2nd Series), London: O.U.P., 1930, pp. 42f.

19

THE PROTESTANT COMMUNITIES

WHAT place is there for religious communities within the
Reformed Churches? All the reformers, Luther, Calvin,
Melanchthon, Zwingli, Bucer rejected the Religious Life, partly on
account of abuses attendant upon it in their day, partly on what
appeared then to be scriptural grounds. They left open two tiny
loopholes. Some of them saw the possible value of quasi-religious
communities for the training of pastors; and Bucer in particular saw
the possibility of a vocation to celibacy for a period of years or even
for life. But all had a strong distrust of external vows.

With regard to the first loophole, the heroic young Lutheran
theologian, Dietrich Bonhoeffer, executed by the Nazis in 1945, had
during their régime created surreptitiously a 'college for the training
of pastors', and, with a view to the realization of this, had written a
book called *Life Together*.[1] I heard it read aloud at meals when enjoying the hospitality of the Swiss Calvinist Sisterhood at Grandchamp,
of which I shall be speaking shortly. When asked how I liked the
book, I could only reply, 'It strikes me as a description of our life at
Mirfield'. It was later discovered from his correspondence with our
Superior, Father Talbot, that Bonhoeffer stayed with us during his
time in England (1933–5). It seems that he was the early forerunner
of the many visitors to us from Protestant religious communities,
Calvinist and Lutheran, men and women, French, Swiss, German,
and Swedish, seeking to enlarge their knowledge of the Religious Life.[2]

No one can any longer say that religious communities are an
intrusion into the life of the Reformed Churches—that they are
imitations of Roman Catholic or medieval or Eastern Orthodox

models. They spring from within their own tradition as spearpoints of a wider renewal—biblical, liturgical and ecumenical.

> They show a remarkable elasticity: they know themselves to be communities *en marche*. To justify their life they avail themselves of the loopholes left by the Reformers, but they go beyond the Reformers' position. . . . For their life-long commitments to celibacy, to community of goods and to acceptance of authority they avoid the word 'vows' and use the French term '*engagements*'.[3]

We are not surprised to find even so intransigent a Protestant as the great theologian, Karl Barth, giving in his *Church Dogmatics* IV 2 a real, though guarded, welcome to the Religious Life in principle and to these modern evangelical communities in particular. Of these communities the Calvinist Brotherhood of Taizé was the earliest to find itself and is the most widely known and honoured.

It was at Christmas 1940 that the young Swiss pastor, Roger Schutz, founder and prior of the Community of Taizé, called upon the already ageing priest-schoolmaster of Lyons, whom he was later to recognize as having the rôle of John the Baptist, the prophet and more than prophet of the ecumenical age. The village of Taizé, from which Roger Schutz came to pay his visit was a remote spot in the region between Dijon and Lyons, close to the little town of Cluny, which claims an eminent place in medieval monastic history, and not too far from the Swiss border. He had bought there a large château, long uninhabited, and had made it a refuge for Jews and other political refugees as well as for abandoned children. Later—in 1942—to escape the Nazi police, he went to Geneva, where he was joined by another theologian and by students of engineering and medicine who shared his desire for the Christian community life. But before the young men's departure to Switzerland, Abbé Couturier, with Père Villain, had made his first visit to Taizé, where they found Roger Schutz living in solitude. The Abbé was to visit Frère Roger and his brethren frequently in years to come, the most welcome and perhaps the most influential of all their visitors.[4]

When peace came, the little brotherhood formed in Geneva returned to Taizé. Their number having been enlarged by would-be brothers from Paris and elsewhere, they undertook the rebuilding of the village, then in ruins, and restored the lovely twelfth-century church, originally the work of the monks of Cluny. In Eastertide 1949 the first seven brethren committed themselves to *engagement* for life. A rule was developed which was first printed only in 1962, after ten years of its practice, and this was followed soon by a commentary. They are moving documents, full of wisdom, the work of the inspiring mind of Roger Schutz. The members of the Brotherhood are drawn from more than one Protestant confession, and it has been from the beginning international in character. Its worship is designed to restore to Protestantism the liturgical treasures of the medieval and earlier centuries, and the Brethren have learned gladly from Eastern Orthodoxy and from the Church of England, as well as from the Liturgical Movement in the Roman Catholic Church. All the brothers engage in some form of labour: several labour with their hands in Taizé itself, including printers, a doctor and a mason, as well as artists in pottery and painting; others work as pastors in parishes; one brother has been engaged in youth work in Africa, others in heavy industrial work. Yet another is occupied in the sale of gramophone records. Agriculture is not neglected: their farm has set a standard in modern techniques. The community has been largely responsible for the publication of the widely influential quarterly theological review *Verbum Caro*.[5] The creative and prophetic mind of the prior, Frère Roger, works in close alliance with another mind of similar devotion and integrity, but more specifically theological and liturgical in its interests and range, that of his friend, Pastor Max Thurian, the theologian of the community.

The Rule stresses the primacy of worship and calls for interior silence, meditation on the Beatitudes, prayer three times a day, and intercession for the Church and the world. The Brotherhood seeks to take the Gospel realistically and to let it speak to men living in the world. Each brother is to do what he believes Christ would have done in the vocation which God has chosen for him. In recent years brothers have been living in such centres of tension and need as Marseilles among the working-classes, the Ivory Coast, and Muslim districts in Algeria, not to mention Coventry and Sheffield.

Some of these activities of the Community have developed since the Abbé's death; but it grew very swiftly in these directions, and in so doing was a great source of happiness to him. No one who reads the Rule and Commentary on the Rule or the more recent works of Roger Schutz translated under the English title *This Day Belongs to God* (Faith Press, 1961) and its sequel *Unity Man's Tomorrow* (Faith Press, 1962) can fail to be impressed by the Community's concern for the renewal of the Church by the recovery of Christian Unity. For example, the preamble of the Rule closes with these words in italics:

> *Never take part in the scandal of the separation of Christians, proclaiming all so easily the love of our neighbour, but remaining divided. Have the passion for the unity of the Body of Christ.*[6]

Frère Roger has given us a moving account of his relations with Abbé Couturier.[7] From his first visit to this unknown priest in his unimpressive setting, to one entirely devoid of pretensions who, so far from being in touch with the aspirations of modern man, struck him as belonging to a past generation, he realized that God had chosen Paul Couturier to be the instrument of a movement whose immensity perhaps even he himself did not divine.

The humble condition in which Abbé Couturier lived, the absence of gifts which might have won him distinction emphasize the manifest action of God, who can, for the great concerns of his Church, make use of instruments of apparently the most modest kind. . . .

His immense charity never led him to deviate from the truth. He expressed himself loyally, and for him, as for many others, the ecumenical dialogue was an opportunity of rethinking doctrine with a solid thoroughness. He expressed the position of his Church with even greater clarity. He declared that the Roman Church was built on rock and rock it would remain. He recalled that his vision of unity would have to take account of the intransigent utterance of a Church which knows what it believes. This growing eagerness to express before Protestants the real attitude of his Church, permeated as it was by a prophetic hope of unity, is in my opinion the truest ground of his authority with all, both Catholics and Protestants.

At the same time the Abbé was far from seeming a stranger to Protestantism. Frère Roger recalls:

> He knew the treasure of the Reformed Church, and spoke of it with simple fervour. He loved its pastors and layfolk. This penetrating insight into our Church was so unexpected on the part of a priest that this alone captured one's attention.

The attendance of Roger Schutz and Max Thurian at the retreat conference of the interconfessional circle held at the monastery of La Trappe des Dombes in September 1942 was, along with the visit of Frère Roger to the Abbé and his return visit to Taizé, a landmark in the history of the Community's foundation. This conference took place two months before the closing of the Franco-Swiss frontier, by which time the brothers had established themselves in Geneva. So it constituted for them a kind of farewell to Christian France—it was not clear that they would return to make their home in France. Roger Schutz had long studied the history of Port Royal, which had exercised a profound influence upon him. He felt immediately at home with the monks and was moved to deep admiration by the silence and realism of the Trappist life. Max Thurian revelled in the theological dialectic of the conference and was stimulated by the biblical and patristic exposition given by the Catholics present, who had drunk deep of the 'new theology', as it came to be called, of which Père Lubac, S.J., of Lyons was the chief protagonist.

Both Roger and Max conceived there a great devotion to the cause of ecumenism. They found themselves in a fellowship of Catholics and Protestants wherein sheep-stealing is regarded with horror, where it is understood that individual 'conversions' retard union; that union is rather advanced by each coming as close in sympathy and humility to Christ indwelling in his fellow-Christians of other confessions as grateful loyalty to Christ in his own heritage allows. In this loyalty we are to pray, worship and hope, not as standing over against schismatics, but as along with fellow-Christians of other confessions within the universal Catholic Church of the baptized—the Body of Christ on whose life Protestants are as dependent as their Catholic brethren, but wherein they claim a

255

God-given prophetic function. All this, which had come to be taken for granted in this circle, was the result of the intuition, the integrity, the prayer and the influence of Abbé Couturier, whose friendship had drawn them to be present. Brethren from Taizé have attended the yearly conferences ever since their full resumption in 1946, and their home at Taizé is usually the place of meeting in the alternate years, when the Protestants are hosts to the conference.

There is no doubt that this very fruitful friendship between the Abbé and the Brethren of Taizé was greatly helped in its early years by that between him and the Calvinist Sisters of Grandchamp near Neuchâtel in Switzerland. Indeed the Abbé's friendship with Grandchamp preceded his friendship with Taizé, and his perfect trust in both communities and his understanding of them must have been one of the bonds between these two Protestant societies before they became a single family in Christ. Abbé Couturier had been consulted about the foundation and formation of the Sisterhood. This grew out of the discovery, by some ladies who had offered hospitality in their home to others seeking the quiet of a periodical spiritual retreat, of the wonderful fruitfulness of such times of recollection. The foundation members belonged to the guild called the *Third Order of Watchers*, founded in 1923 by the great pastor, Wilfred Monod, whose name has several times occurred in this book. It was an association of Christians living as fully as possible in the spirit of the Beatitudes. The word *Watchers* in its title echoed the Saviour's injunction to 'watch and pray': the first words, *Third Order*, are there to recall the Franciscan Third Order, the fellowship surrounding the brothers and sisters who formed the First and Second Orders in the spiritual family of St Francis of Assisi. They are justified only as it were proleptically—as a prophecy of good things to come. Later Frère Roger was to write:

> Wilfred Monod himself in creating the *Third Order of Watchers* looked forward to the two Orders which should uphold it. I rejoice to say that the Second Order is for us the Community of the Sisters of Grandchamp, whose emergence and growth are so marvellous, both as regards profound life in the Church and direct action in the world.

Pastor Monod and Abbé Couturier had been friends since 1938, and prayed daily for one another. They never had the joy of meeting in the flesh, but their letters are those of intimate friends. I had the privilege in 1939 of calling on the old man at the Abbé's request, so that our library at Mirfield became enriched with a graciously inscribed copy of M. Monod's fascinating memoirs, *Après la journée 1867–1937 (Souvenirs et Visions)*.[8] This book closes with the motto of the *Third Order of Watchers*: it consists of three words which unite that guild closely to their great founder, to the First and Second Orders foreseen by him, since his death splendidly realized; in my mind also to Paul Irénée Couturier who was so close in spirit and friendship to all these:

Joy, Simplicity, Compassion.

NOTES

[1] Dietrich Bonhoeffer, *Life Together*, English trans., London: SCM Press, 1954.

[2] The 'College' directed by Bonhoeffer was not formed after any existing model. An attempt was made there to live the life of a Christian community—to show how in the twentieth century a Christian life should be lived in a spirit of genuine brotherhood and how such a life could grow naturally and freely if men belonged entirely to our Lord and were therefore in brotherly love one to another. Young ministers who came to the college from all over the Reich learned this sorely needed lesson. See Memoir of Bonhoeffer by G. Leibholz in D. Bonhoeffer, *The Cost of Discipleship*, complete ed., London: SCM Press, 1959, p. 12.

[3] S. M. Gibbard, S.S.J.E., *Theology* LXV, 1962, pp. 37ff.

[4] A copy of Roger Schutz, *Introduction à la vie communautaire* (Geneva: Labor et Fides; Paris: Editions 'Je sers', 1944) bears the inscription 'To our dear spiritual father, Monsieur l'Abbé Couturier, Roger Schutz, Max Thurian'.

[5] This journal often contains papers read at interconfessional gatherings at Les Dombes or Taizé.

[6] Besides the books by Roger Schutz mentioned and the Rule and Commentary (*La regle . . . avec directives spirituelles,* Taizé, 1962), see *Ecclesia,* No. 154, 1962, pp. 136–41, and K. S. Latourette, *Christianity in a Revolutionary Age,* vol. IV, London: Eyre and Spottiswoode, 1962, pp. 378f.

[7] *Paul Couturier, apôtre de l' Unité chrétienne: Témoignages,* pp. 167–74.

[8] Paris: Grasset, 1938.

20

INFLUENCE ON THE
SCANDINAVIAN CHURCHES

ANOTHER source of happiness during the dark years of war and enemy occupation was the growth of prayer for Christian Unity among the Lutherans of the Scandinavian countries. Here the way was led by a Swedish minister who was to become one of the Abbé's most devoted and understanding disciples—Dr Gunnar Rosendal, the vicar of Osby in southern Sweden. The significance of his ecumenical rôle can only be grasped by recalling the character and history of the Swedish Church.

In Sweden, a country which had great Catholic traditions, the Reformation of the sixteenth century was political rather than religious. Gustaf Vasa, who in 1524 headed the war of independence against Denmark, broke with the Pope. But though under his protection, the chief leaders of the Church were Olaus Petri and Laurentius Petri, two brothers who had studied at Luther's university of Wittenberg and who disseminated the reformer's ideas, along with the spread of Lutheran doctrine, Catholic order and Sacraments were retained. One of his successors (King John III) tried to reunite the Swedish Church with Rome, but was unsuccessful. The Calvinist designs of his successor, Charles IX, failed likewise. In 1593 the Swedes adopted the Augsburg Confession, thus formally committing themselves to Lutheranism. In the eighteenth century pietism and other forms of revivalism had great influence in Sweden despite attempts to repress them by law. In the first half of the nineteenth century there followed a wave of latitudinarianism, succeeded in its turn at the beginning of the second half by an evangelical revival influenced by English Methodism, a revival which stimulated the growth of dissent and within the Church itself almost destroyed sacramental religion. But the main influence of the national Church, however lacking in inspiring power, was throughout orthodox and conservative, so that there was always the possibility of recovery into sacramental and Catholic ways.

· The twentieth century has seen a real revival of church life in Sweden. Until his death in 1931 its history was largely that of the great Archbishop Söderblom, a champion of Christian Reunion, the founder of the 'Life and Work' movement. A challenging critic of conservative orthodoxy, he aimed always within Sweden at a renewal and deepening of Lutheranism. In the Young Church Movement, of which he was the leader, though the recovery of traditional customs encouraged some degree of liturgical recovery, a stress on the importance of personality and on the preaching of the Cross overshadowed the idea of the Church. It was not until 1935 that the publication of a book called *Church Renewal* by Dr Gunnar Rosendal drew attention to the objects of a new movement which may well be called by this title. This movement, which bears the marks of Anglican influence, aims at reviving in Sweden the traditional conception of the Church. 'Church renewal' is centred on a revival of the sacramental life of the Church combined with a new sense of the value of its ministry as derived through the Apostolic Succession from Christ himself.

The movement certainly bears a close resemblance to the Oxford Movement of the 1830s in England. Dr Rosendal has been spoken of as the Dr Pusey of the Swedish Church. Though lacking the erudition of the great Anglican divine, he has a similar devotion to the Church, the same vision as that of the Oxford leader, and he is winning something of the same prestige—or notoriety, as the enemies of both would doubtless have styled it. He has also a great joviality and geniality, notably absent from the temperament and ideals of Dr Pusey. He has taken similar steps towards the revival in the national church life of religious communities. In general he has set on foot a Catholic revival which, if it has not sprung from the universities, has certainly had its effects within them. Of the small but very live Catholicizing party in the Swedish Church Dr Rosendal has indubitably been the leader-in-chief.

Dr Rosendal also resembles the great canon of Christ Church, Oxford, in being as much a man of prayer as he is a man of action. This constituted the bond between him and Abbé Couturier, who sent him in 1936 his article on Universal Prayer. The vicar of Osby replied:

> Yes, I am in absolute agreement, the only way of winning unity is the way of prayer.

He proceeded to hold a meeting of a group of clergy, before whom he gave an outline of Abbé Couturier's teaching with a commentary on it. Next January in the Week of Prayer he celebrated the Eucharist with special intention for unity, regarding this as the foundation-stone of his parochial work for this cause. Before the close of the year, in preparation for the Week of Prayer in the coming January, he circularized bishops, clergy and the Society of St Bridget, a fellowship of devout men and women, asking all to join in the prayer for unity.

> None has the right to pray for the victory of his own Church, but all are to unite in prayer that unity may be realized in the manner and at the moment that God wills.

Where possible, it is urged, there should be not only special prayers, but also a sermon on unity. (This means an extra sermon; for in Sweden the national Minister of Religion, a state official, controls the text for the clergy's Sunday sermons.)

The result of this appeal was gratifying. Six out of the dozen bishops observed the week with devotion. Next year (1939) there was a further advance, including the dissemination of 2,000 tracts, with as many copies of the Litany for Unity and an article in each of the chief papers. At Osby the office of Compline was said daily with an address on unity, a new altar of St Peter was dedicated with this intention, and a retreat of three days was held for clergy specially engaged in this work. Later in this year a conference took place between three Catholic priests and three Swedish pastors. The outbreak of war prevented Dr Rosendal from going to Lyons in January 1940 to give a radio message there for the Abbé. Instead he busied himself with sending out 3,000 tracts and composing articles for ten papers. Seventy-five clergy found their way that year to the Unity Retreat, at which some thirty were expected.

Dr Rosendal had also corresponded with Father Wattson of the Society of the Atonement who seemed to him to share his own passion for unity. But he soon realized that the concord did not go very deep—that it was wholly impossible for him to share in the Intentions that Father Wattson was propagating in his crusade for unity. Each of these demanded the conversion or submission of this or that part of Christendom to Rome. The reply which Dr Rosendal received from Wattson to his protest proved both in tone and content wholly inadequate—Father Wattson could only point to his Anglican Papalist supporters. Abbé Couturier, in a letter already quoted,[1] though assigning to the Society of the Atonement the credit for initiating the January time of prayer, showed himself wholly understanding with regard to this problem of conscience and serenely certain that God awaits this universal prayer expressed in terms of so many spiritual modes that he may himself reward its sincerity with the divine gift of unity. The Abbé's letters opened the eyes of the pastor to the depth of his correspondent's faith in the mysterious power of prayer—power infinite and ever triumphant. But as to this more light was to be given him later when he came to the monastery of La Trappe des Dombes to take part in the conference of the interconfessional circle of pastors and priests. There he was to meet Calvinists for the first time.

Before that he was to be met at the station at Lyons by the priest whose letters had already so much influenced him and whom he was to come to call '*mon Abbé*', regarding himself as 'his monk' in the work for Christian Unity and the Abbé as the Abbot of the Invisible Monastery.

Yes, [the Abbé] was there, just as I had imagined him! At the exit of the Gare de Perrache I saw him with his pale countenance, his features so finely chiselled, his light smile, frail, ascetic, genial and yet very serious, full of silent dignity. He was there with his *béret basque*, his cloak, his black soutane. An aristocrat from head to foot. He seemed a little tired; from year to year he would seem a little more so.

During the gathering at La Trappe des Dombes, Dr Rosendal regaled the company with a description of his Catholicizing, even anti-Protestant, campaigns in Sweden. This news he found was coldly received by all, not only by the Calvinist pastors. He awoke to the realization that his attitude towards his Protestant brethren was in essence just the same as that of Father Wattson towards all non-Catholics: moreover that endeavour after unity cannot ever worthily take the form of a crusade *against* any other form of Christianity.

Four years later he came once again to Lyons to see Abbé Couturier on his way to Rome, where he was received in special audience by His Holiness, conversed with Mgr Montini and with many other distinguished persons. He returned to Sweden with a more realistic grasp of the gulf separating high-church Lutheranism from Rome. There was that in the spiritual atmosphere of Rome where the dogma of the Assumption of the Virgin had been recently proclaimed, which, he wrote, made him admire even more the work of Abbé Couturier. More keenly than ever he prized the wisdom of his Abbé's innocence in calling all in simplicity to unite their wills with the Prayer of Jesus the eternal and sovereign High Priest and to live in spiritual emulation one with another, striving continually to deepen their Church's life and teaching by closer devotion to Jesus Christ, our common Saviour and by greater faithfulness to the guidance of the Holy Spirit, in obedience to whom we are already one in the Holy Trinity.

As regards the other Scandinavian countries, it was another Swedish friend, Dr N. Ehrenström, secretary of the Study Department of the World Council of Churches in Geneva, who did most to help Abbé Couturier to propagate there the universal prayer for unity. He had already been in correspondence with Arne Bugge in Denmark, who diffused his Tracts there, and, at his suggestion, had written articles for the Danish Press. In Norway he had correspondents in the brotherhood, *Ordo Crucis*. Moreover, he had advised Père Villain, who had been invited to Osby, to take any opportunity that might present itself to visit Norway and Denmark as well as Sweden. The opening awaited came through Dr Ehrenström in 1951 —an invitation to address conferences in Denmark, Norway and Sweden, organized by centres in close contact with the World Council. In all these countries Père Villain had an enthusiastic reception. He was able to promote meetings between ministers of the national Lutheran Churches, often overwhelmingly more numerous in proportion, and priests of the tiny Roman Catholic minorities. He did his best to stimulate the growth of the Religious Life. Its witness and work of reparation is plainly needed in Christian communities which, despite their special and sometimes grievous troubles in relation with the State, are so opulent and so securely established. It was not long before two Swedish girls, the first in Sweden to make their profession to the Religious Life since the Reformation, came to Lyons to ask Abbé Couturier for his blessing on their entry upon a life so unfamiliar and strange to the Lutheran Church of the Swedish nation.

NOTES

[1] See pp. 63, 65.

21

THE PRISONER OF THE LORD

DURING the three years of darkness that befell the French nation between its year of warfare, closing in its capitulation, and its liberation in 1944, the Abbé's ministry was chiefly one of prayer and suffering, though the demands made on his priestly care by post were still of dimensions that would have daunted many a priest. In time of peace, though constantly in ill-health, he had always gone short of warmth and food, because only so could he save money necessary for the printing of the tracts and notices and for the postage of his huge correspondence. But now conditions had become incapacitating, France being reduced sometimes in some regions close to famine.

> With the rigorous fast, reduced practically to vegetarian fare, a diabetic can do practically nothing. How many days I have to spend, apart from the inviolable time of prayer, sitting powerless before work which accumulates and correspondence lying in disorderly heaps! A heavy weight, this, to bear *in facie Domini*. But I trust all to him, since he lets things happen thus. *Benedicam Dominum in omni tempore.*

But this was only a small part of his suffering. It somehow happened that a cloud of misunderstanding and calumny wrapped him round in this period, even at times obscuring him from so understanding a mind as that of his Archbishop. There had been in 1939 the refusal of permission to go to England a third time. There was the refusal of permission to go to ecumenical gatherings, including a conference of the interconfessional circle arranged at Taizé.

264

But these were only symptoms of official distrust springing from deeper hostility. He was denounced, vilified, narrowly watched (especially when at a distance from home) with regard to behaviour and actions which were then judged dangerously imprudent, but which were such as now meet with general approval. Some of his prayers were censured because they contained generous phrases identical with those since then found coming from the mouth of Pope John XXIII.

'I have seen him weep', says Père Villain of the Abbé at this time, 'because he was literally punished'. There were currents of *intégrisme* from time to time in the spiritual atmosphere so that minds normally accounted judicious found him guilty alternatively of pietism or of liberalism, along with a subjectivism due to excessive engrossment in psychology. Later, when the phrase 'false irenism' was found in the encyclical *Humani generis* (1950), the words were regarded as constituting an official condemnation of the way followed by Abbé Couturier and his school.

As a matter of fact, those who had seen and heard Abbé Couturier at work read the sentences about Reunion in this encyclical with relief. They seemed to us to contain an index of the faults and perils avoided in the Abbé's interconfessional circles. But some of us were at once aware that the paragraph would be said to contain a condemnation of him. The mystery of iniquity through which the holy city Sion is at the same time Babylon wherein the Lord is crucified has as one of its corollaries the principle defined by the Abbé himself:

> Those who suffer for the Church must also suffer *through* the Church.

It is hard for the keen churchman to remember how close the Catholic temper comes to Pharisaism, and that it is a truly religious zeal—righteousness after the law—which persecutes most keenly God's servants, the prophets. Special blessings are no doubt reserved for those who acknowledge that they have so offended—that through the epiphany and passion of Christ in his hidden servants, the Kingdom of God coming upon them has 'caught them napping'.

But in the meantime none knew better than Paul Couturier how 'going through the vale of misery to use it for a well so that the pools' might fill with the water of life.

> Man proposes and God disposes. . . . Our meeting was not in the plan of God. For you and for us there is only one attitude possible!—Glory be to God! May his will be done! A setback. . . . What a grace! What a test! there is some inner meaning which escapes us and which we must adore in love! Our march towards Unity has just taken a great step forward! God has permitted a setback! ! ! He must then be preparing great things. It is for us to let ourselves be purified, impoverished of our desires, our views, our self-will. We must enter into a great and divine mystery, that of the great suffering—mystery wherein future reconciliations are forged. Does that mean we shall not go on? . . . Of course we shall! With still more prayer, tenacity and submission to his will. But we shall continue on the higher level of thanksgiving which this causes to spring from our souls.

The darkness may be counted as closing in Easter 1944; for after that final stripping, which seemed to many to set a divine seal on his work and life, he was in many ways unassailable. On 11 April (Tuesday in Easter Week) he was arrested by the Gestapo on the stairs of No. 5 Rue du Plat, as he was on his way home to his sister. They pulled him down into the street, but he got up and said in a loud voice for the benefit of bystanders, 'I love Germans, but I hate the Gestapo!' They got him out of the way in a car. So it was that he followed his friend, Professor Richard, of the Seminaire Universitaire (who was later sent to Germany) into the prison of Montluc. Six weeks later it was the turn of his young Swiss Protestant friend, Pastor Roland de Pury, arrested by police spies in church at the opening of the service. Before his release he had dedicated his book, *Living Stones*, to the memory of one whom he believed to have died in prison—'of Abbé Couturier, apostle of Unity, deceased at Montluc in May 1944'. His venerated friend was not dead, but lived and he was to see him again.

It was to Maisie Spens that the Abbé wrote his own impressions of the event:

Why was I arrested? . . . I still don't know; they've never wanted to tell me. I think I'm not far from the truth in believing that it was because of information resulting vaguely from our anti-Vichy sentiments and our love of England; for my sister was searched for, but managed to escape. She had to keep hidden until the liberation. In prison there were six of us, and sometimes seven, in a space of four square metres. I must tell you that the prison of Montluc, one of the most modern in France, was under the supervision of the Wehrmacht, not of the Gestapo, which arrested, questioned and tortured with a view to questioning when it was thought necessary. It didn't torture priests except in special cases. I haven't been tortured. The prison régime was humane as regards nourishment, custody by the soldiers of the Wehrmacht, hygiene. For a long time I believed that my sister was dead, for no news from outside could penetrate and I knew my sister (65 years old) was very fragile.

Speaking generally, this time meant a marvellous grace of detachment. I said my breviary which they had left me, with the proper amplitude of time. What joy! What joy! One day in the cellars of the Gestapo, waiting to be examined, I wrote down in my breviary some inscriptions that prisoners had written on the walls. Two were in English: 'Don't be affraid for so little a thing as pang (*sic*); when all is lost, France stays; O Crux, spes unica, Ave (Holy Week 1944). Let us pray and suffer for the world. It will be born again lovelier and more human.'

On the day of the Abbé's release there came news of the execution of several of his fellow-prisoners, shot in the back by the Germans, including Gérard Maire, a young communist (aged 22), who had for a time shared the same cell with the Abbé. The young man's mother treasures the letter of sympathy she received from Abbé Couturier. It is one which reveals 'something of the wideness of [his] heart, something of the way in which he opened out the word ecumenical, not only to include all Christians, but the whole wide world that God has made'.[1] It might have been assumed that there would have been nothing in common between the elderly priest devoted to the ideal of Christian Reunion and the ardent young disciple of Karl Marx. But the Abbé wrote:

I had a sincere affection for your son. I loved his frank, direct, generous character, his sensitive heart, his enthusiastic nature. He gave me repeated marks of what one may call deference, sympathy and, I think, even friendship.

His memory is for me one of the most moving recollections that I have of Montluc. Separated in many things, it seems to me that at root our souls were alike. It seems to me that they met in an ardent love for what transcends mortal man—what we would both call justice, freedom and goodness. A great ideal animated him. He found access beyond what is visible, beyond time, into the immense, the eternal, the absolute, into another abode beyond death, that strange metamorphosis. . . .

In my Catholic faith I find him again in him in whom we live, God the eternal, God towards whom we travel over the rough roads of this life, God who has created us and who leaves us some time on this earth to learn to know and to love him. I find him again in Christ who has saved him; for without knowing it he was searching for him, since he died for the triumph of Justice and Love. . . . I am sure that you will accept the assurance that in my heart I pray to Christ for him, and that to the end of my life, I will pray for him, and for his Mother and Father, each morning in those moments of unspeakable *grandeur* which you will know at least by name, the most holy Mass. (29 April 1945.)

NOTES

[1] A. M. Allchin, *The Abbé Paul Couturier*, London: Faith Press, 1960, p. 13.

22

YEARS BETWEEN PRISON
AND DEATH

THE captive thus liberated had seven years during which, in arduous labour, he could enjoy his freedom before he was finally prostrated by the illness which ended in his death in the spring of 1953. During these years he was confessedly a man whose physique, always frail, had been undermined beyond repair. 'My health is broken for ever—Praise be to God!' he observed soon after emerging from prison, but his usual programme continued unchanged: early rising, with Mass said at 6.30 in the church of St Martin d'Ainay; ascent to the Institution des Chartreux, where his steady work at his desk continued until 5 o'clock, only interrupted for the mid-day meal with his brethren and the saying of the Divine Office; returning via the General Post Office, where he got rid of his burden of letters, to the Place Bellecour. Crossing there to find the stairway of 5 Rue du Plat, he climbed the 102 steps to the fourth-floor flat, where his sister gave him his light supper if the arrival of visitors did not prevent her. Prayer and still more correspondence served frequently to shorten the night's rest.

But against this unchanged background which, in his further damaged condition, it must have needed heroic firmness to maintain, the Abbé's life in these last years seems to have been specially creative in new directions. It is true that from now onward he would not journey farther from Lyons than to La Trappe des Dombes, Ars, or Châtelard;[1] but over and above the work on the tracts and other articles, the arrangement of the programme for the Week of Unity at

Lyons, preparations for the meetings of the interconfessional circle, and the phenomenal flood of correspondence, there were many new undertakings.

Three of these stand out specially. First, the enkindlement, particularly amongst his fellow-Catholics, of the spirit of reparation for the persecution of fellow-Christians in the past; secondly, the endeavour to bring the leaders of the ecumenical movement centred on Geneva (which was shortly to give birth to the World Council of Churches) and the irenic spirits in the Roman Church to know and understand one another; thirdly, the effort to mitigate or banish doctrinal misunderstandings. Each of these involved the Abbé in new relationships and friendships, and in special new literary tasks.

First the work of reparation. How wonderfully in this century the resonance of such a word has altered! It used to evoke thoughts of an attitude mystical (used as a term of reproach!), exotic, vampiric, perverse. But reparation is now coming to be seen for what it is—for Christians an elementary thing, because baptism is itself sacrificial, involving union with the Saviour's sacrificial death; a very practical thing, being a quasi-sacramental expression of loving penitence sure to elicit love. Moreover reparation for the past is rewarding as giving light for the present.

Cardinal Gerlier once said to me in the Abbé's presence, 'We must not ask who is to blame, but begin from where we are!' The Abbé's standpoint was different. Beginning from where we are, we must insist that *we* are to blame. The responsibility of each of us for the sins of all is a truth movingly expounded in the novels of Dostoevsky. It is quite certain that we are all to blame—Anglicans, Roman Catholics, Methodists, Eastern Orthodox, Lutherans, etc., and that others are also to blame in relation to us. The Abbé loved dearly that prayer of St Ephraim the Syrian which recurs so constantly in the Lenten worship of the Eastern Churches:

> O Lord and Master of my life, grant not unto me a spirit of slothfulness, of discouragement, of lust of power, of vain babbling. But vouchsafe unto me thy servant the spirit of continence, of meekness, of patience and of love. Yea, O Lord, grant that I may

perceive my own transgressions and judge not my brother. For blessed art thou unto ages of ages. Amen.

Every advance towards unity implies a twofold resolve which is yet single in essence—that of liquidating through penitence the faults of the past before men as before God; that of seeking with them to understand the mind of Christ our Saviour with regard to the present and the future. This double movement will mean trans-figuration as well as cleansing for if the past guilt is liquidated by the Precious Blood of Christ, this is effected through its being in one and the same divine act of mercy conquered by his death and trans-figured by his resurrection. *'The blood is the life.'*

It had been at the first meeting of the French-speaking intercon-fessional circle at La Trappe des Dombes in 1942 that the Abbé first sowed the seed of his vision of Christian reparation. It was after supper, during recreation, that he launched the question:

> If a Catholic historian should study the Massacre of St Bartho-lomew's Day in such a way as by elimination of the political factors to bring out in all objectivity the exact responsibility of Catholics in this crime, and if he confessed humbly and in public this respon-sibility, do you think that his act would have any repercussion on the cause of Christian unity?

Silence followed: and then the senior Protestant minister replied:

> Monsieur l'Abbé, I can assure you that the result would be tremendous.

Some weeks later Père Villain recounted to the Abbé an incident reinforcing the impression that the earlier conversation had made on him. At Geneva a friend of his, a pastor, asked him point blank:

> Do you know at Champel the monument erected by us to the memory of Michel Servet who was burnt by Calvin? . . . We Protestants do know what penitence means. But what have you done to wipe out the bloodshed of St Bartholomew's Day?

This was two days after the feast. Père Villain was able to assure his friend that he had celebrated Mass that morning with this in mind, and that he was sure that there were other French priests who had done the same.

So it was that in August 1946 the following circular reached 200 priests and some lay-folk over the signature of Abbé Couturier.

Between our Protestant brethren and ourselves there extends in France a trench full of blood. The Massacre of St Bartholomew's Day, 24 August 1572, the results of the unjust revocation of the Edict of Nantes in 1685: exile, dragooning, removal of children from their parents to put them in convents, all sorts of cruelties. These happenings have left deep wounds in the French Protestant soul. The large-scale reunions at the *Musée du Desert* in le Gard on the first Sunday in September every year are a certain proof of this.[2] 'The descendants of the Huguenots martyred by the Roman Church under the charge of heresy and blasphemy (*vide* the *Martyrologie* of J. Crespin[3]) have hearts still full of tears and a wound still bleeding in the soul. To win a true reconciliation between the children of the executioners and those of their victims, there would be need of the utterance somehow or other of some kind of *mea culpa* (i.e. some confession of guilt).' So wrote Pastor Wilfred Monod in 1939. There is no French Protestant who would not sign this testimony, as is clear to anyone with ecumenical experience.

It is for this *mea culpa* that I am asking.

Allowing for the morals of the time, for the intrusion of the temporal into the spiritual in that epoch, for the fact of our Catholic faith which the martyrs did not entirely share and which is not in question in this act of reparation—it remains true that, sincere to the point of imprisonment or even death in their faith in Christ, these martyrs suffered or died tormented at the hands of Catholics and that their blood remains between us and our Protestant brethren. It is this which we find intolerable. Many amongst us share already these ideas, these sentiments, this suffering, this desire of reparation. They are realists, and 'Reality is Joy'.

It is in this realism that I request your company by inviting you to an effective realization which is within your power.

If you are a priest, I beg of you to offer the most holy Sacrifice on the day of the coming feast of St Bartholomew, 24 August, asking God's pardon for the acts of violence committed by our fathers, entreating him to change the atoning Blood once shed into a spring of living waters wherein the Lamb-Redeemer will enable us to find once more our profound brotherhood in him.

You will be doing a work of justice, a work of charity, a work for the union of hearts, a distant but necessary prelude to the union of minds in the truth of Christ. Group around the altar in union with yourselves the greatest possible number of the faithful who would understand.

If you are one of the faithful (lay-folk), try to interest a priest in this realization. In any case try to join up with some friends so as to communicate that day with the same intentions, sharing and communicating with the most holy sacrifice.

Finally even if you were to be alone in realizing this project, your prayer would already be a great force of reparation and intercession; though in appearance isolated it would in the invisible realm rejoin the measureless co-operative prayer of the 'Invisible Monastery' of Christian Unity.

I should be grateful—even though I cannot hope to thank each of you individually—if you will let me know what you have been able to achieve.

Please accept, M. . . ., the assurance of my Christian sympathy and brotherhood wholeheartedly offered in the charity of Christ.

P. COUTURIER
Institution des Chartreux, Lyons

The response was immediate and excellent. An article by Père Congar appearing in *Témoignage chrétien* at the end of the same month gave weighty and convincing support to this request. A large number of letters, including those from two cardinals, three bishops, and many priests, showed deep approval of the Abbé's initiative.

A Carmelite sister who had been a Protestant until quite late in life disclosed the distress which was hers over the coincidence of this fateful St Bartholomew's Day with the annual thanksgiving in commemoration of the reform of the Carmelite Order. While the Order chanted the *Te Deum*, it was the *De Profundis* that sprang up in her heart.

There is a moving letter from a Protestant, the only one who received the appeal.

How lovely is the gesture of one who comes forward to reconcile! If he rises to confess his guilt, though soiled by all the filth of the world, he is at that moment shining white with that white radiance which shone on Mount Tabor: this, too, even if the other party does not open his arms to welcome him. But then he will do so, for nothing loosens the heart nor makes the soul tremble in its depths nor moves it more than the approach of him who comes forward to humble himself for his sins.

Brother, I am a little lost. Behind you is the whole of Roman Catholicism. Behind me, in me, the whole of Protestantism. And because you come to me, I suddenly know my own sin better for your not telling me of it. Your coming . . . forbids me to compare our sins and enquire which of us has been the greatest sinner, for 'whosoever observes the whole law but sins against one command only, becomes guilty of all'. Your advent inspired by Christ awakes Christ in me, and we both fall on our knees confessing our common misery at the feet of him who awaited us.

Jacob lifted up his eyes and looked: and behold Esau was arriving. Jacob prostrated himself seven times until he was close to his brother. Esau ran to meet him, embraced him, fell on his neck, and kissed him. And they wept. . . .

Brother, after that comes only singing and waves of peace which engulf us in the Unity of love.

Some correspondents developed the familiar theme that 'all have sinned': why then underline our Catholic offences and keep silent about those of others?' The Abbé replied to this grievance some months later in the journal, *Catholicité*:

The attitude which consists in saying, 'Yes, but the other man also is to blame' is from the start a Pharisaical one. It has little value, indeed I believe it has none: it produces a negative attitude before God and man.

He contrasts the attitude of St Ephraim in the prayer quoted above.

Correspondence with Protestants proved him right in his conviction that one man's contrition wakens unfailingly in another the consciousness of his own sin. But it was not until June 1950 that his own *mea culpa* reached the public in the book of essays which he edited under the title *Christian Unity and Religious Toleration*.[4] Besides the Abbé himself, the contributors were Pastor J. Cadier, Mgr Chevrot, Pastor J. Delpech, Réné Fedou, Jean Guitton, André Latreille, Gabriel Marcel, Père M. Metzger, Père M. Pribille, and Pastor Max Thurian—a selection of gifted and competent writers, Catholic and Protestant.

The publication of this book was timely. The emergence at Amsterdam in 1948 of the World Council of Churches had drawn attention everywhere to the problems of ecumenism. The instruction *Ecclesia Catholica* dealing with this, issued by the Holy Office in the following year, pointed towards the Christian principle of freedom in religion. But advance in this direction was hindered by certain survivals of an earlier mentality typified by the situation of the ill-treated Protestant minority in Spain and in parts of South America. The Abbé felt that this issue of a cleavage between doctrinal pronouncements and actual church behaviour must be plainly raised, and that for this there was need of a number of concerted voices. Having enlisted these, he reserved for himself the task of introducing and editing their contributions and the crucial task of elucidating the difficult questions of the persecution of Huguenots in the sixteenth century and of the present plight of Spanish Protestantism.

The introduction seems to me masterly.

Many obstacles encumber the path of Christian Unity. To attain to Unity in the Truth which is to be found at the end of the road of prayer, Christians ought, as they journey, to advance together as under the gaze of Christ, their invisible travelling-companion. Our journey, full of fatigue owing to the overwhelming weight of the past, resembles that of the disciples to Emmaus. It is he who will resolve our difficulties, renew our courage, enkindle our souls and finally reveal himself in the dazzling light which is his as the one and only Saviour of a single visible Church.

Every page of this volume is centred on Christ. The vision of him illuminates them with divers lights, varied irradiations of his love. The articles which speak directly of history, ancient, modern, or recent, resemble the memories which lay heavy upon the hearts of the two disciples, as discouraged they left Jerusalem. . . .

Christian Unity? *Sperabamus*—We were hoping. But look, Christians wrangle and have been wrangling for centuries! Yes . . . but don't you see also that he is explaining for us this sad history of which he is the key, just as he explained to them the Scriptures of which he is the life?

Must not Christ needs suffer? . . . and his Church suffer as he has done . . . and he and she with him be torn from without and from within? Do you not see that resurrection is close to suffering? Christian Unity is already risen though it be hidden from our heavy gaze. It is risen because Christendom has already become obsessed with this issue—exerts itself to lift the stone from the tomb where many believed that it was asleep for ever. Articles like those of Jean Guitton and Monsignor Chevrot demonstrate this resurrection as do the documents printed in the appendix, and Pastor Thurian's article and the pages written by our collaborators Pastors Delbach and Jean Cadier.

One of the most striking proofs of this resurrection marked on the line of the progress of humanity towards the triumph of the Spirit is unquestionably everything in this volume bearing on religious toleration. The new conditions transforming the problem and the higher quality of the solutions considered sound the death knell for mental attitudes which have perished and announce with a joyous chime a victory of the Spirit.

War . . . Intolerance . . . Mutual Respect . . . Spiritual Emulation . . . so many stages traversed by Christians, of which these pages strive to give glimpses. May the whole team engaged on this little book find here the expression of profound gratitude. Hand in hand, we have striven to work together for his Church.

There is no happier part of Abbé Couturier's labours to record than that constituted by his relations with the official ecumenism centred at Geneva and now operating through the World Council of Churches. In 1946 he was overjoyed by the appearance of the Geneva Conference of the provisional World Council which was to be fully established at the Assembly held two years later at Amsterdam. Here he felt was an answer to the cravings which had so long been stirring in the Mystical Body, and, in particular, to his own prayer.

Before his arrest by the Gestapo in the spring of 1944, he had saluted this movement in a small pamphlet published after his exodus from prison, and entitled *Christian Rapprochements in the Twentieth Century*.[5] This is a modest summary, written as from a watch-tower, of all the activities of the first four decades of our century which have operated in the direction of Christian unity. He records an extraordinary diversity of efforts, but all of them seem to him rays, as it were, forerunning the dawn of a new age. The pamphlet might almost be called 'From Solovyev [whose premature death in 1900 seems to him to mark the century with the challenge of that great sage's irenic gesture and intentions[6]] to the Invisible Monastery [which he regards as the crown of the spiritual ecumenism which is the movement's surest ground of hope]'. It is on this background—one of personal and spiritual activity that he views the great new phenomenon of non-Roman official ecumenism.

He speaks here of the long, fruitful co-operation of Lord Halifax and Abbé Portal; of the Appeal for Christian Unity launched by the Anglican bishops in 1920; of the *Conversations of Malines*, held by Cardinal Mercier, occasioned by this Appeal, an event by which the steadfast perseverance of the two friends was rewarded; of the singularly open-hearted Cardinal Hinsley of Westminster, and his movement of the Sword of the Spirit; of many student organizations, and, in particular, of the Anglican and Eastern Orthodox Fellowship of St Alban and St Sergius; of the admirable interdenominational league of Christian teachers, *L'Amitié*; of the first ecumenical journal *Oecumenica*,[7] an Anglican venture, though composed in French; most promising of all, of the development of the ecumenical movement with its two strands, 'Life and Work' and 'Faith and Order', and of its growing purification from the tendencies which Pope Pius XI had condemned in *Mortalium Animos*, his encyclical of 1928. He asks whether it would be wrong to see the great Christian Assemblies of Stockholm ('Life and Work', 1925) and Lausanne ('Faith and Order', 1927) with those that succeeded each of these in 1937 at Oxford and Edinburgh respectively, as first and distant stages on the road leading towards a 'great ecumenical council' such as Christendom had not yet known.

The writer of this pamphlet saw already manifold signs that the

Church of Rome was being stirred in the same way. In monasteries, in universities, in the encyclicals of Pope Pius XII, there are signs that in a Catholic world deeply affected by the experience of suffering and, in some lands, persecution, endured in common with other Christians, the great principle of spiritual emulation is at work. He sees all this institutional activity as undergirded by and owing everything to the more hidden labour of intercession, the chief instrument of which is the Week of Universal Prayer. He describes the emergence of this from the Papalist Octave and its marvellous spread, and closes by speaking of its fulfilment in the Invisible Monastery.

This being his reading of the course of contemporary history, the Abbé was not only eager that Christians of his own and all other Churches should remember the World Council of Churches in their intercession. He desired wholeheartedly that members of the latter should themselves grasp and help others to grasp the great principle of spiritual ecumenism—union with the prayer of Christ—and make it an essential element in the life of the institution. In this he was mightily successful.

From 1939 the Abbé had been in correspondence with Dr Visser 't Hooft, future Secretary General of the Council, the great Dutch leader whose energy, ability and theological insight have been its mainstay. The chief liaison, however, between Geneva and the Institution des Chartreux during the years that followed until the end of the Abbé's life was the Director of the Ecumenical Press and Information Service (SŒPI),[8] M. Alexandre Weymarn, whom we shall meet again at the end. The Abbé greatly valued and frequently commended the bulletins of information that proceeded from SŒPI, and that bureau was indebted to him for much information about Roman Catholic ecumenism. From 1942 onwards its bulletins constantly quoted the tracts or other brochures published by Abbé Couturier.

Once or twice the Abbé had the joy of being received at the offices in the Route de Malagnou, Geneva, and at the *Institut Oecuménique* at Bossey some miles from the city; or that of welcoming representatives of these institutions at Dombes and Presinges. Dr

Visser 't Hooft himself came once to the latter. But most fruitful of all these relationships was that between the Abbé and the secretary of 'Faith and Order', the Rev. Oliver Tomkins, now Bishop of Bristol, the most understanding and widely trusted of all who ever held high position in this field of non-Roman official ecumenism. Oliver Tomkins took a leading part in preparing the conference at Lund through which 'Life and Work' and 'Faith and Order' were integrated into a single whole. He was the Abbé's ally in getting the Week of Universal Prayer espoused by the World Council of Churches. During the four years between the Assembly of Amsterdam (1948) and the Conference of Lund (1952) they engaged in intimate correspondence which was supplemented by their conversation when Oliver Tomkins visited the Abbé in Lyons at Easter 1949. The visit had been preceded by the gift to the Abbé by Oliver Tomkins of his book, *The Wholeness of the Church*, acknowledged by the latter with gratitude—for

> a precious book of great objectivity, full of that sense of sorrow for our divisions which permeates nowadays the whole of Christendom, both Catholic and non-Catholic.

At Lyons they discussed the problem of the extension of the Week of Prayer; its spirit of emulation; the possibility of the inauguration of a centre for developing dialogue between Anglican and Catholic theologians; and a goal most dear to the Abbé's heart, the 'convergent appeal' in which the official leaders of all Christian communions, each in the religious idiom of his own people, should call forth prayer for unity from Christians throughout the world.

Thenceforward the collaboration of the two friends was close and fruitful. Signs of this are to be found in the yearly intentions for intercession published by the Secretary of 'Faith and Order'. We find, for instance, this:

> Let us pray for all those who, although not partaking officially in the preparations for the conference of Lund, regard our work with sympathy and prayer: with special thanksgiving for the manifestation of the ecumenical spirit in the Church of Rome.

279

Abbé Couturier on his side seeks to familiarize his readers with the great movement which is centred at Geneva. So we find in the Tracts such words as these:

> All Christians ought to make a habit of praying for the preparation of the important World Conference of Faith and Order which will take place at Lund (Sweden) during the summer of 1952.

And again:

> All Christians ought to make a habit of praying for the World Council in which are represented practically all the non-Catholic confessions. It is manifestly a great work of the Holy Spirit. 'The Church is united in a *Kyrie Eleison* which we ask others to offer along with us. We have only too few voices joining with ours' (O. Tomkins).
>
> May each Catholic hear this brotherly call which comes from Geneva and understand, Lord, that it is the echo of a call of your spirit.

The Abbé had the joy before he died of finding SŒPI in December 1952 printing his tract of January 1953 side by side with the prayer leaflet of 'Faith and Order' which recommended the observance of the Week of Prayer. The final acceptance of his prophetic message was signalled shortly after his death by the splendid resolution passed by the World Council of Churches at Evanston 1954 in words already quoted, but which will bear repetition:

> The measure of our concern for unity is the degree to which we pray for it. We cannot expect God to give us unity unless we prepare ourselves to receive his gift by costly and purifying prayer. To pray *together* is to be drawn together. We urge, wherever possible, the observance of the Week of Prayer for Christian Unity, 18–25 January (or some other period suited to local conditions) as a public testimony to prayer as the road to unity.

Prophetic words from the Abbé (1949) about ecumenism have surely been vindicated:

> At the outset there might have been cause for fear. What will this young child be? . . . a mixture . . . an alloy . . . a coalition

. . . human unity . . . the Tower of Babel or Pentecost? Ever more clearly the answer comes—it is the action of the Holy Spirit . . . a re-orientation . . . the Passion of the Church . . . the desire to do only the will of Christ . . . a way of renunciation . . . a seeking after his truth . . . anguish at the sin of separation. Verily a great miracle is beginning to be performed on the threshold of a new epoch. It is the beginning of the transformation of broken Christianity into a Christianity truly one according to the unity willed by Christ: nothing else than that Unity, unity in all its mystery, with all that it involves, unity to be reached along all these mysterious ways that lead to it. We will go on to the end. Christ is the only Lord in whom—when Unity has been established among his children—the whole world will find its true peace and rest, in order to rise again more beautiful than ever. These are not dreams. They are realities, clearly shown by numerous texts and actions.

Might not ecumenism, then, be the answer to so much heroism, so much martyrdom for justice, charity, and truth—divine plants springing up on every field of battle, suffering, and misery where, since 1914, death has reaped its finest harvest since that long distant past when it began its sinister journey on earth?

These two facts in their spiritual implication seem to be one. Born of heroism, ecumenism, that powerful source of the ocean of peace which Christian Unity will prove to be, will be maintained and will go forward only if it is sustained by heroic prayer, by suffering, troubled, strenuous prayer which will ascend ever more fully and fervently from the multitude of Christians of both the old and the young Churches. . . . He who should fail to contribute to this gigantic labour to which the Holy Spirit is calling all baptized members of Christ, would be guilty of betrayal. He would have failed to understand his responsibility as a child of the Church.

The subject of the Virgin Mary is a danger point in ecumenical discussions. Protestants feel no doubt that it is in their excessive devotion to the Blessed Virgin and in their doctrine with regard to her that Roman Catholics most clearly exhibit their failure to be faithful to God's Word given in Holy Scripture. But when they are asked to express their own thoughts and sentiments about her, we commonly find them closer than we realize to Catholic tradition.

281

The Eastern Orthodox are equally critical of Roman Catholic dogma, and yet come even closer on this point, at least in their Liturgy, to those whom they criticize. Abbé Couturier wrote to me on 26 September 1938:

> I agree with you about the wealth of devotion to Mary among the Orthodox. I have *lived* the Divine Liturgy innumerable times at great length, and meditated before ikons. They have in their life, in the intuitive thinking springing from that life, what we in our explicit and cut-and-dried formula have defined about the Immaculate Conception. Ask them, 'Can our Lady have known sin?' They will reply, 'Blasphemy! It is blasphemy even to think of it!' Now what is the Immaculate Conception but the articulation of this belief in the form of the 'clear idea'? I am not, be it said, a lover of the 'clear idea'. To be clear it has to be abstract and consequently has limited power to attract the soul. Nevertheless I think it must be agreed that the 'clear idea' has its value as a directive. Moreover the symphonic blending here, as elsewhere, of East and West, and I would add, of the Latin and Anglican soul,[9] would give more profound expression to the reality. We must find a way of discussing all this.

But for the Protestants the need of a right regard for Mary was more urgent. Clearly their need, it seemed to the Abbé, was to recover a love of the Church—not the Church as an idea not as merely invisible, but as the concrete reality, the Church as loved by the Christians of the undivided Christendom. Of this the Blessed Virgin is at once the image and the Mother: so that love of the Blessed Virgin and of the Church stand or fall, increase or dwindle together. Dr Sergius Bulgakov was possessed by the same intuition, as came out in his communication to the Edinburgh Conference of 1937. In 1941 his Protestant friend, Pastor Jean de Saussure gave expression to the same idea in a fine *Meditation on the Virgin, Figure of the Church*, which he sent to the Abbé.

The Abbé loved this meditation, and indeed it is not only a masterpiece of devotional eloquence, but a treasure of mystical theology, springing from the depths of Calvinism, yet striking notes most dear to the Catholic heart.

In form it consists of a prayer to Christ crucified. The author, looking at the Cross, speaks to the Lord about his Mother and the beloved disciple, from both of whom Jesus has parted by an act of supreme detachment. The intimacy of John and Mary is compared to that between the believer and the Church, that Church which Jesus has bequeathed to each of us as a Mother and protectress.

Mary is nothing by herself: from beginning to end of her life her holiness proceeds only from the power of Christ. She can do nothing of herself, but only through submission to Grace, in that relentless, unfailing Amen to the word of Christ through whom she lives. In her soul all the virtues of the Church converge, especially those of poverty and humility, the foundation of the Beatitudes.

Poverty of thy Mother, only wealth of thy Church! Yes, she who conceived thee only by the power of the Most High and who found grace to abide close to thee at the foot of thy cross only by the complete sacrifice of thee, remains the type of those virgin souls free from all human thought and resource and living only by the supernatural work of thy Spirit in them. She is the model of the pure hearts, purified from all that does not come from thee, hearts which thou hast proclaimed *happy, for they shall see God.* She is the patron of that stripping that must be reproduced in all those who must learn to deprive themselves of the goods of this world, of the vain illusions of philosophy, of human traditions, of knowledge, wrongly so-named, of any kind of passion or of the inventions of their own hearts, so as to subsist only by thy grace. She is the image of the poor whom thou proclaimest happy, for the Kingdom of Heaven is theirs. And in fact each time that the Church has allowed herself to be tempted by these false treasures and has thought to say in her heart, 'I am rich, I lack nothing', the weight of them has dragged her to her ruin and downfall. She will never attain salvation, save in the footsteps of Mary; she abides blessed only by conformity to the Virgin's ways. When she becomes worldly, and in doing so, has profoundly turned the world away from thee, it is aways by repeating with Mary, 'Be it unto me according to thy word', whatever it may cost her, and in giving herself up to lose all so as to live by thy Word alone and without any human help that she becomes once more the Mother of numberless believers, each of them hers through supernatural birth.

Humility of thy Mother, sole grandeur of the Church! Yes, the Holy Virgin who always seeks to decrease that thou mayest increase, remains the source of better inspiration for thy Church than the imagination of those hearts that magnify increasingly first Mary and then the Church. For true majesty for the Church also consists not in dominion but in service. And the only rightful way in which she may glorify herself is to be glorified in thee. Those who exalt her in herself do her a double wrong: in the first place, none can exalt thy Church which is only thy Body, save in doing injury to thee; and to do thee injury means doing real harm to her for whom thou art the abiding Head. Further, to honour her, whether consciously or not, apart from thee, brings her down to the standards of the world, for apart from thee nought remains but the world. No, assuredly it is only at the foot of thy Cross, prostrate at thy feet, that the Church preserves its true greatness and its divine mission.

No other glory ascribed to her will add one cubit to her stature, the stature attained by Mary standing at the Cross that day. And since in the Cross it is I who am dying in thee, she, Mary, who stays near that Cross, stays also near me: near each of us who are dying with thee: in her we find in quintessence the presence and help of thy Church, Mother of the faithful. Her tenderness cherishes us Christians in our agony. Thou, as God made man, hast loved in her thy Church made woman. Thou hast given us in her the image of the Church invisible: *behold thy Mother*.

Saviour, thanks be to thee for giving us so fair a Mother. Since in thy mercy thou hast deigned to make us thy brethren, how should thy Mother not be our Mother? And—bond yet more intimate—since she was thy Mother, how could she not belong to us who are the members of thy Body, to us who are one spirit with thee?

The author has succeeded wonderfully in providing (as he makes clear in an enclosed note to the Abbé had been his intention) a 'work positive, not negative', one which for all its succinctness and reserve is matter of 'meditation, prayer, adoration, not of theological controversy'. A few days later M. de Saussure added, 'I should be extremely interested if you could, some day, communicate to me your reflections on the subject of the meditation I sent you'. He has in mind the possibility of publishing the Abbé's thoughts, together with the meditation, in the interests of Reunion.

The two writings were in fact published together, first in one of the brochures entitled *Pages documentaires sur l'Unité chrétienne* (1942). The Abbé, for his part, found it necessary first to make clear that though Jean de Saussure's writing was in conformity with the thought of the great Reformers, there would be few Protestants nowadays to sign it. He proceeds then to develop the ideas of the pastor on the humility of the Virgin finding expression as it does in the Magnificat with its prophecy 'All generations shall call me blessed'. The thought of the mystical Body of Christ draws him on to the thought of the cosmic function of Mary as Mother of the whole Christ. As *theotokos*, Mother of God, her divine maternity has a wholeness which matches that of the whole Christ. The manifold grace of Christ must have an intimate relation with his Mother, who, as Mother of the Word, is through him the Mother of every Christian.

> The Virgin cannot cease in heaven to share maternally—though in a transcendent manner by reason of her entry within the divine mystery wherein she goes ever forward: *They will go from strength to strength*—in the life of the whole Christ.

He goes on to say how the living wealth of this relationship justifies the concepts, dry and juridical in their precision, such as are found in the titles ascribed to Mary of *Mediatrix* and *Distributor of all Graces*, titles which are totally inadequate to express the infinite variety and surety of love involved in the divine motherhood.

The Abbé was not satisfied until the ecumenically vital theme of Mary the Mother of the Lord had been given a less exclusive expression and a fuller presentation to the Christian public: so in 1950 he published a collection of Protestant and Catholic articles with the title *Dialogue on the Virgin*.[10] The meditation of Pastor de Saussure, with his own introductory reflections, is here found in a collection which included seven other contributions: these were by Marshal Booth, the daughter of the founder of the Salvation Army, by a layman of Bernes, M. Schmied, by Pastors Bremond and Vidal, by Frère Max Thurian of Taizé, and by the Roman Catholic theologians, Professor Jean Guitton and Père Ganne, S.J.

Abbé Couturier wrote in the preface:

> Like a faint, distant echo of *Ecce enim beatam me dicent omnes generationes*, this little book gathers together voices varied and unexpected in honour of the humble Virgin Mary.
>
> Because it seems to me strange and indeed a *sign* that these voices come my way to join one another, this little book has come to birth. Is it not a sign that the Mystery of the Virgin is beginning to be revealed in Christian circles where, to all appearances, it has been up to the present ignored?
>
> We must not exaggerate or underestimate the importance of this sign. . . .
>
> A little cloud signifying hope in a heaven which still frowns darkly; some swallows which, without doubt, proclaim tidings of spring, with some twig of quite young olive . . . one can't say more than that. . . .
>
> Just a handful gathered.

Yes, but what jewels this handful contained!

By coincidence rather than design, the little book appeared in 1950, the Holy Year marked by the proclamation of the dogma of the Assumption of the Blessed Virgin Mary. Certainly the darkness of the heavens was by this event intensified. 'The dogma of the Assumption,' wrote later one of the contributors to this book, Frère Max Thurian of Taizé, 'seems to us an insurmountable obstacle'. It was less perhaps the contents of the definition than its imposition as an essential article of faith which makes it insurmountable for the vast majority of non-Roman Christians. The Abbé, though he had never any doubts as to the truth declared, had hoped that there would be no definition, for he feared that it would put off the day of Reunion. However, soon after the proclamation of the dogma, Father Brandreth received a card from the Abbé, containing the words: '*Laus Deo!* Be at peace: she prays also for those who do not accept.' Many of the Abbé's fellow-churchmen who had for the same reason been doubtful also showed the confidence that seems to have welled up in the heart of His Holiness Pope Pius XII that honour given to the august Mother of the Redeemer cannot but hasten the day of the unification of the whole family. The generous reserve with regard to the treatment of the subject of the Blessed Virgin Mary shown by the Second Vatican Council, which introduced it only as a heading in the *schema* on the Church, is perhaps a first vindication of this faith. But her prayers must avail still more mightily for all her children. Pope John XXIII demanded a change in the style of the Church. No more fruitful change could be achieved than a change in the style of the dogmatic utterance of the Church. The distance between the faith of the Magnificat—indeed the faith of the Gospel—and the imposition of such dogmatic definitions safe-guarded by the formula *Anathema sit* is immeasurable. But the Church, which is already in many ways recovering a style worthier of her Lord who 'took the form of a Servant', may yet learn a more convincing mode of witnessing to the truth as it is in Christ Jesus, in particular of honouring his Mother. It is, after all, her image that the Church must wear, the handmaid whose lowliness it is that God regards.[11]

NOTES

[1] See p. 236.

[2] It is at this 'feast of the wilderness' that the Protestants of the Cevennes commemorate their martyrs of the days of the religious wars.

[3] An anthology of extracts from this book has been compiled by T. Monod, Jr, *Livres des Martyrs, 'vie des saints' extraite du Martyrologue Protestant de Jean Crespin*, Neuilly; 1930. There are descendants of these martyrs still living.

[4] *Unité chrétienne et tolérance religieuse*, Paris: Editions du temps présent, 1950.

[5] *Rapprochements entre les Chrétiens au xxᵉ siecle*, Le Puy: Editions Mappus, 1944.

[6] See pp. 192, 229.

[7] Published from 1934 to 1939, when the war made its continuation impossible.

[8] These letters stand for *Service Oecuménique de Presse et d'Information*.

[9] Anglican readers, in following Abbé Couturier's train of thought in this letter, may recall the great hymn of Bishop Thomas Ken (1637–1711), 'Her Virgin eyes saw God incarnate born' (*English Hymnal*, No. 217), in which the classic Catholic doctrine concerning the Blessed Virgin is implicit, but not expressed 'in the form of the "clear idea"'.

[10] *Dialogue sur la Vierge* (Ronds Points, I), Lyon: Vitte, 1950.

[11] Cf. Max Thurian in *Écho-Liberté*, January 1951.

23

AN APOSTLE OF LOVE AND PRAYER

⎯⎯⎯⎯⎯⎯⎯⎯

PAUL Couturier was, we have noted, a *vrai Lyonnais*, who loved every aspect of his city: he was proud of her rich heritage and vigorous life, and felt himself concerned in every episode of her dramatic history. He was French to the finger-tips, but without an atom of the Gallican temperament, realizing that France owes her chief glory to her place in the Church and Commonwealth of Christ. He was a frail man without influence, who for about half a century lived the hidden life, but whose talents were increased through generous self-spending. The riches of mind and spirit thus enlarged did not impair his great simplicity; but it is at the same time true that he was both bourgeois and aristocratic, scientist and mystic, mathematician and humanist, a lover of solitude and a social genius, and that his imaginative sense of the meaning of history harmonized surprisingly with a delight in his own times and an interest in new patterns of liturgy and art.

He has been called an Apostle of Christian unity. He was primarily an apostle of love and of prayer. He came to care for Christian unity first because of his love for the Russians. He has been misunderstood as providing by his formularies and methods a kind of technology for promoting unity amongst Christians, whereas he would have had no use for the unity which could be procured in such a way. His vision and method, in so far as he had any, were profoundly theological. Providence willed that he should not be trained as a professional theologian, but he had many friends among theologians who had a deep respect for his intellectual as well as his spiritual gifts. His ignorance of the academic scene and its special terminology certainly made it easier for him to approach other folk whose very life, like his, consists in theology, if that means growing knowledge of God in Christ, a quality which is not always evident in professional theologians. I write in the Mega Lavra at the foot of Mount Athos, where Paul Couturier's neat signature (though he has never been here) is to be found pasted into a scrapbook. There is here theology to be found more perhaps in the simple peasant monks[1] than in the scholar monks. This fact recalls the era of the foundation of this monastery a thousand years ago, when still the need for a theology of union between heart and mind was better understood, and the intellectualism that tempers much modern academic theology would have been recognized as a sad disease. The formula in which Abbé Couturier gave expression to the prayer which was to rise from Christians of every communion, *that the visible unity of the Kingdom of God may be such as Christ wills and achieved by whatever means he wills* has greater depths than is often observed. It is only intelligible aright if it is understood as a lover of the Gospels understands it—as grounded in the prayer of our Lord Jesus Christ in St John 17. That is why, in the Abbé's scheme, it goes along with prayer for the sanctification of Christian Communions. Our Lord prayed that we may be sanctified in the faith, that all may be one through one indwelling by himself in the triune life of God. Any visible unity not rooted in the interior life of the growing love of God in the Holy Trinity he would have regarded not only as insufficient but also as disastrous. Those who criticize the formula as vague and say that it owes its success to its vagueness have failed to detect its Gospel source or are ignorant of the nature of prayer, being often—because the Gospel and prayer are in essence one—ignorant of both of these. The President of *Unitas* in Rome criticized the petitions demanded in the Week of Prayer for Christian unity for a sanctification of each Christian group as having nothing to do with prayer for Christian unity.[2] This criticism reveals an astonishing conception of holiness. Can members of the Body of Christ, becoming holy, fail to come close to Christ? Can they come close to Christ without coming closer to one another in the Truth? This criticism gives proof of the need for the Second Vatican Council. Abbé Couturier had apprehended from the beginning of his ecumenical career that the prayer of our Lord himself is the only prayer adequate at once to the crucial situation in which Christians find themselves, and to the mystery of unity in Christ with which it has to do. The formulas and methods which he developed in relation to universal prayer for Christian unity are all grounded in that holy of holies of the written word, the seventeenth chapter of St John's Gospel, our Lord's own anaphora or Prayer of Consecration.

Paul Couturier's divinely fruitful intuition as regards the meaning of unity, schism and disunity sprang from his prayer. He was eminently a man of prayer, whose faith in prayer was evidenced and grounded in the proportion of time and energy he spent in this. He was a great master of prayer because he prayed incessantly. The fruit of this has been the evocation of a great and increasing fire of love effected ultimately by the contagious flame of his own prayerful spirit. In the circumstances in which he lived, and with so many claims upon him, it cost him much to make prayer the main work of his life. It involved, besides great hardship, ever-increasing suffering, but his serene joy swallowed up that suffering without destroying its character. Suffering passes away. But to have suffered is something that abides. Prayer which he knew as the bearing of the Cross was for him rooted in the realistic optimism of Christian faith in the Risen Saviour.

To enter into the Prayer of Christ: this demand he made not only of his fellow-churchmen, but also of all baptized Christians. He knew that no man can address Jesus as Son of God, save in the Holy Spirit (I Cor. 12.3; cf. Rom. 10.9; John 15.26; I John 4.2, 3). This fundamental principle, so dear to the apostles, which must have its origin in our Lord's words to St Peter at Caesarea Philippi (Matt. 16.17), was the axiom of Paul Couturier's thought. He knew that prayer in this, the Spirit of God, i.e. in the name and intention of the Lord Jesus, is prayer heard of God, and that it must needs be fruitful. The wealth or poverty of any particular Christian's heritage is irrelevant here: or rather, it is just those who inherit great riches who are in danger of narrowness and complacency, and are most likely to need the aid of intercession offered by Christians less richly endowed. Hence he constantly asked the prayers of Protestants for members of the Catholic Church, as well as securing for his Protestant friends the wonderful help that comes from the intercession of the enclosed religious communities of his own Church. Intercession, thanksgiving, worship are the exercise of our sonship in the Body of Christ the Son of God, and Christian life is unthinkable without them. They constitute a primary part of the life of Charity.

In this larger, deeper sense of constant growth in holy love for God and his children, the vocation to pray and work for unity was seen by Abbé Couturier as a necessary part of the vocation of any Christian. It was impossible for a man or woman, once he or she had realized the implication of baptism, not to accept the responsibility of an ecumenical vocation. God was in Christ reconciling the world unto himself, and committing to us as members of his Body the task of implementing this loving act of reconciliation. We must therefore desire the ever-growing unity of the reconciled. This is and will be found through and in Christ the one new man. He through whom we have access in one Spirit to the Father lives to intercede for us. Our participation in his life and in his Spirit therefore requires our union in his prayer. Hence, as we have seen, the great Liturgies of the Church, Roman, Eastern Orthodox and Anglican alike, all contain prayer for unity. It is also implicit in the Lord's Prayer, the 'Our Father', the Lord's gift to us.

Thus the movement of prayer which is the life of the Church must continually draw us closer together. It will do so more effectively as we become conscious of the essential character of our life as members of the one Apostolic Church, the Body of Christ, gathered in close eucharistic union with our great High Priest, with the faithful departed in his nearer presence, and with one another in him. But apart from this perpetual unitary movement, Abbé Couturier had a childlike belief in the duty, the value and the God-given consequences of prayer of petition—of the *via orationis* as a way of asking. Bishop Charles Gore was constantly warning his disciples not to lose the sense of this elementary aspect of prayer in the quest of more mystical aspects of it. This truth pervades the Scriptures everywhere but is specially emphasized in the teaching of our Lord himself in the Gospels. *Ask and it shall be given. Seek and ye shall find. Knock and it shall be opened unto you.* The Abbé was constantly asking his friends' prayers for particular things and people. He often asked them to pray at particular times, the time of some conference or important interview. When he had some specially important undertaking in hand, such as his journeys to England, he took care to ask for a widespread barrage of prayer.

Our common Christian life of ever-growing co-inherence in Christ, in the harmony of his Body and of the life of the Trinity, seemed to him a golden web which was woven by relationships of holy love. In this friendship played an essential part. He loved to put Roman Catholic, Anglican and Protestant communities into touch with one another, and alert individuals of the different Churches often found through introduction by Abbé Couturier the way to life-long and fruitful friendship in Christ. It was, no doubt, his principle of 'spiritual emulation' in generosity of self-giving, regarded as covering every moment of the day, which was often the most inspiring element in these friendships.

The friendship between Dom Benedict Ley of Nashdom and Sister Maria Gabriella of Grottoferrata (d. 1938) is a well-known instance of this. Unfortunately some of the literature which it has called forth has been marred by the desire to proselytize. This was felt by Abbé Couturier keenly. He wrote:

> I would be glad if, when telling the story of the life and death of Sister Maria Gabriella, you invited the reader to rise higher in his prayer and intention, bidding him observe that it is only a revivified Catholicism which will be able to offer a milieu with which non-Catholic Christians can be integrated—a Catholicism revivified in every field of human life . . . the style of its presentation, the conception of its aesthetic life, its members and its hierarchy overflowing with burning charity, etc. . . . Thus it would be much better to offer one's life for the unity that Christ wishes by the means he wishes. So we show respect with regard to the mystery in which is wrapped the path which is to carry us from the

impoverished Catholicism of our day, already undergoing a magnificent revival, towards the fullness of that renewed Catholicism, in which all our brethren will find the fulfilment of their desires. In that day the life-offerings of Catholics, Protestants, Anglicans and Orthodox will blend in a single flame, a single holocaust, a single burning desire. 'Saviour, the unity that thou desirest for thy Church, the way that thou desirest to lead us thither—we know that it is the sanctification of all Christian groups in thy love.' For this unity, for this sanctification, necessary condition of its arrival, let them offer their lives this man or woman whom thy Spirit is calling authentically to do so.

His own friendships are intimately associated with his offering of the Holy Sacrifice of the altar, the remembrance of each one dear to him being found on the altar in a photograph, a letter or a prayer. As regards this last he wrote:

> If you would like to compose a prayer to Christ, even a confidential one sealed, the contents of which should never be known to any save you and him, and for that prayer to be presented to him on the altar by me, the altar at which each day, as I celebrate the Holy Mysteries, I enter with you into his sacrificial oblation, I would gladly see to that.

He himself in return would give his friends prayers of his own which revealed such depths in his soul as they were able to apprehend, so that they could pray them with and for him. The following prayer was given to one of his Anglican friends, Father Francis Tyndale-Biscoe of the Society of St Francis, Cerne Abbas:

To my beloved brother, Father Francis.

Saviour Jesus, gather together all the children of your love. At the foot of the Cross, all together in anguish by reason of our separations which the voice of our consciences does not for the moment allow us to surmount, we beg pardon for all the sins which prepared, consummated and maintained our terrible divisions. We recognize humbly that we are all guilty. Saviour, forgive us.

Grant us the torment of prayer for Christian unity. We ask it with all our soul, Saviour. We know that there can be nothing that resists prayer when it is the echo of your prayer.

Give my Anglican brethren an ever greater holiness. May your Spirit enlighten them, guide them, direct them all along your way, which leads to your unity, Saviour Jesus! The unity for which you have prayed before your agony in the garden.

Give them the passion of prayer for the Roman Church, that she may be purified and sanctified; that she may walk along the rough way of renewal; that she may find her true dimensions; that she may manifest her true countenance; that she may come forth renewed in the expression and presentation of her thought and life; that, thanks to their prayer, there may come the great day when she will be ready for the joy of the gathering in her bosom of all Christians sanctified and renewed.

> Saviour, pardon us,
> Saviour, sanctify us,
> Saviour, may your Spirit
> penetrate all our souls
> with his love and with his light
> for the greater glory of the Holy Trinity
> in his eternal unity.

P.C.

His sense of the co-inherence of the Body of Christ gave special meaning to exchanges of such intimacies as regards personal aspiration and prayer:

There will be no need to say, 'I pray for this one, for another, unknown to me: or yet to say, I pray in their place.' But it will be right to say, 'I let the other pray in me: I offer him unity by the path of my soul: may the way of my prayer be open to him, the *via orationis*. So at the altar of the Holy Mass, at the Choir Office, at private prayer, with me and in me are praying my brethren, Protestant, Anglican and Orthodox.'

He used to say,

Union will be the work of those who pray. May thy will produce for its fulfilment a *théologie priante—theologia sacra—*it will be luminous because it will be full of prayer.

When I first knew the Abbé, he was 57 years old. He was a priest intrinsically hallowed through the greater part of his life by the discipline of an age-long tradition. There was a notable priestly neatness and cleanliness and careful correctness of attire, combined with obvious poverty. These things were of an order impressive in itself, but not what most impressed. Paul Couturier was, above all things, a man possessed by holy love. There was a radiance which comes from living close to God, but this raised it, in his case, to an apostolic intensity. His countenance, the lines of which were pure, regular, and, as it were, carved in fine ivory, was frail. It was also transparent, and shone with that unique light that marks the saint and seer. He had bright blue eyes which contrasted with his ivory skin. Sometimes the light in his eyes and countenance became flame, but the serenity of his quiet-loving spirit did not change.

The voice had the same quality as his genial appearance. It did not at first strike the hearer as possessing any special characteristics. It was not particularly musical: there were the Lyons accent and intonation and certain clerical mannerisms. All these things were characteristic of his milieu and training, as were perhaps also the combination of frank cordiality and quiet reserve. Suddenly, however, without notice, one would find that the voice had attained a new majesty, speaking slowly and with dignity of some mysterious region inhabited by the speaker, from whose life it derived deep authority. Then he was seen to be no longer ordinary, but clearly the man of God.

How soon we came to realize this! He was endowed with a rare gift of sympathy and friendship, which was given a new quality by grace. He inspired to a unique degree the love of men and women of all types, races, and 'Confessions'. This was because he had the gift of seeing with incomparable perspicacity the Christ in each of them and in their various Churches. He had a sense that as all Christians are responsible for the guilt of division and for the recovery of unity, God has allowed each to retain one gift in particular which he will be allowed to share with all, when sins are done away.

A Catholic, thoroughly Roman in his intransigence, he was generous in his understanding of and sympathy for other Christian traditions—very quick to see the value of the precious ore hidden in the detached rocks of Christendom. Along with this went his

295

ineradicable conviction of the need for each of penitence for the faults of all Christians—above all, for the faults of pride or lack of charity. He thought this penitence not least necessary for the sins of his own Communion, and in those days the majority of his fellow-churchmen were not so persuaded. With regard to this last point—the need of Rome for penitence—his conscience was as inexpugnable as was his assurance of the infallibility of the Church of Rome as the Church of God. Having the gift of seeing Christ in men and women individually, he drew the best out of each, and we found ourselves drawn to greater heights and depths and fresh perspectives beyond any potentialities hitherto suspected. If one failed his expectations, he showed a great capacity for encouragement.

His love for England was very great, and there is no doubt that he had an extraordinary gift for understanding our rather complex ecclesiastical and political heritage, as well as for appreciating the more straightforward excellences of English life and character. He had a surprising diversity of English friends, and his friendship for each was unique in quality. He often unconsciously helped us to appreciate qualities in one another which prejudice might have obscured. So it must have been with Jesus and those who loved him. To think of Paul Couturier is at once to go on to think of Christ. He attached no one to himself, but strove to attach all his friends to his Lord.

His great gift of appreciation made him the most delightful of guests. He was a host of exquisite courtesy and complete devotion, whether in his fourth-floor flat which, it has been observed, would have suited better an Alpinist than a diabetic with a bad heart, or in the streets and holy places of Lyons and Ars. None could make as clear as he did the glories of Lyons in the past or the rich spiritual content and affinities of its present society. Though recognized by folk of all kinds—theologians, priests and pastors, a great variety of Anglicans, and the general public—as endowed with a special mission from God, this did not prevent him from mysteriously achieving a remarkable degree of self-effacement wherever he went. This was because his presence drew out and lit up all that was excellent and beautiful around him. In this he resembled the Abbé

Portal, to whom he said he owed everything. With both of these men one felt oneself in the presence of a man of God—a man marked by God for this particular vocation which he obeyed without deviation, in perfect serenity. Each had the instinct and ability for finding the help of theologians. Each had the art of interrogation and of inviting enquiry. They got men to speak, rather than spoke themselves, but later they would summarize briefly in a way that evoked the wonder of the learned. Each had a deep respect for time, of which God is the Master, knowing that 'there is nothing divine about hurry and no hurry in the divine.' Both had waiting times, as in the thirty years of Nazareth. Every moment has its own place in that mighty stream of grace through which the Church grows. Both lived, studied, spoke, waited, or, when the call came, took action in that light.

Perhaps Paul Couturier's photographs need to be supplemented by his letters to give one the sense of the impression he made. His writing has clarity, precision, *ordonnance*, and relevant intensity (to quote T. S. Eliot's description of the style of Bishop Lancelot Andrews), and for all that it is a little stiff and clerical, every sentence radiates warmth, energy, spirit. When he loves to write of the deep things of God,

> the language becomes heavier and richer of content, the arrangement of phrases takes on a Gothic air; we have brief propositions of grave elevation: the whole letter is an ascension.[3]

There was quite certainly in him a spiritual energy and light which belong to the new creation. I remember one summer, after his health had been ruined by the Gestapo imprisonment, that two of us were together with him on the hill of Fourvière, after paying some visits and seeing some things of interest. The English visitors were almost prostrate with the heat. Our host, who had been up far earlier and was an older man and an invalid, took care to take us into a quiet café and order us a bottle of wine. It was a ludicrously small incident, but it stands for me as evidence that holiness draws from springs of energy to which mediocrity has no access and that this energy is one with a sympathy equally supernatural.

Another friend of the Abbé, Father Brandreth,[4] treasures especially the memory of an incident which occurred in the village church of Ars, whither he had been taken with others by Abbé Couturier.

> We were there on one occasion when a terrifying thunder-storm and rain-storm broke. A group of tourists—tourists, not pilgrims—came into the church to take shelter from the rain, talking and laughing quite loudly. Father Couturier had for more than an hour been a small frail figure kneeling motionless in prayer. He never moved at the interruption, but about fifteen minutes later, when the rain cleared, each of these tourists was kneeling behind him.

A tiny hint this, but surely a significant one, as to the power of holiness!

NOTES

[1] See Archimandrite Sofrony, *The Undistorted Image*, London: Faith Press, 1958, pp. 40–74; cf. Foreword by G. Florovsky, pp. 5f.

[2] C. Boyer, S.J., 'Tendences actuelles de l'oecuménisme Catholique', *Unitas* (French), no. 54/5 (1961), pp. 251–60.

[3] Pastor Rosendal in *Témoignages*, p. 69.

[4] See p. 178.

24

THE PRIEST AND THE PROPHET

MAISIE SPENS has well said:

> In the Abbé, the rôle of priest and prophet not merely combine in rare degree; they are inseparable. He was both priest and prophet of unity. He was priest and victim in oneness with the High Priest our Lord, who prayed—and prays—that all may be one as he and the Father are one, and offered himself as victim to that end. He was prophet of unity, not in the sense of 'predicting'—though he believed steadfastly that this prayer of the total Christ would in God's own way and time obtain from him the gift and miracle of the visible unity of all Christians—but the Abbé was prophet of unity by virtue of symbolizing it in his one life and person, as did the Old Testament prophets symbolize in their lives and persons the several messages committed to them by God.[1]

He was in everything a priest. This was perhaps because his love and understanding of the Liturgy brought him close to the eternal Sovereign High Priest. Yet this same Saviour, our Lord Jesus Christ is also the Sovereign Prophet who discerns the meaning of history as well as the King who directs all its currents. The contrast depicted by Heiler between prophetic and contemplative prayer[2] is in Couturier's experience disproved: for liturgical prayer holds both together in solution as surely as they are thus found in the supreme eucharistic prayer of the eternal *Liturgos* in St John 17.

His love of the liturgy was the mainspring of the Abbé's life. The word 'Liturgy' is used so as to include the divine office as well as the Eucharist which is the sun round which the Liturgy as a whole revolves. Of the seventeen notebooks left to Père Villain which contained his reflections on all sorts of subjects, seven of these contain 'General Notes with notes referring to the Mass' and seven contain material for a commentary on the Mass. Three interests were at work in the compilation of the latter. There was his desire to gain an ever-deeper apprehension of the problem of Christian Unity. There was his eagerness constantly to revivify his priesthood exercised in the offering of Mass, in the saying of the divine office, in the administration of the Sacrament of Penance—the shriving of the nuns of the Convent of St Charles of which he was chaplain—and the giving of Benediction at the same convent. Finally there was the desire to write a book on the Mass. He had chosen the motto for the book he hoped to write: *Laudabo Deum Meum in vita mea.* He was hesitating over his choice of a title, though one favoured is *Liturgy and the Liturgos.*

The notebooks, it has been said, 'revealed the Abbé as possessed of a liturgical temperament of the first order'. Despite the influence upon him of the distinguished Jesuit, Père Albert Valensin, who, through the *Exercises* of the founder of the Society of Jesus, introduced him to the fullness of the life of Christian Prayer, he was far more profoundly marked by his stay at the Benedictine Priory of Amay of which he became Oblate. The word PAX heading his letters was a constant reminder that there was his spiritual home. The chief nourishment of his spirit was Holy Scripture in which he saturated himself through the deliberate slow saying of Mass carefully prepared beforehand and through the contemplative recitation of the divine office. This 'solitary priest who carried the whole Church in his heart, was so convinced of the purity of the official prayer of the Church that he would have thought it harmful to substitute any other'.[3] He noted in one of these books and loved to read to Anglican friends a summary of an audience given on 12 December 1935 by Pope Pius XI to Dom Capelle, Abbot of Mont-César (Louvain) a liturgical writer of eminence:

> Pray, following the spirit of the Church in your prayer. The Church is large. Even at times displays an astonishing largeness of mind. She accepts manners of praying which are very deficient and very imperfect because she has compassion on the weakness of poor

humanity. Well and good!, she says, as you can't pray in any other way, pray like that, provided you do really pray . . . but if one wishes to know the mind of the Church, that is a different thing. . . . The Liturgy is a very great thing. It is the most important organ of the ordinary *magisterium* of the Church. What few things there are below worth caring about—Christ, the soul, the life of the Church! All the rest, what is it worth? . . .

Of this divine discipline which is that of the Church herself, the priest is the Liturgos, and the Abbé with a view to personal behaviour has to define this rôle. So we find a section in which he interprets the consciousness of the Liturgos by the expression 'to be a crowd'.

Liturgy and the Liturgos.

To be a Liturgos is to live and play one's part from *in medio cosmo*—to find oneself a crowd with one countenance open towards God, the other towards the world. It is thus to grasp in oneself the very life of Christ, the Liturgos: to unite in oneself, to unite with one another, to unite with God beings with dispositions entirely at variance with one another. Our liturgical prayer gives utterance to all: sinners, innocents, weak, strong . . . a human voice to animals and plants . . . voice for the life emergent (*ébauchée*) of plant and of animal. This is the life of man. This it is to be Christ.

I am head of creation and brother of all that is and of all its constituents by reason of

1. one's being the *metempsychosis* of the whirlpool of life, microcosm of its inter-related energy

2. having this love of being, of all that is and lives

3. having relations and friends, as one man to another

4. culture as one man to another

5. brotherhood with all [*tous*] and hence with everything [*tout*] in Christ

6. the use of all that is manufactured.

The function of the Liturgos is to descend in order to reascend. It is like that of Christ, like that of the Church—the divine *Agape* which comes to raise up its creation. It is thus a human function and a function of the Church (Christian = priest). All for the act of adoration that is Christ's to his Father. Here is the centre. The Mass is at the centre of the Liturgy and hence of the cosmos.

The leanings of the Abbé in eucharistic theology are made clear in a note which inaugurates a programme: 'to establish a synthesis between Père de la Taille and Dom Vonier'. He often quoted this formula from the second; 'The Mass is the sacrament of the Sacrifice of the Cross.' He himself notes:

> One act alone. The Incarnate Word adores the Father during the whole of his earthly life, the summit of which is the oblation of the death on the Cross. It is by his whole life that the risen Lord is glorified. His whole life is rendered by the Church co-extensive with mankind. Hence the Supper, eminently a focus of Communion, looks toward the Cross, renews itself by the Mass—the act by which the community (stem and branches) lets itself be drawn into his unique Act of maximal adoration which takes place at Calvary.
>
> The Mass is continued by Communion in which he adores within us; by the Reserved Sacrament wherein he adores amongst us; but its normal end is adoration in us by Communion. The Reserved Sacrament comes forth from a Mass with a view to Communion.
>
> *Holy Mass and historical feasts of the liturgy.*
> In the same way as the Holy Supper was eternalized because Christ is God eternal and thus abides, actualized incessantly by the Holy Mass in space-time—so is it with all the historical feasts of Christ: Christmas, Easter, Pentecost (Feast of the Spirit) and all the feasts since all belong to the mystical Body of Christ, extended through space-time and continuing his activity there, eternalizing each of his actions.

Bent on giving new value to the function of the laity in the priesthood of the Church, he found this to consist in the most active possible participation in the liturgy of the Mass.

> What the faithful need to be told emphatically [with regard to the Elevation] is not a word with regard to faith in the Real Presence so much as a word declaring their *sacrificial participation*, a word which, actualizing their entry upon priesthood, at the same time manifests and effects their insertion into the priestly Body of Christ, for which they are personally responsible, each one being a crowd.

With this in mind he hunted for invocations. Those noted include:

'Father we give thee thy Christ our Saviour!'
'Father graciously hear thy Christ in us!'
'To thee, Father, in the unity of the spirit, honour and glory!'
'In thy Christ, to thee Father, honour and glory in the Unity of the
       Spirit!'
'Father, thy Christ in whom we are!' [He notes this as good in
       experience—his own admittedly.]
'Father! thy Christ our Saviour!' [Noted as very good.]
'Father! thy Christ who lives in us!'
'*Pater! de tuis Donis ac Datis!*'
'*Christus tuus . . . Salvator noster*
   . . . In quo omnes sumus
   . . . Et in quo omnia constant!' [What fullness!]

With regard to the differences of eucharistic development in West and East, the Abbé observes:

Visibly Hidden in the Eucharist.
Christ allows western psychology to incline in what is for us a more human direction—visibility. Hence the Monstrance.
He allows oriental psychology to incline in the direction of *hiddenness*, more divine, more mysterious.
Together they might attain equilibrium; together, i.e. by each accepting the other, each following its own line of movement.

In an article entitled 'The Mystery of Wheat',[4] the Abbé draws out the cosmic character of the Eucharist, the aspect so dear to him. We have first paragraphs entitled: 'The sprouting corn—the mystery of the life of vegetation'; 'The corn which nourishes or the mystery of Bread'; 'Bread in the service of Christ'; then 'The Eucharistic mystery of bread'.

Glory of wheat to become under the form of bread, and by the will of Christ, the offering that man is to bring to the altar as a sign of his contrition, his adoration, his supplication, his thanksgiving—this last the very meaning of the word Eucharist, that form of prayer which includes all prayer, as the greater contains the less!
On this bread which has become a natural symbol of human

gratitude falls consecration, veritable fire from heaven, proof of acceptance of our offering by the Father since the Father, covering this bread with his Spirit, effects here the birth, in the sacrificial figure of death, of his Son once crucified for us in his Human form upon the Cross of redemption. Behold then the bread becomes, not—assuredly not!—the habitation of the glorified Christ, but quite simply the Sign that the glorified Christ has resumed relations with our space and time, so truly that he must affirm the presence, *real, hic* in space *et nunc* in time of his real Being which is entirely *spiritual*—Son of God, human soul and body risen and glorified. To signify the real presence of a spiritual reality—this is the high part played by Bread eucharisticized. Thus begins the unfolding of the most Holy Sacrifice of the Eucharist, that sacrament of the Sacrifice of Calvary. This part played by the Bread as *Bread of Sacrifice* it continues by becoming the *Bread of Communion* in the sacrifice offered to the most Holy Trinity. . . . The Bread will be henceforth conserved in all the reality of its character as Bread of Sacrifice and of Communion, to nourish the dying or to receive the adoration of the living, since its presence signifies the Presence, mysterious and real as it is, of the glorified Christ.

If the whole destiny of created being—mineral, vegetable, human, Christian—is to be the visible consummation of a mystery, this means that creation is sacred. It is the sacrament of the Creator. It is his theophany. It is diaphanous with a transparence through which the Trinity reveals himself.

One ought therefore not to approach this mystery of wheat promoted to so great a function in the cosmos save with reverence.

The farther one advances in realizing its holy mysteriality (character as mystery), the more this reverence should declare itself to the point of becoming respect, veneration.

To have this reverence, this respect, this veneration for the wheat is to have with regard to it the sense of the sacred. This sense of the sacred goes far beyond verbal expressions of it, however irreproachably pronounced, or conventional gestures and ritual, however irreproachably performed. This sense of the sacred is the sense of the worship 'in spirit and in truth' of God present through this prodigious destiny which has as its starting-point the death of the grain of wheat in the earth and for its point of arrival the *Sacrificial Bread of communion* on the altar of the most holy Sacrifice.

The author goes on to insist in detail on the sacred character of every point in the procedure of the making of the holy bread for the altar. Then comes a dramatic climax. The sense of the sacred as he displays it is realistic and exacting. For he goes on to speak of the *extreme wretchedness of the hosts.*

How, as a matter of fact, does wheat reach our altars? Paul Couturier was not a mathematician and a scientist for nothing. These faculties of his were in deep harmony with his mystical theological and liturgical instincts. He had prepared a careful enquiry with regard to actual practice. Every part of the human workmanship was carefully examined—weight, manner of baking, shape, the imprinting of holy symbols. At every point there were signs of negligence and lack of integrity. The altar-breads current were wholly unworthy to become signs of the adorable Presence. If ordinary English bread is what we know it to be, a disgrace to civilization, it is not surprising if the bread of the altar has its defects; and if all the beauty and dignity of church worship should have at its central point such symptoms of ugliness, we have here a token of Pharisaism unconscious but undeniable. The recovery of the sense of the sacred at this point of wheat might have far-reaching implications. Care for the integrity of the bread on the altar might induce a new sense of integrity with regard to that which supplies the daily needs of common life. In any case the ethos of a secularized and over-mechanized civilization ruled by Mammon should not be allowed to penetrate thus unobserved at this crucial point of our fellowship with God.

The Divine Office was the joy of Abbé Couturier's life. He longed to share it with the laity. Speaking of a popular substitute, the chaplet, which consists of the rapid recitation in public of the mysteries of the Rosary, he remarked:

What an abbreviation of the great Life of the Spirit—Christ praying freely in us. We must re-introduce the Breviary amongst the faithful, the Breviary in French, whole or in part . . . are they not as capable as Protestant people are of reading the Psalms?

The saying of the Office was a work which he regarded as demanding solitude and time. He could not approve of the habit, sanctioned it is true by canonists, of saying the Breviary rapidly with only 'virtual attention', or of reciting it in 'bus or tram or in the street.

> When one has something of importance to say to a friend one no longer speaks at the Latin speed of conversation: one speaks slowly, one thinks of what one is saying; one makes an affective act of the will. The someone to whom one speaks? God. The something important—some part of the Mass or of the Breviary, prayer.

The Psalter was for him the prayer of Christ himself—Christ as clothed in human nature in all its diverse history.

> It is then the total Christ of all human history (that of humanity and of each individual) who prays in me. Even that which might be left of evil in these prayers would be a cry of distress recalling by the Church which recites them, the exasperation of mankind.
>
> When I say the imprecatory Psalms I ought to have such sentiments expressed, experienced, and consummated by the love which Christ has revealed to us, for love is the perfection of vengeance which is only a first intimation of justice.

He knew portions of the Office by heart and noted thoughts which they suggested to him. So far from regarding an hour sufficient for the Breviary, as some moral theologians advise, it needed the counsel of his confessor to assure him that two hours were enough. He was conscious of wielding great power in his function as Liturgos. Through his faithful and generous application of intentions he included in the Divine Office the Church in her entirety, holding—as he loved to say—that each of us is responsible for the welfare of the Church of God.

At the same time this Liturgos was emphatically a man for whom private devotions held their special place in life. The idea of restricting himself to the official prayer of the Church would have seemed

to him to show misunderstanding of its function as the sacred river
of the City of Christ into which all human aspiration and appeal
found its way freely. The liberty of the glory of the children of God
he regarded as a first principle of our life in the Spirit. The Liturgy
would not be its consummation if it is thought of as restricting the
expression of the particular contribution of prayer unique in each
faithful soul. The prayer of Jesus Christ himself in his Body which
must operate in each several member, would be impoverished without the infinite variety of personal or private prayer.

How greatly he loved that prayer which seems to me the most
satisfying of all prayers of surrender, a prayer which comes to us
from the great saint of Switzerland, St Nicholas de Flüe (1417–87):

> My Lord and God, take from me all that blocks my way to thee.
> My Lord and God, give me all that speeds my way to thee.
> My Lord and God, take this myself from me and give me as thine
> own to thee.

It is possible that Paul Couturier thought of the Jesus Prayer of
the Orthodox Church as standing somewhere between liturgical
prayer and individual devotion.[5] The Jesus Prayer is the fruit of the
hesychast tradition developed on Mount Sinai and later on Mount
Athos. This prayer consists of the incessant repetition of the words,
'Lord Jesus, Son of God, have mercy on me a sinner'. More and more
it eliminates all discursiveness, gradually becoming itself one word,
the name of Jesus. The name echoes continually in the soul, adheres
to the rhythm of breathing, and becomes, in a sense more than
figurative, the breath of life—of the soul and body indissolubly.

> It is the Liturgy interiorized, incessant communion with Jesus
> present in his Name.[6]

Paul Couturier was aware that his emphasis on the prayer of
Christ in us as a principle of prayer for unity might seem difficult to
harmonize with the hallowed tradition of Orthodox spirituality, the
exercise of the Jesus prayer. The second paragraph of his testament
deals skilfully with this. It is headed 'Let Christ pray in us to his
Father for unity', and runs as follows:

No one can say the name of Jesus save through the Spirit of God, St Paul teaches us. To say the name of Jesus signifies: a prayer, a movement [*élan*], an elevation of the soul towards the Father, for the *real* utterance of this Name is an *act*, a 'yes' human and poor, a poor 'yes' of our human misery—we are sinners! and a 'yes' shining forth from our human grandeur—we are free! Sons of his Love! We are his living images. This 'yes' can resound very far in the unexplored regions of our spiritual being. It can be partial or may more or less truly approach totality, though never completely attaining this. The more we ask God to strip us of ourselves, the more we enter into the divine renunciation—'He who loses his soul, saves it'—the more firmly is established in us our capacity to hear Christ praying to his Father in us through his Spirit. There emerges a dissolving of our prayer into his prayer. In the attentive silence of our listening souls there is established our cleaving to him with our whole will, not only with our words, our sentiments, our desires. The more we discover ourselves in him where we really are one, or him in us where he really is, the more efficacious becomes our prayer, since it is now he who prays without the weight of ourselves.

Such an attitude, the work of God, divine liberality, precious pearl bought at the royal price of renunciation, situates us at the Antipodes of an *inert spiritual passivism*. And this attitude has already freedom of the city in vocal prayer, private or corporate, provided that there be assured the gravity of the silence surrounding them and a certain unhurriedness of utterance.

The Abbé found place and need in the life of the Church not only for prayer liturgical and for prayer mental, but for prophetic prayer. Here is an example of his gift for this—the substance of his prayer at the opening of a Bible circle at Lyons:

O Christ our Master, beloved and adored, thou didst say 'Where two or three are gathered together in my name, there am I in the midst of them.'

Look down, we beseech thee, upon some of thy baptized members here gathered together in thy Name. They have come to implore thy pardon, to tell thee how much they suffer by reason of being separated from one another in their faith in thee—and to pray to thee.

Relying on thy word, we believe that although invisible to our bodily eyes, thou art really here in person among us.

We desire, all together, to find one another in thy sufferings on the Cross, in thy agony, in thy death—for we are all here agonizing in thy agony, dying in thy death . . . all redeemed in thy unique and perfect Sacrifice . . . and to take that Redemption to ourselves by saying together once more, with greater fervour, the 'Yes' of our Baptism.

In the very depth of our being we know, we acknowledge, and we confess that we are sinners and that, although justified, we still sin seven times a day.

Pardon us. Purify us. Sanctify us. Send to us thy Spirit.

We have come here chiefly to tell thee, with one heart and one soul, our intense suffering, thine own suffering, thy more intense suffering, that suffering which caused thee to utter that most moving of all the prayers that thou hast left to us:

'*Holy Father . . . the glory which thou gavest me I have given them; that they may be one even as we are one: I in them, and thou in me, that they may be made perfect in one; and that the world may know that thou hast sent me, and hast loved them, as thou has loved me.*'

O Christ, pardon all our guilt in this tragedy of divisions.

This indeed is the greatest of all tragedies than can ever afflict humanity, for thy Church is thyself, and it is not possible for thee to say in one place 'Yes' and in another, 'No'. And the children of thy love—in the sight of their brethren, and as far as it is in their power—make thee appear to contradict thyself. And yet for each of us, it is our own individual Church which, as a Mother, engenders our faith in thee, and at the same time, separates us from our Christian brethren.

O Christ, have pity on our distress.

It is because our fathers and we ourselves have forgotten to love thee, that our vision has become obscured. We no longer know how to read thy thoughts. We can no longer see thy image in our brethren; neither can we recognize them in thee, where all are lovable since by thee they are all infinitely beloved.

We are all guilty of the worst heresy—the heresy against love. To fail to understand thy love and all that thy love involves is indeed the negation of thy command; it is, in the face of the world, to contradict thee. 'By this shall all men know that ye are my disciples, if ye have love one to another.'

The irony of it! O Christ, pardon us!

Grant that all Christians may love one another without reserve. Thou alone canst bring this to pass.

Grant that we may love thee with an unbounded love.

The things which we have in common—thy Book, thy Baptism, our faith in thee, in thine Incarnation, in thy Redemption, and indeed many other beliefs—all this unites us indissolubly, making us in thee, and through thee, children of thy Father.

But the things which separate us, unite us even more closely—though in a different way—than the things which we have in common. For the things which separate us are the cause of intense suffering, the suffering of being separated in our thoughts concerning thy Church: and there is nothing that draws us together and unites us more closely, than suffering.

That is why, this evening, we are here, drawn together by what we have in common, but drawn together still more closely by what separates us.

With one heart and one soul we desire to pray to thee in one and the same prayer. We desire that the prayer which we offer to thee shall arise from thine own Book, from such pages of thy Book as shall tell thee in a new way that we are one in our love and in our suffering.

O Christ, have pity. O Christ, pardon us.

O Christ, make us suffer so intensely by reason of our separation that thy prayer within us may penetrate us, may take possession of us, may have free course in us, and ascend to thy Father.

'*I in them, and thou in me, that they may be made perfect in* ONE!'

NOTES

[1] Broadcast: 'The Way of Life', 22 January, 1960. Cf. *Témoignages*, pp. 177–202.

[2] F. Heiler, *Prayer, a Study in the History and Psychology of Religion* (tr. S. McComb), Oxford: O.U.P., 1932.

[3] Villain, *L'Abbé*. This section of my book draws substantially upon Part III, pp. 269–79, 'Quelques thèmes de réflexion'.

[4] Published in *Maison Dieu*, 1949, No. 18, pp. 122–35.

[5] On Mount Athos it is regarded as good to 'retain' this prayer even during the monastic offices, and it may take the place of such offices if the monk cannot be present.

[6] Paul Eudokimov, 'Saint Seraphim of Sarov (An icon of Orthodox spirituality)', *Ecumenical Review* XV, No. 3, April 1963, pp. 269f. Abbé Couturier's meditation, 'A Cosmic Aspect of Prayer', composed for the Sisters of Grandchamp, dwells on the relations between prayer and breathing. This is to be found in *Oecuménisme spirituel*, pp. 164–75.

PILGRIMAGES AND CHRISTIAN UNITY

Abbé Couturier saw clearly the unique place which pilgrimages must take in the ecumenical movement. The pilgrimage would be amongst other things a means of freeing this movement from the danger of being monopolized by ecclesiastics, intellectuals and specialists. It would make it accessible to all kinds of ordinary folk, bringing it down from the theological level—that is to say from the level of *theologia secunda* (dialectical, doctrinal, dogmatic) in which the theological life of Western Christianity largely consists, to that of *theologia prima* which belongs to all Christians and is primarily thanksgiving and praise. (I owe this valuable discrimination to Dom Sartory, O.S.B., of Niederaltaich.) The pilgrimage may well be the means of awakening in Protestants the incarnational or sacramental instinct, and of teaching Catholics the meaning of that call of the redeemed to transfigure the universe, the realization of which is the heart of Orthodoxy. Moreover, pilgrimages are sure to promote what may be called the practice of the mystery of the communion of saints.

Abbé Couturier shared great understanding of the special vocation in this regard of an American Episcopalian, Miss Barbara Simonds, whom he did much to help and encourage. Miss Simonds is a pioneer in setting on foot such pilgrimages of prayer for Christian Unity. Living in Rome for many years, she was the first to devise schemes by which Christians representing various traditions might in that city together retrace their family history, starting with the apostolic age and the catacombs and gradually moving through the centuries to those more recent ages wherein variant traditions, however acutely divided one from the other, may be apprehended by other groups in the light of their common origins. The Abbé was in the habit of taking his guests on pilgrimages in honour of the martyrs and saints of Lyons, or to the shrine of the Curé d'Ars. He would have been deeply moved by the news of the pilgrimage taken by Pope John XXIII before the opening of the Vatican Council. The decision of Pope Paul VI to go as a pilgrim to the Holy Land itself would have been wholly after his own heart. He regarded Solovyev's *Three Conversations*, composed in Easter 1900, shortly before the author's death, as giving the sign-manual to this century. The meeting described in the last of these ('Short story of Antichrist': Frank, *Solovyov Anthology*, p. 229) between Pope and Patriarch along with the leader of Protestantism in Jerusalem seems strikingly to foreshadow what actually took place close to the Holy City in January 1964.

25

1950–1953: LAST ILLNESS AND DEATH

CERTAINLY there was no excess of purple in the sunset of this faithful and fruitful life. But the last three years have a simple and homely dignity—the solemn peace and creaturely surrender that characterize Compline in the Office of the sons of St Benedict, of whose world-wide, perennial family Paul Couturier was an oblate.

In the summer of 1950 came an invitation from Père Boyer, the head of *Unitas*, to attend at Rome the *Réunion internationale* of twenty-five theologians interested in ecumenism. No doubt the invitation coming so soon after the publication of *Humani Generis* with its denunciation of false irenism was gratifying to the Abbé. But expressing his gratitude, he declined. Others, he knew, would present his convictions, for they had taken stock of his principles and shared his certainty that Reunion must be ultimately a fruit of the interior life of Christians. His own apostolate must go forward now, hidden and detached, within the boundaries of the circle that his labours, co-operating with Providence, had formed around him. 'If a grain of wheat fall into the ground and live, it abideth alone. But if it die, it bringeth forth much fruit.'

In 1951 he was present in the Salle Blanchon to hear his beloved disciple, Père Maurice Villain, speak on the *Real Meaning of Ecumenism*. He was busy himself during the early months with the preparation of a book on Anglican religious communities, to which the chief of these had each contributed an account of their history and of their life and work. Cardinal Gerlier was ready to permit the publication

312

of this valuable work, provided that some English Roman Catholic bishop would give his assent. I tried vainly to secure this. Soon afterwards an attractive book,[1] covering the same ground, by an English Roman Catholic, the well-known author, Peter Anson, was published with the due official sanction from the Roman Catholic side by an Anglican publisher, the S.P.C.K. The author knew how to present his material in such a way as to evade the disapproval of authority.

In the summer of that year, the Abbé was present for the last time at the gathering of his interconfessional circle at the monastery of La Trappe des Dombes. It was specially well attended. The Protestant ministers included the President of the Consistory of Lyons, Pastor Eberhard, Dean Courvoisier, and the distinguished Swiss theologian, Pastor Leuba, and two members from the original circle of Erlenbach. The Roman Catholics present included secular priests as well as Marists, Sulpicians and Jesuits. The subject of the discussion, as in the previous year 1950, was the doctrine of the Sacraments. The Abbé was to prove unable to attend the gathering of 1952, the subjects of which were the Communion of Saints and the Last Things.

For in the middle of November 1951 the Abbé was pronounced dangerously ill with an affliction of the heart. It was clear that he must give up his room in the Institution des Chartreux and be confined henceforth more or less wholly to his sister's flat. He received permission to say Mass there in a private oratory, and he did so daily until his death. This very modest place of worship imprinted its image upon the memory of visitors from many lands who came there to pay to one whom they loved and venerated what they knew might be a final visit. On the table which did duty as an altar stood crosses which recalled three great Christian communions. The bare wooden cross was the gift of the Protestant sisters of Grandchamp; the Eastern Orthodox cross, delicately carved in mother-of-pearl, recalled through its donor, Maisie Spens (an Anglican), the Invisible Monastery, the illimitable vision of which she and the Abbé had seen at the same time independently one of the other. Along with these and his own crucifix there were ikons to recall earlier relations with the Russian refugees. On the wall on the Gospel side a poster by Brother Eric de Saussure of Taizé, depicting Christ in his agony, registered the crucial fact of the suffering of the Saviour for the unity of his people: there was added in 1952 a second poster from the same vigorous hand, which showed the Cross, the all-sufficient sacrifice, to be nevertheless one which all the members of his divided Body must consent to carry together: in January 1953 these were joined by one from another hand containing the single prostrate figure— Humility who to all 'opens the ways that are barred'. There were always visible close at hand the white eucharistic vestments, the present prepared for the Abbé and given to him by the Anglican nuns of the House of Prayer to whom Dom Benedict Ley of Nashdom had introduced him.

Of the friends who managed to find their way there the most privileged were those permitted to be present at Mass and to receive Holy Communion from the Abbé's hands. Others were permitted to pray in this oratory, sometimes accompanied by him. He could not rise to greet his friends, but when a priest visited him, he would request his blessing. Mlle Couturier kept careful guard, seeking to prevent too long or too exacting a visit.

In the Unity week of January 1952 by the Abbé's invitation the great poet-dramatist, Paul Claudel, came to Lyons and enthralled an audience which overflowed the Théâtre des Célestins by a great pronouncement on the theme, 'Why I love the Bible'. The Abbé participated only *in spiritu*, staying in his fourth-floor flat and lifting up his hands to support his brethren in Christ as once Moses interceded for Israel upon the mountain. Perhaps no visit brought the invalid greater joy than one which followed soon after—that of Cardinal Gerlier himself who came to express his gratitude over this event.

In the spring of the same year arrived a letter from Maximus IV the Patriarch of the Greek Catholic Church of the Melchites, which also brought the Abbé much happiness and consolation:

> We, Maximus IV, Patriarch of Antioch and all the East, of Alexandria and of Jerusalem, moved by the desire of expressing our satisfaction and our gratitude to Monsieur the Abbé Couturier of

the Archdiocese of Lyons, who for many years has displayed great zeal in furthering the unity of the Church, specially by publishing writings and organizing prayers with that intention, having obtained permission of His Eminence Cardinal Pierre Marie Gerlier, Archbishop of Lyons, nominate Abbé Paul Couturier Honorary Archimandrite of our Patriarchate of Alexandria and authorize him to carry the appropriate marks of distinction in conformity with Canon law and tradition.

And we bless him with our whole heart in the name of the Father and of the Son and of the Holy Ghost.

From our patriarchal see at Damascus, 11 April 1952,
MAXIMUS IV, Patriarch, etc.

Quotations from two private letters from the East throw light on this event. Mgr Tawil, editor of *Le Lien* (review of the Patriarchate) comments thus:

It is your love of the East and your competence in dealing with its problems which have merited you this distinction. Your call to union in connexion with the Universal Prayer for Christian unity is awaited every year with impatience, and we publish it all the more gladly because it shows us each year some new and interesting aspect of the problem. We are very happy to be counted among your friends.

Père Robert Clément, his cousin and disciple in ecumenism, wrote to the same effect:

This East of yours which you have loved almost next to the Russians and which you do not forsake despite your more recent discoveries—Anglicanism and the various Protestant communions —it is this East which is the first to pay homage to your work. The Archimandrite's cross and the veil which you will be able to wear henceforth will recall that you know how to make yourself all things to all men for the love of Christ.

Who are the Melchites and Maximus their Patriarch? Maximus IV, Patriarch of Antioch and of all the East, of Alexandria and Jerusalem, unlike most of those who carry high-sounding ecclesiastical titles, is a great and significant figure in the church history of our time. The Greek-Arab flock of which he is head, is often spoken of as a Uniat Church. This may well give an erroneous impression. The Uniat Churches are like the Melchites in that they are composed of Christians who accept the claims and doctrines of Rome and yet continue to use an Eastern Rite. But whereas the other Uniat Churches came into being as the result of Roman Catholic pressure, the Melchite Churches—for there are Orthodox as well as Catholic Melchites—are the result of the bifurcation of a single river in periods of misunderstanding. The bifurcation, during the same centuries, of English Christianity into the Papal or so-called recusant stream and the Anglican or conformist stream is a phenomenon which strikes some minds as somewhat similar to that of the Melchite Churches. The Eastern Orthodox heritage of the Uniat Churches seems to be preserved only in externals; but the Greek Melchites under Roman jurisdiction have succeeded in keeping alive the Orthodox character and ethos in their church life.

Patriarch Maximus IV is a living testimony to this. An Arab of great vigour and independence of mind, he lives alternately in his ancient palace close to his cathedral at Damascus and in the new quarter of Faggelah in Cairo. But he is also well known in the Lebanon, where he spends the summer months, and in various European capitals. Wherever he goes this octogenarian, at once venerable and radiant, wins friends and admirers by his integrity, wisdom and courage. He is possessed by a deep conviction as to the two-fold vocation of himself and his flock at this time: on the one hand they must defend the tradition and the prerogatives of the Oriental patriarchal Churches; on the other hand it is their duty to affirm steadfastly their allegiance to the Roman Pontiff. From himself and his able theologians there have proceeded recently important protests against the centralizing tendencies of Roman jurisdiction, especially the usurpation of the rights of Patriarchs by the Curia and the provision by the Roman Congregation of Rites of rubrics for the Oriental Liturgies which betray flagrant negligence with regard to their structure. Maximus IV has recently given forceful expression to his basic convictions in a lecture at Düsseldorf, an English translation of which has been printed in *Reunion*.[2] He has made clear his readiness to resign his office in favour of the Eastern Orthodox Melchite archbishop if the Orthodox Melchites can see their way to accept the Roman claims.

I had the privilege two years ago of meeting the Patriarch Maximus at the home of the Monks of Unity at Chevetogne. He spoke of his happiness over the late Archimandrite Couturier's growing prestige, citing an Arab saying to the effect that the woodman knows of the quality of a tree before it is felled. Since then he has been an exceptionally vigorous and influential participant in the Second Vatican Council.

The conferment of the office of archimandrite on Paul Couturier was noticed by a few Western journals. There was a quiet family feast, the one occasion on which Archimandrite Couturier wore in token of his rank the very simple cross of gilded plate presented to him by friends. Though his new rank gave him the right to be addressed as Monsignor, he remained always 'the Abbé' to his friends, however much they appreciated the Patriarch's discernment. More impression was made in England by the appearance in the *Church Times* of 1 August 1952 of a brief note telling of the Abbé's grave illness and asking for prayers. He was deeply touched by the large number of letters of sympathy he received from English and American friends and admirers, known and unknown.

The January tract of 1953 followed the same lines as usual, save for three last requests:

1. that Christians of different communions, when they meet in friendship or sympathy will not forget to say together the Lord's Prayer;
2. that all Christians will understand that it is their duty to pray for the World Council of Churches;
3. that they will understand that humility, the fruit of prayer, opens all barred roads.

In the same month the Abbé published what has been called his 'spiritual testament', a revised edition of his brochure *Prayer and Christian Unity*, which contained a full and precise statement of this message. Whereas in 1944 it had appeared *ad usum privatum* signed *Irénée*, it carried now the signature of the author and the *imprimatur* of the archdiocese of Lyons.[3]

The last months of his life, when he was no longer engrossed in active ministry, must have been for the Abbé, despite the visits of friends from many lands, a time of greater solitude. A pioneer, especially one in the realm of the Spirit, must needs be a solitary, and this most of all when he is preparing for the end. Since September 1948 the visits of his most intimate disciple, Père Maurice Villain, had been much less frequent, and this for reasons for which the Abbé himself was largely, if indirectly, responsible. Père Villain had given up his work as lecturer in theology at Lyons in order to consecrate himself to the ecumenical ministry which he had found more and more absorbing. For this reason he had left Lyons for Paris. It is true that their union of intention and labour was intensified rather than lessened by loss of this local co-operation; moreover they met from time to time as opportunity served. But both felt the parting considerably.

Their last meeting was in February 1953, when Père Villain passed through Lyons on his return from Morocco where he had proclaimed the message of the Week of Prayer for Christian unity not only to Christians, but also, with episcopal encouragement, to Moslems and Jews. He was received by the Abbé in his little oratory with a certain unusual solemnity. The Abbé began by speaking, not for the first time, of death. He had recently suffered the loss of a beloved aunt, Mère Lepage of the Ladies of Nazareth, to whose affection and holy example he owed so much in earlier years. He spoke also of Dom Gregory Dix of Nashdom, who had died recently, and of Arthur Smallwood, the English pioneer whose vision had been so strangely close to his own. He exhorted Père Villain to solitude with God, the unique condition for realizing, without illusion, the character of our vocation. He advised Maurice Villain to make a day's retreat every month for the purpose of seeking the divine will. Then, after silence, he added,

If one day the Holy Spirit inspires you to make tracts, don't copy mine. Follow the inspiration of the Holy Spirit.

He seemed to his visitor to have attained the highest degree of detachment. The penitential strain, normally so intense in his nature, seemed to have given place to a simpler and gentler state of mind—the humble repose of a child in his Father's arms. He seemed to be resting effortlessly in that abandonment, the *Fiat* of Mary which he so often commended to his spiritual children, and in which he saw the Alpha and Omega of holiness.

He had good news to give his disciple. A postcard had arrived from Cardinal Gerlier, then at Rome, intimating that he had made opportunity to speak to Pope Pius XII of the scheme of prayer for Christian unity and had, on the Abbé's behalf, conveyed a report on this subject, which linked up with the *'appel convergent'* to prayer.

As Père Villain would be passing through Lyons four weeks later, on his way to Geneva, their next meeting was fixed for 24 March.

There were three older friends who remained close to him in these last years. The first was Victor Carlhian, the layman with whom he had spent part of every summer from 1921–38, and to whom, more than any other, he owed the liberation of spirit which had enabled him to find his vocation. M. Carlhian was now president of the Lyons philosophical society, and had attached himself to the church of St Paul, in the parish of which he lived, and which is closely associated with one of the great figures of the Conciliar Movement, Jean Gerson (1363–1429), who had spent his last ten years there and had endeared himself to parishioners by catechizing the children. Gerson had been everywhere admired for his learning and holiness: after his death there had been talk of his canonization, before the triumph of the monarchic papacy caused a lessening of the prestige of the great men of the Councils. It was a suitable place of worship for Victor Carlhian. In 1959, when Abbé Emile Meura of Lille and I brought to Lyons an ecumenical pilgrimage of Roman Catholics and Anglicans to visit the tomb of the Abbé, the Anglicans by chance lodged close to this church and were given permission to have their Eucharist in a chapel or sacristy which belonged to it. On my last visit at that time to Victor Carlhian, whose great part in cherishing the free growth of the French Catholic intellect, not to mention the resistance movement of the war-years I had come to realize, I found that he had just died after a long, painful illness, during which he had offered his sufferings for the cause of unity, so dear to his departed friend. It was good that the Church of England, which he greatly esteemed, should have its representatives at the Requiem Mass for him in the church of St Paul.

There was, secondly, Jean Escoffier, a distinguished businessman, who had been the Abbé's pupil at the Institution des Chartreux, and who, with his charming wife and family, was unfailing in grateful loyalty and kindness to his former schoolmaster.

But most intimate, devoted, and faithful of all was, of course, his sister, Marie Antoinette, two years older than himself, whose collaboration in his ecumenical apostolate had been so keen and steadfast from its first phase, when they were concerned with the care of Russian refugees. It will be recalled that it was owing to her weak health (she suffered from a kind of neurosis) that the Abbé, on the advice of their distinguished uncle, Mgr Planus (also a member of the Chartreux), after spending the day from Mass till evening at the Institution des Chartreux, always took his supper and spent the night at his sister's flat on the fourth floor of 5 Rue du Plat.

There were spiritual advantages and disadvantages in this arrangement. It is a mistake to think that the duty of caring for his sister—an astonishing compound of the lovable, the saintly, and the exacerbating—must be regarded as a God-given means of penance and sanctification of the Abbé. It is true that at the close of the First World War, had it not been for this responsibility, the Abbé would probably have embraced the contemplative life in an enclosed order; but his dear aunt, Mère Lepage, of whose death I have just written, in spite of her deep sympathy for this aspiration, had spoken against this suggestion. She told me of this herself, and we have now the actual words written in her own hand.

It seems to me that in leaving your sister in a situation in which she has real need of you, he [God] is showing you his will.

So the Abbé stayed in the world, free to embrace his vocation as the servant of Christian Unity.

Without such a home, how much less could he have done first for his Russian friends, and later for the separated brethren, Anglican, and Swedish Lutherans, and other Protestants, who visited him in such numbers! For them his sister was a charming hostess, taking the deepest interest in each visitor and keeping them all faithfully in her intercessions, but her volubility in conversation was, at times, shattering! There were also certain limitations in her outlook which made her cautious with regard to her brother's undertakings. It seems to me that her churchmanship, which was fervent, was marked by a certain conservative strictness which indicated the narrow mould of piety from which her brother had been liberated. But all her friends found her tender love and reverence for her brother winning, despite her talkativeness, and there was never any doubt as to who was spiritually in control of the home.

They lived apart only during the summer, when Abbé Couturier was staying with the Carlhians at their country estate as chaplain and tutor to the family, and Mlle Couturier was also away at some home or convent in the country. During these periods of separation, they engaged in extensive correspondence, of which the sister's share has survived. Discovered among her papers after her death in 1959 was a packet on which her brother had written 'Letters from my beloved sister'. The letters are exquisite in their spontaneity and with a genuine strain of old-world holiness. She had sought at times, but in vain, to correct what she felt to be her brother's excess of generosity, and to guide his exuberance into safer, more conventional channels, but she nevertheless co-operated with him keenly in prayer and labour. As far as possible she cared for his health, and did her best to make him take care of it. This is the constant refrain of her letters. He must take a proper measure of rest during his annual holiday. He is advised not to read when he is resting, not to say his Office late at night, not to rise to do his meditation before early Mass. No doubt the Abbé profited greatly from her incessant counsel, though there were times when there was no holding him back from eager self-spending. She wrote:

Don't overdo it. Take your time . . . above all. Don't be all exaggeration when you come out of your retreat. Love God like St Francis de Sales, sweetly and in tranquillity.

She was a faithful, trusted friend, to whom friends and associates of the Abbé owe much. When he wrote to her from a priest-pastor conference at Presinges in 1950, 'The days here have been extraordinarily blessed, due largely to your prayers', he meant what he said.

It is true that he had to correct her sometimes when her anxiety regarding the future was too dominant.

Nothing is perfect in this world [he wrote]. Man is himself the principal artisan of his unhappiness. This comes because his attention is concentrated on what he lacks instead of what he has. The least lack then spoils a situation full of happiness.

The imagination can play the most terrible tricks and can people our lives with a crowd of parasites which form a ring round the solid, lovely reality which divine generosity affords us. I am always the happiest of men; so you must be the happiest of women.

I think constantly of you, and am trying to unite myself with your novena, and will say Mass for you on the 8th. Don't let us torment ourselves. What you ask seems good, but our view is always so short. Isn't it much better to ask only to know and do the divine will? No doubt that is so; for that is the goal of our life.

It was every day that he bore her in his oblation to our Lord in the Holy Mysteries of the altar.

Saviour, I give and abandon to you the dearest gift you have given me after my mother's departure—my sister. Grant her pardon for her sins. Sanctify her. May she offer you her old age each day, and in advance her agony and her death; may she agonize in you and may she die in you; in faith, in hope, in your love. Amen.

After his death, Marie Antoinette chanced to find a farewell letter from her brother.

Pray a great deal. Do much good. Au revoir. Live in the peace of Christ.

The words which follow his signature come from a Jesuit whom she venerated.

> Pray before everything, everything. Trust and total abandonment to the Divine Providence.

His and her trust in the loving Father were to be vindicated in her blessed, peaceful death six years after his own.

Now that her brother was mortally ill, Mlle Couturier was openly vigilant: as eager to spare his becoming over-fatigued, and perhaps as unsuccessful as ever before. When she made clear her conviction that a visitor's departure was overdue, the Abbé would sometimes beg for respite. 'Let us be, Antoinette, let us be', he would say. Sometimes, however, the invalid had to give in. Père Maurice Villain records his disappointment when, having travelled over 300 miles to see his friend, their conversation was limited to a quarter of an hour.

The meeting between Père Villain and the Abbé which had been fixed for 24 March, the eve of the Feast of the Annunciation, never took place. When Père Villain arrived at Lyons on the afternoon of that day, his friend and master was dead. The end had come in the early morning.

On the fourth floor of 5 Rue du Plat, M. Carlhian was awaiting his arrival, and he understood what this meant. As he crossed the threshold, Père Villain noted the marks of the seals imposed by the German secret police eight years earlier. As he came in, he could see through the open door of the oratory the frail figure of the dead priest lying parallel to the altar, upon which stood the chalice covered once more with the veil after his last Mass on St Benedict's Day, three days before. Nearby lay the alb and the white chasuble, gift of the Anglican nuns of the House of Prayer. The burse was full of memorials of those associated in prayer and friendship with his oblation—letters, cards containing prayers, ordination mementos of priests, Roman Catholic and Anglican, whose first Masses he had inspired, claims for intercession: the whole of Christendom was present with him in his eucharist. The Holy Father, the great names of the various hierarchies, the World Council of Churches, the persecutions suffered by Christians, whether inflicted by the enemies of the faith or by one another; Jewry, India, Islam, his agnostic and communist friends—all these found a place here, together with the offering of his own life. No visitor could fail to notice that his head now lay directly beneath the symbolic figure in the poster, humility opening all the barred roads.

A Jesuit priest, Père Girardon, had been summoned from Fourvière at 9 p.m. on Monday, 23 March. There seemed to be no immediate danger; but the Abbé, after making his confession and offering his life for unity, took the priest's hands within his own and said gratefully, 'Thank you for everything'. He died soon after midnight.

The news seemed to move Christians everywhere to join in thanksgiving, in the consciousness that as the Feast of the Annunciation dawned, a faithful messenger of God had returned to behold his face, leaving behind him the certainty that in his mission God had been with him.

The funeral took place on Friday, 27 March 1953. The Requiem was in the church of St Bruno, the big, baroque parish church attached to the house of the *missionnaires Chartreux* and close to the school which had been the scene of the larger part of his ministry. The Cardinal Archbishop of Lyons was there, and gave the Absolutions. The World Council of Churches was represented by M. Alexandre de Weymarn, director of the Press Bureau at Geneva: he brought the Cardinal the sympathy of Dr Visser 't Hooft. Pastor Bäumlin, Pastor de Pury, and Pastor Bruston were among the numerous Protestant friends in the congregation, but there were no Anglicans and only one friend from the Eastern Orthodox Church. This the Abbé would have regretted. Among the Roman Catholics were many priests and members of religious communities, both men and women.

At the close of the ceremony the Cardinal ascended the pulpit. He made it clear that he was aware of departing from the custom of the diocese by which no word is spoken at the funeral of a priest.

If I make an exception [he continued], and it will be, as you may guess, a brief one, it is not in order to place the Abbé Couturier above his colleagues, for he would have been the first to protest against such treatment. It is because of the nature of the apostolate to which he dedicated his whole life, the greatness of the cause which he served with his whole soul. The presence in this congregation of many of our separated brethren would suffice to bring this out. It is not only as a friend, a devoted friend, that I speak, but above all, as Archbishop of Lyons, that I wish to offer to the departed the sorrowful homage of my admiration, my affection and my thanks.

Abbé Paul Couturier was the apostle of unity—the undaunted worker for the unity of all Christian people.

Union, unity, the consolidation of the human community—this is the great aspiration of the world today, and it is found at all poles of thought. Nowhere is it felt more intensely than in the sphere of religion. There is no sterner commandment in the Gospel of our Lord Jesus Christ, whose prayer it was that they may all be one. It is the great scandal of the world that Christians are divided. All those who love Jesus Christ, those also who for love of Jesus Christ love their brethren, are homesick for the unity of Christians such as our Saviour wished.

There is no question here of a sentimental unity realized in equivocation, but the only unity which could be true—unity realized in candour, loyalty, and truth. . . . It was to this task that dear Père Couturier dedicated his life, with a devotion, a fervour, a charity that were truly wonderful. Of course, I do not forget all that he has done in this *Maison des Chartreux*, which was very dear to him; nevertheless the great work of his life was, as I have said, his apostolate for unity. He pursued it with an ardent generosity which sometimes gave rise to certain anxieties in those who had the deepest concern for the doctrinal aspects of the problem, but these same people have always been unsparing in their profound admiration and grateful affection for him.

Abbé Couturier has greatly honoured this diocese. He has been a magnificent servant of the Church. The Church, with my humble voice, thanks him.

May we treasure his spirit; may we always follow the example of his radiant goodness, to which there are innumerable witnesses, and which gained an influence, full of sweetness and authority, over so many souls. Many of these are not within the fold of the Catholic Church, yet they tell us with overwhelming force that he was their light and their guide.

We shall never be able to forget what he has done for the unity of Christians. Our Holy Father recently told me how much he has the unity of Christians at heart, and that it should be the object of our ardent prayer to him who alone is able to grant that it comes to realization as he wills.

He whom we mourn was a precursor, an example. His work will be continued in the same spirit.

I sorrowfully salute the sister of the deceased who was the companion and support of his life, and whose anguish at this ceremony can today be enlightened by so great a hope. Amen.

A few minutes later, at the sanctuary steps, Pastor Roland de Pury, speaking in the name of the religious communities of Taizé and Grandchamp, as well as of the Abbé's Protestant friends in general, paid tribute to the memory of 'a great brother'.

He leaves us the example of tireless patience and charity, resolute in the pursuit of that end at once so clear and so mysterious: the unity of all those who have for their only Lord and Saviour Jesus Christ.

At the cemetery of Loyasse, before a small group of intimate friends there were some final words. These were spoken by M. Alexandre de Weymarn, the industrious and gifted exile from Baltic lands who has made the Press Bureau of the World Council of Churches one of the most helpful and trustworthy of its instruments. He said:

He from whom we have parted was a unique personality: a great Christian, a true priest. If I may be permitted a personal reflection, I should like to add that Abbé Couturier has been for me also a friend, a great Christian and a priest. . . .

For his comrades in the field of ecumenical action this venerable priest of the Roman Catholic Church, whose life was integrally spiritual, was the staunchest of friends. His deep and irenic vision of the aspirations of Christians to unity has constantly sustained

326

and stimulated those who accompanied him on his often arduous way. In the person of Abbé Couturier we have lost a unique personality whose spiritual heritage is precious to us.

The ecumenical programme of Abbé Couturier found its completest expression in *spiritual emulation. . . .* That the ecumenical cause has found in the Roman Catholic Church so venerable a champion is a benediction as much for herself as for the separated Churches. His work is indissolubly tied to the ecumenical ideal which more and more attracts the Christian conscience. The cross on the tomb of this Christian whose perseverance, patience and faith were extraordinary, will be the silent reminder of the aspirations which he has tirelessly sought to share with other Christians —the common witness to the Divine Master of the Church, the crucified and risen Christ. To his last hour the life of Abbé Couturier was directed by the invincible hope of the day when the great distress of the separation of Christians will come to an end.

It was not long before one plot in the cemetery began to receive pilgrims from near and far, some of whose visits have had consequences in life both profound and fruitful. Here lies 'the Abbé', as English-speaking pilgrims always call him, their great sense of the sufficiency of the name perhaps unconsciously indicating their acceptance of this humble priest as abbot-guardian of the world-wide 'Invisible Monastery'. His grave is marked by a simple tombstone, bearing an inscription of which the dignified, masculine reserve expresses the devotion of his old friend, that faithful layman, Victor Carlhian:

HERE LIES
MONSIEUR PAUL COUTURIER
Priest of the Society of St Irenaeus
deceased 24 March 1953
in his 72nd year
HE WAS AN APOSTLE
OF THE UNITY OF CHRISTIANS

Yet it should run not 'was', but 'is'. The verb in the past tense—*was*—alone needs emendation. For what he was, most surely he still *is*, mighty in prayer, awaking Christians everywhere to realize their divisions as an outrage against love, calling them here and now to provide the unique, immediate, invincible remedy for this—total surrender to Jesus Christ of their wills, that free course may be given to his prayer, his sovereign will that *they all may be one.*

NOTES

[1] *The Call of the Cloister* (1955).
[2] *Reunion* VI, No. 55, 1960, pp. 154–64.
[3] A translation of this follows, as Appendix A.

APPENDIX A

Prayer and Christian Unity

———————

Abbé Couturier printed this first in 1944, unsigned *ad usum privatum*. During the winter preceding his death (1952-3) he republished it in a slightly revised form, with his own signature and the *imprimatur* of his archbishop. In this second form he regarded it as his 'ecumenical testament'.

The prayer of Christ in St John 17, prototype of every prayer for Unity

'True prayer is a struggle with God, in which we are victorious through the victory of God' (Kierkegaard). And God wills this struggle. He wishes to give us a share in his work. He who is in us permits us through him to triumph over him. That is why the prayer of Christ after the Last Supper on Maundy Thursday, in which he asks his Father for the Unity of his Church, must find its echo in sorrow and constant supplication in the heart of every Christian. For what follower of Christ could refuse to see in his prayer for Unity the prototype of all prayer for Unity? It would be as blasphemous (the word is no exaggeration) to try to find another approach to prayer for Unity as to look for a model for prayer in general other than that he left us, the 'Our Father'.

Letting Christ pray in us to his Father for Unity

St Paul teaches us that no one can say the name of 'Jesus' except by the Spirit of God. To say the name of 'Jesus' is to express a prayer, a soaring, a lifting-up of the soul towards the Father, for the true utterance of this Name is an act, a 'yes', human and poor, a poor 'yes' from our human misery, for we are sinners! but a 'yes' which breaks forth from our human dignity, for we are free, sons of his Love. We are his living images! This 'yes' can echo far within the unexplored regions of our spiritual being. It may be partial, or almost complete, without ever being able to reach true completeness. The more we implore God to strip us of ourselves, the more we enter into the divine surrender—'He that loses his life shall save it'—and the more able we become to hear Christ praying in us by his Spirit.

An ineffable change takes place by which our prayer is stripped to be reclothed in his prayer. In the attentive silence of our listening soul, our attachment to him is affirmed with our whole will, not only in our words, feeling and desires. The more we find ourselves in him, in whom we truly live, or he in us, in whom he truly lives, the more effectual does our prayer become, since it is he who prays in us, free from our burden of self. Such a state of mind is the work of God, gift of the divine generosity: it is a pearl of great price, bought at the royal price of renunciation. It sets us at the antipodes of inert passivity of the spirit; and vocal prayer, either private or public, will be permeated by this attitude, provided that it can be surrounded by deep silence, and have a certain deliberation of utterance.

An expression of this attitude, given as one example among many other possible ones

'Lord, under the intolerable weight of distress caused by the separations between Christians, my heart fails. I have confidence in thee, O Christ, who has overcome the world. It is the property of love to produce a blind confidence in the beloved. My confidence in thee is boundless, and rightly so, since thou art almighty.

'For my soul to draw near to thee, O God, it were better that she should walk unknowing rather than knowing, exchanging what is comprehensible and variable for the unvarying and incomprehensible which is thyself. My confidence in thee, O Christ, throws me into thy heart where I find thy prayer; "Father, that they may be one, that the world may believe that thou hast sent me, Father, that they may be made perfect in one." My sinner's prayer is thy prayer to thyself, and it is in thy prayer alone that I find peace. Then how will Unity come about? What obstacles are to be overcome? It is thy work: my faith can only bid me pray with thee and in thee, that thy Unity may come, the unity which thou hast not ceased to desire, which thou dost continue to prepare, which thou wouldst have brought about long ago, if everyone—everyone, including myself, had been as crystal between that in the creation which wishes, through the Christian, to ascend to thee, and that which, by the same channel, desires to come down from thee to the world.'

This is a simple and loyal way of prayer. It is a meeting-place where, by virtue of charity, the prayers for unity of all true sons of love, all true Christians, even though separated, may flow together into the heart of Christ. This manner of prayer does not, of course, erase, weaken or obscure in any way the many differences of doctrine which characterize our separations. Each one is fully conscious of this and recognizes it: thus each remains true to himself and sincere towards others. But this kind of prayer, with a great sweep of wings, rises above all differences, and makes it possible for us all to rest together in the heart of Christ.

To rise above (survoler) *is not to deny, still less to forget*

This 'rising above' is by no means negative. It does not imply any dilution or forgetting of our respective beliefs, which are dearer to each other than his own being. This positive action of 'rising above' is as true and right for the Protestant, the Anglican and the Orthodox as for the Catholic, in whatever way each is permitted by his beliefs to envisage the problem of Christian Unity. How many situations there are in everyday life where an interior 'rising above' is encouraged, even demanded, for psychological well-being. When we are crushed by the death of someone dear to us, must we not force ourselves to 'rise above' the memory of the painful separation, to keep faith with the will of the one for whom we mourn, who, being with God, requires of us that we shall be always obedient to the ceaseless calls of the divine will. We must 'rise above' what separates us—death, the grave, grief—to find each other again in the unutterable joy of that presence, albeit invisible, of him who has taken one from this world, leaving the other still here for a time. Must not the sinner 'rise above' the details of his sins, that he may go forward in peace, reconciled by his repentance? The memory of the evil he has done is blurred, though it has power to strengthen his adoration and thanksgiving in the heart of Christ, where he will find the truth of the Master's words: To whom little has been forgiven, the same loveth little. Must not our spiritual stripping make us 'rise above' the good we have been able to do, by allowing God to act in us and through us, that we may advance in divine Love, protected from the ultimate danger of spiritual pride? 'Rising above', then, is seen to be as it were a psychological law, for realizing, freely and intensely, the interior task we must accomplish. It is necessary to forget, to 'rise above' when memory blocks the way, ensnares the feet, breaks the spirit, and takes away the singleness of aim of the soul, or casts some heaviness upon it, and causes sadness to arise in it, preventing us from resting in God, and refreshing ourselves with his peace and joy. The truth of this will be clear to anyone who has really suffered the buffetings of the Christian life. Others, though they imagine they understand, will not do so.

The Catholic Church claims to be the One Church which Christ willed

The Roman Catholic faith claims that the Roman Catholic Church possesses Unity and is the centre of Unity, which cannot exist outside her. She claims to be the one Church from which, in the course of history, other Christian bodies have separated, to a greater or less degree. They are like strong branches, which have been more or less torn away from the age-old tree by violent storms; but which are nevertheless still part of it, to some extent, provided they still cleave to it with some part of their being. This theme is fully developed in a fine article by L. Richard, professor in the Faculty of Theology in Lyons: 'La foi chrétienne chez les non-catholiques' (*Revue Apologétique*, August–September 1938). If the Church affirms that she is one, she also affirms very strongly that her lacerations have mutilated her maternal heart and body, that her life is hereby less rich, and that her message to the world impeded. Further, the Roman Catholic Church declares that if she makes these claims, they are necessitated by the Will of Christ—that she could not modify her faith without destroying herself and cutting herself off from Christ; which is quite impossible, for it was to Peter that was said: 'Thou art Peter, and upon this rock I will build my Church and the powers of hell shall not prevail against it.'

The psychological conviction in the soul of the Roman Catholic as to the Unity of his Church

One would surely look in vain for any way in which the unyielding demands of this belief in the Unity of the Church could prevent the faithful member of the Roman Catholic Church from praying in accordance to the prayer of Jesus.

Indeed, how could he desire or ask of the Father anything other than what Christ himself asks? Christ would no more be the life of his soul. He knows well that when he 'lets Christ pray in him'

Christ asks us to walk in the paths he will choose, however unknown, long, hard and full of suffering they may be. And if, by virtue of his belief regarding this question of the Unity of the Church, the Catholic finds himself in a different intellectual or metaphysical sphere from that in which some other groups of Christians are placed by reason of their beliefs, it is still true that the Catholic faith, as it is developed in the soul of the believer, becomes a psychological reality, apart from which faith would be nonexistent, since it would be in a spiritual vacuum. Now this psychological reality produces a state of mind, with regard to one's beliefs, similar to that created in the mind of one's Protestant, Anglican or Orthodox brothers by the psychological reality of their respective beliefs. It would seem then that, *psychologically, Catholics, Protestants and Orthodox are in a similar position with regard to the problem of Christian Unity.*

Evidence of the psychological identity of the state of mind of all Christians towards the problem of Unity

The witness of Orthodoxy, by Father Sergius Bulgakov, Professor at the Academy of Paris.

'If we suppress or allow to be supressed, even for a moment, the conviction that in belonging to such and such a Church we are in the truth and consequently our conviction of the error of those who do not share our beliefs, do we not become guilty of coldness and lack of faith, and give evidence of an eclecticism which seeks to find a way of escaping from the necessity of bearing witness to the truth and suffering for it? . . .

'Thus there is agreement and opposition, unity and division, the love inspired by the Church and equally the aversion inspired by it—the Church's problem has as it were its own dialectic: thesis and antithesis, characteristics which are closely linked, the one increasing in proportion to the growth of the other. The ecumenical mind of the Church, which is always seeking the way of Unity, is accompanied by an ever more acute and sensitive consciousness of differences of belief, together with a growing sense of deep Christian Unity.' (Quoted from *Russie et Chrétienté*, No. 1 (1934), pp. 40–41—review edited by the Dominican fathers of the Centre Istina.)

Calvanist witness of Karl Barth 'At many points where the diversity of the Churches is evident, we must make a choice and a decision, if we listen to the voice of Christ. We are not above the differences separating the Churches, but right in the middle, and we cannot believe one thing and say that the opposite is also Christian. Those who pretend to be above these differences are in fact only lookers-on at God and themselves. They are deaf except to their own utterances.

'Let us say it again: Jesus-Christ, mediator between God and Man, is the Unity of the Church, the Unity which embraces a multiplicity of parishes, gifts and persons, but excludes a multitude of Churches. It is the duty of the Church to be one Church. We cannot neglect the insistent demand of Christ. It is a duty and a command which our Lord imposes upon the Church, if we truly believe that Jesus is the Unity of the Church, and that the multiplicity of Churches is our wretchedness. If we listen to the voice of the Good Shepherd, the Unity of the Church must needs be a burning question. The union of the Churches does not come about of itself, but we discover and realize it in obedience to Christ in whom unity is already accomplished. . . . The union of the Churches is too great a thing to be the result of a movement, even the best of movements.

'The *first and last word in this situation, practically speaking* (for in the eyes of the Church we are one by right, though in practice we are many), *must be prayer for pardon and sanctification, addressed to the Lord of the Church.* The duty of uniting the Churches coincides essentially with the actual practical task of listening to Christ, which is the presupposition behind every action of the Church. This means in fact that the issue of the Church must be raised in Churches at present numerous and separated, for how can we listen to Christ except in a specific way, namely in the Church to which we belong, to which we are bound by ties of obligation? Ecclesiastically speaking, if we exist at all, it is in separation. The existence of a multiplicity of Churches is evidence of our refusal to face the situation. We cannot listen to our Lord without taking a decision, making an acknowledged choice. Nor can we do it without keeping ourselves apart, and so we approach him in a state of contradiction. Who are we?' (*Oecumenica*, July 1936, pp. 142, 140, 141, 148, 145, 146, 151. The italics are ours.)

Lutheran evidence of Monseigneur Meiser, Bishop of Munich 'Belief in the Body of Christ, one and undivided, causes us to experience personal suffering and distress in the divisions within the Church. What? Is Christ divided? (I Cor. 1.13). Jesus prayed in the high-priestly prayer for the Unity of the Church. The Unity of the Church will therefore always be for Christians a truth perceived by faith and at the same time a duty always imposed afresh. Where external unity is lacking, an essential part of the witness of Christianity to the world is also lacking.

'The place where our concern and Christian love are to be exercised is first of all the religious body which, having brought us to Christ and nourished us in the faith, will always occupy first place in our concern and activity.

'*To strive for understanding does not and should not mean that we are to become* cosmopolitans without a country or Christians situated between the Churches; but rather that we should, corporately and positively, become evangelical and Lutheran in the fullest sense, men who know in their lives the depth and fullness of biblical evangelicalism . . . who, as true Lutherans are receptive to everything authentically Christian.' (A long and remarkable letter dated 11 March 1941 from Bishop Meiser to his people. In the heart of this letter he points out, at some length, that true charity between Christian brothers demands integrity, the affirmation of respective beliefs. This letter states concisely the differences between Lutherans and Catholics and the true way of working for Christian Unity. The italics are ours.)

The Unity of the Church is a revealed truth, but it is also something which is to be

We cannot do more here than glance along a line of thought which it would need a whole book to develop. If the Roman Catholic Church affirms that the Unity of the Church already exists, that it is a revealed truth, it does not therefore deny that unity is still in the future.

In a living organization, whatever it may be, the two apparently opposite terms of being and becoming co-exist harmoniously each in its own right. The whole unifying force of that which will become an oak-tree, the unity of the oak-tree itself, is already present in the acorn when it falls to the ground. This unity in the acorn will open out into a manifold variety of form and structure: it will open—that is, it will grow taller and broader, and will grow beyond itself in the course of its own integral life. Has not the unifying force of the acorn become stronger, and its power to unify greater, when it holds together in due order the whole imposing mass of the oak and the energy which this mass contains, than when it only held in one simple little acorn the little mass which constituted the acorn and the energy contained in that little mass? The unity of a living organism is either dynamic or it is non-existent. Not only does that 'unity' or 'unifying' force become greater with the growth of the organism which it energizes, but never at any moment in the life of the organism does it cease to be active and dynamic; for through it the organism, which each moment is destroying itself and dying through the action of physical and chemical forces, is each moment created anew. It is the story of the whirlpool of life.

This is only a distant analogy, but it can be applied to whatsoever is to become the unity of any organism—even one which is spiritual, supernatural and divine, for then the unity will transcend both its actuality and its future development. And so it is with the Church.

The Catholic Church of the future

The day will come when the peoples of India, China and even Africa, will face the reality and implications of the message of Christ: then within the Church there will be throngs of Asiatics and Africans, rivalling the peoples of the Old World and the New in numbers, influence and sanctity; many things in the Catholic Church will be changed, but nothing essential. The same creed will be stated in different ways, wide horizons of scriptural study, at present hidden, will be revealed; new forms of spirituality will make their appearance far different from our own in their psychological approach; organization and discipline will be modified.

If we were miraculously transported to the Church as it will be in several centuries time, we should be in a strange world, albeit a world of living faith, just as if we had been transported to the Christian community of the first century; but in either situation we should soon find ourselves at home in the faith.

The problem of Christian Unity is not to be thought of in terms of 'returning' but of 'integration', or 're-embodiment'!

Since all things move forward, progress, and change in the process, since God is present in his creation, in humanity, and in every group of Christians whom he leads forward (a fact which none acquainted with them will deny), it follows that the problem of Christian Unity is not purely and simply co-extensive with the idea of 'returning', an ominous and misleading word. History cannot be reversed. Those who left the Roman Catholic Church centuries ago are no longer alive, and their descendants would not recognize the places left empty by their ancestors in the living cathedral, because it has grown and changed. Without any doubt the question of Unity has an historical aspect which is of great importance. But its most significant aspect is one which can be adequately defined by saying that the Christian bodies are at present facing each other as if they had never known each other—they are discovering each other. For they have yet to discover each other, come to a clear understanding and agreement about what they have in common in their Christian life. And this common heritage is much greater and deeper than is generally supposed, because inherited prejudices, lack of concern, and spiritual pride are already present, venomous and blinding. They must above all pray together in Christ, and in Christ's prayer. How are Christians to discover each other, recognize each other, and love each other unless prayer, the source of power, the only power which can move all, is the primary incentive acting upon their souls, which would otherwise be helpless before these crippling separations!

Unity cannot be attained by a great number of individual conversions

We must not delude ourselves into supposing that the vast problem of Christian Unity can be solved by a series of individual conversions, for such a stream very soon slows down to a trickle, and the gains scarcely compensate for the losses. Newman is a classic example of this: his lead, practically speaking, has not been followed, in spite of his great eminence and sanctity. Dom John Chapman, the late abbot of the Catholic Benedictine Abbey of Downside, wrote some eighteen years ago: 'Our gains are offset by our losses: the increase is not proportionate to the increase of population. In fact, it cannot be said that England is being converted to the Roman Catholic religion.' (*Revue apologétique*, page 68 of the issue of January 1937.)

If the impossible happened, and this kind of union were to succeed, it would be through gradual assimilation, progressively destroying rich differences of culture; whereas it is the vocation of all to form one single vast harmony, a symphony of different complementary but concordant strains. The Creator has called all the riches of his creation to form a harmonious whole in Christ. This summons finds its expression on the personal level—for men are conscious that they bring with them a certain cultural heritage, or a past shaped by

Providence, or a certain personal experience. All of these Divine gifts—in the rightful joy each must take in playing his part, adding his note to the whole. This joy should surely be left to him. Each and all should accept and value their present state, if they wish, as they should, to take their part in the thought of their Creator; otherwise how much poorer the Church of Christ would be in its effort to represent the Gospel message to the world! But no one can deny the right of individual conversion to a soul which no longer believes it is in the way of truth. These conversions, provided they are sincere and whole-hearted, are as it were short-cuts and footpaths—it is only conversions of this kind which have any true value, and they will be acts of great nobility of character, which everyone should reverence and respect. There remains the great work, the task of the growth towards maturity of Christian groups, in relation one to another.

Corporate reunion is the normal way of Unity

Like the great mountain roads which climb gently in wide curves, the high roads of corporate reunion develop in their long slow progress the patient preparation of the spirit—that of the laity as well as that of the hierarchy. Later, much later, will come a day, the day ordained by Providence, when corporate reunion will be achieved by the religious leaders, and when the faithful, their hearts now completely disposed towards unity, will all, by their own respective adhesion, set the seal upon this Reunion, the common goal of their deepest desire. The works of God are accomplished slowly, and transcend, even while fulfilling, the laws of our psychology.

Each Christian group has its own particular religious riches, and these will be preserved when Christian Unity is restored within the Unity of the Church. This is a fact I would emphasize. 'For may there not be, among our separated brethren, traditional forms of expression, customs, or even doctrinal developments, which are not so easily perceived in the Mother Church?' (*Revue apologétique*, March 1937, page 343, article by Jean Guitton. The context, needless to say, gives the precise Catholic connotation of the expression 'Mother Church'.)

Preparing for this reconstitution

As a result of this prayer, each Christian group, including Catholics, will deepen their life, perfect their talents, reform themselves in whatever respect reformation is needed, and, mounting towards our Lord, will reach the height where the walls of separation end. Then they will all mutually recognize in their other brethren the Christ whom they adore, knowing him to be truly one Christ in identity, unique in his love, his life *and his thought*. Then dogmatic Unity will be realized, when the spirits of all are united in the unique Thought of Christ; and union will be proclaimed by the voice of Peter. This will perhaps take place in a great Ecumenical Council.

'No one has the right to pray that a Christian Church may be overthrown and that his own Church may reign supreme' (a true observation by Dr Rosendal of Sweden)[1]

We cannot but condemn the attitude of mind which can only see work for unity as a military operation, to be described in military terms of conquest, victory, triumph, struggle, lines of defence, as though they were waging a war. Schism, persecution, tolerance, and indifference—all these are stages in the history of Christian Unity which are now in the past, in spite of some sad, but happily spasmodic modern persecutions among Christians; we are now in an age of mutual respect, of understanding, and of brotherhood founded on our basic unity; we have come, to sum up in a single phrase, to the era of 'spiritual emulation'. The question of good companionship, of what the English call fellowship, between the members of different religious families, seems to be a most important issue in our present civilization, in the new world which is taking shape in the half-light in which we live (J. Maritain, *Who is my neighbour?*). That is why any form of prayer which bears a resemblance to the fulminations of the sons of Zebedee is to be condemned and, we should like to think, banished for ever from every Christian heart; 'Lord, may lightning strike those who do not hurry to rejoin us in our Faith, since they will not listen to us and be converted. Lord, already thy justice scatters them, ruin is upon their house. Show them all the might of thine arm! Among the ruins of their own church they will at last discover the way of truth; then they will come and join us, and Unity will have arrived.' Such a prayer cannot be from above. It is Satan, or Satan's likeness in us, which inspires it. It is Satan alone who destroys; he is turned in upon himself, and can see no good outside himself. This prayer is blasphemy against the work of God among our non-Catholic Christian brethren; and the blasphemer in this case forgets a psychological law which cannot be broken: for every persecution, at any time and in any place, in making martyrs, creates new believers to take their places; and in trying to stifle the faith of the faithful, produces among them, whatever their allegiance may be, concentration and reactions which will preserve it.

Spiritual realism

Should not all Christians endeavour to have the same relationships with and consideration for each other, in the intimacy of their personal prayer, as those which exist between them in the Soul of Christ praying to the Father that all his own should be made perfect in unity? Now, in the Soul of Christ his redeemed do not overpower each other; they are all one in the reconciling power of his Redemption, his Peace, his Joy and his Prayer. They are not opposed to each other; they are intimately united by his thought and his love in the one and only fruit of his Redemption. Let us enter then into the union of his Prayer, letting him freely pray in us. We shall then all dwell in the bountiful realism of the simple and pure Christ-bearing life (*vie 'Christifique'*).

Spiritual realism in the Communion of Saints

Since all who are baptized, either by water or by desire—a great multitude, both of professing Christians and of pagans, seekers of the unknown God through what is positive in their dim beliefs and strange rituals, true Christians, though they did not know it—since all the baptized have in them the Life of Christ, they must be described both corporately and as individuals in the light of the wonderful relationship which St Paul describes in I Corinthians ch. 12. Into my poor prayer, then, runs like lifeblood the prayer of others: their aspirations towards penitence, albeit unexpressed, their faults in need of reparation, the cries of frustration which guilty souls lift to Christ even through their very crimes, misplaced endeavours after happiness, seeing that within their souls the throne of the Living Christ stands empty, and no voice speaks more loudly than a void—absence crying for a presence; the excellent thanksgiving of those who have perceived and known that their lives are full of the mercy of God; the sweet joy of souls at peace—the whole inner life of all men.

Let every Christian be aware of this great flood of prayer, which drives into his own heart to find utterance of that 'Yes' which will let it unfurl like a breaking wave before the very throne of the Divine Majesty.

By this 'Yes' to whatever degree realized I imprint with the seal of my own personal life this flood which has come from the most distant depth of the heart of the human race. I do this at the very moment at which I cast it, or rather Christ casts it on my behalf, before the Father.

In exchange my prayer enters into the prayer of all other men. And if the beloved brother who launches my prayer towards the Holy Trinity lives more intensely the life of the Holy Trinity than I, then through him, even though he may be unknown to me, my poor prayer will make a more rapid flight to the Eternal and have greater efficacy in the presence of God.

At the altar of the Holy Sacrifice at which I celebrate the Holy Mysteries, there is present on its way Godward, finding completion there if needs be—so my Catholic faith affirms—every sacrificial element in what my Christian brethren have retained of the eucharistic *agape* of the first Maundy Thursday.

At the Choir Office, at the breviary prayed alone, in silent prayer, my Protestant, Anglican or Orthodox brothers pray with me and in me in my prayer. And likewise I am present and have my part in the loyal and sincere prayer which is lifted up to God through the splendours of the Divine Liturgy and Offices of the convinced Orthodox. I am present and have my part in the public prayers of Anglicans—those lovely Canticles—Mattins and Evensong, which have never since the sixteenth century ceased to rise to God in every English Cathedral—those masterpieces of the faith of our medieval ancestors—and in the private prayers of fervent Anglicans, and still more in the service of Holy Communion; I am present and have my part in the worship, the prayers, measured and full of faith, and in the profound hymns of Protestantism, and particularly in the fervent commemoration of the Last Supper held by my Protestant brothers.

O God, how can I be unaware that pleasing you depends on the generosity of my reply 'Yes' to your known will, following the example of the Virgin of Nazareth, who remains the Gospel model of all human acquiescence to the divine will: 'Be it unto me according to thy Word.' You allow it to be so—every creature must seek you from its own place on earth, wherever that may be; 'Thou that lightenest every man that cometh into the world', O Word of God become

Christ! We are all, every one, advancing towards the Truth which is yourself, for ever pursued, as we all are, by your love, by your Spirit. We set out upon this journey, always without ceasing. We never arrive. 'Brethren, I count not myself to have apprehended but . . . forgetting those things which are behind, and reaching forth towards those things which are before, I press on towards the mark' (Phil. 3.13). He is the way by which we go, the Truth to which we make our way, on and on, the range is infinite—the Life in which we dwell here below, through the darkness of faith, despite our sin, provided we repent of it; later—yet always soon—in 'the father's bosom'—the home where there is no more sin, and where the spirit walks or rather runs from glory to glory.

All this without vagueness, indifferentism, interdenominationalism

From the complete separation of their different places of worship, the full independence of their beliefs, rites, and types of spirituality, Christians separated from each other will utter from their hearts their prayer for unity, and will let Christ pray in them—he who is the Saviour of all, loved and adored and served by all. 'Thou, Father, art in me, and I in Thee . . . that they may be made perfect in one. . . .'

Parallelaboration—a newly-coined word which expresses very well the temper of the time now at hand when 'spiritual emulation' must be found among all Christians. *Parallelaboration* is the exact opposite of the uneasy and fruitless spiritual collaboration, or, as the theologians call it, '*communicatio in sacris*' which can only tend to create a spirit of religious indifferentism, that is to say the profanation of holy things, since for practical purposes they are treated as identical, when they are in reality different. But it must be borne in mind that '*communicatio in sacris*' does not necessarily take place on every occasion, and we should know how to discriminate, seeing it only where it does in fact exist.

There must be no dream of building a place of worship in a town centre where everyone would come to pray together, deserting their places of worship

In adding this caution, which is purely hypothetical in character. I am thinking particularly of certain timid Catholic souls, whose only conception of the problem of Christian Unity is based on a particular textbook attitude, showing no appreciation of the real nature of the problem; they have an abstract conception formulated by writers who have never really faced the problem of Christian Unity, nor suffered because of it, nor known any souls who have so suffered. It must be added that these timid Catholic souls are often very holy and devout, and admired by all who know them, but they are immature, and there is a lack of priests who can train them. As a matter of fact this dream of thus building has obsessed the minds of a number of liberal Protestants, sometimes most courageous in spirit and noble in mind. They were never very numerous, and indeed where there has been a positive revival of Protestant theology, the number has become smaller and smaller. It may be said that the ecumenical movement has outgrown this pitfall. The chief characteristic of the movement is the ever more ardent search for the 'unique Mind' of Christ who manifests himself to the world through the Church, the continuation of himself on earth. It has been said that the problem of the Church will be the great problem of the twentieth century, and this gives us a well-grounded hope that we shall soon see the rise of the dawn of Christian Unity.

Prayer is the greatest of cosmic forces

After these necessary explanations, let us return to the main subject of these pages: Prayer. Is it the fundamental force whose property is to remake Christian Unity? Or are other forces needed, equally strong, to forge the healing link? Prayer is the fundamental force. It is fundamental because it is the greatest of cosmic forces; it fertilizes and makes fruitful even the highest of other powers: those of the heart and intellect. These powers are separate gifts, given directly to man by God. But it is only as a result of prayer, whether his own or other people's, that man's powers become fruitful for God. It is man's prayer in Christ, or Christ's prayer in man (which is the same thing), which upholds creation in its due order, gives it harmony, makes it pleasing to God, and makes creation sing, through man, the perpetual praise of thanksgiving to the Creator. Prayer transmutes the world of rocks, plants, and animals, into an ordered song: 'O all ye works of the Lord, bless ye the Lord.' What would the violin and the bow be without the artist who makes them sing? Prayer makes us fellow workers, by grace, with God himself, God, in us, waits for his children to hear 'creation groaning and travailing' and when they hear it, they direct it to his glory by the canticle of their prayer.

Since God has made us members of Christ, he has given us, his

343

children, a power which is dreadful and terrible, but of indescribable sweetness—the power to ask and to obtain from him anything which can be brought within the orbit of the 'Our Father', the prototype of prayer his Son left us. The Gospel overflows with clear affirmations of the power of prayer and the conditions in which it is valid—faith, humility and perseverance. Everything which can be asked of the Father in Christ's name is vouchsafed by prayer, that is why all prayer implies surrender, for it is often very difficult to declare that Christ would indentify himself with our petition or our thanksgiving, or even our so-called oblation, adoration and contribution.

Finally, by creating in the soul a condition of the will, prayer causes us to introduce into the universe a metapsychical force with strength proportionate to the strength, calmness and stability of that will. There is nothing in modern science to refute this principle; and much can be inferred from it.

Evidence of Peter Wust

In April 1941 Peter Wust, one of the most attractive of German philosophers and a fine Christian, lay dying. At Christmas 1940, when he knew the end was near, and was rejoicing in God's goodness towards him, he wrote a letter to his students in which he bequeathed to them a 'magic key'. 'This key is not, as you might expect from a philosopher, exercise of the intellect, but prayer. Prayer, understood as the supreme gift of oneself, brings peace, a spirit of childlike simplicity, and a sense of proportion. In my view, a human being grows up within the framework of humanity (not of humanism) in proportion to the quality of his prayer. And by prayer I mean only true prayer, which is marked by extreme humility of the spirit. Only souls who know how to pray will live life to the full. Suffering teaches us prayer better than anything. This is the only key which will unlock every door on the way to Christian Unity.'

Visible Christian Unity will then be attained

This Unity is as it were within the divine plan, a claim made by the Word-made-Flesh, since the Church is his own Self, still dwelling among us. 'We usually seem to forget that disunion is an evil, the greatest of all evils, because as long as it lasts, One God in Three Persons is not and cannot be adored in visible unity by the whole Body of Christ. Yet, it is precisely for this work of adoration, by which alone true human dignity can be obtained, that this Body was created. How then can this reunion be arrived at except by the exercise in this same Body, of penitence, contrition and supernatural hope in God?' (*Essay on the Religious Nature of Unity* by Arthur Smallwood, in the October 1939 issue of *Nouvelle Revue Théologique*.)

It is unthinkable, therefore, that the Church's present state of *ecclesia peregrinans* or of *kenosis* should influence the mind of the Christian so as to accept the state of separated Christendom as normal, however one might try to make out a case or pseudo-defence for this, as being the normal state of affairs. The Church of Christ will one day achieve the splendour of visible Unity; it will become ever more beautiful and more and more holy; although still in the shadow of faith, it will glorify the splendour of Creation in ever wider, deeper and more heartfelt praise of God the Trinity, the Creator. And always, to the end of time, the Church will be confronted by anti-Christ, the symbolic personification of all the evil on earth and of all the perpetrators of that evil. When humanity—work of the Creator who, dwelling within his creation, ceaselessly urges it towards the Truth—when humanity has reached a high degree of spiritual progress through the Church which vivifies and crowns it, the greater will be the danger of sin, and hence of disunion, for the temptation of the sin of pride, the sin of the spirit, will be greater. According to the Scriptures, Satan and anti-Christ will then have their day. This day will be short, soon to be followed by the dazzling final triumph of Christ, the whole Christ, who is the Church.

When will visible Christian Unity be attained?

Visible Christian Unity will be attained when the praying Christ has found enough Christian souls of all communions for him to pray freely in them to his Father for Unity. The silent voice of Christ must sound forth in the voices of all his baptized, in all their supplications made in humility and penitence—for we all bear a terrible burden of guilt in this drama of separation. If this guilt were only guilt of omission, indifference, unconcern or readiness to accept the present state of affairs, it would be terrible enough; but how much spiritual pride has shown itself, and still shows itself on all sides, strengthening the barriers and deepening the ditches? Let each of us examine himself before God.

Because the Catholic affirms the unique nature of the Catholic

Church as an integral part of his Faith, he must be the first to set an example of deep humility, not merely in a passing moment of condescension, but as an habitual expression of his sorrow for broken Christianity—a sorrow which persists as a token of true regret and contrition for the faults of his ancestors, remembering the human history of the Church, at once glorious and full of wretchedness; and remembering also his own faults. It is essential to do this, if his attitude to his beliefs is to be logical; also it will throw the glory of the past into great relief. He is likewise under an obligation, which is inexorable, to take the initiative in a mutual search for imaginative sympathy—the cordial welcome, the outstretched hand, the open and sincere heart, love of one's neighbour in the true, and therefore full sense of the word 'He who humbles himself shall be exalted.' He who loves, provided that his love is persistent and admits of no exception, is he who in the last resort begets understanding. 'Where love is not, set love, and you will receive love back', says St John of the Cross, echoing the great apostle John: 'We have known and believed the love that God hath to us' (I John 4.16).

An undeniable fact

Prayer, the fundamental cosmic force of creation, is found in its completeness in Christ as he prayed for Unity. In that prayer he expressed before his Father his own desire, since Christian Unity is part of his Father's divine plan; his prayer is the expression of his will for his baptized. What has once existed in the mind of Christ exists eternally, for through his mind it becomes part of his person, part of the eternal Word. Christ continues to pray for Unity until the end of time, in the love of the Spirit, the Lamb before the Father's throne. But he desires us to share this prayer with him, for all Christians share his Life. Indeed, he has so willed it that he cannot bring about Christian Unity without us, just as he cannot save us without our co-operation. Each of us can take to himself the words of St Paul, 'I make up . . . in my prayer in him for Unity what is lacking in his prayer.'

God has created us free, in his own image, making us 'free sons in his own Son', and receiving us again into himself by his love; and he could not encroach upon this marvellous gift of freedom without to some extent destroying our personality; far from doing this, he has raised us by the Infinity of the Person of his Anointed One.

Honour and responsibility, thanksgiving and guilt, humility and contrition; such are the two aspects of the human spirit. To hold in our hands the responsibility for Christian Unity—though not for the unity of the Church—to hold such great responsibility that if we were to neglect it, God in his justice would find terrible ways to make us fulfil our role—such is our Christian destiny, as glorious as it is terrifying. But let us take courage; God is love, and he is still our Father.

The circumstances make us recognize all these truths amid the darkness and uncertainty of these days. 'The more we lack on earth the more we shall discover that better thing which the world can give us—the Cross.' (Charles de Foucauld, *Écrits spirituels*, p. 267.)

The annual revival of the Universal Prayer of Christians for the Unity of Christians

As the days pass, this Universal Prayer of Christ in Christian souls, as he prays to his Father for their Unity, will enter and penetrate the whole Christian body; God alone will hear the ceaseless secret whisper in souls, fraternities, and cloisters. But threatened even in the monasteries by routine and by the buzz of manifold occupations, this half-inarticulate melody of prayer would stand a great risk of being interrupted and silenced by indifference and forgetfulness. To be effectual and to bring about the *parousia*, the promised glory of the 'Day of the Lord', this music must enlarge and swell till it becomes the immense, unanimous cry of the whole people of Christ. Only then will Christ's prayer be granted by his Father; for only then will full expression be given to the prayer of the whole Christ, the Risen Christ dwelling in all loyal and sincere souls, true sons of the Father.

But this can only come about if all Christians, even though separated, pray this prayer, so that it pulses and throbs in unison, over and over again—prayed independently here on earth, but convergent in God. For at least one period each year there must be great and visible intercession on the part of all the children of Israel, a true 'revival' of supplication, a living resurgence of the unceasing melody.[2] There are other factors, too, which make it necessary that this prayer should be visible, recurring and simultaneous.

For all Christians share to some extent the responsibility for the fragmentation of Christendom, by which God is offended before all men, and men are justly scandalized. There must therefore be a common, visible and simultaneous act of reparation, as far as such a thing is possible, before God and men, and before creation both visible and invisible; for creation has a mysterious but real relationship with all Christians, vitally bound as they are to Christ, and it is therefore weakened in its Christ-furthering task by the burdensome weight of Christian disunity. The fact that the prayer is prayed by all simultaneously has the advantage that the spiritual forces of reparation and intercession are not merely added together but multiplied. It is because the strands are entwined that 'a threefold chord is not quickly broken'.

It is because the disciples are together (and in our case they will be so as far as possible) that Christ is in the midst of them. In the face of the ugliness of their separations, this simultaneity will allow Christians at last to present to their non-Christian brothers, and to all waiting creation, the moving and visible beauty of the unity of their spiritual efforts; the prelude and measure of Christian unity, transcending any purely human strivings for concord.

Perseverance in prayer . . . passing the torch from hand to hand . . . in space and time

'We must have a sure belief that God is working out his purpose, and that he, to whom a thousand years are as a day, will reveal and consummate the unity of all Christians, in his own time and his own way. It is enough for us that, when our earthly sojourn is ended, we may be found still journeying courageously, ever deepening our unity with each other, ever keeping before our eyes the distant goal, our faces resolutely set towards Jerusalem. We must hope that even though it may not be possible for us, those who come after us will be able to say "our feet shall stand in thy gates". "Wherefore criest thou unto me? Say to the children of Israel that they go forward" ' (Ex. 14.15: extract from the Address of His Grace the Archbishop of Canterbury given on 29 July 1937 in St Paul's Cathedral at the inauguration of the Oxford Ecumenical Conference).

An attempt to show that the prayer of all is absolutely necessary for mutual understanding, which is an essential condition for the realization of Christian Unity

In the last analysis, to 'seek the Kingdom of God' means nothing unless it means to pray. Let us pray therefore and all the rest will be given in addition: and 'all the rest' includes charity, which draws hearts together, by which means alone minds, too, will ultimately be drawn together, and will share the unity of faith—the Unique Thought of Christ, which is infinitely beyond the grasp of our own minds, in his eternal unity.

Psychological unreality

It is strange that the order of purely logical considerations should be reversed. God cannot first bring about unity of minds in the truth and afterwards union of hearts in charity. Psychologically, and in practice, the reverse is the case. When we say, 'it is from unity of faith that the bond of charity must emerge, *Ut Unum Sint*', if by that we mean that unity of faith must be established before anything else so that the bond of charity may emerge from it, afterwards, we are victims of abstraction.

Basis of the supreme importance of charity in the psychological order

Prayer leads to charity and charity to fullness of the faith, which, conforming to its own nature, brings unity in its turn, and from this unity springs an increase of charity, whence flow forth fresh unifying lights of the faith, and so forth. '*Ex igne lux, ut de luce ignis.*' Therein lies the true way to understand the question and to work effectively towards Christian Unity.

Controversy, on the other hand, shuts the door of the soul to the breath of the Holy Spirit, for it immediately produces a defensive attitude, and that results in opposition in two camps, whereas if we look first for what unites us, and not what divides us, 'a union of hearts in prayer is established and a union of minds will follow in the sphere of faith' (Letter of a Carmelite).

In God the Holy Trinity, the Father precedes the Son and the Father and Son precede the Holy Spirit, following a logical but not an actual order, since in eternity they are co-existent simultaneously, related one to the other in their infinite personality according to the demands of the divine life. But Creation is the work of Love, that is to say of the Trinity eternally fulfilled in the Spirit, since God the Holy Trinity has created because he has willed to do so. As this Creation comes directly from God it follows that in this Creation, logically, actually, chronologically, and psychologically, love precedes knowledge, will precedes thought; the union of hearts in charity of necessity precedes and most surely prepares for the unity of minds in the truth. When God wished to reveal to the world the secrets of his Life, he began by the act of Love which is the Incarnation. The Incarnate Word was revealed 'full of grace' so that we might know that he was 'full of truth'.

Difficulties of understanding each other: a typical example

Because we are so half-hearted in our observance of the precept which would enlighten us, 'This is my commandment that ye love one another', we understand each other even less, and though we live in physical proximity, spiritually we are far apart.

During a retreat for fellowship, prayer and study, shared by several pastors and priests, it so happened that, while speaking about the theology of salvation, one pastor, extremely sympathetic towards Catholicism, had to state the Protestant point of view. He began by reading long extracts from three modern Catholic theologians, each of whom expounded the Protestant position in the usual Catholic way. These theologians have the reputation among us of being remarkably well informed, endowed with comprehension and sympathy as well as penetration of thought, and are in fact distinguished both as men and as thinkers. When the pastor had finished reading he added, 'It is with deep sorrow, beloved brethren, that I have to tell you that we cannot recognize ourselves in these lines.' This shed a beam of light upon my soul and I realized how great was the gulf which prevents us from understanding each other. I understand lack of understanding:

> Mankind live here below
> Strangely unknown one to another
> Their hearts no kinship show,
> Not one of us discerns his brother.

(L. Mercier, 'Spleen' in *Voix de la Terre et du Temps*.)

Of the mystery of language and of the mind

Thought has no material substance; we express it in an artificial, conventional and most inadequate combination of words, setting in motion sound waves which we entrust to the passive goodwill of the air. What our hearer receives is a poor imitation of what is in our minds mutilated by the language in which we clothe it, however flawless that language may be. How is the listener to strip it of his own auditory sensations? The phrase, the words, which for us would more or less conjure up our own thought—what will they convey to the mind of someone else? It is astonishing enough that the thought it evokes in him is sufficiently akin to my own for him to answer me, and that we can hold a conversation, and in doing so can contrive to understand each other to some extent; at least we suppose so, and that suffices to order our relationships and to establish some sort of social life. Considerable development is needed here. But a simple appeal to reason makes us realize that if we understand each other by the material contact of words, it is precisely because we have a share in a supreme intelligence, God himself. The existence of language is the proof, moment by moment, both spiritual and tangible, of the existence of God, and of our share in his existence.

To understand, we must therefore dwell in God

The more we dwell in God the more his Life will live in us; that is to say, the more we love him and obey him, the more transparent in him and through him, we shall become to each other. Our words will spring forth from regions ever closer, as our souls draw near to each other in him.

Now there is nothing which will open for us the door to divine Life more than prayer. It is impossible for Christians to understand each other unless they pray. The more they pray, the more they will understand each other, because the same Thought will become more comprehensible to all, the same Word which 'lighteneth every man that cometh into the world'.

General Conclusion

If we were to examine every single difficulty which must be overcome so that progress towards Christian Unity may be made, we should always come to the same conclusion: The problem of Christian Unity is for everyone a problem of the orientation of the inner life, for unless it is orientated, even in secret, towards Christian Unity, how can Christians face this burning question? Unless it succeeds in gripping, even torturing the Christian conscience, what hope is there of its resolution?

PAUL COUTURIER

NOTES

[1] I am using the term 'Christian Church' because it is convenient, and in current use by our non-Catholic Christian brothers, in the sense of what the Catholic Church claims should be called a 'group'.

[2] This revival takes place each year during the Week of Universal Prayer of Christians for Christian Unity, 18–25 January, when Anglicans, Catholics, Orthodox and Protestants, both Lutheran and Calvinist, pray according to the spirit of these pages, and the number of those who pray, already immense, grows from year to year—see the leaflets on this subject which appear every year.

APPENDIX B

The Invisible Monastery

It is thus described by Abbé Couturier himself:

'The Invisible Monastery consists of the company of souls to whom, because they have tried truly to expose themselves to his flame and thus to his light, the Holy Spirit has been able to make known intimately the sorrowful meaning of the separations between Christians—those in whom such knowledge has engendered permanent suffering resulting in habitual prayer and penitence. This fellowship is invisible in its totality, for it is scattered among all Christian communions. In some cases its members are isolated. In others they are found in groups corresponding to their temperaments and their tastes. Sometimes these individuals or groups are in relations more or less visible, more or less frequent one with another, but the reality in its full number remains always invisible, being always hidden with Christ in God. The name of Monastery does nevertheless belong to this unity, because it is the same suffering, the same desires, the same pre-occupations, the same spiritual activity, the same goal which gather together in the heart of Christ this multitude drawn from every nation. . . . Enclosure there is none save that found through dwelling in Christ—his prayer for unity. The spirit is that of this Prayer Universal; the action is spiritual emulation developed in every direction.'

(Its members) 'form a network of luminous points in perfect interdependence one of another, like those points of light which denote the stars. Like the stars they create an atmosphere of health-giving clarity. They cannot be wholly ignorant of one another. Nor can they fail to love one another.'

The life of this family whose members are sealed by baptism, at very least by that of desire, is Eucharistic in character. The Holy Mysteries of the Body and Blood of Christ are the chief meeting-place of its members who grow ever closer to one another through their growing union with Christ. They may well reflect on a note of Paul Couturier which reveals his own disposition with regard to these mysteries:

'I enter into Christ's self-oblation so that through my boundless self-surrender he may blend truly all in me and through me totally with himself, uniting all with his sacrifice and his oblation.'

Paul Couturier: Dates

Birth at Lyons	29 July 1881
Childhood in Algiers	1884–93
Ordination as priest at the cathedral, Lyons	9 June 1906
Work for degree in physical sciences	1906–9
Becomes master in the college des Chartreux	1909
First meeting with M. Carlhian	1920
Care for Russian refugees	1923–35
Stay with the monks of unity at Amay	July 1932
First celebration of the Week ('Octave') at Lyons	January 1933
Becomes oblate of the order of St Benedict	13 August 1933
Meeting with Metropolitan Eulogius (Russian Orthodox)	14 October 1934
Article on the 'Psychology of the Octave'	December 1935
First interconfessional conference—with the first group (German-speaking) at Erlenbach	1936
First visit to England	1937
Article on 'Universal Prayer of Christians for Christian Unity'	December 1937
Second visit to England	1938
Week of Universal Prayer kept for the first time under this name	January 1939
First contacts with the World Council of Churches	1939
First visit to Taizé	1941
Second interconfessional group (French-speaking)—first meeting at les Dombes	1942
Prisoner at Fort Montluc	12 April– 12 June 1944
'Christian Rapprochements in the Twentieth Century'	1944

355

Memorandum sent to Pius XII concerning interconfessional theological conferences	1948
Christian Unity and Religious Toleration (symposium)	1950
Dialogue concerning the Virgin (collected articles)	1950
Grave heart-trouble begins	November 1951
Prayer and Christian Unity (Ecumenical Testament)	1952
Nominated Archimandrite of the Patriarchate of Antioch	1952
Death	24 March 1953
Funeral at the Church of St Bruno	27 March 1953

INDEX

357